Social Democracy in East Timor

Since the end of the Cold War, considerable scholarly debates have been devoted to the nature and scope of international state-building interventions in 'fragile', post-colonial states and their effectiveness in instituting democratic rule.

By examining the construction of political institutions in East Timor, this book highlights the relationship between the social and political realms during these processes. Focusing on the roles of East Timorese leaders and civil society organisations during the independence movement, it analyses the effectiveness of democracy building in East Timor. It examines the processes of drafting the new Constitution, establishing key political institutions (such as the electoral system), and articulating a new vision of citizenship and social justice. The book argues that East Timor offers a relatively successful case of democratic transition, enabled by a consistent set of goals and aspirations, grass-roots political legitimacy and participation, and the development of a democratic civil nation.

Offering a coherent argument for why democracy has been successful in East Timor and the roles of political leaders and civil society during democratic transition, this book will be of interest to those studying Southeast Asian Politics, International Politics, and Democracy.

Rebecca Strating is a lecturer of Politics at La Trobe University Melbourne, Australia. She teaches and researches Southeast Asian Politics and International Relations.

Routledge contemporary Southeast Asia series

1 **Land Tenure, Conservation and Development in Southeast Asia**
Peter Eaton

2 **The Politics of Indonesia-Malaysia Relations**
One kin, two nations
Joseph Chinyong Liow

3 **Governance and Civil Society in Myanmar**
Education, health and environment
Helen James

4 **Regionalism in Post-Suharto Indonesia**
Edited by Maribeth Erb, Priyambudi Sulistiyanto and Carole Faucher

5 **Living with Transition in Laos**
Market integration in Southeast Asia
Jonathan Rigg

6 **Christianity, Islam and Nationalism in Indonesia**
Charles E. Farhadian

7 **Violent Conflicts in Indonesia**
Analysis, representation, resolution
Edited by Charles A. Coppel

8 **Revolution, Reform and Regionalism in Southeast Asia**
Cambodia, Laos and Vietnam
Ronald Bruce St John

9 **The Politics of Tyranny in Singapore and Burma**
Aristotle and the rhetoric of benevolent despotism
Stephen McCarthy

10 **Ageing in Singapore**
Service needs and the state
Peggy Teo, Kalyani Mehta, Leng Thang and Angelique Chan

11 **Security and Sustainable Development in Myanmar**
Helen James

12 **Expressions of Cambodia**
The politics of tradition, identity and change
Edited by Leakthina Chau-Pech Ollier and Tim Winter

13 **Financial Fragility and Instability in Indonesia**
Yasuyuki Matsumoto

14 **The Revival of Tradition in Indonesian Politics**
The deployment of *adat* from colonialism to indigenism
Edited by Jamie S. Davidson and David Henley

15 **Communal Violence and Democratization in Indonesia**
Small town wars
Gerry van Klinken

16 **Singapore in the Global System**
Relationship, structure and change
Peter Preston

17 **Chinese Big Business in Indonesia**
The state of the capital
Christian Chua

18 **Ethno-religious Violence in Indonesia**
From soil to God
Chris Wilson

19 **Ethnic Politics in Burma**
States of conflict
Ashley South

20 **Democratization in Post-Suharto Indonesia**
Edited by Marco Bünte and Andreas Ufen

21 **Party Politics and Democratization in Indonesia**
Golkar in the post-Suharto era
Dirk Tomsa

22 **Community, Environment and Local Governance in Indonesia**
Locating the Commonwealth
Edited by Carol Warren and John F. McCarthy

23 **Rebellion and Reform in Indonesia**
Jakarta's security and autonomy polices in Aceh
Michelle Ann Miller

24 **Hadrami Arabs in Present-day Indonesia**
An Indonesia-oriented group with an Arab signature
Frode F. Jacobsen

25 **Vietnam's Political Process**
How education shapes political decision making
Casey Lucius

26 **Muslims in Singapore**
Piety, politics and policies
Kamaludeen Mohamed Nasir, Alexius A. Pereira and Bryan S. Turner

27 **Timor Leste**
Politics, history and culture
Andrea Katalin Molnar

28 **Gender and Transitional Justice**
The women of East Timor
Susan Harris Rimmer

29 **Environmental Cooperation in Southeast Asia**
ASEAN's regime for trans-boundary haze pollution
Paruedee Nguitragool

30 **The Theatre and the State in Singapore**
Terence Chong

31 **Ending Forced Labour in Myanmar**
Engaging a pariah regime
Richard Horsey

32 **Security, Development and Nation-Building in Timor-Leste**
A cross-sectoral assessment
Edited by Vandra Harris and Andrew Goldsmith

33 **The Politics of Religion in Indonesia**
Syncretism, orthodoxy, and religious contention in Java and Bali
Edited by Michel Picard and Remy Madinier

34 **Singapore's Ageing Population**
Managing healthcare and end of life decisions
Edited by Wing-Cheong Chan

35 **Changing Marriage Patterns in Southeast Asia**
Economic and socio-cultural dimensions
Edited by Gavin W. Jones, Terence H. Hull and Maznah Mohamad

36 **The Political Resurgence of the Military in Southeast Asia**
Conflict and leadership
Edited by Marcus Mietzner

37 **Neoliberal Morality in Singapore**
How family policies make state and society
Youyenn Teo

38 **Local Politics in Indonesia**
Pathways to power
Nankyung Choi

39 **Separatist Conflict in Indonesia**
The long-distance politics of the Acehnese diaspora
Antje Missbach

40 **Corruption and Law in Indonesia**
The unravelling of Indonesia's anti-corruption framework through law and legal process
Simon Butt

41 **Men and Masculinities in Southeast Asia**
Edited by Michele Ford and Lenore Lyons

42 **Justice and Governance in East Timor**
Indigenous approaches and the 'New Subsistence State'
Rod Nixon

43 **Population Policy and Reproduction in Singapore**
Making future citizens
Shirley Hsiao-Li Sun

44 **Labour Migration and Human Trafficking**
Critical perspectives from Southeast Asia
Michele Ford, Lenore Lyons and Willem van Schendel

45 **Singapore Malays**
Being ethnic minority and Muslim in a global city-state
Hussin Mutalib

46 **Political Change and Territoriality in Indonesia**
Provincial proliferation
Ehito Kimura

47 **Southeast Asia and the Cold War**
Edited by Albert Lau

48 **Legal Pluralism in Indonesia**
Bridging the unbridgeable
Ratno Lukito

49 **Building a People-Oriented Security Community the ASEAN way**
Alan Collins

50 **Parties and Parliaments in Southeast Asia**
Non-partisan chambers in Indonesia, the Philippines and Thailand
Roland Rich

51 **Social Activism in Southeast Asia**
Edited by Michele Ford

52 **Chinese Indonesians Reassessed**
History, religion and belonging
Edited by Siew-Min Sai and Chang-Yau Hoon

53 **Journalism and Conflict in Indonesia**
From reporting violence to promoting peace
Steve Sharp

54 **The Technological State in Indonesia**
The co-constitution of high technology and authoritarian politics
Sulfikar Amir

55 **Party Politics in Southeast Asia**
Clientelism and electoral competition in Indonesia, Thailand and the Philippines
Edited by Dirk Tomsa and Andreas Ufen

56 **Culture, Religion and Conflict in Muslim Southeast Asia**
Negotiating tense pluralisms
Edited by Joseph Camilleri and Sven Schottmann

57 **Global Indonesia**
Jean Gelman Taylor

58 **Cambodia and the Politics of Aesthetics**
Alvin Cheng-Hin Lim

59 **Adolescents in Contemporary Indonesia**
Lyn Parker and Pam Nilan

60 **Development and the Environment in East Timor**
Authority, participation and equity
Christopher Shepherd

61 **Law and Religion in Indonesia**
Faith, conflict and the courts
Melissa Crouch

62 **Islam in Modern Thailand**
Faith, philanthropy and politics
Rajeswary Ampalavanar Brown

63 **New Media and the Nation in Malaysia**
Malaysianet
Susan Leong

64 **Human Trafficking in Cambodia**
Chendo Keo

65 **Islam, Politics and Youth in Malaysia**
The pop-Islamist reinvention of PAS
Dominik Mueller

66 **The Future of Singapore**
Population, society and the nature of the state
Kamaludeen Mohamed Nasir and Bryan S. Turner

67 **Southeast Asia and the European Union**
Non-traditional security crises and cooperation
Naila Maier-Knapp

68 **Rhetoric, Violence, and the Decolonization of East Timor**
David Hicks

69 **Local Governance in Timor-Leste**
Lessons in postcolonial state-building
Deborah Cummins

70 **Media Consumption in Malaysia**
A hermeneutics of human behaviour
Tony Wilson

71 **Philippine Politics**
Progress and problems in a localist democracy
Lynn T. White III

72 **Human Trafficking in Colonial Vietnam**
Micheline Lessard

73 **Conflict Resolution and Peacebuilding in Laos**
Perspective for today's world
Stephanie Stobbe

74 **Urbanization in Vietnam**
Gisele Bousquet

75 **Social Democracy in East Timor**
Rebecca Strating

Social Democracy in East Timor

Rebecca Strating

LONDON AND NEW YORK

First published 2016
by Routledge

2 Park Square, Milton Park, Abingdon, Oxfordshire OX14 4RN
711 Third Avenue, New York, NY 10017

Routledge is an imprint of the Taylor & Francis Group, an informa business

First issued in paperback 2018

Copyright © 2016 Rebecca Strating

The right of Rebecca Strating to be identified as author of this work has
been asserted by her in accordance with sections 77 and 78 of the
Copyright, Designs and Patents Act 1988.

All rights reserved. No part of this book may be reprinted or reproduced or
utilised in any form or by any electronic, mechanical, or other means, now
known or hereafter invented, including photocopying and recording, or in
any information storage or retrieval system, without permission in writing
from the publishers.

Notice:
Product or corporate names may be trademarks or registered trademarks,
and are used only for identification and explanation without intent to infringe.

British Library Cataloguing in Publication Data
A catalogue record for this book is available from the British Library

Library of Congress Cataloging-in-Publication Data
Strating, Rebecca, author.
Social democracy in East Timor / Rebecca Strating.
   pages cm. – (Routledge contemporary Southeast Asia series ; 75)
   Includes bibliographical references and index.
   1. Democracy–Timor-Leste. 2. Nation-building–Timor-Leste.
   3. Civil society–Timor-Leste. 4. Timor-Leste–Politics and
   government–2002– I. Title.
   JQ790.A58S77 2015
   320.95987–dc23   2015014655

ISBN: 978-1-138-88532-5 (hbk)
ISBN: 978-1-138-32009-3 (pbk)

Typeset in Times New Roman
by Wearset Ltd, Boldon, Tyne and Wear

Contents

List of figures		x
List of tables		xi
Acknowledgements		xii
	Introduction	1
1	The pursuit of democratic independence	19
2	Exercising self-determination	48
3	International state-building and civil society	73
4	Constitution-drafting and the first elections	98
5	Institutions, leaders and elections	123
6	Social democratic citizenship	156
7	Transitional justice and social democracy	179
	Conclusion	204
	Bibliography	209
	Index	241

Figures

1.1	East Timor's independence movement: first phase	26
1.2	Reorganising the independence movement: stage 1	32
1.3	Reorganising the independence movement: stage 2	33
1.4	Reorganising the independence movement: stage 3	35
4.1	Structure of transitional governments	104
6.1	Types of citizenship rights in East Timor	161
8.1	Evolution of East Timor's political society	206

Tables

4.1	Election results by district	109
5.1	Structure of government	126
5.2	Organs of government and constitutional competencies	127
5.3	Choosing an electoral system	136
5.4	East Timor parliamentary election results, 2007	139
5.5	Parliamentary election results, July 2012	145
6.1	Constitutional rights in East Timor	160

Acknowledgements

There have been several names accorded to East Timor, including Portuguese Timor, Timor-Leste and Timor *Loro sa'e*. Upon achieving independence, the official title of the state became the Democratic Republic of Timor-Leste. The English term 'East Timor' is used throughout the book to minimise confusion, although the Portuguese 'Timor-Leste' is used when appropriate, such as in name titles, quotations and so forth.

This book would not have been written without the tremendous support and friendship of Dr Beth Edmondson. I remain incredibly grateful for your wisdom, encouragement and unfailing willingness to read my work and share ideas. The value of your mentorship is immeasurable. I extend my thanks to colleagues and friends within the former School of Applied Media and Social Sciences at Monash University and Federation University, and the Department of Politics and Philosophy at La Trobe University. I would also like to acknowledge the support and good humour of my friends and family, particularly my husband Lincoln whose kindness and patience knows no bounds.

Introduction

Since the end of the Cold War, considerable scholarly attention has been devoted to the nature and activities of international state-building in 'fragile', post-colonial states.[1] International interventions have occurred within states that are internationally recognised as sovereign but are unable or unwilling to provide 'internal sovereignty' in the form of effective governance.[2] State-building experiments have encompassed extensive roles for states and international organisations in (re)constructing political institutions and establishing political order.[3] The recognition of states' external sovereignty has become linked to their capacities to provide democratic governance as they are increasingly seen to hold particular responsibilities vis-à-vis their population.

This development of 'sovereignty as responsibility' reflects the ideological dominance of liberal-democracy within the post-Cold War international system, which has provided a rationale for interventions within non-democratic states.[4] As Franck argues, the global 'democratic entitlement' entails a belief that meaningful political representation and participation is necessary for the realisation of self-determination as '[i]ncreasingly governments recognize that their legitimacy depends on meeting a normative expectation of a community of states'.[5] This entitlement has permeated virtually all aspects of international law as notions of democratic legitimacy link collective self-determination rights with individual rights to political participation.[6] Consequently, the right to non-intervention held by sovereign states has become increasingly contingent upon their democratic credentials.[7]

Scholarly debates have devoted particular attention to the effectiveness of international interventions in instituting democratic rule in developing states. Liberal democratisation represents the dominant form of state-building and encompasses the twin goals of establishing peace and democratic government; however, in societies unused to democratic rule, these goals may not be complimentary.[8] The first post-Cold War democracy-building mission, in Cambodia in 1992–1993, entailed the United Nations Transitional Authority in Cambodia (UNTAC) establishing elections in an attempt to resolve a protracted civil conflict. Since then, democratic institution building by international actors has occurred in diverse territories including Bosnia and Herzegovina, Kosovo, Afghanistan and Iraq. As Barnett and Zürcher state, 'peacebuilders are expecting

2 Introduction

to achieve the impossible dream, attempting to engineer in years what took centuries for West European states and doing so under very unfavorable conditions'.[9] Although state-building missions have generally been more extensive than traditional peacebuilding interventions, they have largely fallen 'far short' of their goals.[10]

In the case of East Timor, intervention involved the United Nations (UN) undertaking a state-building mission to transform it from a dependent colony to an independent state that has been variously described as 'unprecedented', 'ambitious' and 'unique'.[11] The establishment of the United Nations Transitional Administration in East Timor (UNTAET) reflected a recognition that international assistance was necessary for avoiding a failed East Timorese state. The UNTAET was mandated by the United Nations Security Council to develop internal capacities to govern following the UN-led referendum on 30 August 1999, in which the East Timorese overwhelmingly voted to become independent.[12] Resolution 1272, adopted by the UN Security Council on 25 October 1999, endowed the UNTAET with 'overall responsibility for the administration of East Timor and ... empowered [it] to exercise all legislative and executive authority'.[13] It possessed wide-ranging, comprehensive state-building responsibilities, including immediate humanitarian and security assistance, building state institutions and public administration, restoring the judicial system and capacity-building.[14]

The UNTAET's temporary role as de facto sovereign reflects East Timor's distinctive transition to independence. The UNTAET was charged with establishing political institutions and 'capacity-building' as a condition for international recognition of East Timor's sovereignty. State-building in East Timor hence combined the ambitious tasks of building new and effective state institutions and ensuring democratisation as a requisite component of enabling East Timor's rights to self-determination.

Generally speaking, democratisation theorists have tended to neglect Southeast Asia, perhaps because authoritarian resilience has been the dominant trend in the region.[15] One of only three democratic states in Southeast Asia, East Timor is currently a 'flawed democracy' insofar as new state-based institutions have endured since independence but are yet to consolidate.[16] East Timor's democratic statehood has experienced serious political setbacks, including widespread riots in 2006 and assassination attempts on key leaders in 2008. Issues relating to corruption, internal security, weak rule of law, economic development, crime, and unemployment continue to challenge East Timor's transition from a weak state to a consolidated democracy.[17]

Institutional consolidation is a lengthy process. Free, fair and relatively peaceful elections held with minimal international assistance in 2012 reinforced East Timor's 'legitimacy to be fully politically autonomous'.[18] Certainly, more civil liberties are currently enjoyed by citizens in East Timor's liberal democracy than under the Indonesian dictatorship.[19] The state has also reduced its dependence upon foreign assistance since the withdrawal of the Australian-led International Stabilisation Force (ISF) in 2012. In 2013, East Timor ranked 43 of 167 states in the Democracy Index Report, ahead of established states such as Poland, Brazil and Indonesia.[20] Within the Southeast Asian context, extensive international assistance saw the creation of elections in Cambodia which subsequently entrenched an authoritarian, hegemonic party regime under the long-time leadership of strongman Hun Sen.[21] In contrast, East Timor has avoided a hegemonic strong party regime and power transfers have occurred peacefully and in accordance with electoral results. To the extent that democratic institutions have thus far persisted, East Timor can be considered a relatively successful case of externally-assisted democratic transition.

This book sets out to address how and why East Timor transitioned to democracy by examining the values and ideas underpinning the independence movement and the ways these were maintained and/or challenged through the state-building and post-independence phases. The pursuit of the twin goals of independence and democracy made it possible for East Timor to become a sovereign state. Establishing democratic independence required international recognition of East Timor's collective self-determination rights and the establishment of a free and fair election to enable those rights to be exercised. While East Timor's democratic transition occurred within a context of international state-building, so-called 'Western' values around freedom and human rights were not simply imposed upon East Timor. A state-based identity was formulated around principles of pluralism, social justice, democracy and wealth distribution during the independence movement, and these values were used to unify and sustain the resistance movement and justify self-determination claims to the international community.

A range of materials, including international law, speeches, government and policy documents, civil society and media documents, inter- and non-governmental reports, memoirs and secondary sources are used to analyse the discussions and debates around East Timor's statehood before and after independence. A model of social democracy that entails the presence of participatory, deliberative structures of political engagement provides a useful lens for examining the relationships between social and political realms in state formation. As Peou points out, democratisation often 'depends on the interests of and power relations between social and political actors at different levels and how these actors manage to prevent one another from subverting democratic rule'.[22] Since independence, social democratic ends have been pursued by successive East Timor governments, although political decisions have not always matched ideals.

East Timor's delayed independence

The *República Democrática de Timor-Leste*/Democratic Republic of Timor-Leste's (East Timor) acceptance into the United Nations on 27 September 2002 completed a long path to decolonisation that begun in 1974.[23] Since World War Two, the international normative framework has privileged norms of self-determination in post-colonial states and delayed independence has been

4   *Introduction*

increasingly rare.[24] Decolonisation rapidly changed the membership of the international community as 'quasi-states' were accorded *de jure* sovereign status irrespective of internal capacities to 'provide civil and socio-economic goods for their population'.[25] Many post-colonial 'quasi' states would not survive if it was not for the 'normative and material benefits' and legal protection of sovereign recognition and UN membership.[26]

The principle of self-determination underpinning decolonisation was outlined in the United Nations Charter which asserted its primary function to 'develop friendly relations among nations based on respect for the principle of equal rights and self-determination of people'.[27] Self-determination entailed the 'collective right of a people to be itself' and freedom from foreign subjugation.[28] In 1960, this right was further consolidated with the Declaration on the Granting of Independence to Colonial Countries and Peoples, which called for a 'speedy and unconditional end' to colonialism.[29] Key international human rights treaties recognised collective self-determination as encompassing three distinct entitlements: rights to freely determine political status, freely pursue economic, social and cultural development, and freely dispose of natural wealth and resources.[30] Collective self-determination was considered by international human rights covenants as necessary for creating legal systems that protect other human and civil rights.[31]

Self-determination rights are limited as they are generally only granted to people in mandated territories, trust territories and non-self-governing territories in colonial situations.[32] In 1960, East Timor was recognised in the Declaration on Decolonisation as 'a non-self-governing territory' under Portuguese colonial rule since the early 1700s.[33] In 1962, the UN General Assembly Resolution 1807 called upon Portugal to immediately recognise people's right to self-determination and independence in the territories under its administration, including East Timor.[34]

Following a 1974 military *coup* in Portugal that replaced the right-wing Caetano dictatorship with a left-wing government, a shift in policy allowed Portuguese colonies to exercise self-determination.[35] On 13 December 1974, UN General Assembly Resolution 3249 welcomed Portugal's decision and reaffirmed 'the inalienable right' of the East Timorese people to self-determination and independence.[36] On 28 November 1975, following a brief civil war in East Timor across August and September, pro-independence political party FRETILIN unilaterally declared independence and established the Democratic Republic of Timor-Leste (RDTL). This first attempt at establishing East Timorese independence was suspended when Indonesia formally invaded East Timor on 7 December 1975.[37] Successive UN General Assembly resolutions dismissed Indonesia's claims that the East Timorese chose to join Indonesia, declaring that 'the people of East Timor must be enabled freely to determine their own future'.[38] Every year between 1975 and 1982, East Timor's right of self-determination was upheld by the UN General Assembly, and the UN Security Council called upon all states to respect the inalienable rights of East Timor and the territorial integrity of Portugal as the administering authority.[39]

Introduction 5

However, these acknowledgements of East Timor's right to self-determination were not supported by tangible activities that would persuade Indonesia to vacate East Timorese territory.[40] Few states were prepared to recognise the legitimacy of the RDTL.[41] Between 1977 and 1999, the United Nations Security Council did not debate the East Timor question, largely because Indonesia's Western allies wanted the issue kept off the agenda.[42] East Timor was thus unable to make its independence 'real' due to a lack of external support and an inability to expel Indonesia. Subsequently, from 1975 to 1999 Indonesia held effective de facto control over the East Timorese population and territory.

International political factors explaining the delay in East Timor's independence included the Cold War, the threat of communism and the prioritisation of 'friendly' relations with Indonesia by states such as the United States of America and Australia. Additionally, perceptions that East Timor was too underdeveloped and small to become a sovereign state hindered its claims to independence.[43] These factors enabled Indonesia to consolidate the widely held belief that its occupation of East Timor was a *fait accompli*.[44] In 1985, Australia formally recognised Indonesian sovereignty over East Timor and in 1989 Indonesia and Australia signed the Timor Gap treaty concerning the exploitation of oil and gas reserves in the Timor Sea.[45] According to Marker, Australia's policy decisions generated only slight international criticism as many states in the 1980s considered Indonesia's annexation of East Timor as 'irreversible'.[46]

Despite the apparent intractability of Indonesia's occupation, on 30 August 1999 a referendum provided the East Timorese population the opportunity to exercise self-determination.[47] On 11 June 1999, the United Nations Security Council Resolution 1246 established the United Nations Mission in East Timor (UNAMET) to establish a ballot for the East Timorese to decide their future as an independent state or autonomous region.[48] On 30 August 1999, a decisive 78.5 per cent of voters elected for East Timor to become an independent sovereign state.

Self-determination encompasses internal and external dimensions: the internal aspect refers to citizens' rights to political participation, which is supported by democratic institutions and systems.[49] External self-determination is commonly conflated with the achievement of independent statehood.[50] The rights of the East Timorese to ongoing political participation were contingent upon international recognition of their rights to self-determination.[51] East Timor's commitment to democracy and human rights during the independence movement supported their claims to self-determination rights. In turn, the role of the international community was crucial to the achievement of East Timor's sovereign independence as the free and fair ballot provided a legitimate act of self-determination.

International democracy-building

International recognition of sovereignty is increasingly contingent upon domestic authority structures as it imposes a set of responsibilities upon states to pursue democracy and human rights. New states enter a pre-existing normative fabric

6 Introduction

that governs the international community and privileges democratic political systems.[52] As democracy bestows international legitimacy upon states, the validity of an independence struggle is at least partly determined by its commitment to democratic government.[53] International political society is crowded with institutions that uphold 'Western' values around human rights, democracy and free market economics. Dependency upon international institutions can limit the capacities of weak states to make authoritative choices about the types of political, social and economic structures they will develop and sustain.

State-building in East Timor was, in part, a technical exercise in constructing the institutions found in modern, centralised 'Weberian' states. These states are 'formed by a legally constituted and highly differentiated administrative apparatus ... [that] monopolize the legitimate means of violence'.[54] Security Council Resolution 1272 invested broad powers in the UNTAET to build institutions such as elections and electoral systems, the judiciary, the military and the police.[55] As part of this mandate, the UNTAET was also responsible for building institutions that conformed to the ideological demands of the international community.[56] The United Nations mandate that established the UNTAET stressed that its responsibilities be carried out 'with a view to the development of local democratic institutions, including an independent East Timorese human rights institution'.[57] Building institutions required organising agencies and departments 'to discharge their functions both effectively and democratically' in a way that would enable independent East Timor to govern.[58]

Simultaneously, however, the UNTAET was constrained by its duty to respect East Timor's right to self-determination by not imposing a particular form of government on the East Timorese.[59] As states are viewed as representative of a self-determining people, sovereign entitlements include supreme political authority and rights to non-intervention within a bounded territorial jurisdiction, and rights to establish governance structures of their own choosing. This highlights a key tension that resided between ideals of self-determination and the need for international assistance to build economic and judicial capacities in East Timor. While establishing a democracy that permits the exercise of self-determination is one of the primary purposes of contemporary international state-building missions, they temporarily 'deny both to the people over whom they govern'.[60] For some scholars, the 'hubristic' nature of state-building represents a new form of Western imperialism that imposes liberal-democratic structures upon a reluctant population, which not only reflects a denial of self-determination rights but also diminishes prospects of institutional durability after the state-builders have departed.[61]

The need to generate political legitimacy represents a stumbling block for international missions attempting to transpose centralised institutions upon 'traditional' socio-political structures found in developing states.[62] International state-builders in East Timor initially regarded the territory as a 'blank slate' and problematically ignored pre-existing socio-political structures.[63] The socio-political organisational system of *sukus* (villages) continues to underpin the day-to-day life of ordinary East Timorese and their 'tribal-traditional' identities.[64]

Introduction 7

But while customary structures and local patterns of allegiance provide sources of friction in centralised state-building, most, if not all, contemporary states are defined by 'multi-layered and diverse patterns of allegiance and identity'.[65]

A modern 'Weberian' state relies upon the supremacy of legal-rational authority based upon formal and institutionalised law and beliefs in 'natural law' (reason), bureaucracy and the 'rule of law'.[66] The capacities of modern states to request and receive civic compliance depends upon a belief among those governed that the government is legitimate and 'morally justified in exercising political power'.[67] Political legitimacy is a necessary condition for authority as citizens are required to recognise rules as binding.[68] Democratic legitimacy relies upon a belief that citizens have an obligation to comply with the rules of the state.[69] If compliance is voluntary, the need to establish other modes of social control, such as violence or coercion, is diminished.[70]

'Real' power in democratic systems equates to political authority, meaning the 'rightfulness to rule', which is derived from citizens' belief in the legitimacy of key state institutions. The extent to which states can create order and rule of law within society relies upon their capacities to exercise political authority. For a new democratic sovereign state, such as East Timor, legitimate institutions, including constitutions, legislature, courts and government, are essential for internal sovereignty.[71] As political institutions are embodied by the allegiances of citizens towards 'a set of norms, beliefs, and practices', contests in legitimacy can present serious issues to establishing effective statehood.[72] Hence, democratic theorists have argued that developing a democratic political culture is critical to institutionalising and legitimating structures.[73]

Building 'capacity' for self-government would only be possible through 'nation-building', which entails the binding of people to political institutions through mechanisms designed to encourage 'ownership' and 'participation'. Nation-building is necessary for building legitimacy and broad public support for new institutions as 'it is in the realm of ideas and sentiment that the fate of states is primarily determined'.[74] Nation-building is critical for minimising tensions between formal state-based institutions and 'traditional', 'local' or 'customary' forms of authority.

A significant challenge for state-building was fostering a collective identity necessary for developing a democratic political community 'oriented towards practices of engagement, accountability, responsiveness and participation'.[75] Brown suggests that building this kind of civic democratic 'nation' relies upon 'expansive, participatory processes of state formation' and 'an inclusive form of interchange and communication'.[76] Much of the literature criticised the lack of opportunities for the East Timorese to participate in the state-building phase, blaming an 'authoritarian' approach that failed to adequately reconcile competing 'paradigms'.[77] In 2000, UNTAET head Sérgio Vieira de Mello described his role as:

> authorised to impose directives and policies as well as to use force more or less at will. There is no separation of the legislative or judicial from the

8 *Introduction*

> executive authority. There are no positive models on how to exercise such broad powers … the question remains open how the UN can exercise fair governance with absolute powers in societies recovering from war and oppression.[78]

Critiques of the UNTAET corresponded with views in the broader international state-building literature that state-builders tend to implement Western, 'Weberian' structures irrespective of existing local political structures or dynamics.[79] Chopra predicted independence would be problematic in East Timor as the public was 'forced to swallow' Western political ideals.[80] Hohe emphasised the ways the new democratic structures were incompatible with local customary governance structures.[81] She suggested that East Timor's interventions relied upon establishing 'free and fair' electoral processes that failed to 'resonate with local communities and that are not translated into their paradigm'.[82]

However, these commentaries reflected a tendency to overlook the consistent commitment shown by the East Timorese independence movement and leaders to democratic principles, social justice and human rights. For East Timor, becoming a sovereign state was necessary for establishing a democracy and fulfilling the visions of the independence movement.[83] While the UNTAET did not always live up to ideals of 'participatory intervention', civil society organisations were important for service-delivery and keeping the UNTAET and East Timorese political leaders accountable to the public. One priority of the UNTAET was to collaborate and consult with East Timorese leaders as a way of engendering 'local ownership' of political institutions. Multiple UN reports on state-building processes emphasised consensus-building, consultation and dialogue between international experts, East Timorese leaders, and public more generally.[84] Several changes were implemented by the UNTAET to 'Timorise' state-building processes, and East Timorese leaders ultimately played significant roles in establishing their constitution, making choices about the institutional political framework, and articulating citizenship rights and the envisaged relationship between state and society.[85] This challenges the notion that new 'Western' state institutions were simply imposed by the international community, as political elites and civil society were invested in processes of state identity formation and nation-building.

The democratisation of East Timor

East Timor's political transition can be understood as a process of democratisation, which is often presented in two stages, beginning first with the establishment of democratic structures (democratic transition), and followed by the institutionalisation of these structures within the polity (democratic consolidation).[86] Democratic transitions are:

> complete when sufficient agreement has been reached about political procedures to produce an elected government, when a government comes to

Introduction 9

power that is a direct result of a free and a popular vote, when this government de facto has the authority to generate new policies, and when the executive, legislative and judicial power generated by the new democracy does not have to share power with other bodies *de jure*.[87]

This definition reflects several important elements for democratic transition: agreement among political leaders regarding political institutions; establishment of the procedural elements of democracy including fair and competitive multiparty elections; divisions of power between political institutions (entailing the creation of a constitution); and, subservience of non-elected bodies, such as the military, to elected civilian representatives.

As democracy primarily concerns the ways political power can be peacefully transferred, the right to win government through competitive, free, fair and universal elections is crucial. However, the above criteria suggest the presence of 'elections' is not a sufficient condition for democracy.[88] While democracy might be the dominant value set in the realm of international law, many states are only nominally democratic or not at all. Levitsky and Way's term 'competitive authoritarianism' captures the reality that many developing states are not on a pathway to democratic development but have co-opted elections as a way of legitimising authoritarian control.[89] Indeed, the stalled transitions and democratic roll-backs of the twenty-first century highlight the problems with teleological progress models that continue to underpin orthodox theories of political development. Universal, free and fair elections require citizens to hold minimum civil rights and freedoms, such as rights to vote and to run for office, and freedom of expression, press and speech. Elections that cannot achieve the desired democratic ends of popular sovereignty, collective choice and internal self-determination do not meet the minimum requirements.

The pre-conditions required for a successful transition to democracy have been the subject of much scholarly debate, some of which are relevant for examining East Timor's pathway to democratic independence. Scholars, such as Lipset, have argued that socio-economic development is strongly correlated with democratic development.[90] As basic subsistence becomes less of an everyday concern in developing states, the expanding middle-class begins to agitate for more civil and legal liberties. Growing affluence contributes to an expanded class of literate and educated people who demand a greater say regarding state policies.[91] The relationship between economic development and democratisation, however, cannot explain East Timor's transition. In 2002, East Timor was ranked among the least developed states in the world, and it remains one of the poorest states in Southeast Asia.[92] East Timor's democratic transition preceded economic development, which necessitates finding alternative explanations for East Timor's democratic transition.

Others scholars have attempted to explain the importance of values and beliefs using the concepts of cultural receptivity. 'Culturalists' have assumed that certain non-liberal philosophies, including Islam and Confucianism, resist democratic development, although this perspective struggles to explain

10   *Introduction*

transitions in states such as Indonesia and the Philippines.[93] Diamond states that 'democracy requires a distinctive set of political values and orientations from citizens: moderation, tolerance, civility, efficacy, knowledge, participation'.[94] Habituating political rules and behaviours among leaders and citizens is essential for making democracy a viable system of political organisation within a polity, as beliefs, attitudes and values have 'bearing particularly on the persistence or breakdown of democracy'.[95] The relatively consistent promotion of democratic political values throughout and beyond the independence movement is important for explaining why democracy has persisted.

Perceptions of democracy as the only legitimate form of political organisation need to be shared by two key groups: elites and civil society. Transition literature has often focused on the roles of political 'elites' and power networks in permitting and promoting democracy. Elites, generally conceptualised as a 'small, privileged leadership sector', are important 'facilitators and impediments' to democratic transition and development.[96] As Huntington argues, '[D]emocratic development occurs when political leaders believe they have an interest in promoting it or a duty to achieve it'.[97] Democratisation rests upon a change in ideas about what constitutes legitimate socio-political structures: if political or military elites are successful in undermining democratic principles – such as the separation of powers, civil rights or constitutional authority – then democracy will not consolidate.[98] Widespread acceptance among elites of the validity of democracy is viewed as strongly beneficial for institutional endurance. Whether or not a clearly defined 'elite' existed in East Timor during independence is contestable, however many of the agents of East Timor's political independence, including resistance leaders, student protesters and exiled diplomats, would go on to become the new, state-based political elite in East Timor. These activists include former Prime Ministers Xanana Gusmão, José Ramos-Horta and Mari Alkatiri, and current President Taur Matan Ruak and Prime Minister Dr Rui Maria de Araújo. Consequently, the architects of independence became the new vanguard for protecting the democratic vision of sovereign statehood that developed through resistance against Indonesia.

Gill argues that civil society and political participation beyond elites is a crucial element to transition that is often neglected in democratisation literature.[99] 'From-below' explanations seek to explain how civil society 'forces' work to provoke elite buy-in to the project of democratisation. Accordingly, elites and civil society are often viewed as oppositional forces. In East Timor, the distinctions between political and civil society realms of participation were blurred by the independence movement, which was largely a civil society campaign for recognition of rights to self-determination. It carried out an armed resistance movement through clandestine organisations, such as the National Council of *Maubere* Resistance (CNRM) and the National Armed Forces for the Liberation of East Timor (FALINTIL); it established manifestoes and visions of statehood to unify the nation and harness popular support; and, importantly, it waged a diplomatic battle for self-determination within international civil society.[100] The future East Timorese political 'elite' were hence key drivers of

Introduction 11

civil society activism before and during state-building processes. The support of both elites and civil society organisations is crucial for understanding East Timor's democratic transition and the resilience of democratic, state-based political institutions.

Social democracy in East Timor

Social democratic aspirations have been present in East Timor since the beginnings of the independence movement in 1974. In contemporary times, states have become increasingly responsible for ensuring the social and economic welfare of its citizens under international law.[101] Social forms of democracy believe in the necessity of formal, legally protected rights, characterised by Berlin as the 'negative' liberties which give citizens the freedom to live without impediment from other individuals or the state. They also believe that the state holds responsibilities to ensure 'positive' liberties, defined as the means or the capacities of individuals to act upon their freedom.[102] Viewing the state as responsible for equalising the opportunities of all citizens to enjoy basic socio-economic rights is the basis of distributive justice. Social rights enable negative rights 'to become meaningful in the "real world" and not just on paper'.[103]

The key features of social democracy include beliefs that:

1 The state should guarantee civil, political and socio-economic rights;
2 Wealth and income redistribution is necessary for guaranteeing these rights;
3 The state should operate on principles of justice that citizens can agree upon;
4 Civic participation is necessary for the capacities of citizens to deliberate on the nature of rights-based justice.

The first and second features emphasise the importance of 'social' or 'distributive' justice, the central aim of which is bringing individuals up to a minimum standard of living.[104] For those individuals disadvantaged by state institutions, the state is responsible for guaranteeing their socio-economic rights through redistribution.[105] However, the provision of positive liberties presents particular challenges for low income states such as East Timor given the scarcity of resources.[106]

The third and fourth conditions understand stable state institutions, necessary for internal sovereignty, as predicated upon a widespread belief among citizens about their justness.[107] According to Rawls, political order can only be attained if everyone accepts the same principles of justice, and they are aware that others also consent to these principles.[108] This perceives social democracy through the lens of social contract theory, whereby the consent of citizens is required for institutions to be considered legitimate. Only if they are considered valid by citizens can institutions work to create 'real' order. Wealth redistribution provides both equal and differentiated citizenship rights, which Rawls advocates as a means for establishing 'just' institutions.

12 *Introduction*

Creating the conditions of social consent is predicated on substantive consultation, debate and the political participation of citizens beyond voting in elections. While 'procedural' Schumpeterian models of democracy emphasise the importance of elections and majority rule, deliberative Habermasian models focuses upon alternative spheres of political participation and electoral systems that seek to represent a diversity of political viewpoints, including those which may be considered to be in a minority. Advocates of participatory democratic models have noted that democracy must not be imposed upon a people, but rather must be seen as a 'grass-roots', bottom-up participatory process.[109]

Developing a political culture that supports democracy is critical for institutionalising and legitimating democratic structures.[110] A 'civic community' based upon active participation and an interest in public issues creates a sense of civic competence and co-operation in developing a democratic nation.[111] Habituating political rules and behaviours among leaders and citizens is essential for making democracy a viable system of political organisation within a polity, as beliefs, attitudes and values have 'bearing particularly on the persistence or breakdown of democracy'.[112] Building personal experiences with democratic engagement – such as voting in elections, participating in consultation mechanisms or involvement with a civil society organisation – is the best way of developing political culture among a people with little democratic experience.[113]

Civil society is a conduit for consensus-oriented democratic engagement, particularly in new states where people are unfamiliar with democratic processes.[114] Civil society includes 'formal and informal networks, modern and traditional associations, [and] political advocacy groups'.[115] It exists in the 'public sphere', which is 'located between the official and private spheres' and entails direct participation by bodies and citizens that hold particular interests.[116] Within the public sphere, individuals create 'autonomous, organised and collective activities of various kinds ... [and] citizens relate to each other and give collective expression to their demands and judgements on collective affairs'.[117] Civil society is vital to the transformation to democracy because it can support political participation, work with and monitor governments, and lobby for social justice mechanisms.[118]

Civil societies can also prevent the state from becoming too strong or domineering.[119] The capacities of local non-governmental organisations (NGOs) in building coalitions, promoting dialogue and debate about policy issues, and promoting public participation in planning and transition are crucial for engaging citizens in political processes.[120] Following independence, contests about the nature of political participation between elected representatives and civil society organisations often mirrored the distinctions between procedural and deliberative forms of democracy. As the following chapters demonstrate, civil society organisations pressed for more consultative and inclusive mechanisms of engagement throughout transition and have continued to play substantive roles in East Timor's democracy.

Chapter overview

The following chapters track East Timor's independence movement, state-building and post-independence phases. Rustow argued that the first stage of democratisation is often a 'prolonged and inconclusive struggle', which aptly describes East Timor's independence movement examined in the first two chapters. Chapter 1 examines the establishment of East Timor's political parties, and the evolution of peak bodies that unified the movement around democracy and human rights, to demonstrate their importance for East Timor's pursuit of independence. It argues that the independence movement was driven by a desire to create an independent democracy that could articulate and protect human rights. Chapter 2 examines the roles of civil society organisations within and beyond East Timor in pressuring Indonesia to recognise the self-determination rights of the East Timorese. External recognition of sovereignty was essential for the capacities of the East Timorese to establish internal sovereignty and democratic structures. As such, international and domestic non-governmental organisations and solidarity movements were crucial to the eventual achievement of a referendum on East Timor's independence.

Chapters 3 and 4 examine the processes of state-building. Chapter 3 examines the opportunities provided to individuals and civil society organisations to contribute to East Timor's transition to independent statehood. It argues that nation-building requires binding people to a new set of political institutions because democracies require a set of values and orientations on behalf of citizens in order to operate effectively.[121] Developing political culture and a democratic 'civil' community are integral to the democracy-building task. Chapter 4 demonstrates that East Timorese leaders were given the authority to write their Constitution, which would provide an outline for the future state encompassing particular values about the nature of statehood. Deliberative mechanisms of consultation can create a sense that the constitution is 'authored' and 'owned' by the public, which is important for legitimating it as a key political structure.[122] East Timor's first democratic elections were held in August 2001 to establish the Constituent Assembly responsible for preparing the Constitution. These processes of constitution-building could be considered the first 'test' for democracy in East Timor.

Chapters 5, 6 and 7 examine the exercise of social democratic statehood following independence. Chapter 5 discusses the 'institutional design' of East Timor. Institutions are necessary for the effective running of democracies because they establish the operational rules of the system.[123] This chapter focuses particular attention on the construction of a semi-presidential government structure and the Proportional Representation electoral system as key institutions that can shape the pattern and operation of democracy. Chapter 6 examines citizenship in East Timor and the nature of political, civil and socio-economic rights granted to the East Timorese. East Timor's Constitution contains an extensive array of rights that reflect the aspirations of the independence movement that conformed to the visions of social democratic statehood set out during the

14 *Introduction*

independence movement. Chapter 7 examines the various transitional justice mechanisms employed in East Timor during and after transition, particularly the Commission for Reception, Truth and Reconciliation (CAVR), which incorporated 'customary' justice mechanisms in order to legitimise reconciliation processes. Social justice – a cornerstone of social democracy – was embedded in both the practices and discussions around transitional justice.

East Timor's model of statehood aspired to protect and promote an extensive array of civil, political and socio-economic rights, as well as emphasising consultation, dialogue and reconciliatory forms of justice to promote feelings of 'local ownership' and self-governance. The pursuit of democratic independence, social justice and human rights mattered for the creation of East Timor's political structures. East Timorese citizens have held high expectations that the state will deliver upon the promises of modern statehood, and have been disappointed at various times. Nevertheless, East Timor's democratic institutions have endured since independence and are in the process of consolidation.

Notes

1 Helman and Ratner, 'Saving Failed States', 3.
2 Jackson, *Quasi-States.*
3 See for example Sutter, 'State-Building or the Dilemma of Intervention', 5. See also Paris, 'Saving Liberal Peacebuilding', 339; Cooper, *The Breaking of Nations*, 65–69; Fukuyama, *State-Building*, 92–93; Krasner and Pascual, 'Addressing State Failure', 153–163; Fearon and Laitin, 'Neo-Trusteeship and the Problem of Weak States', 5–43; Rotberg, 'The Failure and Collapse of Nation-States: Breakdown, Prevention and Repair', 1–50 and Chandler, 'Great Power Responsibility and "Failed States"', 15.
4 Bellamy, 'Kosovo and the Advent of Sovereignty as Responsibility', 40; Zaum, *The Sovereign Paradox*, 234 and Chandler, *Empire in Denial*, 36–40. See also Fukuyama, *The End of History and the Last Man.*
5 Franck, 'The Emerging Right of Democratic Governance', 46.
6 Ibid. and Fox and Roth, 'Democracy and International Law', 327–352. See also Halperin, 'Guaranteeing Democracy', 105–122 and Cerna, 'Universal Democracy', 328.
7 Reisman, 'Sovereignty and Human Rights in Contemporary International Law', 866–876.
8 Roberts, 'Hybrid Polities and Indigenous Pluralities', 63.
9 Barnett and Zürcher, 'The Peacebuilder's Contract', 23.
10 Ibid. Not all scholars believe peacebuilding missions have 'failed'. See for instance Dobbins and Miller, 'Overcoming Obstacles to Peace', 103–120.
11 See Beauvais, 'Benevolent Despotism', 1101 and 1104; Downie, 'UNTAET', 29; Matsuno, 'The UN Transitional Administration and Democracy Building in Timor-Leste', 53; Wilde, 'From Danzig to East Timor and Beyond', 583; Nakamura, *Reflections on the State-Institution-Building Support in Timor-Leste*, 3 and Chesterman, 'East Timor in Transition', 45–49.
12 United Nations Security Council, *Resolution 1272.*
13 Ibid., 2–3.
14 Ibid.
15 Case, 'Low-Quality Democracy and Varied Authoritarianism', 255 and Slater, 'Democracy and Dictatorship do not Float Freely', 55.

Introduction 15

16 Case, ibid. and Economist Intelligence Unit, *Democracy Index 2013: Democracy in Limbo*, 4–8.

17 Feijó, 'Timor-Leste: Challenges to the Consolidation of Democracy', 1.

18 Ibid.

19 Peou, 'The Limits and Potentials of Liberal Democratisation in Southeast Asia', 29–30.

20 Economist Intelligence Unit, *Democracy Index 2013: Democracy in Limbo*, 4–8.

21 Ibid., 20; Paris, 'Saving Liberal Peacebuilding', 341 and Levitsky and Way, *Competitive Authoritarianism*.

22 Peou, 'The Limits and Potential of Liberal Democratisation in Southeast Asia', 20.

23 United Nations General Assembly, *Unanimous Assembly Decision Makes Timor-Leste 191st United Nations Member State*.

24 People in some territories, such as Vietnam and Algeria, experienced a period of delayed independence while they fought for their independence. Delayed independence also occurred in Western Sahara, however unlike East Timor, it remains a non-decolonised territory. See Franck and Hoffman, 'The Right of Self-Determination in Very Small Places', 335–342.

25 Jackson, *Quasi-States*, 1, 5 and 9 and Philpott, *Revolutions in Sovereignty*, 153.

26 Jackson, ibid.; Federer, *The UN in East Timor*, 4 and Onuf, 'The Constitution of International Society', 18.

27 United Nations, *Charter of the United Nations*.

28 CAVR, *Chega!*, 3–4.

29 United Nations General Assembly, *Declaration on the Granting of Independence to Colonial Countries and Peoples*.

30 United Nations General Assembly, *International Covenant on Economic, Social and Cultural Rights* and United Nations General Assembly, *International Covenant on Civil and Political Rights*.

31 Castellino and Gilbert, 'Self-Determination and Indigenous Peoples and Minorities', 161 and Vidmar, 'The Right of Self-Determination and Multiparty Democracy', 240.

32 Hannum, *Autonomy, Sovereignty, and Self-Determination*, 48 and 49 and Susanne Linton cited in CAVR, *Timor-Leste Self-Determination and the International Community*, 9. See also United Nations General Assembly, *Declaration on the Granting of Independence to Colonial Countries and Peoples*.

33 United Nations General Assembly, ibid.

34 United Nations General Assembly, *Territories under Portuguese Administration*. See Krieger, *East Timor and the International Community*, 31.

35 CAVR, *Chega!*, Chapter 3, 13.

36 United Nations General Assembly, *Question of Territories under Portuguese Domination*.

37 CAVR, *Chega!*, Chapter 3, 58–62.

38 United Nations General Assembly, *Question of East Timor*, United Nations General Assembly Resolution 36/50.

39 CAVR, *Chega!*, Chapter 7, 1, 84 and 124–127 and Krieger, *East Timor and the International Community*, 129–133. The UN General Assembly affirmed East Timor's rights to self-determination in the following Resolutions: United Nations General Assembly, *Question of Timor*, General Assembly Resolution 3485; United Nations General Assembly, *Question of Timor*, United Nations General Assembly Resolution 31/53; United Nations General Assembly, *Question of East Timor*, General Assembly Resolution 32/34; United Nations General Assembly, *Question of East Timor*, United Nations Resolution 33/39; United Nations General Assembly, *Question of East Timor*, General Assembly Resolution 34/40; United Nations General Assembly, *Question of East Timor*, United Nations Resolution 35/27; United Nations General Assembly, *Question of East Timor*, United Nations General Assembly Resolution 36/50 and United Nations General Assembly, *Question of East*

16 *Introduction*

Timor, United Nations General Assembly Resolution 37/30. The UN Security Council affirmed East Timor's rights to self-determination in the following resolutions: United Nations Security Council, *Resolution 384* and United Nations Security Council, *Resolution 389*.

40 Franck and Hoffman, 'The Right of Self-Determination in Very Small Places', 349.

41 CAVR, *Chega!*, Chapter 7:1, 80.

42 Philpott, 'East Timor's Double Life', 143.

43 CAVR, *Chega!*, Chapter 7:1, 66. The various explanations for East Timor's delayed independence are covered in detail in the literature. See for example Cotton, *East Timor, Australia and Regional Order*; Hainsworth and McCloskey, eds., *The East Timor Question*; Fernandes, *Reluctant Saviours* and Burchill, *East Timor, Australia and Indonesia.*

44 CAVR, *Chega!*, Chapter 7:1, 67.

45 Burchill, 'East Timor, Australia and Indonesia', 170.

46 Marker, *East Timor: A Memoir of the Negotiations for Independence*, 127. See also Fernandes, *The Independence of East Timor*, 98.

47 CAVR, *Chega!*, Chapter 3, 134.

48 United Nations Security Council, *Resolution 1246*. Elections were delayed and UNAMET's mandate was extended for one month until 30 September. See United Nations Security Council, *Resolution 1257*.

49 Philpott, 'In Defense of Self-Determination', 354–357.

50 See for example Cassese, *Self-Determination of Peoples*, 5; Fan, 'The Missing Link between Self-Determination and Democracy', 176–177 and Miller, 'Self-Determination in International Law and the Demise of Democracy?', 608.

51 Hannum, *Autonomy, Sovereignty and Self-Determination*, 30.

52 See Fukuyama, *The End of History*, 45 and Pevehouse, 'Democracy from the Outside-In?', 515–516.

53 Dahl, *Democracy and its Critics*, 207–208 and Held, *Models of Democracy*, 1.

54 Habermas, 'The European Nation-State', 281.

55 United Nations Security Council, *Resolution 1272*; Downie, 'UNTAET', 30 and Borgerhoff, 'The Double-Task', 103.

56 United Nations Security Council, ibid.

57 Ibid.

58 Ottaway, 'Rebuilding State Institutions in Collapsed States', 1004. See also Krasner, *Power, the State, and Sovereignty.*

59 Kondoch, 'The United Nations Administration of East Timor', 260.

60 Zaum, 'The Authority of International Administrations in International Society', 456. See Chandler, *Empire in Denial*, 41.

61 See for example Richmond and Franks, 'Liberal Hubris?', 27–48. See also Richmond, 'De-Romantising the Local, De-Mystifying the International'.

62 Traditional authority is based upon customs, and authority is generally hereditary as it is passed down through generations. Charismatic authority is where authority is invested in an extraordinary leader who has the capacity to inspire and unite people. See Weber, *From Max Weber*, 251. See also Mearns, *Looking Both Ways.*

63 Chesterman, *You, the People*, 136.

64 Trindade, 'Reconciling Conflicting Paradigms', 161 and Grenfell, 'Governance, Violence and Crises in Timor-Leste', 88. For an Indonesian perspective on culture, identity and linguistic diversity in East Timor, see Hadiwinata, 'Sejarah Perbatasan Indonesia-Timor-Leste', 67.

65 Krause and Renwick, 'Introduction', xi.

66 Kingsbury, *East Timor: The Price of Liberty*, 10 and Weber, *From Max Weber*, 251.

67 Buchanan, *Justice, Legitimacy and Self-Determination*, 233.

68 Weber, *From Max Weber*, 71–72.

Introduction 17

69 Alagappa, 'Introduction', 2; Buchanan, *Justice, Legitimacy and Self-Determination*, 232 and 238 and Franck, 'The Emerging Right of Democratic Governance', 51.
70 Holsti, *The State, War, and the State of the War*, xi.
71 March and Olsen, *Rediscovering Institutions*, 155.
72 Fukuyama, *State-Building*, 26; Sahin, 'Building the Nation in Timor-Leste', 225 and March and Olsen, *Rediscovering Institutions*, 161.
73 Diamond, *Developing Democracy*, 162; Diamond, 'Cause and Effect', 238–239 and Putnam, *Making Democracy Work*, Chapter 10.
74 Holsti, *The State, War, and the State of the War*, 84. See also Lemay-Hébert, 'State-building without Nation-building?', 21–45.
75 Brown, 'The Nation-Building Agenda in Timor-Leste', 30; Mearns, 'Imagining East Timor Again' and Kingsbury and Leach, 'Introduction', 2.
76 Brown, ibid.
77 Beauvais, 'Benevolent Despotism', 1101; Chopra, 'Building State Failure in East Timor'; Hohe, 'The Clash of Paradigms'; Morison, 'Democratisation and Timor-Leste after UNTAET', 179–184 and Trindade, 'Reconciling Conflicting Paradigms', 163–164.
78 Chopra, ibid., 981.
79 Wesley, 'The State of the Art on the Art of State Building', 374 and Ottaway, 'Rebuilding State Institutions in Collapsed States', 1002.
80 Chopra, 'The UN's Kingdom of East Timor', 33.
81 Hohe, 'The Clash of Paradigms', 570 and 587. See also Cummins, 'Democracy or Democrazy?', 899–900.
82 Chopra and Hohe, 'Participatory Intervention', 291–292.
83 Linz and Stepan, *Problems of Democratic Transition and Consolidation*, 7 and 17 and Linz, 'Democracy Today', 120–121.
84 UN Security Council Resolution 1272 emphasised co-operation and consultation in Section 8. See United Nations Security Council, *Resolution 1272*, Section 8. Various reports emphasised consultation in areas, such as political decision-making, civic education, development, agriculture, the constitution, the Commission for Reception, Truth and Reconciliation and post-UNTAET plans. See United Nations Security Council, *Report of the Secretary-General on the United Nations Transitional Administration in East Timor*, 1; United Nations Security Council, *Report of the Secretary-General on the United Nations Transitional Administration in East Timor (for the period 27 July to 16 January 2001)*, 1; United Nations Security Council, *Interim Report of the Secretary-General on the United Nations Transitional Administration in East Timor*, 1 and 5; United Nations Security Council, *Report of the Secretary-General on the United Nations Transitional Administration in East Timor*, 6 and United Nations Security Council, *Progress Report of the Secretary-General on the United Nations Transitional Administration in East Timor*, 4, 6, 8 and 10.
85 Chesterman, *You, the People*, 72.
86 Pridham *et al.*, 'Introduction', 1.
87 Linz and Stepan, *Problems of Democratic Transition and Consolidation*, 3.
88 Diamond, *Developing Democracy*, 9.
89 Levitsky and Way, *Competitive Authoritarianism*. See also Peou, 'The Limits and Potential of Liberal Democratisation in Southeast Asia', 21–22 and Hadenius and Teorell, 'Pathways from Authoritarianism', 147–148.
90 Huntington, 'After Twenty Years', 4.
91 Ibid.
92 Harris and Goldsmith, 'The Struggle for Independence Was Just the Beginning', 3.
93 Peou, 'The Limits and Potential of Liberal Democratisation in Southeast Asia', 33–34 and Huntington, 'After Twenty Years', 6.
94 Diamond, *Developing Democracy*, 162.

18 *Introduction*

95 Ibid., 161. Civic communities are not without conflict but they are tolerant of opposing views. See Putnam, *Making Democracy Work*, 89.
96 Schrader, 'Elites as Facilitators or Impediments to Political Development?', 70.
97 Huntington, 'After Twenty Years', 9.
98 Ibid. See also Dobbins and Miller, 'Overcoming Obstacles to Peace', 115.
99 See Gill, *The Dynamics of Democratization*, 6–8, 44 and Chapter 4.
100 CAVR, *Chega!*, Chapter 7:1, 76.
101 Marshall, 'Citizenship and Social Class' and Rawls, *A Theory of Justice*.
102 Meyer and Hinchman, *The Theory of Social Democracy*, 58.
103 Ibid., 2.
104 Miller, 'Democracy and Social Justice', 18.
105 Rawls, *A Theory of Justice*.
106 Meyer and Hinchman, *The Theory of Social Democracy*, 58.
107 Rawls, *A Theory of Justice*, 3.
108 Ibid.
109 Kaufman, 'Community Power, Grassroots Democracy, and the Transformation of Social Life', 1–26. See also Manor, 'Democratisation with Inclusion', 5–29.
110 Diamond, *Developing Democracy*, 162.
111 Almond and Verba, *The Civic Culture*, 9 and Putnam, *Making Democracy Work*, 87 and 120.
112 Diamond, *Developing Democracy*, 161.
113 Ibid., 171.
114 Anheier, *Civil Society*, 21–22.
115 Lovell, 'Promoting Democracy: The Challenge of Creating a Civil Society', 333.
116 Eisenstadt, 'Public Spheres and Civil Society in Selected Pre-Modern Societies', 2.
117 Hollaway cited in Shires, *Situation Analysis of Civil Society Organisations in East Timor*, 10.
118 Meyer and Hinchman, *The Theory of Social Democracy*.
119 Gellner, *Conditions of Liberty*, 5.
120 Patrick, 'East Timor Emerging from Conflict', 55.
121 Diamond, *Developing Democracy*, 164.
122 Feldman, 'Imposed Constitutionalism', 880.
123 March and Olsen, *Rediscovering Institutions*, 16.

1 The pursuit of democratic independence

Democratisation literature has long held the view that the support of political elites is a necessary condition for sustainable transition to democracy. In a broad sense, the political values propagated by East Timorese 'elites' during the independence movement were consistent with the democratic institutions that were ultimately built in East Timor. While appeals to democracy justified claims to self-determination to the international community, social democratic ideals were used to unify clandestine organisations working within East Timor during Indonesia's occupation and formed the basis of the platforms of peak independence bodies. From 1974 to 1999, key leaders of East Timor's independence movement promoted democratic political ideals, including rights to political participation, collective freedom from foreign domination and protection of human rights.

There were two distinct phases in the East Timorese independence movement. The first phase was characterised by the formation of political parties in 1974–1975, during which time ideas about East Timor's future political status were developed. The collapse of the Portuguese government in 1974 provided a pathway to decolonisation as it replaced Portugal's dictatorship with a socialist democratic government committed to granting rights of self-determination to Portugal's overseas provinces.[1,2] The main political parties were *União Democrática Timorense*/Timorese Democratic Union (UDT), the *Associação Social Democrática Timorense*/Timorese Social Democratic Association (ASDT, later *Frente Revolucionária de Timor Leste Independente*/Revolutionary Front for an Independent East Timor or FRETILIN) and the *Associação Popular Democrática Timorense*/Timorese Popular Democratic Association (APODETI).[3] While debates revolved around whether East Timor should be independent, and whether independence should entail a 'thoroughgoing revolution', there was in essence little ideological difference in the vision of social democratic statehood and citizenship rights developed by the main parties.[4] Each party committed a future East Timorese government to democratic principles, including freedom, equality and human rights.[5] Nevertheless, the divergent perspectives on East Timor's status led to civil conflict in 1975 and exposed East Timor to invasion by Indonesia.[6]

The second phase began with Indonesia's annexation of East Timorese territory, which transformed the independence movement into a war of liberation

20   *The pursuit of democratic independence*

working on multiple fronts. Occupied with resistance and survival in the late 1970s, it was not until the early 1980s that a coherent movement began to emerge. With the unification of different groups under the leadership of Xanana Gusmão, the independence movement became increasingly defined by peak bodies rather than political parties. These peak bodies, including the *Conselho Nacional da Resistência Maubere*/National Council of *Maubere* Resistance (CNRM) and the *Conselho Nacional de Resistência Timorense*/National Council of Timorese Resistance (CNRT), were devoted to serving the national goals of self-determination and independence. They incorporated various political parties and organisations, including FRETILIN, the *Resistência Nacional dos Estudantes de Timor Leste*/National Resistance of East Timor Students (RENETIL), and *Organização de Juventude e Estudante Católica de Timor-Leste*/East Timorese Catholic Youth Organisation (OJECTIL).[7] The peak bodies were intended to unify the independence movement and coordinate the activities of the different groups pursuing independence.[8]

Among the goals of the CNRM and CNRT was the establishment of a democratic state in East Timor through recognition of East Timor's sovereign independence. The creation of the CNRM was part of Gusmão's strategy to establish a unified national movement based upon democratic principles rather than revolutionary Marxism.[9] It framed East Timor's claims to independence within the discourse of fundamental human rights, including establishing East Timor's right to establish an independent democratic state. By the 1990s, the movement had unified around a basic vision of statehood which included the demand for collective and individual freedoms.

The Commission for Reception, Truth and Reconciliation's *Chega!* report notes that the end of the Cold War played a role in underscoring the independence movement's focus on democracy and human rights.[10] This international context was important because the international diplomatic efforts, complemented by armed resistance strategies, were required for international recognition of self-determination rights under international law, a prerequisite for constructing an East Timorese social democratic sovereign state.[11] In 1998, the CNRM was replaced by the National Council of Timorese Resistance (CNRT), the key resistance body that ultimately oversaw the processes of East Timor's decolonisation and represented the East Timorese people within the international community.

East Timor was not a political 'blank slate' prior to the 1999 referendum. Indeed, ideals of social democracy and human rights were disseminated and supported by the peak independence bodies and leaders and justified East Timor's claims to statehood. The social democratic vision of statehood that was developed during the resistance subsequently represented a political promise that would need to be fulfilled following the 1999 independence referendum. An enduring belief in democracy among the key independence leaders who would go on to become the political 'elite' of an independent state is important for understanding East Timor's democratic transition.

Emergence of East Timor's independence movement: 1974–1975

On 25 April 1974, the Salazar-Caetano regime in Portugal was overthrown by the Portuguese Armed Movement (AMF) during the 'Carnation Revolution'.[12] The new leftist-Portuguese government sought democracy and decolonisation following violent conflicts that had been occurring for over a decade in African provinces such as Angola, Mozambique and Guinea-Bissau.[13] It quickly began the process of granting decolonisation to all Portuguese 'provinces', including East Timor, by promulgating law number 7:1974 recognising 'independence as an acceptable outcome of the process of self-determination in the colonies'.[14] Soon after, on 5 May 1974, the Portuguese Governor of East Timor issued a proclamation permitting the establishment of political parties and enabling a level of political freedom not previously experienced under former Portuguese administrations.[15]

Portuguese colonial rule had provided little culture for self-governing at an official state level in East Timor.[16] While traditional forms of political organisation existed at local levels, formal authority primarily rested with the Portuguese governor.[17] Only one political party had been permitted under the Portuguese administration, the *Acção Nacional Popular*/National Popular Association.[18] According to Mário Carrascalão, there was only one clandestine anti-colonial movement in East Timor in 1974, the Revolutionary Movement for the Liberation of Timor (MORELT).[19]

Observers, such as Jolliffe, Taylor and Dunn, generally agree that the Portuguese revolution galvanised East Timor's political movement because it presented new possibilities concerning its political status.[20] The *coup* 'immediately transformed the political landscape of Portuguese Timor', which had previously experienced low levels of political activity.[21] East Timorese independence leader Xanana Gusmão argues that the East Timorese were happy the Carnation Revolution occurred as they held high hopes for new political freedom and 'had been waiting for this to happen'.[22] According to Domingos de Oliviera, before 25 April 1974, people were 'scared because the authorities would shoot them, so they did not talk openly'.[23]

While the changes initially had little effect on the rural population, among the educated urban community it signalled an opportunity for the East Timorese to pursue new political ideas and arrangements and anti-colonial associations quickly emerged.[24] In the early 1970s, many young intellectuals who would play important roles in the independence movement, including José Ramos-Horta, Nicolau Lobato, Xavier do Amaral, Domingos de Oliviera and Mari Alkatiri, held meetings regarding East Timor's political status and contributed political commentary to *Seara*, a Catholic newspaper not subject to censorship laws.[25] However, not all East Timorese were supportive of the news and East Timor's preparedness for full sovereign independence created some concern among other states.[26] Mário Carrascalão recalled his concern about the economic situation in East Timor as it relied heavily upon support from Portugal.[27]

22 *The pursuit of democratic independence*

In the months following the Carnation Revolution, this group of intellectuals moved to form political parties, provoking political discussion among the East Timorese.[28] Many of the politically inexperienced young men who drove the initial independence movement were children of *liurais* (tribal chiefs) and educated at the same Jesuit seminary school in Dare.[29] The intellectuals generally had 'privileged' backgrounds, including land ownership, and some, such as the Carrascalão brothers and José Ramos-Horta, were children of Portuguese *deportados*.[30] To put the education of these 'intellectuals' in context, there was only one secondary school in East Timor in 1975, with approximately 250 students enrolled, and no university.[31] No schools in Portuguese Timor taught politics formally, although some Jesuit teachers discussed the national independence movements occurring across Asia and ideas about economic development.[32] According to Pinto and Jardine, these teachers 'helped engender a sense of Timorese identity among the students by discussing East Timor's colonial predicament and its future'.[33] Most intellectuals in Dili had little practical political knowledge, such as how to organise political parties.[34] Yet despite these limitations, by the end of May 1974, three new political parties had formed in East Timor.

Political parties and their visions for East Timor's future

Sovereign independence was not necessarily a certain outcome of Portugal's decolonisation of East Timor. There were three realistic options: a continuing association with Portugal; sovereign independence; or, integration within Indonesia.[35] The first party to emerge, the Timorese Democratic Union (UDT, 11 May 1974), advocated the first option by declaring that East Timor should become a federated state within Portugal.[36] The platform of the UDT party was mostly conservative due to the organising committee's ties with the old Portuguese regime.[37] The UDT program expressed the founding members' belief in 'progressive autonomy' and increased East Timorese participation in public administration under the Portuguese flag.[38]

The UDT party became known as the 'pro-Portuguese' party and was supported by higher-level civil servants, *liurais*, plantation owners, the Portuguese community and ethnic-Chinese businessmen.[39] Those who supported the UDT party generally held authority or an advantageous political or social status.[40] The original leadership of the UDT consisted of Francisco Lopes da Cruz (President), Cèsar Augusto da Costa Mouzinho (Vice-President), Mário Carrascalão (head of the Organising Committee), his brother João and Domingos de Oliveira (Secretary-General).[41] Some of the UDT founding members, including Lopes da Cruz, Mário Carrascalão and da Costa Mouzinho, had been part of the Portuguese administration and members of the National Popular Association.[42]

The UDT manifesto outlined East Timor's rights to self-determination within a Portuguese federation and rejected integration with any other state, including Indonesia.[43] Some of the basic democratic principles espoused in their manifesto included freedom of thought and association, and protection of universal human rights. It also demonstrated a belief in equitable distribution of wealth, which is a central tenet of social democratic political systems.[44] Domingos de Oliveira, for instance, described the fundamental principles of the UDT's platform as the defence of universal human rights, fair distribution of wealth, democratisation of East Timor and the repudiation of any attempts by Indonesia or other states to annex East Timor.[45] Many leaders, including Mário and João Carrascalão were 'moderates' who rejected a radical agenda involving rapid or extensive change of economic, political and social structures, instead favouring 'the kind of reform that would have established the basis for a conventional developing world democracy'.[46]

While initially advocating Portuguese administration, after meeting with community members on 1 August 1974, the UDT shifted its platform to achieving eventual independence following a 15–20 year transitionary or preparation period during which infrastructure and strategies for effective self-government would be developed.[47] On an Australian fact-finding mission, Dunn observed that the parties who did not advocate independence could be 'safely ignored' because the idea of independence was so popular among the East Timorese.[48] Indeed, Ramos-Horta identified two key reasons for the UDT's position change: first, the East Timorese people were highly supportive of independence; and second, Portugal was reluctant to stay in East Timor.[49]

The UDT's promotion of complete independence was also triggered by the formation of a rival political party, the Timorese Social Democratic Association (ASDT), whose firm pro-independence stance contributed to its growing popularity.[50] On 20 May 1974, the ASDT was formed by mostly young intellectuals who had previously engaged in political activities against Portugal.[51] Many of the organising committee were Catholics who had trained at the Jesuit seminary in Dare and were employed as public servants and teachers. Founding members included elder statesman and nationalist Francisco Xavier do Amaral, independence 'hero' Nicolau Lobato (killed in 1978) and future Prime Ministers Mari Alkatiri and José Ramos-Horta.[52] In May 1975, the independence leader and future President and Prime Minister of the RDTL, Xanana Gusmão, joined FRETILIN and became a member of its Central Committee in September 1975.[53]

The ASDT manifesto declared the rights of the East Timorese people to independence and rejected any form of colonialism. Among the leaders of the ASDT, greater awareness of the features of colonialism – including discrimination, economic under-development and exploitation – fostered their opposition to imperialism.[54] The ASDT manifesto called for the 'immediate participation of competent Timorese in the local administration and government', and appealed to nationalist and anti-colonial sentiments by promising to 'declare immediate independence and to drastically change the colonial administration structure'.[55] In reality, the ASDT, like the UDT, promoted a transition period to prepare for independence.[56] However, they sought a shorter period of transition (eight to ten years) and thoroughly rejected imperialism from the outset. Their vision of self-determination rested upon East Timor's complete sovereign independence.[57]

24 *The pursuit of democratic independence*

The ASDT's platform was based upon the 'universal doctrines of socialism and democracy', and José Ramos-Horta's influence in naming the party reflected his beliefs in social democracy.[58] Ramos-Horta advocated social justice, mixed economy, income distribution and a democratic political system for a future East Timorese state.[59] In August 1974, he linked social democracy to a 'tradition of village level democracy': 'we call our party social-democratic – not in the European sense, but in the tradition of *Mauberism* [*Maubere* meaning 'my brother', *Mauberism* 'removing inferiority']'.[60] A founding member of the ASDT, Justino Moto, argued that the 'ASDT was social democratic, with the emphasis on democratic. It was formed to defend the idea of the right to independence'.[61] Moderate nationalists Xavier do Amaral and Nicolau Lobato also sought social democracy and opposed full capitalist and full socialist systems.[62]

Members of the ASDT largely agreed that a range of conditions would be necessary for independence, including literacy programs, agricultural development, political consciousness-raising, full Timorese participation in political structures and cultural reassertion.[63] The leadership at the time was influenced by the ideas of Marxist educationalist Paulo Freire, author of *Pedagogy of the Oppressed* (1970), who advocated co-operation, unity, organisation and cultural synthesis as the key to breaking the bonds of oppression.[64] In the months after its formation, the ASDT worked intensively to implement literacy programs and raise East Timorese political consciousness. The ASDT used local languages, historical myths and traditional concepts to ground ideas of social democracy within Timorese culture.[65]

On 27 May 1974, the Popular Democratic Association (APODETI) was formed by supporters of East Timorese integration into Indonesia.[66] Leaders Arnaldo dos Reis Araújo and Guilherme Gonçalves were given favours from the Indonesian State Intelligence Coordinating Agency, *Badan Koordinasi Intelijen Negara* (BAKIN), in return for their work in the APODETI. According to Taylor and Ballard, the APODETI was very much a product of BAKIN from its inception.[67] Although a small party, never comprising more than a few hundred supporters, the APODETI nonetheless became an important vehicle for Indonesian propaganda inside and outside East Timor.[68] According to APODETI member Gabriel da Costa, the party considered joining neighbouring Indonesia a better option than staying with distant Portugal.[69] The pro-integration stance of the APODETI was underpinned by predictions that East Timor would be unviable as an independent sovereign state and that Indonesia would probably seize it anyway.[70] The APODETI also focused upon the close ties between East and West Timor, which was initially colonised by the Dutch and became a province within post-colonial Indonesia.[71]

Like the other parties, the APODETI appealed to key social democratic values in order to gain support for their political agenda, including 'human rights, freedom, a just income distribution, free education, free medical treatment and the right to strike'.[72] The APODETI's manifesto declared a commitment to basic civil rights and freedom of expression, despite the fact that these would not have been provided under an Indonesian constitution. Along with the other two

The pursuit of democratic independence   25

parties, the APODETI advocated freedom of religion and anti-discrimination laws and were opposed to corruption.[73] The narrow ideological divide between the main parties might be explained by a lack of political experience among the main actors.[74] However, it also suggests that values of social justice, civil liberties and human rights were important for attaining the support of the East Timorese people. However, APODETI's popularity was compromised by its unwillingness to support East Timorese independence.

In August 1974, there were accusations by members of the Indonesian media that the ASDT were communist and had adopted an increasingly radical position. On 12 September 1974, the ASDT changed its name to FRETILIN as some members became dissatisfied with the term 'social-democracy' and its 'bourgeois' implications.[75] A small group of left-wing students had returned from Lisbon and suggested remodelling the ASDT on the successful Mozambique Liberation Front (FREMILO).[76] According to Taylor, the ASDT had 'encountered the demand for a more immediate transition' to sovereign independence and FRETILIN consequently altered the policies of the ASDT.[77]

FRETILIN's manifesto continued to advocate social democracy.[78] In 1974–1975, ASDT-FRETILIN engaged in a significant grass-roots campaign called *'consciencialização politica'* (political conscientization) designed to promote political ideas of social democracy.[79] Francisco Xavier do Amaral argued that FRETILIN engaged the East Timorese people in the struggle for independence, whereas the UDT focused their attention on gaining the support of the *liurais* who were considered the social 'elites' before and during the Portuguese occupation.[80] The Portuguese revolution created a power vacuum that needed to be filled, and FRETILIN envisaged a shift in authority from Portuguese backed elites to a new guard supported by democratic legitimacy bestowed by the will of the people. Do Amaral explained the strategy of starting with the grass-roots and moving up declaring 'I don't need the *liurai*, they are with the Portuguese. I need the people'.[81] Gathering support for independence meant raising consciousness among the people about the existence of the nation and its capacity for self-rule. Such political rhetoric touched upon concepts of racial equality, freedom from foreign oppression, and rights to self-govern, and drew upon anti-*malai* (foreigner) sentiments.[82]

FRETILIN were interested in improving living standards and employing a mixed-economy based on free enterprise conditions.[83] While the university students argued for a more radical agenda for FRETILIN, and opposed the social democracy agenda, observers close to the events in East Timor at the time doubted that FRETILIN had any serious intention of trying to establish a communist state.[84] FRETILIN propaganda documents continued to emphasise a program of social and economic justice that included the abolishment of forced labour, equal pay, rights to education and universal participation in political life.[85] Dunn commented that FRETILIN were 'more popularist than socialist in their perception of how to work out a model for the future state of East Timor'.[86] Similarly, Hoadler observed at the time that FRETILIN's communist streak was nothing more than revolutionary rhetoric found among young idealists across the

26 *The pursuit of democratic independence*

globe.[87] In some regards, the left-wing rhetoric of 1974–1975 in East Timor mirrored Portugal's transformation from a dictatorship to a socialist democratic regime.

Whereas the ASDT was formed amid realistic expectations of independence, FRETILIN's transformation into a resistance front was shaped by the increasing likelihood of an Indonesian invasion.[88] Mari Alkatiri, for example, suggested that 'internal and regional realities' compelled the ASDT to create a movement capable of preparing people for a long independence struggle.[89] He argued that an ordinary political party could not resist external threats and would require armed forces.[90] Figure 1.1 illustrates the relationships at the beginning of the independence movement and resistance in East Timor. On 19 and 20 August 1975, FRETILIN created an armed wing, the *Forças de Defesa do Povo Maubere* (FDPM), later known as the *Forças Armadas da Liberação Nacional de Timor Leste*/Armed Forces for the National Liberation of East Timor (FALINTIL).

Civil conflict and the Indonesian invasion

Australian Consular representative James Dunn's personal impressions in 1975 led him to believe FRETILIN was the most popular party in East Timor, particularly among the *Maubere* (ordinary people).[91] Taylor concurs, arguing that FRETILIN had 'undoubtedly become the leading party by the beginning of 1975'.[92] The presence of multiple parties undermined the establishment of a unified vision of independence: as Xavier do Amaral observed, party campaigns created confusion among the East Timorese despite little actual difference in the ideologies of the UDT and the ASDT/FRETILIN.[93] FRETILIN engaged in new programs in the areas of health, education, justice and reconstruction, and became increasingly nationalised and radicalised, claiming to represent all Timorese patriots.[94] This resulted in a significant rise in support for FRETILIN compared with other political parties.[95]

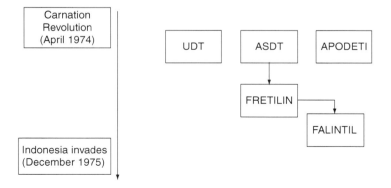

Figure 1.1 East Timor's independence movement: first phase.

The pursuit of democratic independence   27

The *Chega!* report argues that rifts between the UDT and FRETILIN were caused by 'the militant ideologues on their extremes who accused each other, and by extension each other's parties, of being "fascist" or "communist"'.[96] In January 1975, the UDT and FRETILIN had formed a coalition in order to seek East Timor's independence and had agreed to form a transitional government.[97] They envisioned immediate *de jure* independence followed by a staged transitional period leading in 1982 to a transitional government comprised of members of FRETILIN, the UDT and the Portuguese government, which would be responsible for preparing a constitution.[98] The Constitution would then form the basis of East Timor's de facto independence.

Despite the coalition, both parties continued to broadcast propaganda about each other and their antagonistic relationship was stoked by a mutual distrust which gave rise to incidences of violence.[99] The UDT formally withdrew from the coalition on 27 May 1975, following the clear victory of FRETILIN in the elections of chiefs in a number of villages and its subsequent claims as the 'sole legitimate representative of East Timor'.[100] The coalition could not overcome the suspicion held by the parties towards each other and tensions increased following the split.[101]

Dunn observed that Indonesia's strategy involved 'winning over' the UDT by falsely informing them that FRETILIN were planning a *coup* and smuggling arms from their communist allies in China.[102] In early August 1975, leaders of the UDT assured the Indonesian General Ali Murtopo that FRETILIN was not a communist movement, and that a UDT government would expel any communists within FRETILIN to Portugal. However, while moderate leaders Nicolau Lobato, Xavier do Amaral and José Ramos-Horta were abroad in August 1975, the radical left of FRETILIN became more vocal.[103] The anti-communist UDT were fearful that Indonesia might intervene if FRETILIN took control of East Timor.[104] Mário Carrascalão contends that the 'UDT was concerned that if FRETILIN had a Marxist-Leninist ideology Indonesia would use this as an excuse to invade Timor'.[105] While Carrascalão's testimony could be interpreted as defending the UDT party's role in the civil conflict, there is evidence to suggest that Indonesia strategically used the communist threat in order to create conflict between the inexperienced leaders. General Murtopo indicated to the UDT leader João Carrascalão that FRETILIN was planning a *coup* on 15 August 1975.[106] On 11 August 1975, the UDT made a pre-emptive strike against FRETILIN in what was then described as an 'anti-communist' *coup d'etat*.[107] On 19 August, FRETILIN responded with a counter-*coup* against the UDT.[108]

Throughout August and September 1975, FRETILIN and the UDT engaged in a short but brutal campaign for political control of East Timor with fighting taking place across the territory.[109] Both political parties employed violent tactics and violated their opponents' human rights in their quest to establish legitimate rights to rule in East Timor and enact their vision of independence. Around 1,200 to 1,500 people are estimated to have died during the civil conflict, which divided and weakened the pro-independence movement. The conflict compelled the hasty withdrawal of Portuguese administration, which had previously planned to stay in the territory to complete decolonisation in October 1976.[110]

28 *The pursuit of democratic independence*

The conflict between the UDT and FRETILIN reflected social divisions among the East Timorese which stifled the development of national unity. In testimonies to the Commission for Reception, Truth and Reconciliation, East Timorese leaders used the lack of experience and communication as a common justification for the emergence of the conflict between the two parties.[111] While independence was popularly supported, relative political inexperience meant the parties fought each other rather than addressing the larger threat posed by Indonesia.[112] Gusmão blamed both the UDT and FRETILIN for the civil conflict, suggesting that both of their claims to be the sole legitimate representatives of the 'people' left no space for talking or negotiation.[113] East Timorese independence leaders lacked experience in a democratic system involving multiple parties with different opinions and values because the Portuguese had not prepared them for this style of political engagement.[114]

The Indonesian State Intelligence Coordinating Agency, BAKIN, had been conducting covert operations in East Timor from around April 1974 without the Portuguese military intercepting Indonesian intelligence officers travelling to and from Dili.[115] The Portuguese military presence had been reduced just before the Indonesian intelligence-seeking mission *Operasi Komodo* began in December 1974, suggesting that Indonesia's operation was known and intervention anticipated.

After the civil conflict ended in early September 1975, FRETILIN formed government in East Timor while continuing to acknowledge and respect Portuguese sovereignty.[116] The FRETILIN interregnum involved establishing an effective de facto administration in East Timor, an incredibly difficult task given the lack of professionals, technicians and tradesmen left in East Timor. FRETILIN became responsible for dealing with the humanitarian situation and a severe food shortage (with the assistance of international NGOs such as the Red Cross), establishing security, attempting to re-build the civil bureaucracy and stimulating the economy.[117] According to Dunn, by mid-October Dili was functioning close to normal and the interim government 'clearly enjoyed widespread support or cooperation from the population, including many former UDT supporters'.[118] On 28 November 1975, FRETILIN declared East Timor's independence, justifying the unilateral declaration by claiming that their territory 'had been a victim of aggression by Indonesia by land, sea and air'.[119] In response, a coalition of rival political parties, including the UDT and the APODETI, declared that the proclamation of independence contradicted 'the real wishes of the people of Portuguese Timor to exercise an act of self-determination'.[120]

On 8 December 1975, Indonesia formally invaded East Timor by conducting a full-scale air and sea assault, deploying up to 70,000 troops and killing approximately 60,000 people within its first year of occupation.[121] FRETILIN's army, FALINTIL, comprised approximately 10,000 troops defending East Timorese territory using NATO-grade weapons left behind by Portugal; however this proved inadequate for expelling the Indonesian military.[122] Indonesia's early occupation was characterised by widespread displacement of citizens lacking shelter, healthcare or food, summary executions and massacres of the civilian

The pursuit of democratic independence   29

population.[123] The Indonesian military initiated a widespread famine that was responsible for many deaths in the early occupation.[124] Approximately 30 per cent of East Timor's population died during the war with Indonesia, the majority during the 1977–1979 campaign of 'annihilation and encirclement'.[125]

The conflict enabled Indonesia to claim that there was a crisis in East Timor that justified immediate intervention.[126] On 15 December 1975, during UN Security Council debates, the Permanent Representative of Indonesia to the UN, Ambassador Anwar Sani, argued that the civil conflict had produced a dire humanitarian situation with tens of thousands of refugees fleeing East Timor in great numbers due to FRETILIN aggression.[127] Accordingly, the Indonesian government argued they were 'under increasing pressure to take action to protect those people'.[128] Indonesia also provided Portugal's neglect of East Timor as another justification for intervention.[129] Even after East Timor's independence, Indonesia continued to defend the intervention on the basis of the effects the political and security environment potentially held for other states in Southeast Asia, including Indonesia.[130]

Indonesia also claimed they were invited by popular consent.[131] On 29 November, leaders from the UDT, the APODETI, the KOTA and Trabalhista parties signed the 'Balibo Declaration' outlining their support for East Timor's integration into Indonesia.[132] Mário Carrascalão testified later that the political leaders had been indoctrinated by Indonesia, with Domingos de Oliveira reporting that Indonesia coerced leaders to sign it.[133] On 15 December 1975, Indonesian Ambassador Anwar Sani told the UN Security Council that the actions of Indonesia were 'to assist the majority of the people of East Timor upon its own request against the minority [FRETILIN] which wishes to impose its will by force of arms'.[134] In December 1975, Indonesia formed a provisional East Timorese government headed by APODETI leader Arnaldo dos Reis Araújo. A 28-member 'Popular Assembly of East Timor' was formed on 28 May 1976 and, claiming to represent the whole population, unanimously approved integration with Indonesia.[135] In this way, Indonesia sought to persuade the international community that a legitimate act of self-determination had occurred in East Timor.[136]

East Timor's delayed independence: the international context

Many observers have agreed that the international context of the Cold War was a significant reason why the international community acquiesced to Indonesia's occupation of East Timor. Ramos-Horta believes that Indonesia would not have successfully annexed East Timor if it were not for the Cold War.[137] Jusuf Wanandi, an Indonesian political and security strategist, and James Dunn both argue that Indonesia feared that Vietnam, the Soviet Union or China would expand their influence in the Southeast Asian region if their troops were invited to East Timor.[138] The *Chega!* report notes that communist gains in Asia after victories in Vietnam, Laos and Cambodia also 'alarmed the US and its allies and

30 *The pursuit of democratic independence*

worked against Timor-Leste's interests'.[139] The Cold War confounded East Timor's ambitions for self-determination largely because Indonesia had successfully cultivated the image of FRETILIN as communist, propagating a fear that an independent East Timor might become an 'Asian Cuba'.[140] Preventing a Marxist form of government operating in the eastern tip of the 'democratic' Indonesian archipelago provided a rationale for the reluctance of states, such as the United States, to recognise East Timor's claims to self-determination.[141]

At a national party conference in May 1977, members of FRETILIN's Central Committee, including Mari Alkatiri, Roque Rodrigues and António Carvarinho, formally adopted Marxist-Leninism as its central platform.[142] Extreme left ideologues in FRETILIN, such as Roque Rodrigues and António Carvarinho, persuaded more moderate members to adopt a Marxist revolutionary program, including Alarico Fernandes, who became committed to Marxism despite rejecting it prior to Indonesia's invasion. The group met in East Timor (without moderate leader Francisco Xavier do Amaral) to declare Marxist-Leninism as the central doctrine of the party. With the leadership split over the question of Marxism, do Amaral was arrested for 'high treason'.[143] While FRETILIN was a 'broad church' encompassing moderates, conservatives and radicals, Shoesmith argues that the left faction of the FRETILIN Central Committee, inspired by the Vietnamese Revolution and Mao Zedong's Cultural Revolution, were 'disproportionately influential in the decision-making machinery'.[144] By May 1977, groups of FRETILIN members studied and debated *The Thoughts of Chairman Mao* and his theories of war. From September 1977 until February 1979, however, questions of ideology were superseded by Indonesian attacks that left the FRETILIN Central Committee 'virtually destroyed'.[145] From this point, Xanana Gusmão began re-building the resistance, convinced that 'something less doctrinaire' than radical Marxism was necessary for East Timor.[146]

There is debate about how strong the desire to implement a Marxist regime was among the FRETILIN membership in the period of 1977–1984.[147] Mari Alkatiri suggests that FRETILIN's 'revolutionary' and occasionally violent position was necessary 'to bring about a revolutionary social change to address the illiteracy, hunger and poverty of colonised Timor-Leste', and as such reflected a leftist – but not necessarily communist – vision.[148] Alkatiri declared that only 'one or two' FRETILIN members self-identified as communist.[149] However, these comments might be interpreted as historical revisionism: Shoesmith places Alkatiri in the radical left, contending he had a significant role in inserting the 'nationalist-Marxist policies into the Fretilin platform'.[150] Kiernan acknowledges that 'intense' political and ideological divisions were apparent within FRETILIN even during its Marxist-Leninist period.[151] Similarly, Hill suggests that 'a very strong current within FRETILIN' thought Marxist policies would only provoke Indonesia, and Smith argued that any Marxist tendencies were 'much exaggerated by some observers and foreign governments'.[152]

In any case, support for radical left ideology began to decline after FRETILIN authorised the intimidation and execution of opponents, which alienated moderate FRETILIN members, such as Xanana Gusmão.[153] According to

The pursuit of democratic independence   31

Gusmão, elements of the leftist wing of FRETILIN were responsible for assassinating people they perceived as reactionaries and traitors.[154] FRETILIN's attempts to include China in its plan to secure international support and recognition compounded the suspicion of communist or 'Maoist' influences in the region. However, Chinese assistance only lasted until 1977, and the Soviet Union showed little interest in East Timor (despite supporting several leftist liberation movements during the Cold War).[155] Despite East Timor's lack of support from communist states, Indonesia was able to exploit FRETILIN's alleged links to Marxism.[156] Regardless of the extent of FRETILIN's support for communism, its time as a Marxist-Leninist party certainly assisted the Indonesians in justifying its occupation to its valuable Western allies.[157]

The 'communist' justification for intervention disguised one of the key motives for Indonesia's occupation of East Timorese territory, which was the prevention of a viable democratic state being formed within the Indonesian archipelago that could give hope to other secessionist movements.[158] The emergence of either a communist or a democratic East Timorese sovereign state would have been problematic for the goals and priorities of the New Order Indonesian regime.[159] Without downplaying the intensity of anti-communist sentiments during the Cold War, the core reason for Indonesia's invasion was not necessarily FRETILIN's communist leanings. Rather, the real issue for Indonesia was that East Timor's desire to establish an independent democracy undermined its goals of consolidating political control and unification of the entire archipelago.[160] Hence, the Cold War context obscured East Timorese democratic aspirations as Indonesia and others exaggerated the communist elements in FRETILIN for their own ends.

Unifying the independence movement: formation of the CNRM and the CNRT

Following the Indonesian invasion, FRETILIN resistance operations pitted pro-independence forces against pro-Indonesian elements and the Indonesian military.[161] Domestically, FRETILIN had established itself as the dominant resistance movement despite its near destruction in 1978 due to the Indonesian campaign.[162] In the late 1970s, the movement was preoccupied with resistance against the Indonesians as FALINTIL, the armed wing of FRETILIN, employed guerrilla tactics to fight Indonesian troops.[163] By the 1980s, attention shifted to unifying the independence movement around principles of democracy.

FRETILIN's dominance began to decline following a restructure of the resistance initiated by Xanana Gusmão's rise to leadership as National Political Commissar and Commander-in-Chief of FALINTIL in 1981.[164] During the reorganisation of the National Conference in March 1981, the *Conselho Revolucionário de Resistência Nacional*/Revolutionary Council of National Resistance (CRRN) was formed under Gusmão's leadership and adopted a policy of promoting national unity among the different organisations working for independence.[165] As represented in Figure 1.2, the CRRN was created as 'an umbrella forum for all pro-independence elements, not only FRETILIN'.[166] Significantly,

32 *The pursuit of democratic independence*

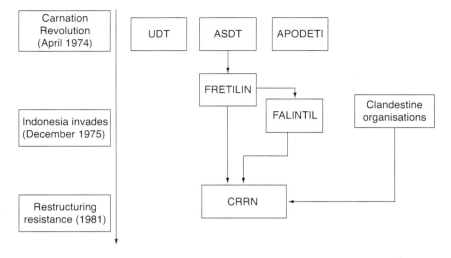

Figure 1.2 Reorganising the independence movement: stage 1.

this restructure represented a movement away from the radical Marxist policies adopted by FRETILIN in 1977.

In 1983, Gusmão began advocating pluralism and multi-party democracy for a future East Timorese state, recognising the failures of Marxist policies in creating the national unity necessary for a long-lasting resistance campaign.[167] Gusmão, while making attempts to understand Marxism, had increasingly found himself opposing FRETILIN'S 'ideological extremists'. He negotiated a ceasefire with Indonesia, and travelled around East Timor advocating democracy, free elections, and respect for key human rights.[168] By 1983, FRETILIN's Central Committee had similarly acknowledged the need for national unity and subsequently altered several of its earlier radical policies in order to broaden its appeal. In 1984, the radical Marxist-Leninist policies of FRETILIN were officially revoked.[169]

One of the central aims of Gusmão's leadership was nationalising and unifying the independence movement comprised of various clandestine associations and political parties.[170] According to Philpott:

> Gusmão began promoting a pluralist, multi-party vision of national unity in which FRETILIN would be a broad national movement embodying competing ideological standpoints. He also guaranteed FRETILIN's respect for freedom of expression, conscience and association and apologised for its earlier excesses.[171]

This suggests that Gusmão considered the centrist ideals of democracy and pluralism as integral to broadening the support base and bringing together the disparate components of the independence movement.

The pursuit of democratic independence 33

Refusing to accept the primacy of any one party in East Timor, Gusmão formally left FRETILIN in 1987.[172] His resignation coincided with the formation of the National Council of *Maubere* Resistance (CNRM), a 'non-partisan nationalist movement', illustrated in Figure 1.3.[173] Members of FRETILIN had sought to establish East Timorese nationalism by turning the term '*Maubere*' into a synonym for the East Timorese 'common' man, and using the Tetum slogan *ukun rasik an* meaning independence or self-government.[174] The formation of the CNRM was a turning point in the independence movement: as Shoesmith suggests, this was part of Gusmão's plan to 'remove the struggle from FRETILIN control'.[175] Its establishment diminished ideological differences between the pro-independence groups and furthered the unification of, and support for, the national resistance project. Independence became linked to national unification rather than revolution as Gusmão sought to counter the radical Marxist influence by promising that FALINTIL would not allow a leftist regime in East Timor. He stated:

> I publicly declare my total and wholehearted rejection of those doctrines that promote suppression of democratic freedoms in East Timor. I publicly declare that the FALINTIL *aswain* [warrior] will not permit the installation of a leftist regime that not only intends to provoke internal disintegration, but also to destabilize the whole area in which East Timor is situated.[176]

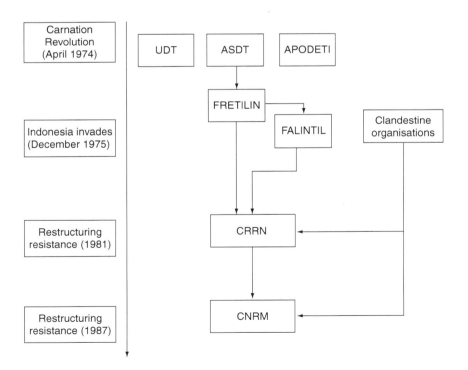

Figure 1.3 Reorganising the independence movement: stage 2.

34 *The pursuit of democratic independence*

The constitution adopted by the CNRM guaranteed the defence of 'individuals and collective freedoms and the respect of the interests of all citizens and social classes in East Timor'.[177] For Gusmão, the ideals of democracy were more likely to establish a unified national movement than revolutionary Marxist doctrine.[178]

Indeed, Gusmão found the Marxists to be guilty of 'political infantilism' and 'thoughtless adventurism', arguing that radicalism had led the East Timorese 'to put many compatriots on the same footing as the criminal aggressor'.[179] He identified radicalism as divisive and overly prescriptive, and instead advocated principles of plural democracy as beneficial for uniting diverse interest groups around the common goal of independence. Gusmão requested members of FRETILIN's left faction to 'correct' previous political ideas and remove ideological rigidity.[180]

The creation of the CNRM was a significant step in the non-partisan unifying and nationalising of the independence movement, and it would become the key umbrella body of the resistance.[181] The CNRM was not, however, a political party: it was an umbrella civil society organisation designed to bring together those working towards independence, including students, political parties and the armed faction. The restructuring of the resistance movement along 'inclusive, non-partisan lines' corresponded with the decision by FRETILIN to abandon its self-image as the only legitimate representative of the East Timorese people.[182] In recognition of this unification, FALINTIL, under the leadership of Gusmão, separated from FRETILIN and became a 'neutral' organisation operating alongside all factions under the CNRM umbrella.[183]

In detention (following his arrest by the Indonesian military in 1992) Gusmão called upon the East Timorese diaspora in 1998 to hold a National Convention in order to re-evaluate the strategies of the independence movement, in light of Indonesian President Suharto's fall from leadership.[184] This political transition in Indonesia presented new possibilities for a negotiated solution for East Timor. In April 1998, the CNRM held a National Convention in Penichè, near the Portuguese capital Lisbon, with the aim of unifying all five pro-independence parties and overcoming divisions, in addition to discussing preparations for potential statehood.[185] A letter from Gusmão stressed: 'we shall make it crystal clear, and as forcefully as possible, to the regime and the world that the East Timor people demand the right to self-determination and independence'.[186] The 218 delegates sought to do this by strengthening the movement through dialogue, consensus-building and increasing 'international confidence in its capacity' as a key resistance body representative of the majority of East Timorese people.[187] The organisation was democratic insofar as conference delegates and office bearers were elected, setting patterns for future representative government in East Timor.[188]

At the conference, the CNRM changed its name to National Council of Timorese Resistance (CNRT), illustrated in Figure 1.4. This was largely symbolic; the UDT was incorporated into the resistance structure for the first time, and the divisive term '*Maubere*' was removed from the title of the independence movement's umbrella body as the term 'Timorese' was considered

The pursuit of democratic independence 35

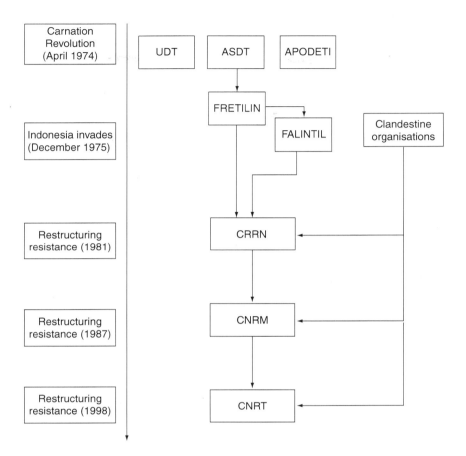

Figure 1.4 Reorganising the independence movement: stage 3.

more inclusive.[189] For the first time, the UDT also acknowledged Xanana Gusmão as the leader of the independence movement, and he was elected President of CNRT with José Ramos-Horta as Vice-President.[190] For the international community, the CNRT 'gave focus to the resistance and presented itself as a skeleton of a possible East Timorese state, perhaps even a government of national reconciliation'.[191]

The evolution of the independence movement, from division and radicalism to moderate pluralism and unification, can be traced through the creation of these key peak bodies. The names of independence organisations reflect these shifts in the independence movement, moving from 'Revolutionary' bodies (FRETILIN/CRRN), to the grass-roots *Maubere*-focused organisation (CNRM), and finally, to an all-inclusive 'Timorese' national council (CNRT). As Walsh observes, the CNRT represented a 'rejection of party politics in favour of an inclusive,

36 *The pursuit of democratic independence*

pluralist system'.[192] It was the end product of an independence movement that had struggled to locate 'the vehicle, ideology and strategy best suited to advance the nationalist agenda'.[193] It represented the final stage of unification under the leadership of Xanana Gusmão.

Visions of the unified independence movement for an East Timorese state

The end of the Cold War coincided with a shift in the policies of the East Timorese resistance leaders, particularly in how they approached international diplomacy.[194] In the 1990s, the international context played an important role in the decisions of the National Council of *Maubere* Resistance (CNRM) and National Council of Timorese Resistance (CNRT) to focus explicitly on establishing inclusive democratic structures. Gusmão's leadership of the independence movement propelled a shift toward nationalising the movement and unifying people around common goals of inclusive social democracy, human rights and freedom.

The shift back to democratic aspirations in East Timor mirrored what was occurring in the international realm. According to Ramos-Horta, the world completely changed in the early 1990s when the Soviet Union collapsed. He suggests the military might of the Soviet Union could not save it because its people rejected its empire built upon fear, suspicion and repression of human rights.[195] The ideological war between communist and capitalist forces came to an end, eliminating the need for 'containment' of communist resistance movements. During the 1990s, Indonesia's justification for the annexation of East Timor did not hold the same currency as it did in the 1970s and 1980s.

The end of the Cold War meant liberal democracies had effectively won the ideological battle against communism and shifted the global balance of power. Corresponding with this 'liberal triumph' and the promise of a 'new world order', the East Timorese independence movement shifted toward peaceful resistance and a greater focus on human rights, emphasising the campaign of international diplomacy as a strategy for gaining international recognition of sovereign statehood.[196] The CNRM, under the leadership of Gusmão, challenged the idea that the independence movement was a radical project and focused instead on human rights and democracy.[197] According to Niner, following the construction of the CNRM, FRETILIN's leftist ideology became further diluted.[198] Independence leaders working outside of East Timor, including José Ramos-Horta, presented the international community with pathways for peace that emphasised the need for human rights protections (in accordance with UN rights covenants), democratically representative and consultative political structures, and reconciliation.[199]

The CNRM supported their claims for independence by appealing to political values that were broadly accepted by the international community, especially established Western states. According to Gusmão, the East Timorese leadership was 'committed to building a free and democratic nation, based on respect for the freedoms of thought, association and expression, as well as complete respect

The pursuit of democratic independence   37

of Universal Human Rights'.[200] On 5 October 1989, Gusmão produced a 20-page document of guidelines for East Timor's independence which was circulated domestically and internationally.[201] It defended the 'inalienable right of the Maubere people to an act of self-determination' and proposed dialogue with Indonesia and the UN in order to resolve the issue of colonialism in East Timor.[202] Gusmão's plan proposed a discussion about the legality of Indonesia's invasion and argued that providing individual human rights was the key to lasting peace. He appealed for international assistance in holding a referendum to ensure its validity and 'respect for the supreme wishes of the people of East Timor, as freely and democratically expressed'.[203] The proposal hence advocated for a democratic independence ballot to provide a legitimate act of self-determination.

Gusmão proposed establishing a transitional administration headed by a representative from Portugal for a maximum of five years. Portugal's provision of a transitional administration would include facilitating a quick and 'harmonious development of East Timor's potential'.[204] During this time, dates for general elections would be set, and the formation of a 'National Unity Government' would take a period of five to 15 years, to be decided between Portuguese and East Timorese leaders. The timeline presented by Gusmão was similar to those outlined in the manifestos of the UDT and the ASDT in 1974.

In 1992, a Peace Plan proposed by the CNRM included a three-stage plan for independence and reflected the independence leaders decision to create democratic structures.[205] This plan was developed and presented to the European Parliament by the CNRM's Special Representative José Ramos-Horta.[206] Its purpose was to draw international attention to the struggle for East Timorese independence, the continuing conflict and human rights violations, and to ask member states of the European Union for assistance in brokering an acceptable solution. As the *Chega!* report notes, it was during this stage that Gusmão became increasingly recognised as a leading figure in the search for a solution to the 'question of East Timor'.[207]

Phase One of the Peace Plan involved a suspension of armed activity and the 'restoration' of all basic human rights, including rights to political activities and assembly (rights typically associated with representative and participatory forms of government).[208] This would include the introduction of an independent Human Rights Commission in Dili and a representative of the UN Secretary-General.[209] Additionally, this stage would oversee an expansion in the activities and presence of non-government human rights organisations, such as the Red Cross and UN specialised agencies.[210]

Among other things, Phase Two anticipated East Timorese autonomy through democratic self-government. Importantly, the Peace Plan indicated that the independence movement leaders desired election of a local assembly, which would take place 'according to universally accepted democratic norms under UN supervision and technical assistance'.[211] This indicates the leadership's efforts to legitimise its vision of statehood by promising the European Union and the international community that internationally accepted democratic political structures would be established.

38 *The pursuit of democratic independence*

Phase Three, self-determination, would be constituted by a vote for independence. Upon approval, there would be an election of a constituent assembly and the creation and adoption of an East Timorese constitution, application for UN membership, ratification of all international human rights instruments and membership of regional institutions, such as ASEAN.[212] These steps indicate that the leadership viewed the institution of democratic structures and the restoration of human rights previously denied – in addition to shaping future relations with other states in the international community – as being important for an East Timorese state. The leadership envisaged relying upon international and regional support to achieve independence and transition to effective democratic statehood.

While the CNRT was not a political party as such, it developed policies that the political parties in the future state would be expected to uphold. The CNRT committed East Timor to a 'pluralist, multi-party, democratic system based upon the rule of law and separation of State and religion'.[213] Gusmão made it clear to the political parties that they must put their ambitions aside in order to present a unified front for independence.[214] He called upon all organisations working within the CNRT to accommodate various political positions in order to advance the prospects of democracy in East Timor.

At the CNRT's 1998 National Convention, the Magna Carta concerning Freedoms, Rights, Duties and Guarantees for the People of East Timor was adopted which 'defined the principles of a future national constitution'.[215] The Magna Carta provided a blueprint for a constitution in the event of East Timor's independence, and was adopted unanimously.[216] It outlined a shared vision of statehood and reflected a firm resolve that independence would be achieved through the 'international rule-of-law'.[217] Achieving this relied upon 'self-determination and independence, social justice, equal rights and responsibilities between the peoples'.[218] It stated that an East Timorese state would respect the United Nations Charter, the Universal Declaration of Human Rights, the International Covenant on Civil and Political Rights and the International Covenant on Economic, Social and Cultural Rights, in addition to other international rights treaties.[219] Tanter, Seldon and Shalom described the Magna Carta as displaying 'CNRT's impressive commitment to building an East Timor that will be a model of social democratic constitutional democracy with strong protection for human rights'.[220] Upon independence, these international treaties became the basis of human rights law in the East Timorese Constitution, and reflected efforts to link international human rights norms to their struggle for independence.

Political rights were listed as 'fundamental freedoms' in the Magna Carta, including freedom of movement, rights to information and speech, and freedom of conscience and religious belief.[221] These rights would be protected by various safeguards including constitutional guarantees, the creation of a democratic legal system based on the rule of law and the punishment of 'authoritarian' actions that might curtail civil liberties.[222] Political rights are widely acknowledged as integral to the effective operation of a democratic political system, and as such, are recognised under international human rights law as requisite for the effective political participation of people within their state.

The pursuit of democratic independence 39

The commitment to inclusive pluralism was demonstrated in several ways: for example, the document rejected any discrimination on the basis of race, age, colour, gender, origin, religious belief or social status.[223] The Magna Carta outlined the cultural rights of the East Timorese, including the responsibilities of the state to promote and respect 'the culture, customs and traditions and religious values of the majority and minority groups who comprise the rich fabric of our nation'.[224] Additionally, the document declared the need for religious tolerance to promote 'solidarity, co-operation and harmony between adherents of different religions, as well as agnostics and atheists, and promotion of ecumenism and mutual respect between faiths while upholding the principle of the separation of State and religion'.[225] The CNRT argued that East Timor had the right to create a plural state based on traditional and modern political and legal institutions.[226]

The CNRT contended that the East Timorese population had rights to implement a peaceful and progressive democratic political system and equal rights to education, property and healthcare services.[227] The Magna Carta states that rights to healthcare and services for mothers and children would be protected through the adoption of laws that 'give priority to public health and preventative medicine'.[228] This reflects a belief that citizens possess socio-economic rights that extend beyond the basic freedoms necessary for making a democracy operational. The Magna Carta offers further evidence of the leadership's preference for developing a social democratic model of statehood and citizenship based on equalising life opportunities through wealth redistribution.

Peace and reconciliation consultations in East Timor, such as Dare I and Dare II, also outlined East Timor's rights to democratic independence and the protection of its peoples' human rights.[229] Dare I was held soon after Indonesia announced in January 1999 that it would allow a referendum for the East Timorese to choose autonomy within Indonesia or independence. Both Dare I and Dare II brought together anti- and pro-independence groups with the aim of beginning dialogue and halting violence between them.[230] All parties involved in the discussion agreed upon guaranteeing democracy, tolerance and respect for difference of opinion.[231]

From 25 to 30 June 1999, in Jakarta, Bishops Carlos Belo and Basilio do Nascimento initiated and promoted the Dare II conference as a pathway to reconciliation and a durable solution.[232] As with Dare I, its principal purpose was to stimulate dialogue between conflicting groups to establish a ceasefire. While considered by some as a failure, basic principles were agreed upon, including that 'every individual in Timor Lorosae has civil, political, social, cultural, religius [*sic*] and economic rights'.[233] The discussions again demonstrated an interest among the participants in creating a democratic state that provided political, legal and socio-economic rights, and freedom from oppression.[234]

Following the referendum in 1999, the CNRT held five commissions in East Timor during 2000 and achieved consensus among the participants on a range of issues. The first commission adopted the 'Pact of National Unity', which committed the political parties to uphold national unity and independence, the rights outlined in the Magna Carta and free, fair and universal elections.[235] In several

40 *The pursuit of democratic independence*

resolutions throughout the commission, the Congress unanimously adopted the Magna Carta, a national action plan on human rights and a resolution of women's rights. It was during these commissions that other crucial decisions were made, including the adoption of Portuguese as the official language (to be replaced by Tetum after 5–10 years development), reconciliation and a republic with a presidential system. These commissions reinforced the Magna Carta as the key document outlining the vision of East Timorese independence.

Conclusion

Creating a democracy focusing upon human rights and social justice was a consistent goal throughout East Timor's independence movement and their transition to statehood. To different degrees, all the major political parties that emerged following the Carnation Revolution pursued a vision of independence grounded in the principles of social democracy and human rights. Ideas of social justice and social democracy largely informed the Carnation Revolution and the decolonisation of Portuguese territories, and also became important in East Timor's independence movement.[236]

During the 1980s and 1990s, the independence movement sought to build a national identity centred upon the shared pursuit of self-determination and sovereign independence. The evolution of peak bodies – from the CRRN to the CNRM and the CNRT – highlighted the failure of revolutionary communism to unify the independence movement. The leadership, driven by Xanana Gusmão, instead used principles of human rights and democracy to strengthen both domestic support for the resistance movement and their claims for self-determination. The evolution of the peak bodies demonstrates the goals for an inclusive, plural and multi-party democracy in East Timor, which was most clearly manifested in the construction of the CNRT and its Magna Carta.

As the following chapters demonstrate, these democratic aspirations remained broadly consistent during and after the state-building mission. The leaders who promoted democratic independence within and beyond East Timor would go on to play influential roles in the state-building process and as politicians in the Democratic Republic of Timor-Leste (see Chapters 3 and 4). As the basis of the Constitution, the Magna Carta demonstrates the CNRT's commitment to protecting and preserving social democracy and human rights in East Timor. The extensive list of political, civil, social, economic and cultural rights pursued during the independence movement would be incorporated in East Timor's Constitution (see Chapters 5, 6 and 7).

Notes

1 CAVR, *Chega!*, Chapter 3, 13–14; Dunn, *Timor: A People Betrayed*, 56; Jolliffe, *East Timor: Nationalism and Colonialism*, 60–61; Kingsbury, *East Timor: The Price of Liberty*, 41 and Nicol, *Timor: The Stillborn Nation*, 22.
2 CAVR, *Chega!*, 14.

The pursuit of democratic independence 41

3 CAVR, *Chega!*, Chapter 3, 16. Other parties formed in the same time frame included *Klibur Oan Timor Asuwain* (KOTA), *Associação Democrática para a Integração de Timor-Leste Australia* (ADLITA) and *Trabalhista* (Labour). These parties also wanted to maintain strong ties with Portugal. See Saldanha, 'Anatomy of Political Parties in Timor-Leste', 70.
4 Philpott, 'East Timor's Double Life', 140.
5 Shoesmith, 'Timor-Leste: Divided Leadership', 231–252.
6 Niner, 'A Long Journey of Resistance', 17.
7 Pinto, 'The Student Movement', 31–34. See also Kiernan, *Genocide and Resistance*, 184–192.
8 Kiernan, ibid., 187.
9 See Niner, *Xanana*.
10 CAVR, *Chega!*, Chapter 7:1, 5.
11 Kiernan, *Genocide and Resistance*, 139.
12 Taylor, *East Timor: The Price of Freedom*, 25.
13 Ballard, *Triumph of Self-Determination*, 7 and CAVR, *Timor-Leste Internal Political Conflict 1974–1975*, 63.
14 CAVR, *Chega!*, Chapter 3, 14; Saldanha, 'Anatomy of Political Parties in Timor-Leste', 70 and Taylor, *East Timor: The Price of Freedom*, 25.
15 Wise, *Exile and Return Among the East Timorese*, 23. See also Kingsbury, *East Timor: The Price of Liberty*, 43.
16 CAVR, *Chega!*, Chapter 3, 7.
17 Nicol, *Timor: The Stillborn Nation*, 21.
18 Taylor, *East Timor: The Price of Freedom*, 26.
19 Mário Carrascalão cited in CAVR, *Timor-Leste Internal Political Conflict 1974–1975*, 38.
20 Dunn, *A Rough Passage to Independence*; Jolliffe, *East Timor: Nationalism and Colonialism* and Taylor, *East Timor: The Price of Freedom*, 26
21 CAVR, *Chega!*, Chapter 3, 23.
22 Ibid., 33 and Taylor, *East Timor: The Price of Freedom*, 25.
23 Domingos de Oliviera cited in CAVR, *Timor-Leste Internal Political Conflict 1974–1975*, 102.
24 Taylor, *East Timor: The Price of Freedom*, 26 and 48.
25 Jolliffe, *East Timor: Nationalism and Colonialism*, 56–57. See also CAVR, *Chega!*, Chapter 3, 24 and Pinto and Jardine, *East Timor's Unfinished Struggle*, 11.
26 CAVR, ibid., Chapter 3, 14.
27 CAVR, *Timor-Leste Internal Political Conflict 1974–1975*, 38.
28 Xanana Gusmão cited in CAVR, ibid., 33.
29 Jolliffe, *East Timor: Nationalism and Colonialism*, 8 and CAVR, *Chega!*, Chapter 3, 12 and 24.
30 Jolliffe, ibid., 69 and CAVR, ibid., Chapter 3, 11.
31 CAVR, ibid. and Franck and Hoffman, 'The Right of Self-Determination', 343.
32 Pinto and Jardine, *East Timor's Unfinished Struggle*, 10–11.
33 Ibid., 11.
34 Mário Carrascalão cited in CAVR, *Timor-Leste Internal Political Conflict 1974–1975*, Fox, 'A District Analysis of the East Timor Elections 2001–2001, 37.
35 Dunn, *A Rough Passage to Independence*, 43 and Hoadley, *The Future of Portuguese Timor*, 2. For a political history of Timor-Leste from the perspective of socialist politician Avelino Coehlo, see Coelho, *Dua Kali Merdeka*. In Indonesian, see also Sanches, *Mengenal Pemerintahan Timor-Leste*, 14–19.
36 Mário Carrascalão cited in CAVR, *Timor-Leste Internal Political Conflict 1974–1975*, 38 and Saldanha, 'Anatomy of Political Parties in Timor-Leste', 70.
37 CAVR, *Chega!*, Chapter 3, 15 and Ramos-Horta, *Funu*, 31. See also Taylor, *East Timor: The Price of Freedom*, 26; Dunn, *Timor: A People Betrayed* and Jolliffe, *East Timor: Nationalism and Colonialism*, 62.

42 The pursuit of democratic independence

38 Dunn, *A Rough Passage to Independence*, 49 and Hoadley, *The Future of Portuguese Timor*, 3.
39 Hoadley, ibid. and Taylor, *East Timor: The Price of Freedom*, 26.
40 Dunn, *Timor: A People Betrayed*, 49 and Ramos-Horta, *Funu*, 30.
41 Mário Carrascalão cited in CAVR, *Timor-Leste Internal Political Conflict 1974–1975*, 38
42 Taylor, *East Timor: The Price of Freedom*, 26. See also CAVR, ibid., 38 and Walsh, 'East Timor's Political Parties and Groupings: Briefing Notes', 21.
43 CAVR, *Chega!*, Chapter 3, 15 and Taylor, ibid., 26.
44 Dunn, *A Rough Passage to Independence*, 49.
45 Domingos de Oliviera cited in CAVR, *Timor-Leste Internal Political Conflict 1974–1975*, 57.
46 Dunn, *A Rough Passage to Independence*, 50.
47 Ibid., 49. Domingos de Oliviera cited in CAVR, *Timor-Leste Internal Political Conflict 1974–1975*, 39 and 102 and CAVR, *Chega!*, Chapter 3, 15.
48 Dunn, *A Rough Passage to Independence*, 50 and Department of Foreign Affairs, *Australia and the Indonesian Incorporation of Portuguese Timor, 1974–1976*.
49 Ramos-Horta, *Funu*, 31.
50 Mário Carrascalão cited in CAVR, *Timor-Leste Internal Political Conflict 1974–1975*, 38; Dunn, *A Rough Passage to Independence*, 50 and Taylor, *East Timor: The Price of Freedom*, 27.
51 Mari Alkatiri cited in CAVR, ibid., 52. See also Taylor, ibid., 27.
52 On founding members of FRETILIN, see Hill, *Stirrings of Nationalism in East Timor*, 61–67.
53 Xanana Gusmão cited in CAVR, *Timor-Leste Internal Political Conflict 1974–1975*, 33 and Niner in Gusmão, *To Resist is to Win!*, xii.
54 CAVR, *Chega!*, 23.
55 Hoadley, *The Future of Portuguese Timor*, 4.
56 Taylor, *East Timor: The Price of Freedom*, 27.
57 Dunn, *A Rough Passage to Independence*, 51.
58 Ibid., 51; Mari Alkatiri cited in CAVR, *Timor-Leste Internal Political Conflict 1974–1975*, 135 and Taylor, *East Timor: The Price of Freedom*, 27.
59 Ramos-Horta, *Funu*, 35.
60 Hill, *Stirrings of Nationalism in East Timor*, 72–74.
61 Taylor, *East Timor: The Price of Freedom*, 27.
62 Dunn, *A Rough Passage to Independence*, 52 and Jolliffe, *East Timor: Nationalism and Colonialism*, 70.
63 Niner, 'A Long Journey of Resistance', 16; Philpott, 'East Timor's Double Life', 140 and Taylor, *East Timor: The Price of Freedom*, 27.
64 Kiernan, *Genocide and Resistance*, 153 and Hill, *Stirrings of Nationalism in East Timor*, 67. See for example FRETILIN, *East Timor: Indonesia's Vietnam*, 3 and FRETILIN, *What is Fretilin?*
65 Hill, *Stirrings of Nationalism in East Timor*, 72–73.
66 Dunn, *Timor: A People Betrayed*, 70.
67 Ballard, *Triumph of Self-Determination*, 7. Taylor suggests that it was written by members of BAKIN. Mário Carrascalão claims the APODETI manifesto was written by Portuguese military officer Major Arnao Metelo. Mário Carrascalão cited in CAVR, *Timor-Leste Internal Political Conflict 1974–1975*, 39 and 41 and Taylor, *East Timor: The Price of Freedom*, 28.
68 Dunn, *A Rough Passage to Independence*, 59.
69 CAVR, *Timor-Leste Internal Political Conflict 1974–1975*, 124.
70 Dunn, *Timor: A People Betrayed*, 70.
71 Dunn, *A Rough Passage to Independence*, 59.
72 Taylor, *East Timor: The Price of Freedom*, 28.

The pursuit of democratic independence   43

73 Dunn, *A Rough Passage to Independence*, 58 and 62.
74 Saldanha, 'Anatomy of Political Parties in Timor-Leste', 71.
75 Dunn, *A Rough Passage to Independence*, 55 and Ramos-Horta, *Funu*, 35.
76 Nicol, *Timor: The Stillborn Nation*, 79 and Niner, 'A Long Journey of Resistance', 16.
77 Taylor, *East Timor: The Price of Freedom*, 33.
78 See FRETILIN, *What is Fretilin?*
79 Ramos-Horta, *Funu*, 38.
80 Francisco X. do Amaral cited in CAVR, *Chega!*, Chapter 3, 5.
81 Ibid. and CAVR, *Timor-Leste Self-Determination and the International Community*, 64.
82 Jolliffe, *East Timor: Nationalism and Colonialism*, 91.
83 Dunn, *A Rough Passage to Independence*, 180.
84 See Ramos-Horta, *Funu*, 38 and Ramos-Horta cited in CAVR, *Timor-Leste Internal Political Conflict 1974–1975*, 45 and Niner, 'A Long Journey of Resistance', 16.
85 FRETILIN, *East Timor, Indonesia's Vietnam*, 32.
86 Dunn, *A Rough Passage to Independence*, 52 and 180.
87 Hoadley, *The Future of Portuguese Timor*, 4.
88 Taylor, *East Timor: The Price of Freedom*, 33 and Mari Alkatiri cited in CAVR, *Timor-Leste Internal Political Conflict 1974–1975*, 136.
89 CAVR, ibid.
90 Ibid., 137.
91 Dunn, *A Rough Passage to Independence*, 57.
92 Taylor, *East Timor: The Price of Freedom*, 39.
93 Francisco X. do Amaral cited in CAVR, *Timor-Leste Internal Political Conflict 1974–1975*, 64–65.
94 Ibid., 77 and CAVR, *Chega!*, Chapter 1, 6.
95 Taylor, *East Timor: The Price of Freedom*, 35 and Kiernan, *Genocide and Resistance*, 146–152.
96 CAVR, *Chega!*, Chapter 3, 23. João Carrascalão suggests alternatively that the UDT did not really consider FRETILIN to be communist. Cited in CAVR, *Timor-Leste Internal Political Conflict 1974–1975*, 131. However, Kiernan suggests that the UDT 'aimed to eradicate the so-called "communist" elements within FRETILIN'. See Kiernan, ibid., 137.
97 Fernandes, *The Independence of East Timor*, 32.
98 Ibid.
99 Ibid., 34 and CAVR, *Chega!*, Chapter 3, 23.
100 CAVR, ibid., 27. See for example speeches by Nicolau dos Reis Lobato in Do Reis Lobato, *Fretilin e a liberdade do povo em marcha*.
101 Fernandes, *The Independence of East Timor*, 34–35.
102 Dunn, *A Rough Passage to Independence*, 140.
103 Ibid., 141.
104 Mari Alkatiri cited in CAVR, *Timor-Leste Internal Political Conflict 1974–1975*, 55.
105 Mário Carrascalão cited in ibid., 42 and see also ibid., 106.
106 Dunn, *A Rough Passage to Independence*, 35 and 140.
107 Ibid., 14. See also Fernandes, *The Independence of East Timor*, 35.
108 Coelho, *Dua Kali Merdeka*, 32–34.
109 CAVR, *Timor-Leste Internal Political Conflict 1974–1975*, 14–15.
110 Saldanha, 'Anatomy of Political Parties in Timor-Leste', 70.
111 Mário Carrascalão cited in CAVR, *Timor-Leste Internal Political Conflict 1974–1975*, 42.
112 Personal ambition was also a factor. See Coelho, *Dua Kali Merdeka*, 27–28.
113 Xanana Gusmão cited in CAVR, *Timor-Leste Internal Political Conflict 1974–1975*, 35.

44   *The pursuit of democratic independence*

114 CAVR, *Timor-Leste Internal Political Conflict 1974–1975*, 77.
115 Mário Carrascalão cited in ibid., 40.
116 CAVR, *Chega!*, Chapter 3, 46.
117 Dunn, *Timor: A People Betrayed*, 207–210. See also do Amaral, *Nao ha duvida de que a Indonesia invadiu um pais livre neutro, pacifico, soberano, independente e nao-alinhado.*
118 Dunn, ibid.
119 Communique issued by the Portuguese National Decolonization Committee, 29 November 1975. See Krieger, *East Timor and the International Community*, 39–40. For an Indonesian perspective see Indonesia Departemen Luar Negeri, *Pelaksanaan Politik Luar Negeri Indonesia Pasca Pemisahan Timor Timur*, 13.
120 Joint Proclamation by APODETI, UDT, KOTA and the Partido Trabilhista, issued at Batugade, 30 November 1975, in Krieger, ibid., 40–41.
121 Kingsbury puts 70,000 as an upper estimation of the number of troops that landed in the days after 7 December. See Kingsbury, *East Timor: The Price of Liberty*, 50. The CAVR *Chega!* report estimates that between 102,800 to 183,000 East Timorese died from 1975–1999, many in the early years. See CAVR, *Chega!*, Chapter 6, 3.
122 CAVR, ibid., 60.
123 Ibid., 70.
124 Fernandes, *The Independence of East Timor*, 47.
125 Ibid. See also CAVR, *Chega!*, Chapter 3, 75–81 and Taylor, *East Timor: The Price of Freedom*, 53.
126 Dunn cited in CAVR, ibid., 114. Niner estimates that 1,500 to 3,000 people died. See Niner, 'A Long Journey of Resistance', 17.
127 United Nations Security Council, *Resolution 384*. Extracts of the debates preceding this resolution can be found in Krieger, *East Timor and the International Community*, 54–87.
128 Krieger, ibid., 62.
129 Kuntari, 'Timor Timur Satu Menit Terakhir', 43.
130 Indonesia Departemen Luar Negeri, *Pelaksanaan Politik Luar Negeri Indonesia Pasca Pemisahan Timor Timur*, 11.
131 Burchill, 'East Timor, Australia and Indonesia', 170. See also Strating, 'Contested Self-determination'.
132 Communique issued by the Portuguese National Decolonization Commission, 29 November 1975, in Krieger, *East Timor and the International Community*, 39–40. See also Appendix C in Jolliffe, *East Timor: Nationalism and Colonialism*, 341 and Coelho, *Dua Kali Merdeka*, xiii.
133 Mário Carrascalão cited in CAVR, *Timor-Leste Internal Political Conflict 1974–1975*, 47.
134 Cited in Krieger, *East Timor and the International Community*, 63. See also Republic of Indonesia, *Government Statements*, 15–16; Suharto, *Address before the Extraordinary Sessions of the Regional House of the People's Representatives of East Timor*, 6; Department of Foreign Affairs, Republic of Indonesia, *Process of Decolonization in East Timor*, 5; Department of Foreign Affairs, Republic of Indonesia, *East Timor: Building for the Future: Issues and Perspectives* and Kartasasmita, *East Timor*, 49. Indonesia has continued to maintain that the majority of East Timorese chose to join Indonesia. See Indonesia Departemen Luar Negeri, *Pelaksanaan Politik Luar Negeri Indonesia Pasca Pemisahan Timor Timur*, 12 and 14.
135 Nicol, *Timor: The Stillborn Nation*, 314.
136 Strating, 'Contested Self-determination'. For an East Timorese perspective, see Gusmão, *Timor Lorosae: perjalanan menuju dekolonisasi hati-diri*, 5.
137 Ramos-Horta cited in CAVR, *Timor-Leste Internal Political Conflict 1974-1975*.
138 Wanandi and Dunn cited in CAVR, ibid., 72 and 111.

The pursuit of democratic independence   45

139 CAVR, *Chega!*, Chapter 7:1, 5 and Dunn cited in CAVR, *Timor-Leste Internal Political Conflict 1974–1975*, 111.
140 Philpott, 'Post-Colonial Troubles', 137–139 and CAVR, *Chega!*, Chapter 7:1, 5. See Mari Alkatiri cited in CAVR, *Timor-Leste Internal Political Conflict 1974–1975*, 58 and Coelho, *Dua Kali Merdeka*, 25.
141 CAVR, ibid., Chapter 7:1, 66. See also Sastrosatomo, *Indonesia di tengah pergolakan perang dingin*, Chapter 1.
142 Nicol, *Timor: A Stillborn Nation*, 94; Philpott, 'East Timor's Double Life', 141 and Shoesmith, 'Timor-Leste: Divided Leadership', 231, 235 and 239.
143 Kiernan, *Genocide and Resistance*, 116–117 and Shoesmith, ibid., 237–239.
144 Shoesmith, ibid., 237.
145 Kiernan, *Genocide and Resistance*, 124–125, 128.
146 Ibid.,129.
147 Shoesmith, 'Timor-Leste: Divided Leadership', 238. See also da Silva, 'Popular Social Democracy', 171.
148 Alkatiri cited in CAVR, *Timor-Leste Internal Political Conflict 1974–1975*, 53.
149 Ibid., 58.
150 Shoesmith, 'Timor-Leste: Divided Leadership', 235, 237 and 238.
151 Kiernan, *Genocide and Resistance*, 116–117 and 121–122.
152 Hill, *Stirrings of Nationalism in East Timor*, 94 and Smith, 'East Timor: Elections in the World's Newest Nation', 146.
153 Philpott, 'East Timor's Double Life', 140.
154 Kiernan, *Genocide and Resistance*, 117.
155 CAVR, *Chega!*, Chapter 7:1, 39–46 and 68.
156 Ibid., Chapter 7:1, 5–6.
157 Garrison, *The Role of Constitution-Building Processes*, 14 and Ramos-Horta cited in ibid., 92.
158 Philpott, 'East Timor's Double-Life', 140.
159 See for example FRETILIN, *East Timor, Indonesia's Vietnam*, 10–11.
160 Ibid., 139 and Falk, 'The East Timor Ordeal', 152–153. For an Indonesian perspective on the use of state violence to quell nationalist movements, see Munir, 'Kekarasan Negara', 25–31.
161 Taylor, *East Timor: The Price of Freedom*, 85–88. The 'encirclement and annihilation' military campaign ran from August 1977 until August 1978. See CAVR, *Chega!*, Chapter 3, 75–78 and Kiernan, *Genocide and Resistance*, 138.
162 CAVR, ibid., Chapter 3, 94.
163 See ibid., Chapter 3, 76–77, 82–83 and 93.
164 Ibid., Chapter 3, 97 and Chapter 5, 27–29; Niner, 'A Long Journey of Resistance', 20 and Shoesmith. 'Timor-Leste: Divided Leadership', 240.
165 CAVR, *Timor-Leste Internal Political Conflict 1974–1975*, 53 and Kiernan, *Genocide and Resistance*, 169.
166 CAVR, *Chega!*, Chapter 3, 96.
167 Niner, 'A Long Journey of Resistance', 20–21.
168 Shoesmith, 'Timor-Leste: Divided Leadership', 240.
169 CAVR, *Chega!*, Chapter 3, 98.
170 Not all FRETILIN leaders approved the policies of national unity. Some members, led by Reinaldo Correira, attempted a *coup* against Gusmão. See Kiernan, *Genocide and Resistance*, 174.
171 Philpott, 'East Timor's Double Life', 141.
172 Shoesmith, 'Timor-Leste: Divided Leadership', 235.
173 Philpott, 'East Timor's Double Life', 141.
174 CAVR, *Chega!*, Chapter 3, 27. Martinho Gusmão argues the philosophy of *Ukun Rasik An* is based on egalitarianism and solidarity, and individualism may undermine

46   *The pursuit of democratic independence*

respect for other people. See Gusmão, *Timor Lorosae: perjalanan menuju dekolo-nisasi hati-diri*, 25–35.
175 Shoesmith, 'Timor-Leste: Divided Leadership', 240. See Niner, *Xanana*, 111.
176 Gusmão, *To Resist is to Win!*, 135 and Shoesmith, ibid., 241.
177 Niner, *Xanana*, 112.
178 Ibid., 115.
179 Ibid., 112 and Shoesmith, 'Timor-Leste: Divided Leadership', 240–241.
180 Niner, *Xanana*, 112.
181 CAVR, *Chega!*, Chapter 3, 107 and Walsh, 'East Timor's Political Parties', 10.
182 Walsh, ibid.
183 Ibid. and CAVR, *Chega!*, Chapter 3, 107–108.
184 Niner, *Xanana*, 176.
185 Land, 'East Timorese Convention a Success'.
186 Ibid.
187 Walsh, 'From Opposition to Proposition'.
188 Ibid.
189 Niner, *Xanana*, 177.
190 Ibid.
191 Philpott, 'East Timor's Double Life', 142.
192 Walsh, 'From Opposition to Proposition'.
193 Ibid.
194 CAVR, *Chega!*, Chapter 7:1.
195 Ramos-Horta, 'Human Rights, Democracy and Rule of Law', 4.
196 CAVR, *Chega!*, Chapter 7:1, 115.
197 Ibid., Chapter 7:1, 87.
198 Niner, 'A Long Journey of Resistance', 22.
199 Ibid. and Pinto and Jardine, *East Timor's Unfinished Struggle*, 251–254.
200 Xanana Gusmão cited in CAVR, *Chega!*, Chapter 7:1, 88.
201 Gusmão, *To Resist is to Win!*, 139–140.
202 Niner, *Xanana*, 119 and 139.
203 Ibid., 139.
204 Ibid., 140.
205 Pinto and Jardine, *East Timor's Unfinished Struggle*, 251 and Walsh, *From Opposition to Proposition.*
206 CAVR, *Chega!*, Chapter 3, 120.
207 Ibid., Chapter 3, 115.
208 Pinto and Jardine, *East Timor's Unfinished Struggle*, 251.
209 Ibid.
210 Ibid.
211 Ibid., 253.
212 Ibid., 254.
213 Walsh, *From Opposition to Proposition.*
214 Ibid.
215 CAVR, *Chega!*, Chapter 7:1, 90 and Niner, *Xanana*, 177. See also National Council of Timorese Resistance, *Magna Carta.*
216 Land, *'East Timorese Convention A Success'.*
217 Ibid.
218 National Council of Timorese Resistance, *Magna Carta.*
219 Ibid.
220 Tanter, Seldon and Shalom, 'East Timor Faces the Future', 245.
221 National Council of Timorese Resistance, *Magna Carta.*
222 Ibid.
223 Ibid.
224 Ibid.

The pursuit of democratic independence   47

225 Ibid.
226 CAVR, *Chega!*, Chapter 7:1, 90.
227 National Council for Timorese Resistance, *Magna Carta*.
228 Ibid.
229 Niner, 'A Long Journey of Resistance', 24.
230 Soares, 'Political Developments', 68.
231 Ibid.
232 CAVR, *Chega!*, Chapter 1, 138 and Niner, 'A Long Journey of Resistance', 24.
233 East Timor and Indonesia Action Network, *Dare II Agreements*.
234 CAVR, *Chega!*, Chapter 1, 138. See Soares, 'Political Development', 69.
235 Walsh, *From Opposition to Proposition*.
236 Kingsbury, *East Timor: The Price of Liberty*, 43.

2 Exercising self-determination

For much of its occupation of East Timor, Western states, including United States and Australia, viewed maintaining friendly relations with Indonesia as in their strategic and national interests. In the Cold War context, Indonesia was geopolitically significant in terms of position, population and physical size and its role as a major oil producer, and the seaways bisecting the archipelago provided key trading routes between the Pacific and Indian oceans.[1] In September 1974, the Australian government led by Prime Minister Gough Whitlam had informed Indonesian President Suharto of its preference for Indonesian integration above East Timorese independence. Questions over the capacity of East Timor to self-govern such a small territory and population partly underpinned concerns about an East Timorese state. While the United Nations (UN) never legally recognised Indonesia's territorial claim, the actions of a number of states in the international community, including the United States and Australia, undermined East Timorese independence.

As sovereign statehood is an identity established through mutual recognition among 'like-units' (states) based on collectively created and understood political, social and geographic boundaries, debates around East Timor's independence played out in international forums and the UN. Given East Timor was not recognised as a part of Indonesia by the UN, Indonesia also attempted to persuade fellow states of the legitimacy of East Timor's incorporation.[2] Independence rested upon the community of states permitting it to join the 'club' of sovereign states. These dynamics of mutual recognition are complicated when self-determination claims clash with the territorial claims of an existing sovereign state. In these circumstances, the international community tends to privilege existing sovereign states. While international assistance would be necessary for supporting and conducting a ballot through which the East Timorese could exercise their right of self-determination, this ultimately needed to occur with Indonesia's consent.

Civil society groups and non-governmental organisations (NGOs) played significant roles in supporting East Timor's claims to democratic entitlement and its pursuit of sovereign independence.[3] Civil society organisations in many states across the globe – including Portugal, Australia and Indonesia – in conjunction with exiled independence leaders, utilised human rights and principles of democracy and freedom to advance East Timor's cause. A range of organisations were established specifically to support self-determination and human rights in East Timor, including East Timor Relief Association (ETRA, Australia), East Timor Action Network (ETAN, North America), *Forum Solidaritas untuk Rakyat Timor Lorosae* (FORTILOS, Indonesia) and *Comissão para os Direitos do Povo Maubere*/Commission for the Rights of the *Maubere* People (CDPM, Portugal).[4] Alongside large international human rights NGOs, such as Asia Watch and Amnesty International, these organisations contributed to raising awareness of East Timor's desire for democratic independence and self-determination at the UN, and lobbied governments to adjust their policies on East Timor.[5] Collecting and disseminating information on human rights violations in East Timor was important for sustaining international interest in the independence movement.

The 'grass-roots' solidarity movements operating at domestic and international levels, in conjunction with the 'diplomatic' front of the independence movement, pressured Indonesia and the international community to find a peaceful solution to the situation in East Timor.[6] Exiled members of FRETILIN, including Mari Alkatiri and José Ramos-Horta, played key roles in lobbying governments and shoring up support for the independence movement.[7] Social organisations used international diplomatic spheres to persuade states of the illegitimacy of the Indonesian incorporation in East Timor.[8] The Santa Cruz massacre in 1991, the arrest of Xanana Gusmão in 1992 and the awarding of the Nobel Peace Prize to Bishop Carlos Belo and Ramos-Horta in 1996 garnered extensive global media attention and damaged the image of Indonesia's regime in East Timor.[9]

The pressure from international organisations increased in the late 1990s to complicate Indonesia's rule in East Timor, and contributed to Indonesian President B. J. Habibie's eventual acceptance of a self-determination referendum.[10] The end of the Cold War at the beginning of the 1990s 'created new space for challenging both the Indonesian occupation and Western support for Jakarta'.[11] As the care-taker President – following President Suharto's resignation in 1998 – Habibie instituted political reforms to appease domestic 'pro-democracy' activists, which included dealing with East Timor's political status. East Timor's achievement of independence was in a large part due to Indonesia's democratic transition that was compelled by a grass-roots *reformasi* movement. International pressure from states and civil society organisations compounded internal dissent and made the question of East Timor difficult for the new Indonesian regime to negotiate, ultimately contributing to Habibie's decision to grant the East Timorese a self-determination ballot.

The UN conducted and monitored East Timor's independence referendum in August 1999 to ensure the validity of East Timor's self-determination ballot, along with the assistance of international and domestic civil society organisations. While there are a number of precedents for international assistance in conducting elections in existing territories, including in Cambodia and the autonomous region of Kosovo, there are fewer examples of internationally-run

50 *Exercising self-determination*

ballots that establish new states, such as those that occurred in East Timor or South Sudan in 2011. An act of self-determination relies upon free choice, and it could result in sovereignty, an autonomy arrangement or free association within the same or a different state.[12] The East Timorese were given the choice to accept or reject autonomy: the latter option would result in East Timor's separation from Indonesia.[13]

Indonesia, Portugal and the UN agreed in their pre-referendum negotiations that an external body would monitor and conduct the democratic referendum in order to provide an internationally acceptable solution to the question of East Timor.[14] While acts of 'liberal peacebuilding' have their fair share of critics, in this case, East Timor would not have become a sovereign state without international assistance. East Timor's decision about its future had to be the outcome of 'an informed, fair and democratic process, free of outside intervention and threats, conducted impartially and preferably supervised by the United Nations'.[15] Accordingly, United Nations Security Council Resolution 1246 made the United Nations Mission in East Timor (UNAMET) responsible for ensuring a universal, secret and democratic ballot.[16] The referendum would involve a legitimate act of 'internal self-determination' – the democratic political participation of people to determine their political future – to achieve 'external self-determination' (political autonomy). On 30 August 1999, 78.5 per cent of voters in East Timor's referendum elected for East Timor to become an independent state.[17]

Civil society and international pressure

One of the first decisions of the short-lived government of the Democratic Republic of Timor-Leste (RDTL) in 1975 was to send a delegation of ministers overseas to lobby and network with diplomats and politicians in order to gain international recognition of their government.[18] The external delegation of exiled leaders included José Ramos-Horta (Minister for External Relations and Information), Mari Alkatiri (Minister for Political Affairs), Rogerio Lobato (Defence Minister), Abilio Araújo (Minister for Economic and Social Affairs), Guilhermina Araújo (Deputy Minister for Economic Relations) and Roque Rodriques (Ambassador Designate to Mozambique).[19] They lobbied governments and attempted to maintain the question of East Timor's status on the international agenda. While the original purpose of the international delegation was to secure international recognition of FRETILIN's leadership, their activities led the way for the international campaign for East Timor's right to self-determination.[20] According to the *Chega!* report, the FRETILIN delegation 'opened key diplomatic fronts in Europe, Africa, the United States and the UN ... [and s]trong and lasting links were also fostered with civil society organisations in many countries'.[21]

At the UN, the RDTL delegates would go on to lead the external push for independence as they attempted to participate in sessions and advance East Timor's self-determination claims.[22] From 1975 onward, East Timor's delegate

Exercising self-determination   51

to the UN, José Ramos-Horta, was responsible for lobbying diplomats, monitoring information, and building networks with UN staff, journalists and members of international civil society groups.[23] He suggests that between 1976 and 1982, FRETILIN was 'virtually alone' in the lobbying effort for East Timor's self-determination at the United Nations.[24] As the RDTL was not recognised as a government, representatives had no formal status as 'ministers' or 'diplomats'.[25] Consequently, members of the RDTL were not given observer status in the United Nations (a status that had been afforded to other non-state actors making claims to statehood), which hampered their abilities to participate in meetings.[26] Ideological and leadership divisions among the FRETILIN international delegates compounded representation issues that accompanied the decision of the Central Committee to turn FRETILIN into a Marxist-Leninist party in the late 1970s.[27] Given their lack of formal political status, East Timorese independence leaders could be considered a part of international civil society working to establish self-determination in East Timor.

Throughout the Indonesian occupation, international alliances were formed between civil society groups, parliamentarians and East Timorese leaders.[28] Periodic meetings were held during the 1970s and 1980s across Europe, in states such as Portugal, the Netherlands and Britain, which supported the international solidarity movement.[29] Non-governmental organisations, such as Amnesty International and Human Rights Watch, provided reports on human rights conditions considered more credible than official Indonesian reports.[30] An organisation called Parliamentarians for East Timor (PET), formed in 1988, at one point comprised 900 members across 40 states.[31] Members of PET presented the issue of East Timor to the UN Secretary-General and recommended Bishop Belo and José Ramos-Horta for the Nobel Peace Prize.[32] Politicians, such as Ken Fry in Australia, criticised the positions of their governments and attempted to keep the spotlight on the issue of East Timor at national and international levels. For example, in 1996 Fry testified to the United Nations Security Council on behalf of the East Timorese independence movement.[33]

Independence leaders operating outside of East Timor, such as Ramos-Horta, established links with international civil society organisations and media in order to raise awareness of East Timor's struggle for self-determination.[34] The support provided by civil society organisations to the independence movement was critical given that East Timor had few resources and lacked state allies.[35] For instance, the Australian East Timor Association (AETA) funded FRETILIN's first mission to the United Nations in 1975.[36] Many FRETILIN members of the East Timorese diaspora were also members and key organisers of civil society organisations. In major Australian cities, FRETILIN was well established by the late 1980s, and its members created links with churches, civil society organisations and the media, in addition to organising community demonstrations.[37] The presence of East Timorese refugees was important in sparking interest in the movement within Australia.[38]

Throughout the 1980s, organisations from Portuguese civil society played important roles in publicising and advocating the plight of East Timor both in

52 *Exercising self-determination*

Portugal and abroad.[39] Some took up East Timor's cause at the international level, including the *Comissão para os Direitos do Povo Maubere*/Commission for the Rights of the *Maubere* People (CDMP) which operated from 1983 to 2002, and the *Centro de Informação e Documentação Amilcar Cabral*/Anti-Colonial Information and Documents Centre (CIDAC), an NGO established in 1974 to report and monitor the situation in East Timor.[40] Luisa Teotonio Pereira, a member of both organisations, testified at the Commission for Reception, Truth and Reconciliation hearings that she had petitioned the UN Sub-Commission on Discrimination and the Protection of Minorities on behalf of Timor-Leste on four occasions during the 1980s.[41]

International NGOs presented and argued East Timor's case at international levels and provided much needed support to the 'diplomatic' front of the East Timorese independence movement. In 1986, the United Nations Special Committee on Decolonisation allowed NGOs to make submissions. Every subsequent year, around 20–25 international NGOs, including large organisations, such as Asia Watch, would travel to New York to petition for East Timor's rights to self-determination. The *Chega!* report suggests that these efforts made East Timor perhaps the most argued topic on the agenda.[42] Teotonio Pereira asserts that the most important work undertaken by the international solidarity movement was the collection, processing and dissemination of information.[43] She recounts 'an avalanche of petitions' supported by East Timorese eye-witness accounts sent to the United Nations Decolonisation Committee every year from 1986.[44] Some members of civil society organisations (particularly Portuguese NGOs) were in contact with East Timorese people inside and outside the territory, rendering them important sources of information about events in East Timor.[45]

The *Chega!* report notes that solidarity movements were beneficial to East Timor as they provided the backbone of international civil society's support for East Timorese self-determination.[46] Human rights and peace activists, in addition to solidarity movements, became important players in raising awareness and internationalising the East Timor independence movement.[47] They tended to focus on East Timor's pursuit of self-determination as a moral issue, which enabled broad coalitions to form across civil society, including the East Timorese diaspora and independence movement.[48] The East Timor question was also widely considered in terms of human rights violations, particularly as organisations appealed to a minimum international 'standard of civilisation' that encompassed democracy and liberal ideals, articulating the crucial link between 'internal' and 'external' self-determination.[49] The aim of many pro-East Timor groups was to 'promote Timor-Leste as a human rights issue, not a pro-FRETILIN or anti-Indonesian issue'.[50] Some organisations, such as the Campaign for an Independent East Timor (CIET), actively supported FRETILIN and accepted East Timor's political status as independent.[51] However, other advocates, including Human Rights NGOs and Australian Consul to East Timor James Dunn, focused specifically on advocating peace and human rights.[52] According to Simpson, one of the challenges facing international civil society organisations was moving the discourse from human rights in East Timor to self-determination.[53]

Exercising self-determination 53

Some solidarity groups in Australia represented FRETILIN, however these members were often 'a minority in a mainly UDT community and, as refugees, the community feared being expelled if they sided overtly with Fretilin against Indonesia'.[54] FRETILIN organisers within the Australian diaspora, such as Lay Kuon Nhen and Abel Guterres, took part in a large public rally in Melbourne in 1983 that was addressed by FRETILIN leaders Abilio Araújo and Roque Rodriques.[55] The first official FRETILIN Committee was established in Sydney in 1986, and by the late 1980s FRETILIN 'was well established in many parts of Australia, including Darwin, Sydney, Melbourne and Perth and had good contact with the Resistance in Timor-Leste'.[56]

Australia was an important site for civil society activities promoting self-determination and human rights for the East Timorese.[57] Collecting and disseminating information was integral to the work of civil society organisations in Australia: for example, a group of Australian aid agencies, including the Australian Catholic Relief and Community Aid Abroad, funded James Dunn's trip to Portugal in 1975 to interview East Timorese refugees and confirm reports from FRETILIN about human rights abuses.[58] East Timor was on the agenda of a number of Australian journalists, human rights activists, academics, aid agencies, churches, students and politicians. The Australian Council for Overseas Aid (ACFOA), a key resistance body of 70 national NGOs, advocated for East Timorese self-determination for 24 years at home and abroad, researching human rights conditions in East Timor and fostering networks with NGOs and civil organisations overseas.[59] Similarly, the Timor Information Service (TIS) sought to provide credible information and analysis and raise public consciousness of East Timor's status.[60]

The Santa Cruz massacre

The end of the Cold War was largely considered a turning point in East Timor's campaign for independence as support rapidly intensified in the international civil sphere.[61] Certainly, international awareness of East Timor's claims for self-determination expanded following the 'massacre' at the Santa Cruz cemetery in Dili on 12 November 1991, where Indonesian military fired at East Timorese attending the burial of pro-independence student, Sebastio Gomes.[62] At the burial, members of the independence movement had sought to gain the attention of a Portuguese delegation in Dili at the time by protesting against Indonesia's repressive regime.[63] Footage of the Indonesian military's crackdown on the peaceful protest taken by photographer Max Stahl was smuggled out of the territory by Dutch journalist Saskia Kouwenberg, and employed 'as compelling evidence of the use of systematic military violence against ordinary East Timorese'.[64] This footage captured Indonesian soldiers firing directly on the crowd, and there were allegations that troops bayoneted wounded protesters and killed those taken to the hospital.[65] Members of the foreign press who witnessed the Santa Cruz protest, including two US reporters and a British photographer, were also badly beaten. In the days that followed, the Indonesian military conducted a

54 *Exercising self-determination*

series of executions, and hundreds of East Timorese were detained and given lengthy jail sentences. It was estimated that 271 people were killed, although Indonesia claimed only 19 died.[66]

Santa Cruz was considered by many as a turning point in East Timor's efforts to achieve rights to self-determination and a 'major setback for Indonesian diplomacy'.[67] The massacre raised international attention to a point where East Timor was temporarily at the centre of global political debate.[68] In the United States, for example, editorials in the Washington Post, the New York Times and other influential newspapers condemned the massacre.[69] Although it was not the worst massacre committed by Indonesia in East Timor, the media attention generated by the event raised sympathy for East Timor's cause as it demonstrated the readiness of Indonesia to use force against East Timorese protesters.[70]

Stahl's video footage validated the claims of human rights violations that had been made by international NGOs and independence leaders, such as José Ramos-Horta, who had previously been accused of fabricating stories of violence and human rights abuses by Indonesia and its allies.[71] Indonesian Foreign Minister Ali Alatas, despite blaming 'a small group of agitators and pro-independence youth', described Santa Cruz as the moment where international political support for Indonesian occupation waned as '[c]ountries that formerly supported us were shocked'.[72] The majority of US senators called upon then US President George W. H. Bush to assist East Timor's right of self-determination by introducing to the UN General Assembly a resolution 'instructing the United Nations Commission on Human Rights to appoint a Special Rapporteur for East Timor'.[73] The international outcry that followed the Santa Cruz massacre was compounded by the widespread coverage of the arrest of resistance leader Xanana Gusmão in 1992, and the awarding of the Nobel Peace Prize to Bishop Carlos Belo and José Ramos-Horta in 1996.[74] The Nobel Peace Prize had the effect of legitimating and affirming Ramos-Horta in the international diplomatic sphere, in spite of Indonesia's persistent efforts to discredit him and his accounts of the situation in East Timor.[75] These events renewed international interest throughout the 1990s, increased pressure on Indonesia, and provided a morale boost for civil society organisations that supported East Timor's struggle for self-determination.[76]

In a statement to the UN General Assembly in 1994, Amnesty International argued that the international community shared responsibility for the Santa Cruz massacre and other human rights violations.[77] The East Timor Action Network (ETAN), PET, Asia-Pacific Conference on East Timor and British Coalition for East Timor also petitioned the General Assembly deploring human rights abuses, including forced sterilisation, the killing of newborns, and the imprisonment of Xanana Gusmão.[78] The British Coalition and ETAN in particular used the events to condemn their own governments and pressure for change.

The membership of ETAN, an NGO working across North America, expanded rapidly following the Santa Cruz massacre.[79] Formed in December 1991, ETAN applied pressure on the US Congress to take a tougher stance on Indonesia through a public information campaign and lobbying.[80] Similar to the

Portuguese solidarity organisations, ETAN's first priority was to increase media coverage and awareness of East Timor's situation and the complicity of the United States by providing credible information for journalists, policy makers, researchers and so forth.[81] Simpson argues that ETAN was able to 'carve out a niche ... [and] have a discernible impact on U.S. policy'.[82] They also attempted to persuade US Congress that East Timor's self-determination required imposing sanctions on Indonesia.[83]

In 1992, the ETAN's lobbying resulted in the creation of a bill to stop funding the International Military Education and Training program, which provided US training for the Indonesian military.[84] Fernandes and Simpson both attribute the successful passage of this bill to the sustained pressure of the ETAN, and a campaign by university students who telephoned thousands of people in key electorates.[85] A number of senators and members of Congress took a particular interest in East Timor, which was also useful for the independence movement. Newly elected President of the United States, Bill Clinton, decided to ban 'the sale of small and light arms, riot-control equipment, helicopter-mounted weaponry and armoured personnel carriers to Indonesia'.[86] Special Advisor to the President Stanley Roth reportedly received 'more letters on East Timor ... than any other country in Asia'.[87] Domestic pressure of this kind affected the relations between the United States and Indonesia as the Clinton administration took steps to prevent further human rights abuses in East Timor.

The Santa Cruz massacre also attracted significant public attention in Australia, generating the creation of new groups and increasing the membership of existing groups.[88] The East Timor Relief Association (ETRA), for example, was an activist NGO formed in 1992 in Sydney that soon spread to other capital cities. To raise awareness, it held demonstrations at the Department of Foreign Affairs and the Indonesian embassy and established conferences and seminars throughout Australia and abroad.[89] The ETRA also produced East Timorese music, art exhibitions and theatre pieces to place East Timor's independence movement in a cultural context and maintain East Timorese identity in the diaspora.[90] These organisations worked with independence leaders such as José Ramos-Horta: ETRA President Abel Guterres recalled following the leaders as they 'worked to support East Timor from the outside'.[91]

The Asia region also became an important site for the formation of civil society organisations following the Santa Cruz massacre.[92] By 1995, there were East Timor support organisations in over 20 states and the International Federation for East Timor was formed as a transnational umbrella body to coordinate their activities at international organisations such as the UN.[93] According to human rights activist, Sister Monica Nakamura, the 'International Initiative for Dialogue', a Philippines NGO, assisted organisations to convene a regional forum, the Asia-Pacific Coalition for East Timor (APECT). This was held in Manila in 1994 as the beginning of an 'ongoing, co-ordinated solidarity for Timor-Leste across Asia'.[94] The purpose was to pressure Indonesia's neighbours to support East Timor's self-determination. A second conference of the APECT in Kuala Lumpur in 1996 generated 'much-welcomed publicity' when all foreign

56 *Exercising self-determination*

participants were deported by the Malaysian government in a sign of support for Indonesia.[95] Mass protests were also held across the region calling for UN intervention in East Timor.[96]

The Indonesian pro-democracy student movement

One of the most significant civil society movements that contributed to the struggle for East Timor's self-determination was the Indonesian student pro-democracy movement. Movements supporting East Timor's independence and Indonesian democracy established links through the East Timorese student activists. This was facilitated by Indonesia's policies to 'normalise' the region by increasing educational opportunities in East Timor: in 1985, Governor of East Timor, Mário Carrascalão, introduced a policy allowing East Timorese students to study at universities across Indonesia. In 1988, the National Resistance of East Timor Students (RENETIL) was established in Bali and would become an important vehicle for student activism.

Indonesian solidarity organisations, such as FORTILOS and Solidarity for Peace in East Timor (SOLIDAMOR), supported East Timorese claims to self-determination.[97] FORTILOS was a clandestine organisation working to raise awareness among Indonesians about the military campaign in East Timor.[98] A member of FORTILOS, Nugroho Katjasungkana, recalled that in the 1990s the pro-democracy movement in Indonesia was focused upon removing the Suharto regime and other issues such as environmental destruction and oppression.[99] East Timorese students had been developing links with pro-democracy and human rights groups throughout the 1990s as their commonalities extended from a desire for greater political liberty and freedom from oppressive government.

The pro-democracy movement in Indonesia and the East Timor solidarity movement shared the same view that the root of their problems was Suharto's authoritarian New Order regime.[100] Katjasungkana argues that the 'underlying and primary motivation was freedom for the grass-roots people, in Indonesia, Timor-Leste and other countries suffering similarly'.[101] Support for East Timor's self-determination was part of the broader goal of achieving democratic freedom.[102] Indonesian and East Timorese student activists viewed Indonesian democratisation as a prerequisite for the achievement of East Timorese self-determination, recognising that Indonesia's authoritarian New Order regime would not permit East Timor's separation.[103] The Indonesian pro-democracy protests against President Suharto intersected with, and supported, East Timor's independence movement.[104]

Indonesia's transition to democracy

Indonesia's transition to democracy was a result of a number of key forces, including economic crisis, political mobilisation at the grass-roots level, international pressure and regime disunity.[105] The Asian Financial Crisis of 1997–1998, high rates of unemployment and rising food prices undermined

Exercising self-determination 57

President Suharto's supposed economic competence and led to mass protests across Indonesia in April and May 1998.[106] On 19 and 20 May 1998, a coalition of activists from 14 university campuses across Indonesia, FORKOT, announced plans for a massive demonstration at the Indonesian Parliament, and students took over the National Assembly building.[107] Indonesian civil society played a significant role in compelling Indonesian military and political elites to reassess their preferences in regards to democratisation. The *Reformasi* movement gained support from the middle-class and some Indonesian elites, including Indonesia's People's Consultative Council leader Harmoko Dewantono and military chief General Wiranto.[108]

As Harold Crouch argues, democratisation in Indonesia relied in part upon the willingness of the *Tentara Nasional Indonesia* (TNI, Indonesian military) to disentangle itself from the 'doomed' Suharto regime.[109] Reform-minded members of the TNI were convinced that a negotiated re-setting of the military and political spheres was necessary for ensuring their own political survival.[110] The *Reformasi* movement triggered the resignation of President Suharto on 21 May 1998 as he lost the political capital that sustained his rule.[111] The removal of President Suharto from power provided an opportunity for East Timor's independence movement to gain significant traction.[112] Indonesia's democratic transition prompted the resurgence of several secessionist movements, particularly East Timor's.[113] In June and July 1998, major demonstrations were held in East Timor calling for a referendum with little resistance from Indonesia, and these grew into a general mass strike with the civil service shutting down.[114]

The United Nations and the international community also used the fall of President Suharto to 'increase its pressure on Indonesia for a solution to the issue of Timor-Leste'.[115] Indonesia's leadership shift from Suharto to care-taker President B. J. Habibie proved decisive in the eventual achievement of East Timor's rights to self-determination.[116] The New Order 'strong-state' regime had taken seriously the risks of secessionist movements in East Timor, Aceh, West Papua and other regions breaking up the Indonesian archipelago and any potential 'domino affect' East Timor's independence might pose to national unity.[117] Indonesian Foreign Minister Ali Alatas suggestion to President Suharto that he offer special autonomy to East Timor was flatly rejected.[118] The possibilities of East Timor securing independence under President Suharto were, at best, remote.[119] However, the weaker Habibie administration in a new democratic Indonesia presented new possibilities for East Timor's quest for a referendum.[120]

A series of factors led President Habibie to seek resolution on the issue of East Timor. According to Soares, one of his most active campaigns was the resolution of the Timor issue and the restoration of Indonesia's human rights image abroad.[121] Habibie can be considered a 'soft-liner' more susceptible to international pressure than his predecessor, and his relative openness to international liberal norms was part of a strategic distancing from the policies of Suharto.[122] Habibie could also hardly ignore the *Reformasi* movement's request for reforms given its significant role in removing Suharto from power.[123] He moved quickly to institute limited democratic reforms across Indonesia to settle protestors,

58   Exercising self-determination

including in East Timor. These reforms included recognition of rights to assembly, reducing limits on press freedoms and freedom to form political parties.[124] The 'mood for change' both domestically and internationally compelled Habibie to find a solution to the problem of East Timor.[125]

In Indonesia, NGOs and members of the solidarity movement called upon leaders to provide the East Timorese with a free choice to remain with Indonesia or separate.[126] Many Indonesian civil society organisations dedicated to East Timorese independence were established or regenerated during this period of relative freedom immediately following the fall of Suharto as people were able to engage in protests and demonstrations.[127] Indonesian pro-democracy activist Yeni Rosa Damayanti observes: 'Back then we had one objective: to make Indonesians understand what the East Timor issue was all about. We had freedom to do it openly and we could approach the new political figures who came out with reforms'.[128] To achieve this aim, organisations such as SOLIDAMOR, which emerged after Suharto vacated power, engaged in political activities such as the *Timor Timur Fair* (promoting Timor independence), and arranged meetings between Xanana Gusmão, Indonesian political figures and members of political parties.[129] They also lobbied Dewi Fortuna Anwar, a key advisor to President Habibie.[130] These activities corresponded with an 'explosion of information on East Timor', with books, postcards, posters, t-shirts, stickers and other merchandise distributed across Indonesia.[131]

In June 1998, amidst international and domestic pressure, Habibie offered East Timor a 'special status' within Indonesia, consisting of wide-ranging autonomy as an 'end-solution to the question of East Timor'.[132] This new policy suggestion 'came under close international scrutiny'.[133] In a CNN interview 13 days after he came to power, Habibie suggested that something needed to be done about East Timor, offering a broad autonomy package as an option, but maintaining the view that East Timor should remain a province of Indonesia.[134] That this autonomy option was offered within a fortnight of Habibie's ascension to power, and on a global news media channel such as CNN, signals that the international attention on Indonesia was a factor in Habibie's offer of autonomy. Moreover, some commentators argued that the autonomy package was a 'trade-off' for much needed restructuring loans from the International Monetary Fund.[135]

According to Ballard, President Habibie's offer of autonomy 'produced a diplomatic and media sensation that would, in turn, eventually create the conditions for United Nations intervention in East Timor, and Timorese independence'.[136] It was rejected by many East Timorese, and Xanana Gusmão refused to accept anything less than a vote for self-determination.[137] Between June and September 1998, hundreds of East Timorese, particularly youth, protested in the streets of Dili and openly opposed the autonomy package.[138] Protesters demanded a UN-sponsored referendum and the full exercise of their rights to self-determination.[139] Tamrat Samuel described the political climate in November 1998: 'Many East Timorese, emboldened by the political transformation sweeping Indonesia and the weakening of the military's position, have seized the opportunity to seize and consolidate new political space in East Timor'.[140]

Exercising self-determination 59

This new political openness corresponded with increased violence between pro-independence and pro-autonomy groups, which made it dangerous for international delegations to travel to East Timor and monitor the human rights situation.[141] Australian and US intelligence discovered that Indonesia's declaration at the end of 1998 that it had reduced troop numbers by 6,000 in East Timor was a sham: Indonesia had actually increased troop numbers from nearly 16,000 to 18,000.[142]

Indonesia experienced other forms of international pressure as its Western allies began to question East Timor's political status and human rights became 'more prominent in Washington and Canberra's thinking'.[143] In June 1998, representatives from Austria, the United Kingdom and the Netherlands visited East Timor and concluded that the only way of resolving the conflict was through a referendum.[144] In July 1998, the US Senate called for a referendum in East Timor, and in October 1998, the United Nations raised serious concerns about escalating levels of violence.[145] Ballard reports that international concern about the violence in East Timor had 'grown significantly in Portugal, the UN, Great Britain, the United States and many other nations'.[146] Throughout the 1990s, the East Timor question had been 'a problem for Indonesian diplomacy', and both President Habibie and Foreign Minister Ali Alatas were keen to repair Indonesia's damaged human rights image abroad.[147]

In December 1998, Australian Prime Minister John Howard sent President Habibie a letter encouraging him to enter into direct negotiations with the East Timorese and offered New Caledonia as a model of self-determination.[148] It differed from Habibie's autonomy package because it left open a possibility for East Timorese independence.[149] Howard had intended to confirm Australia's support for East Timor's integration in Indonesia; however his letter triggered independence and insulted the Indonesians with its comparison between East Timor's integration and French colonialism.[150] On 5 January 1999, the Australian government reversed its *de jure* recognition of Indonesian sovereignty over East Timor, proclaiming that the East Timorese held self-determination rights while still positioning autonomy as the best solution.[151] Public opinion in Australia was increasingly critical of the government's stance on East Timor, due in part to the active East Timorese diaspora and the work of independence leaders, especially José Ramos-Horta, in raising human rights issues in the Australian media.[152] Former Foreign Minister Alexander Downer stated that 'no foreign policy issue ... captured the public interests in Australia more than East Timor' during his time as Foreign Minister.[153] Australia's stance on East Timor was significant given the 'weighty and substantive nature' of the relationship between Australia and Indonesia.[154]

On 27 January 1999, Habibie announced that he would allow a referendum in East Timor whereby rejection of the offered autonomy package would result in independence.[155] Foreign Minister Ali Alatas had described East Timor as a pebble in Indonesia's shoe: in the economic climate following the Asian Financial Crisis, some Indonesian leaders and academics decided Indonesia would be better off without East Timor.[156] Habibie argued that if 'the East Timorese still

60 *Exercising self-determination*

refused to accept integration [after 25 years], then norms of democracy and justice would suggest that they should peacefully exercise their right of self-determination'.[157] He wrote 'if, after 22 years, the East Timorese people cannot feel united with the Indonesian people ... it would be reasonable and wise if ... East Timor can be honourably separated from the unitary nation of the Republic of Indonesia'.[158] This statement points to the existence of a unique East Timorese collective identity that had not been successfully integrated into the broader Indonesian nation.[159]

Indonesian journalist Sabam Siagian suggested the decision reflected Habibie's character and was one that surprised society.[160] Critics also argued the decision was unconstitutional and violated Habibie's authority as a transitional President.[161] Conversely, in an Indonesian publication, Singh argued that Habibie had solved an intractable international problem, and, given the costs of maintaining East Timor's territory and the widespread perception among other provinces that East Timor was privileged, Indonesians should not see East Timor as a loss.[162] Habibie's emphasis on the 'norms of democracy' as underpinning self-determination suggest that the Indonesian pro-democracy campaign had successfully packaged East Timor's right of self-determination as part of the broader need for political reform in Indonesia.[163]

However, observers such as Fernandes and Lloyd believe that both Habibie and Alatas genuinely believed the East Timorese would choose autonomy within Indonesia.[164] Habibie also believed the plebiscite would be popular among the Indonesian people given the pressure for change that had emerged from the *Reformasi* movement.[165] As the Personal Representative of the United Nations Secretary-General for East Timor Jamsheed Marker observed: 'the near revolutionary changes that occurred in the political life of Indonesia, following the downfall of Suharto, were generated by forces which were manifestations of popular will'.[166]

The international community also welcomed the ballot 'as an unprecedented democratic gesture that showed the President's willingness to distance himself from Suharto's past wrongs'.[167] Habibie's decision was a culmination of various 'from above' and 'from below' pressures exerted by domestic and international civil society organisations and states that had become increasingly persuaded that Indonesia's sovereign claims to East Timor were untenable in the post-Cold War environment.[168] While the referendum was partly a result of a fortuitous mix of circumstances, the international legitimacy of East Timor's claims to self-determination relied upon the grass-roots campaigns that linked East Timor's collective rights to self-determination with civil and human rights of individuals.

The 'popular consultation' in East Timor

Official tripartite talks held since 1983 had contributed little to resolving the East Timor question, but would become increasingly important to negotiating the operation of the referendum.[169] The East Timorese were not represented in the negotiations due to the difficulties in determining which leaders or groups were

Exercising self-determination 61

sufficiently 'representative'.[170] On 5 May 1999, Indonesia's Foreign Minister, Ali Alatas, Portugal's Foreign Minister Jaime Gama and the Secretary-General of the UN Kofi Annan finally negotiated a settlement on the question of East Timor, rendering the UN responsible for conducting a referendum on independence in East Timor.[171] The 'May 5 Agreement' set the ground rules for a direct, secret and universal ballot in East Timor, referred to as a 'Popular Consultation'.[172] The question put to the voters was:

> Do you accept the special autonomy for East Timorese within the Unitary State of the Republic of Indonesia? (accept). Or do you reject the proposed special autonomy for East Timor leading to East Timor's separation from Indonesia? (reject).[173]

The May 5 Agreement contained a constitutional framework for the Special Autonomous Region of East Timor (SARET) that would have been implemented had the East Timorese chosen autonomy.[174] Publishing this plan allowed the East Timorese to consider what autonomy under Indonesia would entail. Some commentators, such as Lloyd, suggested an alternative option of delayed independence should have been permitted, although this was clearly undesirable for Indonesia.[175] Habibie had rejected Australian Prime Minister John Howard's idea of a period of autonomy, arguing that Indonesia would not act as a 'rich uncle' for 15 years.[176]

The May 5 Agreement made Indonesia responsible for ensuring security so that the Popular Consultation could be 'carried out in a fair and peaceful way'.[177] This arrangement was widely criticised on the basis of the violent, repressive measures employed during the occupation by the Indonesian military toward supporters of the East Timorese resistance movement.[178] There were also doubts that the TNI accepted Habibie's decision to allow a referendum.[179] Links between the Indonesian military and the East Timorese pro-integration militia were already well-established and the militia were trained, funded and supported by the Indonesian military in the lead up to the referendum.[180] This relationship undermined Indonesia's capacity or willingness to provide a secure environment for the vote.[181]

A report commissioned by the Office of the High Commissioner for Human Rights on the violence in East Timor states that '[i]n the period before the ballot, suspected supporters of independence were subjected to persistent threats and acts of violence by pro-Indonesian militia groups'.[182] A UN General Assembly Commission of Inquiry also found members of the TNI and militias involved in the 'systematic and widespread intimidation, humiliation and terror, destruction of property, violence against women and displacement of people'.[183] There were several examples of mass killings before the popular consultation perpetrated predominantly by pro-integration militias, with pro-independence supporters the main targets.[184] In one instance, on 6 April 1999, a militia group surrounded a church in Liquiça that was sheltering refugees, and threw tear gas into the building.[185] When the refugees fled the church, the militia attacked them and killed

62   *Exercising self-determination*

more than 50 people.[186] News of the massacre spread across the world and led UN Secretary-General Kofi Annan to strongly condemn the violence.[187] United States President Bill Clinton called upon Habibie to take measures to control the violence, again placing pressure on Indonesia to act responsibly towards the East Timorese.[188] By July 1999, more than 50,000 East Timorese were classified as internally displaced.[189]

Under the terms of the May 5 Agreement, UN Security Council Resolution 1246 established the United Nations Mission in East Timor (UNAMET) on 11 June 1999 which was responsible for organising and conducting the Popular Consultation and activities relating to voting.[190] The UNAMET, consisting of 241 international staff members, 420 UN volunteers, 280 civilian police and 4,000 local staff, were responsible for conducting the democratic vote in fair and impartial conditions.[191] The arrival of the UNAMET also oversaw the growth of an international media presence in East Timor: over 600 journalists were given official accreditation to cover the referendum and inform the rest of the world about the events in East Timor.[192]

The responsibilities of the UNAMET included a wide-scale public information campaign necessary for the East Timorese to make an informed choice. Local radio broadcasts across East Timor in Bahasa Indonesian, Portuguese, Tetum and English ran for three hours a day explaining the purpose, objectives and impartiality of the UNAMET and emphasising the need for a secret ballot.[193] They also explained the implications of an 'accept' or 'reject' vote.[194] Printed material in four languages explained the May 5 Agreement, utilising symbols for illiterate people, including the National Council of Timorese Resistance (CNRT) flag for a 'reject' vote.[195] They also explained how to vote, informing the East Timorese that there would be one vote per person, the types of identification required and how to mark the ballot and place it in the box correctly.[196] Bishop Belo and other members of the Catholic Church worked hard to reassure the East Timorese that they were free to vote how they wanted with no moral obligation to follow traditional 'blood oaths' between *liurais* and individuals.[197]

These information sessions were important for ensuring people's votes reflected their views. Other declarations of 'self-determination' in East Timor's past included the unilateral declaration of independence by FRETILIN in 1975, the Balibo declaration and the 'election' of a Provisional Government of East Timor in 1976.[198] All had failed 'the fundamental test of freedom of choice' required for an exercise of self-determination and were never widely considered legitimate in the international community.[199] Part of the UNAMET's mission was to explain to voters that the referendum would be freer and fairer than anything experienced in the past, and that the United Nations would not leave after the vote.[200] A free and fair vote under the close watch of the international community supported electoral legitimacy by providing evidence that the outcome accurately reflected the will of the East Timorese.

The official period for political campaigning was set by the UNAMET, in consultation with both pro-integration and pro-independence groups, to run from 14 August until 26 August.[201] The strict rules about where and when supporters

Exercising self-determination   63

could campaign were designed to limit intimidation and potential violence.[202] Parties had signed an agreement not to intimidate, stab, shoot or beat campaigners, although as Martinkus notes, this had little effect on instances of political violence.[203] Ian Martin, head of the UNAMET, acknowledged that the security situation prevented the establishment of a 'level playing field' in the campaign period as the pro-independence coalition, the CNRT, were not able to campaign openly.[204] Independence leaders were openly targeted and forced to flee Dili. The CNRT were forced to close its offices after its new Dili headquarters were burnt down just eight days after opening.[205] Despite the rising levels of violence, pro-independence students continued their activism, opting for a low-key door-knocking campaign around remote villages.[206] Thirteen-hundred copies of a newspaper titled *Vox Populi*, produced by pro-independence groups, were circulated every two days.[207] Due to the dangers, the CNRT and other pro-independence activists waged an information campaign rather than organising public rallies, confident that a sense of East Timorese nationhood had sufficiently consolidated over the 24-year resistance.[208]

On 30 August 1999, after two postponements of the referendum, 98.5 per cent (451,792) of registered East Timorese voted in the Popular Consultation, a remarkably high number given the atmosphere of violence and intimidation.[209] The UNAMET thought they would be lucky to see 50 per cent of registered voters take part.[210] In many rural areas, people walked for hours and waited in long queues in order to submit their preference.[211] Twenty-one-point-five per cent (94,388) voted in favour of the autonomy package, and 78.5 percent (344,580) chose independence by rejecting special autonomy in Indonesia.[212] Although there were some charges of voting irregularities, and some regions experienced violence and intimidation during the vote, the ballot was considered to have been administered under mostly fair and democratic conditions.[213] The referendum was declared by the UN as an 'accurate reflection of the views of East Timorese people'.[214] On 3 September 1999, UN Secretary-General Kofi Annan announced: 'After 24 years of conflict, East Timor now stands on the threshold of what we all hope will be a process of orderly and peaceful transition towards independence'.[215] The democratic exercise of self-determination provided the pathway for East Timor to become internationally recognised as a sovereign state.

Following the announcement of the referendum results, a 'shocked' Indonesia and pro-integration supporters accused the UNAMET of lacking neutrality.[216] According to observers, major breaches of ballot rules were in fact largely instigated by pro-integration groups, including attacking civilians, burning homes and intimidating people.[217] It was also suspected that the criticisms of the UNAMET and the campaign of intimidation were designed to cast doubt over the legitimacy of the result.[218]

The violence perpetrated by the pro-integration militia rapidly escalated following the referendum as the Indonesian military neglected their responsibilities to provide security in East Timor.[219] Indonesian Colonel Tono Suratman warned in an interview before the ballot that 'if the pro-independents do win ... all will

64 *Exercising self-determination*

be destroyed'.[220] 'Operation Clean Sweep' was a three-week 'scorched earth' campaign in East Timor adopted by the Indonesian military and pro-independence militia.[221] It was estimated that 70 per cent of the physical infrastructure was deliberately burnt or rendered uninhabitable across East Timor, and street-by-street burnings destroyed 95 per cent of some areas.[222] Robinson estimates that 2,000 people were killed during Operation Clean Sweep, with around 400,000 people (approximately half the population of East Timor) forced to flee their homes.[223] An estimated 230,000–250,000 of those were forced across the border into West Timor and the remainder took refuge in the mountains of East Timor.[224] Some prominent East Timorese leaders, including Bishop Belo and Xanana Gusmão, were evacuated to Darwin.[225]

While Indonesia denied responsibility and blamed pro-integration militias, it appears the operation was planned, systematic and coordinated under the orders of the Indonesian military.[226] The 'Garnadi Document', prepared on 3 July 1999 by high-ranking Indonesian official Major-General H. R. Garnadi, was considered by many (including human rights advocacy group *Yayasan HAK*) as the initial blueprint for the scorched earth policy as it recommended the extensive destruction of infrastructure should the autonomy proposal be rejected.[227] The UN Commission of Inquiry on East Timor held the Indonesian military ultimately responsible for acts of political violence before and after the consultation.[228]

This 'reign of terror', as Ballard described it, appeared to be an act of revenge for the independence vote and a strategy to push FALINTIL, the pro-independence armed forces, into a civil war, thus complicating the transition to independence and casting doubt over East Timor's legitimate exercise of self-determination.[229] It was also a lesson to other restive communities in Indonesia about what would happen if they attempted to secede.[230] The victims of violence were overwhelmingly real or alleged supporters of independence, including 'CNRT leaders, local authorities, alleged traitors, villagers in pro-independence base areas, members of the Catholic clergy, students and young people, locally employed UNAMET staff, women and girls, and small children'.[231] The majority of the UNAMET staff were forced to leave the territory.[232]

The post-ballot violence led to an international outcry and calls for a multinational peacekeeping force in East Timor with international pressure increasing after the United Nations sent a mission to East Timor and Jakarta on 6 September.[233] Indonesia initially rejected international calls for a Multinational Force, arguing it could handle the security situation.[234] No state would commit to sending in forces unless Indonesia consented.[235] Various governments sought to pressure Indonesia, including United States President Bill Clinton, who set economic sanctions and issued warnings to Indonesia to stop the violence.[236] A series of mass protests were held in Sydney and Melbourne in early September involving approximately 20,000 to 30,000 people.[237] These demonstrations forced the reluctant Australian government to lead a peacekeeping force, although Indonesian government reports viewed Australia as quite willing to institute a new model of intervention in the region.[238] On 7 September, Martial

Exercising self-determination   65

Law was instituted in East Timor and failed to improve the situation. Five days later, international pressure forced Habibie to request a multi-national peace-keeping team.[239] On 15 September, the United Nations authorised the establishment of the peacekeeping body International Force for East Timor (INTERFET), which arrived in East Timor on 20 September 1999 to restore peace and stability.[240]

Conclusion

While it is difficult to determine the precise impacts that civil society pressure had in compelling policy change, East Timor's path to independence suggests that grass-roots movements within states and international civil society played an important role in pressuring governments and the United Nations to act. Without consistent support from civil society organisations, including funding, information sharing, demonstrating and lobbying, the international 'diplomatic' arm of East Timor's resistance movement would have struggled to raise international consciousness.

The resignation of Indonesian President Suharto was driven to a large extent by pro-democracy protests in Indonesia, which worked in conjunction with the East Timor student independence movement. The resignation of President Suharto provided opportunities for the East Timorese independence movement to actively pursue their goals of democratic independence and publicise the situation in East Timor. Protest movements in Australia, United States and elsewhere regarding East Timor's independence were factors in altering the policies of Western states. This suggests that civil society and grass-roots organisations were influential in establishing East Timor's rights to vote for self-determination at an international level.

International civil society organisations driven by East Timorese leaders, NGOs and the diaspora pressed for an end to foreign oppression as both a pathway to peace and as a way of providing fundamental rights and freedoms. United Nations Secretary-General Kofi Annan argued that the contribution of international civil society was crucial to resolving the conflict in East Timor as it 'earned legitimacy and respect in its advocacy for Timor-Leste by promoting core values' such as human rights, peace and democracy.[241] Independence was seen as the only guarantor of the restoration and preservation of human rights in East Timor, and the only acceptable pathway to political freedom.

East Timor's pursuit of democratic independence enabled the vote for independence after nearly 25 years of Indonesian occupation. East Timor's external self-determination rights were contingent upon the UN-led Popular Consultation, which utilised democratic principles of universal political participation in decision-making. This ensured that the will of the nation regarding East Timor's political status would be properly measured and abided by. While a commitment to democracy supported East Timor's claims to self-determination, it is also evident that its path to independence was driven by a desire to establish democratic structures and institute human rights and freedoms.

66 *Exercising self-determination*

Notes

1 Dunn, *Timor: A People Betrayed*, 346.
2 See Strating, 'Contested Self-determination'. For an Indonesian perspective, see Indonesia Departemen Luar Negeri, *Pelaksanaan Politik Luar Negeri Indonesia Pasca Pemisahan Timor Timur*, 15–24.
3 Fernandes, *The Independence of East Timor*, 162.
4 CAVR, *Timor-Leste Self-Determination and the International Community*, 17 and Simpson, 'Solidarity in the Age of Globalization', 456.
5 CAVR, *Chega!*, Chapter 7:1, 94.
6 Ibid.
7 Shoesmith, 'Timor-Leste: Divided Leadership', 238.
8 Strating, 'Contested Self-determination'.
9 Fernandes, *The Independence of East Timor*, 151; Kingsbury, *East Timor: The Price of Liberty*, 60–63 and Philpott, 'East Timor's Double Life', 142.
10 Soares, 'Political Developments', 61.
11 Simpson, 'Solidarity in the Age of Globalization', 458.
12 Unrepresented Nations and Peoples Organization, *The Question of Self-Determination: The Cases of East Timor, Tibet and Western Sahara Conference Report*; Suzanne Linton cited in CAVR, *Timor-Leste Self-Determination and the International Community*, 9 and United Nations General Assembly, *Declaration on the Granting of Independence to Colonial Countries and Peoples*.
13 United Nations General Assembly and United Nations Security Council, *Question of East Timor: Report of the Secretary-General*.
14 Ibid.
15 CAVR, *Chega!*, Chapter 7:1, 4.
16 United Nations Security Council, *Resolution 1246*.
17 United Nations Security Council, *Secretary-General Informs Security Council People of East Timor Rejected Special Autonomy Proposed by Indonesia*.
18 CAVR, *Chega!*, Chapter 7:1, 78.
19 Kiernan, *Genocide and Resistance*, 168 and Ramos-Horta, *Funu*, 128.
20 CAVR, *Chega!*, Chapter 7:1, 79.
21 Ibid.
22 Ibid., Chapter 7:1, 80.
23 Ibid., Chapter 7:1, 81.
24 Ramos-Horta, *Funu*, 128.
25 CAVR, *Chega!*, Chapter 7:1, 81.
26 Ibid.
27 Ibid., 83.
28 Ibid., Chapter 7:1, 18.
29 Ibid. and Simpson, 'Solidarity in the Age of Globalization', 456.
30 CAVR, *Chega!*, Chapter 7:1, 106.
31 Ibid.
32 Ibid.
33 Ibid., Chapter 7:1, 97.
34 Ibid., Chapter 7:1, 78 and Ramos-Horta, *Funu*.
35 CAVR., ibid., Chapter 7:1, 79.
36 Ibid., Chapter 7:1, 98.
37 Ibid., Chapter 7:1, 80.
38 Simpson, 'Solidarity in the Age of Globalization', 456.
39 Pereira cited in CAVR, *Timor-Leste Self-Determination and the International Community*, 17. See also Pinto and Jardine, *East Timor's Unfinished Struggle*, 244.
40 Fernandes, *The Independence of East Timor*, 77.
41 Ibid.

Exercising self-determination 67

42 CAVR, *Chega!*, Chapter 7:1, 92.
43 Pereira cited in CAVR, *Timor-Leste Self-Determination and the International Community*, 19. See also Simpson, 'Solidarity in the Age of Globalization', 454.
44 CAVR, ibid.
45 Ibid. Indonesia cut off access to East Timorese territory from 1975 until 1989.
46 CAVR, *Chega!*, Chapter 7:1, 6.
47 Pinto and Jardine, *East Timor's Unfinished Struggle*, 249.
48 CAVR, *Chega!*, Chapter 7:1, 81.
49 Zaum, *The Sovereign Paradox*, 43.
50 CAVR, *Chega!*, Chapter 7:1, 100.
51 Ibid., Chapter 7:1, 99–101.
52 Ibid. See Jolliffe, *East Timor: Nationalism and Colonialism*, 180.
53 Simpson, 'Solidarity in the Age of Globalization', 459.
54 CAVR, *Chega!*, Chapter 7:1, 79.
55 Ibid., Chapter 7:1, 80.
56 Ibid.
57 Ibid., Chapter 7:1, 97.
58 Ibid. and Taylor, *East Timor: The Price of Freedom*, 202.
59 CAVR, *Chega!*, Chapter 7:1, 97–100; Dunn, *Timor: A People Betrayed*, 147 and Taylor, ibid., 55–56.
60 CAVR, ibid., Chapter 7:1, 100.
61 Simpson, 'Solidarity in the Age of Globalization', 459. See also Indonesia Departemen Luar Negeri, *Pelaksanaan Politik Luar Negeri Indonesia Pasca Pemisahan Timor Timur*, 12 and 25.
62 CAVR, *Chega!*, Chapter 3, 116. See also Singh, 'Habibie Melempar Bola Panas Ke Tangan PBB', 41.
63 Fernandes, *The Independence of East Timor*, 89 and Kingsbury, 'East Timor to 1999', 23.
64 Fernandes, ibid., 90 and Philpott, 'East Timor's Double Life', 142.
65 Fernandes, ibid. and Kingsbury, 'East Timor to 1999', 24.
66 CAVR, *Chega!*, Chapter 3, 117.
67 Fernandes, *The Independence of East Timor*, 90; Kingsbury, *East Timor: The Price of Liberty*, 62; Lloyd, 'The Diplomacy on East Timor', 83; Philpott, 'East Timor's Double Life', 142 and Soares, 'Political Developments', 65. For an Indonesian perspective, see Mashad, 'Indonesia menjawab tantangan global', 192–193.
68 Philpott, ibid.
69 Fernandes, *The Independence of East Timor*, 91.
70 Kingsbury, 'East Timor to 1999', 24.
71 CAVR, *Chega!*, Chapter 3, 166.
72 Alatas, *Pebble in the Shoe*, 57–59 and Fernandes, *The Independence of East Timor*, 90.
73 Ibid., 91.
74 Mashad, 'Indonesia menjawab tantangan global', 194.
75 Ballard, *Triumph of Self-Determination*, 14. See also Indonesia Departemen Luar Negeri, *Pelaksanaan Politik Luar Negeri Indonesia Pasca Pemisahan Timor Timur*, 25.
76 CAVR, *Chega!*, Chapter 7:1, 113.
77 Krieger, *East Timor and the International Community*, 185–186.
78 Ibid., 187–196.
79 CAVR, *Chega!*, Chapter 7:1, 109 and Simpson, 'Solidarity in the Age of Globalization', 459.
80 Simpson, ibid. and Fernandes, *The Independence of East Timor*, 92.
81 Simpson, ibid, 495 and 463.
82 Ibid.

68   *Exercising self-determination*

83 Fernandes, *The Independence of East Timor*, 92.
84 Ibid. and Ambrosio, 'East Timor Independence, 124.
85 Simpson, 'Solidarity in the Age of Globalization', 460 and 476–467.
86 Fernandes, *The Independence of East Timor*, 93.
87 Stanley Roth cited in ibid.
88 Ibid., 99.
89 Ibid. and CAVR, *Timor-Leste Self-Determination and the International Community*, 21.
90 CAVR, *Chega!*, Chapter 7:1, 92.
91 Abel Guterres cited in CAVR, *Timor-Leste Self-Determination and the International Community*, 21.
92 Ibid., 44.
93 Simpson, 'Solidarity in the Age of Globalization', 461.
94 Monica Nakamura cited in CAVR, *Chega!*, Chapter 7:1, 110.
95 CAVR, *Timor-Leste Self-Determination and the International Community*, 45.
96 CAVR, *Chega!*, Chapter 3, 117.
97 CAVR, *Timor-Leste Self-Determination and the International Community*, 31 and Fernandes, *The Independence of East Timor*, 125. See also CAVR, *Chega!*, Chapter 3, 119.
98 CAVR, ibid.
99 Nugroho Katjasungkana cited in ibid.
100 CAVR, *Chega!*, Chapter 3, 119.
101 Nugroho Katjasungkana cited in CAVR, *Timor-Leste Self-Determination and the International Community*, 32–33.
102 Ibid., 33.
103 Ibid., 32 and CAVR, *Chega!*, Chapter 3, 119–120. Newspapers, such as *The Voice of the Maubere People*, were circulated by pro-democracy groups around Indonesia.
104 See CAVR, *Timor-Leste Self-Determination and the International Community*, 36.
105 Gill, *The Dynamics of Democratization*, 18–25.
106 Ambrosio, 'East Timor Independence', 115; Ballard, *Triumph of Self-Determination*, 33; Lloyd, 'The Diplomacy on East Timor', 84; Marker, *East Timor: A Memoir of the Negotiations for Independence*, 80 and Pietsch, 'Australian Imperialism and East Timor', 13. For an official Australian perspective on the events of 1998, see Department of Foreign Affairs, *East Timor in Transition 1998–2000*, 14–37.
107 Ballard, ibid., 33 and Fernandes, *Reluctant Saviours*, 33.
108 CAVR, *Chega!*, Chapter 3, 125.
109 Crouch, *Political Reform In Indonesia After Soeharto*, 3. See also Yulianto, *Hubungan sipil militer di Indonesia pasca Orba*, 348–353 and Manning and Van Diermen, eds., *Indonesia di Tengah Transisi.*
110 Strating, 'The Indonesia-Timor-Leste Commission of Truth and Friendship'.
111 Ibid.; Ballard, *Triumph of Self-Determination*, 33; Fernandes, *Reluctant Saviours*, 3; Marker, *East Timor: A Memoir of the Negotiations for Independence*, 80; Philpott, 'East Timor's Double Life', 142 and Pietsch, 'Australian Imperialism and East Timor', 13.
112 Ballard, ibid., 40 and Fernandes, ibid., 33. See also Anwar, 'Implementasi Kebijakan Luar Negeri dan Pertahanan Australia terhadap Indonesia', 101–104.
113 Pietsch, 'Australian Imperialism and East Timor', 13.
114 Ibid.
115 CAVR, *Chega!*, Chapter 3, 124.
116 Chesterman, *You, the People*, 61 and Philpott, 'East Timor's Double Life', 142.
117 Marker, *East Timor: A Memoir of the Negotiations for Independence*, 96.
118 CAVR, *Chega!*, Chapter 3, 125.
119 Ballard, *Triumph of Self-Determination*, 41; Chan cited in CAVR, *Timor-Leste Self-Determination and the International Community*, 50 and Lloyd, 'Diplomacy on East Timor', 84.

Exercising self-determination 69

120 Ballard, ibid.
121 On 'hardliners' and 'softliners' see Gill, *The Dynamics of Democratization*, 50.
122 Soares, 'Political Developments', 64; CAVR, *Chega!*, Chapter 3, 139 and Marker, *East Timor: A Memoir of the Negotiations for Independence*, 129.
123 Pietsch, 'Australian Imperialism and East Timor', 14.
124 CAVR, Ibid., Chapter 3, 113 and 125.
125 Lloyd, 'The Diplomacy on East Timor', 80.
126 Marker, *East Timor: A Memoir of the Negotiations for Independence*, 88.
127 CAVR, *Timor-Leste Self-Determination and the International Community*, 38.
128 Yeni Rose Damayanti cited in ibid., 37.
129 Ibid.
130 Ibid.
131 Ibid., 38.
132 Marker, *East Timor: A Memoir of the Negotiations for Independence*, 87.
133 Ambrosio, 'East Timor Independence', 129.
134 Ibid., 130 and Ressa, *Indonesia's Habibie Faces Daunting Task*.
135 Lloyd, 'The Diplomacy on East Timor', 84.
136 Ballard, *Triumph of Self-Determination*, 26.
137 Ibid., 34 and CAVR, *Chega!*, Chapter 3, 126.
138 Lloyd, 'The Diplomacy on East Timor', 85.
139 Marker, *East Timor: A Memoir of the Negotiations for Independence*, 87–88.
140 Ibid., 104.
141 Ballard, *Triumph of Self-Determination*, 34. Kuntari emphasised the intimidation of FRETILIN. See Kuntari, 'Timor Timur Satu Menit Terakhir', 47–67.
142 Ballard, ibid., 34 and Martinkus, *A Dirty Little War*, 81.
143 Ambrosio, 'East Timor Independence', 115.
144 Lloyd, 'The Diplomacy on East Timor', 86.
145 Ibid.
146 Ballard, *Triumph of Self-Determination*, 36.
147 Soares, 'Political Developments', 61 and 65 and Alatas, *Pebble in the Shoe*, 57.
148 Ibid., 66 and Marker, *East Timor: A Memoir of the Negotiations for Independence*, 128.
149 See Lloyd, 'The Diplomacy on East Timor', 88. Dewi Fortuna Anwar suggests Howard lacked the closeness with Indonesia of former Australian Prime Minister Paul Keating. See Anwar, 'Implementasi Kebijakan Luar Negeri dan Pertahanan Australia terhadap Indonesia', 101–104 and 110–112.
150 For an Indonesian perspective, see Indonesia Departemen Luar Negeri, *Pelaksanaan Politik Luar Negeri Indonesia Pasca Pemisahan Timor Timur*, 30–34. See also CAVR, *Chega!*, Chapter 7:1, 3 and Department of Foreign Affairs, Australia, *East Timor in Transition 1998–2000*, 29–33.
151 Marker, *East Timor: A Memoir of the Negotiations for Independence*, 121. See Lloyd, 'The Diplomacy on East Timor', 89.
152 Marker, ibid., 128.
153 CAVR, *Chega!*, Chapter 7:1, 114.
154 Marker, *East Timor: A Memoir of the Negotiations for Independence*, 121. See also Department of Foreign Affairs, Australia, *East Timor in Transition 1998–2000*, 38–54.
155 CAVR, *Chega!* Chapter 3, 130.
156 Lloyd, 'The Diplomacy on East Timor', 84. See Alatas, *Pebble in the Shoe*.
157 Habibie cited in Marker, *East Timor: A Memoir of the Negotiations for Independence*, 128.
158 Habibie cited in Fernandes, *Reluctant Saviours*, 41–42 and Alatas, *Pebble in the Shoe*, 151.
159 Strating, 'Contested Self-determination'.

70 *Exercising self-determination*

160 Cited in Indonesia Departemen Luar Negeri, *Pelaksanaan Politik Luar Negeri Indonesia Pasca Pemisahan Timor Timur*, 32 and 33.
161 Ibid., 34.
162 Singh, 'Habibie Melempar Bola Panas Ke Tangan PBB', 28–29.
163 Wibisono Makarim, 'Dunia Menilai Indonesia Konsisten Dengan Demokrasi', 51–52.
164 CAVR, *Chega!*, Chapter 7:1, 130; Fernandes, *Reluctant Saviours*, 33–34 and Lloyd, 'The Diplomacy on East Timor', 91.
165 Marker, *East Timor: A Memoir of the Negotiations for Independence*, 129.
166 Ibid.
167 Soares, 'Political Development', 66–67.
168 CAVR, *Chega!*, Chapter 7:1, 93.
169 Lloyd, 'The Diplomacy on East Timor', 79. For the perspective of Indonesian ambassador to the UN, see Wibisono Makarim, 'Dunia Menilai Indonesia Konsisten Dengan Demokrasi', 48–51. For Ali Alatas' perspective, see Alatas, *Pebble in the Shoe*, Chapters 2, 3 and 5. See also Indonesia Departemen Luar Negeri, *Pelaksanaan Politik Luar Negeri Indonesia Pasca Pemisahan Timor Timur*, 24–28.
170 Marker, *East Timor: A Memoir of the Negotiations for Independence*, 93.
171 United Nations General Assembly and United Nations Security Council, *Question of East Timor: Report of the Secretary-General*.
172 See CAVR, *Chega!*, Chapter 3, 132 and United Nations, *Press Conference by Secretary-General Kofi Annan, His Personal Representative for East Timor, and Foreign Ministers of Indonesia and Portugal*.
173 United Nations General Assembly and United Nations Security Council, *Question of East Timor: Report of the Secretary-General*.
174 Ibid.
175 Lloyd, 'The Diplomacy on East Timor', 94–95. See also CAVR, *Chega!*, Chapter 3, 130.
176 Marker, *East Timor: A Memoir of the Negotiations for Independence*, 128.
177 United Nations General Assembly and United Nations Security Council, *Question of East Timor: Report of the Secretary-General*. Indonesia would retain control over foreign affairs, currency, defence and finance.
178 Lloyd, 'The Diplomacy on East Timor', 95.
179 Pietsch, 'Australian Imperialism and East Timor', 15.
180 Ibid. and van Klinken, 'Taking the Risk, Paying the Price', 45. See also Bartu, 'The Militia, the Military, and the People of the Bobonaro District', 81–98.
181 United Nations Security Council, *Question of East Timor: Report of the Secretary General*, S/1999/705, 22 June 1999, 4.
182 Robinson, *East Timor 1999 Crimes against Humanity*, 1.
183 United Nations Office of the Commissioner of Human Rights, *Report of the Commission of Inquiry on East Timor to Secretary-General*.
184 The UNAMET only substantiated two examples of pro-integration supporters being killed by pro-independents. See ibid and CAVR, *Chega!*, Chapter 3, 131 and 142.
185 Fernandes, *Reluctant Saviours*, 56.
186 Ibid.
187 Marker, *East Timor: A Memoir of the Negotiations for Independence*, 141.
188 Ibid.
189 Soares, 'Political Development', 72.
190 United Nations Security Council, *Resolution 1246*, 1–2 and United Nations Security Council, *Question of East Timor: Report of the Secretary-General*, 1.
191 United Nations Security Council, *Resolution 1246*, 2.
192 CAVR, *Chega!*, Chapter 3, 136.
193 Smith, 'The Popular Consultation in the Ermera District', 29 and 31.

Exercising self-determination 71

194 United Nations General Assembly and United Nations Security Council, *Question of East Timor: Report of the Secretary-General*, 24–25.
195 United Nations Security Council, *Question of East Timor: Report of the Secretary General*.
196 Smith, 'The Popular Consultation in the Ermera District', 30.
197 Ibid., 30 and 37.
198 Krieger, *East Timor and the International Community*, 39 and 44.
199 CAVR, *Chega!*, Chapter 7:1, 19–20.
200 Smith, 'The Popular Consultation in the Ermera District', 31.
201 Martin, *Self-Determination in East Timor*, 64.
202 Ibid., 63–64.
203 Martinkus, *A Dirty Little War*, 250.
204 Ibid., 254 and Martin, *Self-Determination in East Timor*, 75.
205 Martin, ibid.
206 Martinkus, *A Dirty Little War*, 250 and Soares, 'Political Developments', 67.
207 CAVR, *Chega!*, Chapter 3, 140.
208 Ibid.
209 Soares, 'Political Developments', 73. See United Nations General Assembly and United Nations Security Council, *Question of East Timor: Report of the Secretary-General*, 24.
210 Kingsbury, 'The TNI and the Militias'.
211 CAVR, *Chega!*, Chapter 3, 143.
212 United Nations Security Council, *Secretary-General Informs Security Council People of East Timor Rejected Special Autonomy Proposed by Indonesia*.
213 Ballard, *Triumph of Self-Determination*, 53; CAVR, *Chega!*, Chapter 3, 143 and Smith, 'The Popular Consultation in the Ermera district', 29 and 39.
214 United Nations Security Council, *Secretary-General Informs Security Council People of East Timor Rejected Special Autonomy Proposed by Indonesia*.
215 Ballard, *Triumph of Self-Determination*, 54.
216 Alatas, *Pebble in the Shoe*, 196 and 211 and Indonesia Departemen Luar Negeri, *Pelaksanaan Politik Luar Negeri Indonesia Pasca Pemisahan Timor Timur*, 35–37.
217 Kingsbury, 'The TNI and the Militias', 69 and Smith, 'The Popular Consultation in the Ermera District', 29, 33 and 36–37.
218 Lloyd, 'The Diplomacy on East Timor', 92.
219 Ballard, *Triumph of Self-Determination*, 68; Robinson, *East Timor 1999 Crimes against Humanity*, 3 and Soares, 'Political Developments', 68.
220 Burchill, 'East Timor, Australia and Indonesia', 179.
221 Chopra, 'The UN's Kingdom of East Timor', 27.
222 Ibid. and CAVR, *Chega!*, Chapter 3, 145. See Robinson, *East Timor 1999 Crimes Against Humanity*, 44 and United Nations Office of the Commissioner of Human Rights, *Report of the Commission of Inquiry on East Timor to Secretary-General*.
223 Robinson, ibid., 1 and Beauvais, 'Benevolent Despotism', 1103. The *Chega!* report also records evidence of torture, bodily mutilation and rape that occurred during this time. See CAVR, *Chega!*, Chapter 3, 145.
224 Beauvais, ibid. and Robinson, *East Timor 1999 Crimes Against Humanity*, 42.
225 CAVR, *Chega!*, Chapter 3, 149. See for example Alatas, *Pebble in the Shoe*, 168 and 189–193.
226 Martin, *Self-Determination in East Timor: the United Nations, the Ballot, and International Intervention*, 124.
227 Yayasan HAK, *MajGen (ret) H R Garnadi*. See also Soares, 'Political Developments', 57 and Crouch, 'The TNI and East Timor Policy', 157.
228 United Nations Office of the Commissioner of Human Rights, *Report of the Commission of Inquiry on East Timor to Secretary-General*. See Indonesia National Human Rights Commission. *Commission for Human Rights Violations in East Timor (KPP-HAM)*.

72   *Exercising self-determination*

229 Ballard, *Triumph of Self-Determination*, 55.
230 Kingsbury, 'The TNI and the Militias', 77.
231 Robinson, *East Timor 1999 Crimes Against Humanity*, 4. The UN report found only a small number of the victims of violence were members of pro-Indonesian groups.
232 Beauvais, 'Benevolent Despotism', 1103.
233 CAVR, *Chega!*, Chapter 3, 150.
234 Lloyd, 'The Diplomacy on East Timor', 100 and Soares, 'Political Development', 72.
235 CAVR, *Chega!*, Chapter 3, 149.
236 Lloyd, 'The Diplomacy on East Timor', 101.
237 Fernandes, *Reluctant Saviours*, 3, 46 and 89–94.
238 Indonesia Departemen Luar Negeri, *Pelaksanaan Politik Luar Negeri Indonesia Pasca Pemisahan Timor Timur*, 37. See also CAVR, *Chega!*, Chapter 7:1, 149.
239 CAVR, ibid. and Lloyd, 'The Diplomacy on East Timor', 101. Alatas suggests it was at the behest of General Wiranto. See Alatas, *Pebble in the Shoe*, 214.
240 United Nations Security Council, *Resolution 1264*.
241 Kofi Annan cited in CAVR, *Chega!*, Chapter 7:1, 95.

3 International state-building and civil society

Studies in democratisation and international state-building across a variety of contexts have suggested that democracy must be accepted at grass-roots level to establish the long-term legitimacy and functionality of the political system.[1] As Manor suggests, creating political institutions alone is insufficient for building a democratic state; rather, he advocates a model of 'democratisation with inclusion' through grass-roots participation and citizenry engagement, supported and facilitated by a free and open civil society.[2] The proposition that successful implementation of democracy is more likely through 'bottom-up' rather than 'top-down' processes presents a number of issues for international state-builders in facilitating democracy in new, weak states.

Zaum has argued that a new regime of 'positive sovereignty', in the form of legitimate authority expressed as a relationship between society and state, has emerged as the principal function of international transitional administrators.[3] However, critics of liberal peacebuilding have noted that transposing 'Weberian' state structures upon existing socio-political institutions leads to a 'sovereign gap' between society and states that diminishes prospects of institutionalisation.[4] The capacities of domestic and international agents to create sustainable and robust institutions depends upon models of engagement and partnership that ensure a widespread feeling of 'local ownership' over new state structures and perceptions of legitimacy among citizens. In East Timor, the United Nations Transitional Administration in East Timor (UNTAET) was mandated to institute international norms of democracy, establish political order and create viable institutions that could resist state failure.

Building a functional social democratic state based upon political legitimacy in East Timor required both state-building and nation-building as co-constitutive processes. The term 'nation-building' is often used interchangeably with state-building, however these terms describe different activities.[5] State-building refers to establishing new states by 'building effective systems and institutions of government'.[6] Nation-building, on the other hand, refers to the processes of integrating the new state and society and binding the nation to new political structures.[7] Whereas international state-building activities focus on establishing peace in conflict areas and (re-) building political structures within a territory, civic nation-building entails establishing and consolidating relationships between

74 *International state-building and civil society*

state and society, uniting competing social groups and developing a robust civil society as a site of reasoned deliberation and participation.[8] This is crucial to establishing a system that is compatible with the local context: as Migdal argues, understanding the basis of internal political struggles requires focusing not just on state formation but 'society formation' understood as a 'melange of social organisations' providing the 'civic bases of association'.[9]

For East Timor, the creation of a democratic civil society was necessary for supporting effective internal sovereignty and supporting processes of legitimation whereby citizens willingly comply with the authority of the state.[10] Social democracy in particular emphasises a robust connection between the social and political spheres of public life through citizenry participation and engagement. The *raison d'etre* of the state, according to this perspective, lies in its capacities to ensure citizens the political and socio-economic rights necessary for the attainment of full citizenship. This vision of social democracy sees the social and political realms as co-constitutive and mutually supportive.

In considering East Timor's state-building processes, this chapter examines the direct participation and capacities for decision-making by East Timorese leaders, many of whom experienced their own transition from civil society activists advocating independence to state-builders and, ultimately, politicians. The development of civil society organisations and their roles during East Timor's transition period (1999–2002) validated the importance of citizenry participation in forming a democratic political culture. East Timorese leaders and civil society organisations were active and critical participants in state-building processes and held the UNTAET and other actors to account. In many respects, building functional state 'capacities' entails implementing strategies for inclusion and participation, not only to increase the likelihood of building domestic sovereignty and independence for the new state but also providing opportunities for citizens to practice democratic behaviour.

This chapter evaluates three strategies employed by the international community in the first phase of transition to increase participation of the East Timorese in the project of state-building. These included the National Consultative Council (NCC), the National Council, (NC) and the World Bank's Community Development Project, which were designed to facilitate community participation and representation. While these provided some scope for participation, international dominance in the transition period limited the extent to which these programs could assist in developing a democratic civic nation and, to some extent, stifled democratic opportunities in East Timor's transition. The UNTAET responded to criticisms regarding a lack of consultation by moving toward increasingly participatory models of transition, and the following chapter examines the second phase of transition.

During the transitional period the willingness of East Timorese individuals and civil society organisations to involve themselves in the construction of their new state signalled the emergence of an embryonic democratic political community in East Timor. As Kingsbury notes, the first sign of a civic nation emerged when 98.5 per cent of registered East Timorese voted in the 1999

International state-building and civil society 75

referendum.[11] In that instance, and in the elections that followed, voter turnout was significantly high, particularly compared with more established democracies. The willingness of many East Timorese to engage in debate and discussion throughout the transition period reflected the beginnings of a political culture based on democratic behaviours, participation and engagement.

The authority of the United Nations Transitional Administration in East Timor

United Nations Security Council Resolution 1272 established the UNTAET, which became responsible for ensuring that East Timor could become a viable, independent democratic state.[12] It was also responsible for establishing East Timor's international legitimacy, which 'imposes a set of responsibilities on the state ... in regards to their own population'.[13] These responsibilities entail the establishment of 'positive sovereignty' by guaranteeing basic rights, developing an organised political bureaucracy, maintaining rule of law and adhering to international law and norms – what Zaum refers to as 'the standard of civilisation'.[14]

The May 5 Agreement between the UN, Portugal and Indonesia had directed the United Nations to play a significant role in East Timor, regardless of the results of the plebiscite.[15] Portugal and Indonesia had agreed in negotiations that in the instance autonomy was rejected, sovereign authority would not be transferred immediately to the East Timorese. Rather, the May 5 Agreement stipulated that 'the governments of Indonesia and Portugal and the Secretary-General shall agree on arrangements for a peaceful and orderly transfer of authority in East Timor to the United Nations'.[16] On 15 October, it was agreed between Indonesia and the UN that all 'assets' would be handed over to the UN.[17] On 19 October, Indonesia rescinded its 1976 law, which had incorporated East Timor as a province of Indonesia.[18]

By the time INTERFET entered East Timor in September 1999, Operation Clean Sweep had created a humanitarian crisis in East Timor that presented significant obstacles for East Timor's political transition. The physical destruction had drastic humanitarian consequences and caused significant challenges to East Timor's abilities to re-establish law and order and build state institutions.[19] As Joel Beauvais suggests, 'all semblance of government and financial institutions essentially had ceased to exist'.[20] Members of the Indonesian administration in East Timor fled the territory, creating a 'governance vacuum' that threatened 'to plunge East Timor into Somalia-style crisis'.[21] Resolution 1272 articulated several issues facing state-builders in East Timor, including the widespread displacement of citizens, large numbers of refugees in West Timor, border security weaknesses and the 'systematic, widespread and flagrant violations of international and humanitarian and human rights law'.[22]

Given the circumstances, the Security Council considered the continuing situation in East Timor as a 'threat to peace and security', and thus of legitimate concern to the international community.[23] The creation of the UNTAET delayed East Timor's independence as neither de facto (effective) nor *de jure* (legal)

76 *International state-building and civil society*

sovereignty was immediately transferred to the East Timorese people.[24] The referendum itself was not enough to secure East Timor's sovereign independence: a mission in East Timor was necessary for re-establishing security, filling the resultant power vacuum and establishing centralised state-based institutions.

On 25 October 1999, the United Nations Transitional Administration in East Timor (UNTAET) was established by unanimous vote in the Security Council.[25] Security Council Resolution 1272 bestowed responsibility for 'all legislative and executive authority, including the administration of justice' on the UNTAET.[26] The mandate required the UNTAET to:

- provide security and maintain law and order throughout the territory of East Timor;
- establish an effective administration;
- assist in the development of civil and social services;
- ensure the co-ordination and delivery of humanitarian assistance, rehabilitation and development assistance;
- support capacity building for self-government; and,
- assist in the establishment of conditions for sustainable development.[27]

Resolution 1272 provided authority for a period of 'shared sovereignty' between the UNTAET and East Timor with the purpose of establishing the institutions necessary for independent democratic self-government, although the power balance was considerably weighted in favour of the UNTAET.[28]

International lawyers have argued that Resolution 1272, along with Indonesia's consent to the establishment of the UNTAET, constituted a limited transfer of sovereign power to the international community in East Timor.[29] In what was a unique situation, the UNTAET was given de facto sovereign powers, which are generally only conferred to states as representatives of a group of people possessing rights to self-determination. During the political transition, *de jure* sovereignty was not held by any entity.[30] United Nations Security Council Resolution 1272 gave the Transitional Administrator, Sérgio Vieira de Mello, 'the power to enact new laws and regulations and to amend, suspend or repeal existing ones'.[31] In a rather undemocratic arrangement, legal responsibility for operating and reconstructing state functions during the transition period was invested in the Transitional Administrator rather than the people of East Timor, leading Beauvais to describe the situation as a 'benevolent despotism'.[32] According to the typology developed by Doyle, the arrangement could be considered an example of 'supervisory authority' comprised of full executive and law-making powers.[33]

The transitional administration in East Timor was officially a peacekeeping operation.[34] The authority to create the UNTAET stemmed from Chapter VII of the Charter of the United Nations, which mandates the Security Council to take measures to 'maintain and restore international peace and security'.[35] The transitional authority was established to 'provide security and maintain law and order' through a 8,500 strong military component.[36] Political stability required the effective operation of key state apparatuses following the withdrawal of

International state-building and civil society   77

Indonesia. This ambitious task involved employing hundreds of international advisors and placing them into civil administrative positions in state departments and institutions.[37] The reliance on non-East Timorese technocrats was partly due to a lack of a human skills base in East Timor as Indonesians who had previously filled administrative roles rapidly evacuated the territory after the referendum.[38] The absence of a history of self-government in East Timor at national levels justified international assistance in building East Timor's capacity to effectively and independently self-govern.

Although state-building is not new in the history of the United Nations, the scope of international assistance in establishing political institutions in East Timor was widely described as 'unprecedented'.[39] In comparison, the United Nations Transitional Administration in Cambodia's (UNTAC) responsibilities were limited to ensuring peaceful conditions and running elections, a limited mandate compared to the UNTAET.[40] At the time, the UNTAC – an 18-month mission costing US$1.8 billion – was considered an extensive peacekeeping mission.[41] The United Nations Mission in Kosovo (UNMIK) was tasked with a range of institution-building responsibilities similar to those of the UNTAET, but without a clear settlement on the question of sovereign independence.[42] While more recent interventions in Afghanistan and Iraq imposed democracy through a violation of sovereignty, international actors backed away from the extensive UNTAET model, replacing it with a less successful 'light footprint' approach.[43] Several examples of failed state-building suggest more extensive external support should be offered for democratisation.[44] However, this largely depends upon how state-building is conducted: the administrative structure and processes must encourage self-determination and capacity-building to counteract the problems posed by a foreign imposition.

State-building and the problem of legitimacy

The United Nations Security Council Resolution 1272 recognised the importance of collaboration between the international authority and local actors in fulfilling the twin obligations of institution- and capacity-building in East Timor.[45] State-builders were mandated to construct the features of statehood necessary for East Timor's transition from a dependent colony to a sovereign state in partnership with the East Timorese. United Nations Security Council Resolution 1272 stressed 'the need for the UNTAET to consult and cooperate closely with the East Timorese people in order to carry out its mandate effectively with a view to the development of local democratic institutions'.[46] The UNTAET reflected the movement towards exporting Western-style democratic governance to non-democratic states.[47] Beauvais describes the task of the UNTAET as moving East Timor from a situation in which there was 'virtually no administrative class, organised civil society, or history of self-rule, to a viable, independent, and democratic state'.[48] International 'democratisation' efforts support the notion that all people, irrespective of their cultural or ethnic identifications, are entitled to democratic governance and attendant citizenship rights as it is 'increasingly

78 International state-building and civil society

promoted and protected by collective international processes'.[49] These responsibilities reflect an international normative framework that privileges democratic systems ahead of alternatives.[50]

Paradoxically, the actual activities of international transitional administrations can undermine democratic principles regarding self-determination and political participation. This was particularly pronounced in Cambodia, the first example of post-Cold War democracy assistance, where external state-builders faced a number of challenges.[51] Since its independence in 1954, Cambodian politics had been the product of regional power dynamics and interventions by United States, China and Vietnam.[52] While East Timor's transition was preceded by a war of liberation, Cambodia's civil conflict had endured between opposing parties since 1970.[53] The 1991 Paris Peace Agreements, negotiated between four Cambodian political parties and 18 states, including the USA and Vietnam, mandated democratic transition to end an era of brutal conflict.[54]

While the internationally organised 1993 elections were considered a high-point of the UNTAC's administration, the power transition that resulted was not. A significant problem for external state-builders was managing the existing power dynamics and political violence and getting on board the elites who mattered.[55] The UNTAC largely failed to negotiate existing arrangements of power and authority, particularly the grass-roots patronage networks that governed party politics.[56] The UNTAC did not manage to disarm or demobilise all parties or implement a successful ceasefire, which led to a political environment that could not be considered 'neutral'.[57] The limited mandate of the UNTAC failed to take into account key agents of conflict, such as the Khmer Rouge militia, who were not 'incentivised' to give up activities that undermined new democratic imperatives.[58] Despite the royalist FUNCINPEC party gaining the highest percentage of the vote (45 per cent), the ruling party Cambodian People's Party (CPP) (which received 38 per cent) negotiated a 50:50 sharing arrangement with the CCP leader Hun Sen strong-arming his way to the Prime Ministership he had possessed since 1984.[59]

As Roberts explains, the elections failed 'to contribute to the consolidation of democracy because they were not a product of Cambodian society'.[60] Consequently, since the 1993 elections, Cambodia has maintained a hybrid 'competitive authoritarian' regime.[61] Paradoxically, a key issue for Cambodia's democratisation was not just that elections were a foreign product, but that the international community exited almost immediately, allowing existing patterns of authoritarianism to return in a different guise.[62] As Roberts argues, 'democratic transition was quite clearly impeded by resistance from elite political culture'.[63] The international state-builders failed to recognise Cambodia's existing political culture that fostered ideas of the 'absolutism' of political power contrary to democratic ideals.[64] Additionally, Levitsky and Way point out that civil society in Cambodia was 'virtually non-existent'.[65] The failed power transfer set a trend in Cambodia whereby democratic elections would be used to consolidate the 'legitimacy' of the authoritarian, non-democratic regime.[66] Cambodia hence provides a salient lesson on how the failure to institute democratic

International state-building and civil society 79

and participatory state-building processes undermines the end goal of producing a democratic state. It also represents an instructive case-study of what happens when elites and citizens are not invested in the democratising process.

While it was assumed that the UNTAET would build democracy in East Timor, this raised the potential problem of displacing accepted 'traditional' forms of socio-political organisation with culturally incongruous 'modern' structures. As the Cambodia example highlights, ignoring existing socio-political institutions and dynamics is fraught. Developing opportunities for the East Timorese to participate in the creation of new political structures was essential for ensuring that state-based institutions would not be viewed as 'imposed' or incompatible with East Timorese culture.

Nation-building connects the social and political spheres through participation, communication and social integration. The mass mobilization of people and the capacities of people to relate to each other in the public realm are important for building relationships between state and society that are required for effective nation-building.[67] Nation-building is conceived of as scaffolding positive and interactive relationships between political and social actors. Fostering 'national unity' and 'cohesion' is important for transitioning states like East Timor, as national ideas 'determine the structural and operational parameters of democratisation'.[68] Shared perceptions of the legitimacy of democratic institutions are unlikely to be facilitated by international actors. Nation-building entails the establishment of an internal relationship between society and the state and is predicated upon people participating in democratic processes, including the construction of new state institutions. A level of national unity – defined broadly as the regulation of social conflict – is necessary for democracy to flourish, as political violence and instability undermine democratic principles of equality, non-violent conflict resolution and rule of law.[69]

According to Borgerhoff, nation-building entails the 'deliberate interest- and ideology-based formation of a national format which creates a collective identity and affiliation of the population with the nation-state'.[70] For East Timor, this required establishing a democratic nation based on a shared civic democratic culture rather than ethnic or linguistic homogeneity, emphasising an inclusive national identity that could overlay existing forms of local and cultural identity. The coherence between ideas of national sovereignty and democratic government is reflected in the belief that free and equal citizens possess sovereignty, including the right to consent to their political institutions.[71] As such, the reification of democratic norms and political culture in the 'nation' is a condition of democratic transition, as democracy needs to be habituated, ritualised, and institutionalised as the 'only game in town'.[72]

The democratic civic nation is advanced through the participation of people in democratic activities that foster a nuanced understanding of the kinds of behaviours and orientations that effective democracies require. Building a nation, as a socio-cultural community within a political jurisdiction, is important for democracy because it views sovereignty as residing with the people.[73] Democratic legitimacy requires the majority of the population sharing a belief in the

80 *International state-building and civil society*

authority of political institutions, processes and behaviours, and a willingness to conform to the laws of the state. Consequently, democratic theory justifies the presence of the state by perceiving sovereignty as owned by citizens, and positioning people as the ultimate judges of democratic legitimacy as it 'reflects the depth of commitment [found in citizens] to the substance of the political system'.[74] In the 'age of popular sovereignty', the sovereignty of the state is grounded in the people: when a state is unable to maintain a sense of civic nationhood, 'the legitimacy of the state itself is in question'.[75] This suggests that collectively, citizens hold considerable political agency and responsibility in consolidating and maintaining democracy.

Civil society and state-building in East Timor

Civil society is an important space for nation-building and facilitating a sense of political culture, which, in turn, supports the binding of people to their structures and the development of national unity and cohesion based on democratic principles.[76] Civil societies are important for democracies because they provide alternative spaces for political and social engagement for individuals and organisations.[77] They are also essential for developing democratic behaviours and embedding democratic norms within social structures. During the transition period from September 1999 until May 2002, local non-state actors in East Timor were involved in a variety of areas, including agriculture, education, health, economic development, water and sanitation and media. Civil society organisations contributed to service provision, advocacy, training and awareness and basic health and education services.[78]

Prior to the 1999 referendum, civil society in East Timor consisted mostly of the clandestine movement opposing the Indonesian occupation, and the few non-clandestine NGOs that existed did so with many restraints.[79] Indonesia had banned civil society organisations in East Timor until the late 1980s, when a small number of international non-for-profits were permitted to operate.[80] Even after this policy shift, civil society organisations members faced persecution and aggression.[81] The Roman Catholic Church was viewed as acceptable to the Indonesian state, and although it was the most active civil society organisation, its influence was largely limited to health and education.[82] One of the first NGOs was the Catholic *Delegado Sosial* (DELSOS), which evolved into *Caritas Dili*.[83] Another long running civil society organisation was the East Timor Agriculture and Development Project Foundation (ETADEP), which concentrated on providing services to farmers.[84] Local NGOs concerned with social issues such as women, human rights, children, water and sanitation were established around 1997, including *ETWAVE, Fokupers, Pronto Ata Serbi, Yayasan Bia Hula* and *Yayasan HAK*.[85] Around this time, student and youth organisations also flourished, including the East Timor Students Solidarity Council, which in July 1998 organised a political demonstration in Dili of almost 10,000 people and sought to raise awareness about self-determination.[86]

The NGO Forum (FONGTIL), an umbrella organisation for NGOs, was established in 1998 comprising 14 registered NGOs involved mostly in advocacy and human rights work.[87] It was initially created to coordinate emergency assistance during the 1997–1998 drought and was supported by international NGOs, such as the Australian Council for Overseas Aid (ACFOA) and Oxfam.[88] In June 1999, 14 East Timorese NGOs met to reactivate the NGO Forum and formalise organisational structures again with support from international humanitarian aid organisations.[89] Following the referendum, the NGO Forum became a co-ordinating body for local and international NGOs in East Timor and participated actively in shaping political institutions in the new state.[90]

The 1999 referendum in August provided a catalyst for a rapid rise in the number of NGOs. Prior to the referendum, there were 14 NGOs recorded in East Timor. In January 2000, there were 34; by September 2000, there were 124; and by November 2000, there were over 190 local NGOs.[91] By early 2002, 231 NGOs were registered with the NGO Forum, although many of these were thought to be inactive.[92] This rapid increase in the number of NGOs reflects the opening up of civil space that had previously been suppressed by Indonesian rule. The expansion of the civil sphere indicated a desire for East Timorese individuals and groups to participate in the reconstruction and political transformation of East Timor. The United Nations Development Programme reported in 2002 that the East Timorese were 'freely forming civil society organisations, the number of which has grown rapidly and the environment in which they are operating is broadly supportive'.[93] During East Timor's transition, civil society organisations, such as local NGOs, were important sites of community participation and dialogue. In addition, they advocated the adoption of formal deliberative mechanisms to expand the opportunities of people to participate in political decision making.

Civil society during transition largely consisted of 'political' agencies such as the CNRT, local community-based organisations, the Roman Catholic Church, NGOs as well as professional associations, media and citizens more generally.[94] Student and youth organisations convened a congress on 4–6 May 2002 to address social and political issues and formed their own umbrella body called *Conselho Nacional Juventude Timor-Leste.*[95] Community-based organisations that were formed to address a specific need or social issue tended to be less structured operations than NGOs.[96] The NGOs were more likely to be based in Dili, and there was a significant gap in resources and capacities between urban and rural NGOs.[97]

Non-state organisations are not in themselves neutral observers, and there are risks in perceiving social organisations as wholly altruistic: civil societies can also reflect tensions in post-conflict communities.[98] Civil society is not homogeneous as not all organisations work on behalf of the 'common good' or even share a common understanding of what the common good might entail. Civil society is also not synonymous with non-for-profit sectors as it is constituted by a wide-range of informal relationships and associations in the public sphere. While it is problematic to assume that civil society organisations are representative of East Timorese

82 *International state-building and civil society*

citizenry more broadly, during transition several organisations, including the NGO Forum, *La'o Hamutuk* (East Timor Institute for Reconstruction Monitoring and Analysis) and *Yayasan HAK* (Foundation of Law, Human Rights, and Justice) provided a critical voice to the discussions about the role and effectiveness of state-building processes in East Timor under the UNTAET.[99] These organisations played an important role in providing civic education, drafting the Constitution and promoting human rights.[100] The common theme among these social organisations was the need for greater political participation of people, reflecting the idea that East Timorese citizens should have a voice in shaping the new state and its institutions.

By promoting the diverse needs of community members, local NGOs in East Timor were important in encouraging key features of democratic political culture, including accountability and responsiveness of government. In lobbying governments, NGOs worked to ensure political institutions reflected the needs and wants of particular groups in society.[101] East Timor's civil society organisations were important for expressing the voices of citizens and largely perceived themselves as 'architects of development'.[102] According to Lovell:

> [i]nstitutionally, governments must fairly accurately reflect their citizens' views and demands, be accountable to citizens for their actions, and uphold the rule of law. More broadly, citizens must have confidence that their government is effective, and their own political efficacy is high. But established democracies also display a large measure of tolerance of diversity. This spirit of accommodation is developed in a truly civil society.[103]

The accommodation of diverse beliefs and opinions can be problematic if they contradict or undermine democratic ideals and practices. However, building acceptance of democracy through participation, collaboration and reciprocal communication is crucial to informing people of governmental policies and citizenship rights, and promoting trust in the political system.[104] It is also paramount in allowing those who build the structures, make political decisions and create policies to 'know' the interests of diverse groups of people and establish links between state and society.[105]

According to Ian Patrick, the growth of civil society provided 'a means for East Timorese to gain wider experience with plural politics'.[106] As nation-building entails building democratic state/society relations and civic culture, civil society can provide individuals with an opportunity to be involved in bottom-up, participatory planning processes to establish state institutions.[107] It can also assist in building a nation 'that values the participation of people in the day-to-day operation of democratic structures'.[108]

Non-governmental organisations and community based organisations in East Timor informally represented and empowered local communities and citizens within the public sphere. They also strengthened collaboration between state and society by using local knowledge and understanding of East Timorese culture to bring about positive transformations in society and shift political control to a

International state-building and civil society 83

local level.[109] Kaldor recognises the significance of civil society as an 'alternative vehicle for deliberation, for introducing normative concerns, [and] for raising the interests of the individual'.[110] According to Purdue, civil society can be described as 'the cradle of democracy' insofar as it represents a 'complex social fabric, consisting of a diverse set of organisations, with more active participation by a greater number of citizens'.[111] Civil society is a political arena where citizens seek to advance their goals and interests, a complex space or arena for social and political interactions, collaboration and activities.[112]

Civil society organisations can advocate particular viewpoints, lobby governments to create or change policy on issue areas, keep governments and formal institutions or bureaucracy accountable, provide civic education and express plural interests held by members of the nation.[113] Organisations can present the diverse voices of ordinary people in the public sphere and promote grass-roots activism, which is important given that elections alone are generally not enough to produce a 'democracy'.[114] Patrick views these dialogical aspects of civil society as important for balancing any authoritarian tendencies that might arise in post-conflict states like East Timor, which have little practical experience of operating a democracy.[115] The organisation *La'o Hamutuk*, established in Dili in April 2000, played an important role in keeping the UNTAET accountable through periodic newspapers and radio broadcasts devoted to monitoring and analysing the construction of the East Timorese state.[116] It invested time and skill into analysing policy positions and the processes of development during transition.[117] *La'o Hamutuk* itself was largely democratic, employing a non-hierarchical structure where decisions were made by consensus, although other civil society organisations employed less democratic structures.[118]

While it is difficult to measure the impacts that such advocacy had on the activities and policies pursued by the UNTAET, Harmer and Frith note that *La'o Hamutuk* provided greater advocacy and accountability 'than would otherwise have been accorded the East Timorese during this crucial period in their history'.[119] Civil society organisations, such as *Yayasan HAK*, devoted themselves to monitoring human rights abuses and consolidating their visible profiles by documenting rights violations and undertaking advocacy.[120] Importantly, *La'o Hamutuk* existed in a coalition of sorts with other domestic and international NGOs working in East Timor at the same time, such as the Human Rights Monitoring Network and the Core Group on Transparency.[121] Common interests were held by many East Timorese civil society organisations wishing to participate in, and monitor, the building of the new East Timorese democracy. Civil society organisations entered into 'partnerships with the transitional administration in the execution of projects administered by the World Bank and other donors'.[122] Among other things, these organisations rehabilitated schools by building and delivering furniture, fixed roads and repaired water and irrigation systems.[123]

The rapid growth in civil society organisations from 1999–2001 meant that many lacked the technical experience and resources to properly fulfil their roles as social advocates and development partners, which limited their capacities to contribute to East Timor's political transition and socio-economic development.

84 *International state-building and civil society*

This was compounded by many international NGOs' reluctance to involve local NGOs in their projects.[124] The NGO Forum complained that international NGOs had overtaken local ones, who then felt reduced to 'observers and critics who have to ask for what they want'.[125] As such, many local organisations felt that they had been marginalised from the processes of state-building.[126] Patrick argues that local participation and involvement of the community was given inadequate attention in the transition phase and local NGOs were largely under-resourced, suggesting that the UNTAET did not develop adequate strategies for promoting the inclusion of non-governmental social actors.[127] However, the next section argues that efforts were made by the UNTAET to collaborate with the East Timorese leaders and citizens as per Resolution 1272 in the initial stages of the transition period, although these opportunities were often limited. The critical advocacy role of civil society groups and leaders was important not only for ensuring that more participatory structures were instituted during transition, but also for assisting the development of a democratic political culture in East Timor based on discussion, debate and accountability.

Participation in the first phase of transition: August 1999–August 2001

A key objective of the UNTAET was to ensure that the East Timorese community 'became major stakeholders in their own system of governance and public administration, first by intensive consultation … and then through early and progressive development of their capacity to carry out necessary functions'.[128] There are various reasons to support the involvement of the local community in transition. For example, Hohe contends that it is 'crucial for the international community to understand local structures and ideas of political authority and legitimacy'.[129] A more inclusive and culturally relevant transition period would allow international state-builders to anticipate potential hurdles in establishing an operating and effective democracy.[130] Advocates of 'participatory intervention' recommend a longer-term period of transition based on extensive citizenry participation, providing 'time for an indigenous paradigm to coexist with, or to gradually transform during the creation of, modern institutions'.[131] Greater opportunities for self-determination within United Nations missions would engender new structures with the legitimacy they require for institutionalisation.

References to the importance of collaboration and consultation with the East Timorese people in the United Nations Security Council Resolution 1272 were rather vague, and (perhaps deliberately) did not provide clear strategies for the UNTAET to enable participation.[132] This section examines the first phase in transition that was largely defined by the political authority possessed by the UNTAET in East Timor's political transition. The second phase, constitution-building, entailed a shift in political decision-making responsibilities to elected East Timorese leaders and will be examined in the next chapter.

While the administration of the UNTAET could be described as a 'shared sovereignty' arrangement, ultimately Sérgio Vieira de Mello retained authority

International state-building and civil society   85

over the state-building process.[133] Commentators, such as Beauvais and Chopra, argued that authority was, in fact, not adequately 'shared'.[134] In the initial stages of state-building, the UNTAET viewed itself as exercising authority on behalf of the East Timorese, with consultation as a central part of this leadership dynamic.[135] Benzing suggests that this was preferred ahead of an alternative model that involved the UNTAET sharing power with East Timorese leaders until a point was reached where power could be completely devolved.[136] The nature of the UNTAET's extensive authority presented a challenge to building a democratic nation encompassing participation and community empowerment. However, as the transition period progressed, efforts were made by the UNTAET to make transitional decision-making structures more inclusive and participatory.

a National Consultative Council

To meet the directive to collaborate and consult with the East Timorese population, in December 1999, the UNTAET began by establishing a non-elected body, the National Consultative Council (NCC), which comprised 15 members selected by the Transitional Administrator Sérgio Vieira de Mello.[137] The idea for the consultative council was initially developed after discussions between Vieira de Mello and East Timorese leaders, including Xanana Gusmão.[138] The NCC was established 'as the primary mechanism through which the representatives of the East Timorese [could] participate in the decision-making process'.[139] The UNTAET regulation 1999/2 defined the roles of the NCC as representing the views, concerns, traditions and interests of the East Timorese people, and advising the Transitional Administrator on policy-related matters.[140] Village and sub-district councils were established at the local level.[141]

The NCC was initially comprised of Gusmão, a representative from the Roman Catholic Church, seven members of pro-independence coalition the CNRT, one representative each from political parties FRETILIN, the UDT and KOTA, and four UNTAET personnel, including Vieira de Mello.[142] The CNRT was regarded by the UNTAET as broadly representative of the East Timorese people and hence it was used as 'a vehicle through which the UNTAET attempted to carry out its mandate to consult with the Timorese population'.[143] The UNTAET disallowed the acceptance of new parties in the NCC, handing almost full exclusivity to the CNRT (which at the time included both FRETILIN and the UDT).[144] Pro-integration political party APODETI and other pro-Indonesia groups did not participate because they had little political support in East Timor and had mostly fled to West Timor.[145]

The NCC was designed by the UNTAET as a bridge between East Timorese political leaders and society and the UN administration, and its purpose was to give advice to the Transitional Administration in the hope of engendering community participation in state-building processes.[146] It also reviewed and endorsed any UNTAET regulations.[147] In January 2000, the report of the UN Secretary-General noted that the NCC had been a 'unique means for the UNTAET to head

86 *International state-building and civil society*

and to respond to the needs of the East Timorese and for the latter to participate in important policy decisions'.[148] The report considered the UNTAET to have established close consultative and collaborative links with East Timorese political and social actors.

While the NCC was designed to engender a sense of East Timorese ownership over the creation of political structures through participation, civil society organisations and community members were sceptical about the extent of representation that these organisations could provide.[149] Many organisations felt that the NCC was limited in its capacities to represent a broad cross-section of the community and give voice to different interest groups in the processes of state-building. Complaints from civil society organisations highlighted the exclusion from representation in the NCC of particular groups in society, such as women, youth and traditional leaders.[150] Moreover, Chopra observed that political elites in these advisory positions were often 'self-appointed' rather than genuinely representative.[151] There was also the question of the representative capacities of the urban leadership for the majority of East Timorese who live in rural areas. These issues highlighted the problem of establishing the legitimacy of civil society organisations and the East Timorese political leadership during the transition period in regards to their representative capacities.

La'o Hamutuk argued that the NCC was not permitted to contribute to the UNTAET's policy making and that the NCC 'not only deprived Timorese people of the chance to practice decision-making during the transition, but created an atmosphere of mistrust and disempowerment'.[152] Despite his involvement in the creation of the NCC, East Timorese political leader Xanana Gusmão described it as 'tokenistic' because it only held an advocacy role: all decision-making authority remained invested in the Transitional Administrator.[153] While FRETILIN had 'particularly deep roots in the community as a result of their leadership in the resistance movement', its capacities to assist in transition were hampered by the nature of the NCC as a purely advisory body.[154] This was a consequence of the UNTAET's desire to follow the 'principle of impartiality' in their relations with local parties, despite FRETILIN's popularity among the East Timorese population.[155] Building a civic nation required the participation of individuals and civil society organisations to forge the bonds between the state and members of society. While consultation was acknowledged as an important source for building internal sovereignty and for engendering political legitimacy, in practice the NCC was widely considered by the East Timorese civil society organisations as an insufficient nation-building mechanism.

b National Council

In July 2000, the UNTAET responded to these complaints of civil society organisations and East Timorese leaders about the deficiencies of the NCC by creating a 33 (later 36) member National Council designed to give greater political authority to East Timorese leaders and enhance political participation.[156] This demonstrated a willingness from the UNTAET to alter structures in the face of

International state-building and civil society 87

advocacy and lobbying of East Timorese organisations and leaders. On 7 August 2000, an interim cabinet titled the East Timor Transitional Administration (ETTA) was established by the UNTAET consisting of four (later five) East Timorese and four international staff who were given their positions by the Transitional Administrator rather than being elected by the people.[157] By August 2000, both FRETILIN and the UDT ended their participation within the CNRT, which further complicated the UNTAET's relationship with the CNRT.[158] FRETILIN continued to concentrate on consolidating its influence at local levels, which reflected its aim of achieving a high number of votes in the first round of elections (discussed further in Chapter 4).[159] On 23 October, the NCC was replaced by the National Council and the interim Cabinet, and become collectively known as 'the first Transitional Government'.[160] The Transitional 'Government' was designed to integrate East Timorese leaders into decision-making portfolios and was responsible for 'executive tasks', although, as Benzing notes, the nine portfolios did not reflect the range of functions normally performed by governments.[161]

The National Council consisted of representatives from each of East Timor's 13 districts, seven from civil organisations (including the NGO Forum), 13 from political parties and three from religious groups.[162] Members of the National Council were permitted to choose a speaker who could set the agenda and chair sessions.[163] Xanana Gusmão was elected speaker and Milena Pires was elected deputy speaker.[164] Transitional Administrator Sérgio Vieira de Mello asked for nominations for the positions on the National Council, and was responsible for choosing all of the appointments himself.[165] This method of appointing members to the National Council was criticised extensively by civil society organisations, on the basis that they were not democratically elected by the population.[166] This was not an entirely fair criticism: the NC was only designed to be a temporary mechanism of representation until formal elections could provide a new leadership with electoral legitimacy. Elections might have been held earlier, however it is also important to bear in mind the competing priorities of the UNTAET, including the immediate challenges of establishing peace and security. Importantly, the decision to create the National Council was made in collaboration with the CNRT, who were given the option of whether to choose a 'technocratic' (expert) or 'political' model of state-building.[167] The CNRT chose a political model 'whereby East Timorese people would share political decision-making responsibilities with the UNTAET and hold portfolios in the interim government'.[168]

In any case, many of the representatives would go onto to play significant roles as elected leaders in independent East Timor. Xanana Gusmão was influential in the selection of the cabinet members, which ultimately reflected the political allegiances that were established during the independence movement. Two of the original members of the ETTA cabinet were from FRETILIN (Ana Pessoa and Mari Alkatiri), one from the UDT (João Carrascalão) and one from the Catholic Church (Fr. Filomeno Jacob).[169] The fifth member to join was former FRETILIN member José Ramos-Horta. The creation of the cabinet was designed to

88 *International state-building and civil society*

ensure key East Timorese decision-makers could assume political responsibilities early in the transition process.[170] However, the National Council was also denied any legislative powers.[171] While it held the competence to draft, modify and recommend regulations, the Transitional Administrator retained final decision-making authority.[172] This model of participation was again based upon an advisory rather than a decision-making role, which domestic actors criticised as effectively disempowering the East Timorese. This reflected the difficult balance between the necessity of international intervention on the one hand, and the need to engender the transitional process with local legitimacy on the other.

The East Timorese were involved in decision-making processes, although not to the extent that many leaders and civil society organisations had hoped. By criticising the lack of consultation, however, they were able to make a constructive contribution to the development of the public sphere through debate, advocacy and discussion. Respect for democratic ideals relating to participation in the public sphere, including freedom of expression and tolerance of diverse opinions, are necessary conditions for the establishment of democratic civic nation. The National Council was established in the hope of achieving greater consultation and collaboration with the East Timorese, as civil society organisations and East Timorese political leaders criticised the lack of local participation in creating new political structures. Consultation and participation among members of the community is important for facilitating political culture among people as discussion and debate are considered cornerstones of democracy.[173] Widespread consultation contributes to fostering responsive and accountable governance, whereby governments and public service work in the interests of the people.

Civil society organisations became concerned about the role of the National Council in representing the East Timorese community, and East Timorese leaders, such as Xanana Gusmão, accused the UNTAET of failing to share power in practice.[174] In a statement to the National Council and the UNTAET, the NGO Forum of East Timor argued that many of the decisions made by the National Council were not adequately debated and that it did not have enough facilities or funding to engage in broad consultation with the East Timorese population.[175] Consequently, the NGO Forum argued that 'many people, particularly those living in villages in East Timor ... [did not] feel that their voices ... [were] being represented in the National Council sessions'.[176] In March 2001, the National Democratic Institute reported that the East Timorese in focus group discussions expressed the view that the UNTAET's attempts at community consultation were inadequate and the National Council was not representative.[177] The reports noted dissatisfaction in the community about the opportunities to be involved in their political transformation that they were offered.[178]

At the time, the NGO Forum suggested:

> The people of East Timor want to see that members of the National Council are those that can represent the aspirations of the people. National NGOs under the NGO Forum want to support an East Timorese National Council which is capable and responsible to the people of East Timor.[179]

International state-building and civil society 89

Rather than being a representative and consultative body that could engage with the broader community, the National Council was perceived as an opportunity for unelected political elites to participate in decision-making. The first phase of transition under the UNTAET involved an attempt to render the process more consultative. The second phase entailed the next steps in the evolution of participatory mechanisms in East Timor's political transition, including elections.

c Community Empowerment and Local Governance Project

There were other international community projects concerned with enhancing democracy in East Timor during transition. The World Bank, for example, established the 'Community Empowerment and Local Governance Project' (CEP), co-sponsored by the Asian Development Bank, which was a nation-building project initially intended to support village and sub-district councils composed of equal numbers of elected men and women.[180] This was envisaged by the World Bank as providing a useful model for democratic governance and allowing people to feel ownership over East Timor's transition to democratic statehood. According to Chopra, the UNTAET 'bitterly opposed the project and attempted at all costs to stop it' because they would not control the US$35 million set aside for the project.[181] One argument offered by the UNTAET against the CEP was that 'international staff needed to dictate community empowerment'.[182] *La'o Hamutuk* argued that the UNTAET feared that the decision-making bodies established by the CEP would circumvent the UNTAET's governance structures.[183]

According to the project description, CEPs were designed to provide a foundation for local governance and encourage 'democratic accountability from the bottom-up'.[184] As *La'o Hamutuk* noted, the CEPs were designed to establish transparent, democratic and accountable structures in local areas, as part of a broader project of instilling principles of democratic practice at a grass-roots level.[185] A second aim was to increase local ownership by using and developing indigenous capacities in special community programs designed for reconstruction.[186] These CEPs were another mechanism designed to facilitate the transition of authority from the UNTAET to independent government. As a World Bank report in 1999 argued, CEPs emphasised collaboration and joint consultative planning in order to promote ownership and involvement of the East Timorese in community development.[187] The CEPs proved successful at increasing women's participation in governance and community development planning, although local councils were not always elected democratically.[188] Importantly, *La'o Hamutuk's* assessment of CEPs suggests that they enhanced capacity-building within the districts and villages.

Grants were offered to communities that allowed them to make choices about the programs that they needed and wanted.[189] Forty-three per cent of first round funding went to constructing community meeting halls, and 25 per cent for building roads that linked to bigger roads.[190] A total of 600 projects were supported. A US$2 million grant was initially offered for 'cultural heritage' programs designed to document and display peoples recollections of recent history

90 *International state-building and civil society*

and become a part of archival records for future generations.[191] Other projects included building community libraries, and linking a culture program with civic education campaigns in collaboration with the CNRT, NGOs and the Roman Catholic Church.[192]

Chopra argues that the UNTAET continued to oppose the CEPs 'with the consequence that the transitional administration never had much of a presence below the district level, where 80 percent of the population' lived.[193] More local control over these governmental functions would have enhanced this exercise of nation-building. As a result, the councils could not debate broader social and political issues and they became instruments for funnelling donor funds from the World Bank to local communities.[194] Matsuno argues that the program was limited because the village councils were only set up to handle development funds and they did not exercise any legislative, executive or judicial powers. However, the CEP design was still sufficiently democratic.[195] While there were some challenges to effective implementation, the programs themselves recognised the need for the East Timorese to participate in their own state- and nation-building projects.

Conclusion

As previous chapters have demonstrated, the demand for a democratic political system was a central pillar of the East Timorese independence movement. During transition, surveys conducted of the East Timorese population found that participants largely perceived democracy as linked to freedom from oppression and individual rights.[196] Inculcating democratic political culture through political engagement during transition was important, as many East Timorese had limited practical experience with, and knowledge of, democratic structures and behaviours.[197]

Questions were raised during the transition period concerning the capacities of the UNTAET to engage in nation-building, and the lack of deliberative mechanisms to engage the East Timorese in the processes of democracy-building. The nature of the state-building operation in East Timor posed challenges to democratic engagement and local decision-making because sole authority was invested in the Transitional Administrator, Sérgio Vieira de Mello, which provided a problematic model for governance in East Timor.[198] De Mello himself conceded that 'we did not, we could not involve the Timorese at large as much as they were entitled to'.[199] Complaints were made by observers, East Timorese political leaders and civil society organisations that there were limited opportunities for leaders and East Timorese public to participate in decision-making during the transitional period.[200]

However, international and domestic civil society held important roles in attempting to build an inclusive and participatory democracy in East Timor. East Timor's local NGOs saw themselves as key partners in East Timor's nation-building, and they sought to create 'relations of co-operation, co-ordination and partnership with government'.[201] As Diamond argues, 'there is no better way of

International state-building and civil society 91

developing the values, skills and commitments of democratic citizenship than through direct experience with democracy, no matter how imperfect it may be'.[202] Building political 'organisations' is necessary for democracy, however such organisations can only become institutions when they become both useful and legitimate within the national political community.[203]

The public sphere is pivotal for lending legitimacy to the institutions being built, but in spite of the critiques of the UNTAET and their lack of involvement of the local community, East Timorese civil society contributed to the development, service delivery, the monitoring of the UNTAET and transitional government and to the provision of information and policy analysis.[204] Civil society organisations also held important positions on the National Council, as well as contributing to the Constitutional Commissions and Planning Workshops.

Different understandings of the appropriate levels of citizenry participation are commonly expressed by the demarcation between deliberative, consensus-driven forms of democracy and procedural, 'majoritarian' forms. Despite the initial concerns about the levels of local political participation and the decision-makers, East Timorese leaders were given the opportunity to write their Constitution, design their institutional framework and develop and articulate a vision of citizenship. The following chapters suggest that the type of democracy instituted in East Timor was largely developed by East Timorese leaders and corresponds with the visions held by peak resistance bodies throughout the independence movement.

Notes

1 See for example Crook and Manor, *Democracy and Decentralisation in South Asia and West Africa;* Kaufman, 'Community Power, Grassroots Democracy, and the Transformation of Social Life'; Manor, 'Democratisation with Inclusion'; Westergaard, *People's Participation, Local Government and Rural Development* and Rustow, 'Transitions to Democracy', 337–338.
2 Manor, ibid., 6.
3 Zaum, *The Sovereign Paradox.*
4 See Ghani, Lockhart and Carnahan, *Closing the Sovereignty Gap*, 14 and Bickerton, 'State-Building: Exporting State Failure', 108.
5 Brahimi, *State-Building in Crisis and Post-Conflict Countries*, 5.
6 Ibid. For an Indonesian perspective see Soesastro and Subianto, eds., *Peace Building and State Building in East Timor.*
7 Stephenson, *Nation-Building.*
8 Sahin, 'Building the Nation', 226.
9 Migdal, 'Integration and Disintegration: An Approach to Society-Formation', 91 and 104.
10 Migdal, *Weak Societies and Strong States*, 28 and 33.
11 Kingsbury, *East Timor: The Price of Liberty*, 14.
12 United Nations Security Council, *Resolution 1272.*
13 Zaum, *The Sovereign Paradox*, 226.
14 Ibid., 38.
15 United Nations General Assembly and United Nations Security Council, *Question of East Timor: Report of the Secretary-General.*
16 Ibid., 10.

92 *International state-building and civil society*

17 Lloyd, 'The Diplomacy on East Timor', 103.
18 CAVR, *Chega!*, Chapter 3, 152.
19 See Robinson, *East Timor 1999 Crimes Against Humanity*, 44.
20 Beauvais, *Benevolent Despotism*, 1104.
21 Ibid., 1108–1109.
22 United Nations Security Council, *Resolution 1272.*
23 Ibid.
24 See Jackson, *Quasi-States*, 26–31 and Zaum, *The Sovereign Paradox*, 38.
25 United Nations Security Council, *Resolution 1272* and Lloyd, 'The Diplomacy on East Timor', 103.
26 United Nations Security Council, *Resolution 1272*.
27 Ibid.
28 Hooper and Williams, 'Earned Sovereignty', 360.
29 Benzing, 'Midwifing a New State', 318.
30 Ibid., 319.
31 United Nations Security Council, *Resolution 1272.*
32 Beauvais, 'Benevolent Despotism'.
33 See Croissant, 'Perils and Promises of Democratization Through United Nations Transitional Authority', 657.
34 Nakamura, *Reflections on the State-Institution-Building Support in Timor-Leste*, 3.
35 United Nations, *Charter of the United Nations*, Article 39, Chapter VII.
36 Nakamura, *Reflections on the State-Institution-Building Support in Timor-Leste*, 9 and United Nations Security Council, *Resolution 1272*, Section 3:c.
37 Nakamura, ibid., 3.
38 Chopra, 'The UN's Kingdom of East Timor', 27.
39 Beauvais, 'Benevolent Despotism', 1101 and 1104; Chesterman, *You, the People*, 6 and Matsuno, 'The UN Transitional Administration and Democracy Building in Timor-Leste', 53.
40 See United Nations Security Council, *Resolution 745*, S/RES/745, 28 February 1992.
41 Ibid., 73 and Gallup, 'Cambodia's Electoral System', 30.
42 At the time of the UNMIK's establishment, Kosovo was part of the former Federal Republic of Yugoslavia. The Resolution reaffirmed 'the commitment of all member states to the sovereignty and territorial integrity of the Federation Republic of Yugoslavia'. See United Nations Security Council, *Resolution 1244*.
43 Chesterman, *You, the People*, 75.
44 Chesterman, *You, the People.*
45 United Nations Security Council, *Resolution 1272.*
46 Ibid.
47 Morison, 'Democratisation and Timor-Leste after UNTAET', 179.
48 Beauvais, 'Benevolent Despotism', 1104.
49 Franck, 'The Emerging Right of Democratic Governance', 46 and Zaum, *The Sovereign Paradox*, 231.
50 Franck, ibid., 43.
51 Roberts, *Political Transition in Cambodia 1991–99*, xiv.
52 Chesterman, *You, the People*, 73.
53 Croissant, 'Perils and Promises of Democratization through United Nations Transitional Authority', 653.
54 Marks, 'The Process of Creating a New Constitution in Cambodia', 207.
55 Barnett and Zürcher, 'The Peacebuilder's Contract', 44–45.
56 Levitsky and Way, *Competitive Authoritarianism*, 330. See also Roberts, *Political Transition in Cambodia 1991–99.*
57 Marks, 'The Process of Building a Constitution in Cambodia, 207–208; Croissant, 'Perils and Promises Democratization through United Nations Transitional Authority', 660 and Gallup, 'Cambodia's Electoral System', 30.

International state-building and civil society 93

58 Croissant, 'Perils and Promises of Democratization through United Nations Transitional Authority', 662.

59 Levitsky and Way, *Competitive Authoritarianism*, 335; Roberts, 'Political Transition and Elite Discourse in Cambodia', 105; Un, 'Patronage Politics and Hybrid Democracy', 210 and Gallup, 'Cambodia's Electoral System', 33.

60 Roberts, *Political Transition in Cambodia 1991–99*, xiv.

61 Levitsky and Way, *Competitive Authoritarianism*.

62 Chesterman, *You, the People*, 75 and Levitsky and Way, *Competitive Authoritarianism*, 309, 328 and 332.

63 Roberts, 'Political Transition and Elite Discourse in Cambodia', 109.

64 Ibid., 108.

65 Levitsky and Way, *Competitive Authoritarianism*, 331.

66 Ibid., 4 and Croissant and Haynes, 'Inequalities and Democracy in Southeast Asia', 776.

67 Pye, *Politics, Personality and Nation-Building*.

68 Rustow, 'Transitions to Democracy', 350–351; Mearns, 'Imagining East Timor Again', xiii–xxv and Sahin, 'Building the Nation in Timor-Leste', 221.

69 Sahin, ibid., 222.

70 Borgerhoff, 'The Double-Task', 103.

71 Sahin, 'Building the Nation in Timor-Leste', 225.

72 Linz and Stepan, *Problems of Democratic Transition and Consolidation*, 5.

73 Ibid., and Sahin, 'Building the Nation in Timor-Leste', 225.

74 Diamond, *Developing Democracy*, 169.

75 Jacobson cited in Migdal, 'State Building and the Non-Nation-State', 22.

76 Diamond, *Developing Democracy*, 161–162.

77 Putnam, *Making Democracy Work*, 96.

78 See Shires, *Situation Analysis of Civil Society Organisations in East Timor*, 13 and Brunnstrom, 'Another Invasion', 310–321.

79 Australian Council for International Development, *Timor-Leste Civil Society Analysis*, 2; Hunt, 'Building a New Society', 16 and Patrick, 'East Timor Emerging from Conflict', 58–59. Around 10–15 international NGOs were permitted to operate in East Timor after 1989.

80 Brunnstrom, 'Another Invasion', 312.

81 Ibid.

82 Hunt, 'Building a New Society', 16 and Patrick, 'East Timor Emerging from Conflict', 58–59.

83 Shires, *Situation Analysis of Civil Society Organisations in East Timor*, 16.

84 United Nations Development Programme, *Ukan Rasik A'an*, 40.

85 *Fokupersi* and *ETWAVE* were established as women's rights NGOs, *Pronto Ata Serbi* was a health NGO, *Yayasan Bia Hula* dealt with water and sanitation, and *Yayasan HAK* was concerned with human rights. See ibid. and Hunt, 'Building a New Society', 16.

86 Shires, *Situation Analysis of Civil Society Organisations in East Timor*, 16 and United Nations Development Programme, *Ukan Rasik A'an*, 41.

87 Patrick, 'East Timor Emerging from Conflict', 58 and Hunt, 'Building a New Society', 16–17.

88 Shires, *Situation Analysis of Civil Society Organisations in East Timor*, 19 and United Nations Development Programme, *Ukan Rasik A'an*, 41.

89 Shires, ibid., 20 and United Nations Development Programme, ibid.

90 Meden, 'From Resistance to Nation Building'.

91 Hunt, 'Building a New Society', 17 and Patrick, 'East Timor Emerging from Conflict', 59.

92 Hunt, ibid., 9; United Nations Country Team, *Building Blocks for a Nation* and Australian Council for International Development, *Timor-Leste Civil Society Analysis*.

94 *International state-building and civil society*

93 Shires, *Situation Analysis of Civil Society Organisations in East Timor*, 4.
94 United Nations Country Team, *Building Blocks for a Nation*, 109.
95 Shires, *Situation Analysis of Civil Society Organisations in East Timor*, 17.
96 Engel, 'Reaching for Stability', 174.
97 Hunt, 'Building a New Society', 18 and Patrick, 'East Timor Emerging from Conflict', 60.
98 Patrick, ibid., 54.
99 Harmer and Frith, '"Walking Together" Toward Independence?', 239.
100 Hunt, 'Building a New Society', 17.
101 Shires, *Situation Analysis of Civil Society Organisations in East Timor*, 47.
102 Australian Council for International Development, *Timor-Leste Civil Society Analysis*, 3 and United Nations Development Programme, *Ukan Rasik A'an*, 44.
103 Lovell, 'Promoting Democracy', 340.
104 Engel, 'Reaching for Stability', 171–172.
105 Ibid.
106 Patrick, 'East Timor Emerging from Conflict', 61.
107 Ibid., 54.
108 Shires, *Situation Analysis of Civil Society Organisations in East Timor*, 49.
109 United Nations Development Programme, *Ukan Rasik A'an*, 3 and Patrick, 'East Timor Emerging from Conflict', 49.
110 Mary Kaldor cited in Harmer and Frith, '"Walking Together" Toward Independence?', 240.
111 Purdue, 'Introduction: Dimensions of Civil Society', 2.
112 Held, *Models of Democracy*, 141.
113 Ibid., and Shires, *Situation Analysis of Civil Society Organisations in East Timor*, 47.
114 Lovell, 'Promoting Democracy', 333.
115 Patrick, 'East Timor Emerging from Conflict', 53.
116 Harmer and Frith, '"Walking Together" Toward Independence?', 241–242. *La'o Hamutuk* (Tetum for 'Walking Together') is an NGO that monitors, analyses and reports on the activities of international agencies and government in East Timor. *La'o Hamutuk* described itself as a resource centre, providing and analysing information and literature for various sectors of domestic and international societies. See La'o Hamutuk, *The La'o Hamutuk Bulletin* 1, no. 1 (21 June 2000), 1.
117 Shires, *Situation Analysis of Civil Society Organisations in East Timor*, 47.
118 Harmer and Frith, '"Walking Together" Toward Independence?', 242.
119 Ibid., 239.
120 Patrick, 'East Timor Emerging from Conflict', 59. *Yayasan HAK* is an NGO 'that works to realize a Timorese society that is self-sufficient, open, and democratic in a social order based on popular sovereignty'. See Yayasan HAK, *The HAK Association.*
121 Harmer and Frith, '"Walking Together" Toward Independence?, 242.
122 Meden, 'From Resistance to Nation Building'.
123 Ibid.
124 Australian Council for International Development, *Timor-Leste Civil Society Analysis*, 3.
125 The NGO Forum cited in Patrick, 'East Timor Emerging from Conflict', 57. See also Brunnstrom, 'Another Invasion'.
126 Australian Council for International Development, *Timor-Leste Civil Society Analysis*, 3.
127 Patrick, 'East Timor Emerging from Conflict', 49 and United Nations Country Team, *Building Blocks for a Nation*, 110.
128 United Nations Security Council, *Report of the Secretary-General on the United Nations Transitional Administration in East Timor*.
129 Hohe, 'The Clash of Paradigms', 570.

International state-building and civil society 95

130 Ibid.
131 Chopra and Hohe, 'Participatory Intervention', 289; Chopra, 'Building State Failure in East Timor' and Morison, 'Democratisation and Timor-Leste after UNTAET'.
132 Benzing, 'Midwifing a New State', 344 and United Nations Security Council, *Resolution 1272*.
133 Hooper and Williams, 'Earned Sovereignty', 360 and 364.
134 Beauvais, 'Benevolent Despotism' and Chopra, 'The UN's Kingdom of East Timor'.
135 United Nations Security Council, *Report of the Secretary-General on the Situation in East Timor*.
136 Benzing, 'Midwifing a New State', 345.
137 Baltazar, 'An Overview of the Constitution Drafting Process in East Timor' and Matsuno, 'The UN Transitional Administration and Democracy Building in Timor-Leste', 56. The same regulation that created the NCC also established joint Sectoral Committees comprised of East Timorese and international experts to advise in the areas of agriculture environment, education, finance, human rights and local administration. See Hooper and Williams, 'Earned Sovereignty', 364.
138 United Nations Security Council, *Report of the Secretary-General on the United Nations Transitional Administration in East Timor*, 2.
139 United Nations Transitional Administration in East Timor, *On the Establishment of a National Consultative Council*.
140 Ibid.
141 Benzing, 'Midwifing a New State', 348.
142 Baltazar, 'An Overview of the Constitution Drafting Process in East Timor' and United Nations Security Council, *Report of the Secretary-General on the United Nations Transitional Administration in East Timor*, 2.
143 Chesterman, 'East Timor in Transition', 64.
144 Chopra, 'The UN's Kingdom of East Timor', 991.
145 Ibid., 990; Benzing, 'Midwifing a New State', 348 and Department of Foreign Affairs, *East Timor in Transition 1998–2000*, 160.
146 United Nations Security Council, *Report of the Secretary-General on the United Nations Transitional Administration in East Timor*, 2.
147 Chesterman, 'East Timor in Transition', 64–65.
148 United Nations Security Council, *Report of the Secretary-General on the United Nations Transitional Administration in East Timor*, 2.
149 La'o Hamutuk, *The La'o Hamutuk Bulletin* 6, no. 13 (August 2005), 2.
150 A civil society organisation associated with RENETIL argued that 'the Transitional Administrator personally excluded … representatives of women, youth groups, traditional leaders and others [from the NCC]. In reaction, Timorese opposed such an unrepresentative body. Already it was an appointed body without any popular will behind it'. See Asia Pacific Support Collective Timor Lorosa'e, *A Popular Challenge to UNTAET's Achievements*.
151 Chopra, 'Building State Failure in East Timor', 999.
152 La'o Hamutuk, *The La'o Hamutuk Bulletin* 6, no. 13 (August 2005), 2.
153 Dodd, 'Gusmão Gives UN Team a Serve'. See also Eurich, *Factors of Success in Mission Communication Strategies in Post-Conflict Settings*, 183.
154 Garrison, *The Role of Constitution-Building Processes in Democratization*, 9. See also Chesterman, *You, the People*, 135.
155 Gorjão, 'The Legacy and Lessons of the United Nations Transitional Administration in East Timor', 316.
156 The United Nations provided for an additional three representatives from the CNRT selected by the Transitional Administrator. See United National Transitional Administration in East Timor, *To Amend Regulation No. 2000/24 on the Establishment of a National Council* and United Nations Security Council, *Report of the*

96 *International state-building and civil society*

Secretary-General on the United Nations Transitional Administration in East Timor (for the period 27 July 2000 to 16 January 2001).

157 United Nations Transitional Administration in East Timor, *On the Establishment of the Cabinet of the Transitional Government in East Timor*. Refer to Figure 4:1 in Chapter 4.

158 Garrison, *The Role of Constitution-Building Processes in Democratization*, 9 and Goldstone, 'UNTAET with Hindsight', 90.

159 Chopra, 'Building State Failure in East Timor', 998.

160 Benzing, 'Midwifing a New State', 349.

161 Ibid. and Charlesworth, 'The Constitution of East Timor', 327.

162 Brunnstrom, 'Another Invasion', 312; United Nations Security Council, *Report of the Secretary-General on the United Nations Transitional Administration in East Timor (for the period 27 July 2000 to 16 January 2001)*, 2. See also Meden, 'From Resistance to Nation Building'.

163 Matsuno, 'The UN Transitional Administration and Democracy Building in Timor-Leste', 58.

164 United Nations Security Council, *Report of the Secretary-General on the United Nations Transitional Administration in East Timor (for the period 27 July 2000 to 16 January 2001)*, 2.

165 United Nations Transitional Administration in East Timor, *Selection of National Council* and Garrison, *The Role of Constitution-Building Processes in Democratization*, 10.

166 Benzing, 'Midwifing a New State', 349.

167 Chesterman, 'East Timor in Transition', 66.

168 Ibid.

169 See also Department of Foreign Affairs, Australia, *East Timor in Transition 1998–2000*, 161–162.

170 Ibid.

171 Chopra, 'Building State Failure in East Timor', 991.

172 United Nations Transitional Administration in East Timor, *On the Establishment of a National Council*.

173 Diamond, *Developing Democracy*, 174.

174 Smith, 'East Timor: Elections in the World's Newest Nation', 149.

175 East Timor NGO Forum, *Statement to the National Council and the Transitional Government UNTAET/ETTA*.

176 Ibid.

177 Della-Giacoma, *Timor Loro Sa'e is Our Nation*, iv.

178 Ibid.

179 East Timor NGO Forum, *Statement to the National Council and the Transitional Government UNTAET/ETTA*.

180 Chopra, 'Building State Failure in East Timor', 992.

181 Ibid., 993 and La'o Hamutuk, *The La'o Hamutuk Bulletin* 1, no. 4 (December 2000), 6.

182 Chopra, ibid., 993.

183 La'o Hamutuk, *The La'o Hamutuk Bulletin* 1, no. 4 (December 2000): 6.

184 World Bank, *East Timor Community Empowerment and Local Governance Project*.

185 La'o Hamutuk, *The La'o Hamutuk Bulletin* 1, no. 4 (December 2000), 6.

186 World Bank, *East Timor Community Empowerment and Local Governance Project*.

187 Ibid.

188 La'o Hamutuk, *The La'o Hamutuk Bulletin* 1, no. 4 (December 2000), 6.

189 World Bank, *East Timor Community Empowerment and Local Governance Project*.

190 La'o Hamutuk, *The La'o Hamutuk Bulletin* 1, no. 4 (December 2000), 6 and Matsuno, 'The UN Transitional Administration and Democracy Building in Timor-Leste', 59.

International state-building and civil society 97

191 World Bank, *East Timor Community Empowerment and Local Governance Project.*
192 Ibid.
193 Chopra, 'Building State Failure in East Timor', 993.
194 Ibid.
195 Matsuno, 'The UN Transitional Administration and Democracy Building in Timor-Leste', 60.
196 Della-Giacoma, *Timor Loro Sa'e is Our Nation*, iii.
197 Ibid.
198 See Chopra, 'The UN's Kingdom of East Timor'.
199 de Mello cited in Chesterman, *You, the People*, 138.
200 Ibid., 135–140; Beauvais, 'Benevolent Despotism'; Chopra, 'Building State Failure in East Timor'; Fan, 'The Missing Link between Self-Determination and Democracy'; Hohe, 'The Clash of Paradigms'; Morison, 'Democratisation and Timor-Leste after UNTAET' and Trindade, 'Reconciling Conflicting Paradigms'.
201 Shires, *Situation Analysis of Civil Society Organisations in East Timor*, 45.
202 Diamond, *Developing Democracy*, 162.
203 Ottaway, 'Rebuilding State Institutions in Collapsed States', 1005.
204 United Nations Development Programme, *Ukan Rasik A'an*, 44.

4 Constitution-drafting and the first elections

Constitution-drafting from September 2001 to March 2002 was the first opportunity for East Timorese leaders to make political decisions regarding the structures of the new state.[1] As the previous chapter established, civil society organisations and leaders criticised the lack of decision-making opportunities for the East Timorese during the first phase of transition and the perceived 'neo-colonialist' tendencies of the international administration.[2] They called for elections to decide who should represent the East Timorese community, which occurred when state-wide democratic elections in August 2001 formed the Constituent Assembly. The second phase of transition involved creating a constitution, a significant task that requires articulating the political institutions and the legal framework of the future state. The Constituent Assembly was responsible for drafting the Constitution in collaboration with civil society organisations and the people of East Timor. This process was conducted by East Timorese political leaders, almost entirely free from international intervention. The political party FRETILIN achieved a large majority of the votes and were thus able to wield significant influence in writing the Constitution. This period was particularly important for analysing the willingness of East Timorese political leaders to establish patterns of democratic engagement, set boundaries of appropriate political practice and build the capacities and credentials necessary for self-government.

Constitutions are important for establishing and consolidating democracy in new independent states as they articulate the rules and frameworks necessary for establishing internal sovereignty. According to Habermas, internal sovereignty is present when government has the capacity to maintain law and order: in democracies, this supreme power relies upon authority commonly expressed as 'the right to rule'.[3] While effective 'Weberian' states maintain a monopoly on the use of violence, in democracies political order is not instituted through widespread use of force.[4] Hence, developing 'a normatively positive appreciation' of primary democratic institutions among citizens is a core condition of democratisation.[5] The legitimacy of the democratic system of rule is predicated on 'rational legal' authority, which exists when laws are obeyed by people not out of fear, but because the majority view them as valid.[6] The success of democratisation is also predicated on the support of the political elite. This renders the involvement of

Constitution-drafting and the first elections 99

electorally legitimised leaders in constitution-building as crucial to its future capacities to shape and constrain the behaviours and activities of the political elite.

Constitutions are essential for establishing rule of law.[7] According to Linz and Stepan:

> a democratic regime is consolidated when governmental and non-governmental forces alike, throughout the territory of the state, become subjected to, and habituated to, the resolution of conflict within the specific laws, procedures and institutions sanctioned by the new democratic process.[8]

Consequently, becoming an independent democracy requires political and legal processes to work within the operational political and legal parameters outlined in the constitution.

The processes of constitution-drafting reflect and reveal core political values about democratic systems and can establish political behaviour and the practices of political and social actors. These ideas about participation and consultation reflect practices of 'new constitutionalism', a term Hart uses to refer to contemporary methods of constitution-building.[9] New constitutionalism is underpinned by a belief that democratic processes in constitution-building are requisite in establishing a democratic constitution. In transitioning states such as East Timor, new constitutionalism entails the establishment of inclusive and responsive mechanisms to allow citizens opportunities to have their voices heard. In permitting greater inclusion, constitution-building processes can establish democratic patterns of consultation and debate, and levels of responsiveness of political leaders to social demands. In short, processes matter for outcomes: democratic processes matter both for the creation of a democratic constitution and a democratic system.

It is important to note that the 'needs, hopes and aspirations' of the people in East Timor were not homogeneous and thus the Constitution could not feasibly include the views and visions of all people. Pluralism does not mean all views should be viewed equally valid as constitutions outline the scope of acceptable diversity. However, a durable constitution depicting and institutionalising the broadly understood aspirations of 'society' and including the voices of people not often heard by political leaders, could provide the basis of a lasting peace.[10] In other words, deliberation is important for understanding the needs of a diverse constituency. Deliberative mechanisms involving citizenry consultation and participation in East Timor established an inclusive and responsive model of democracy capable of addressing the needs of a plural society, despite FRETILIN's attempts to restrict the political discourse at times. This was important for effective democracy because it established the terms of reasonable pluralism and diversity of public opinion without violence.[11]

Deliberative mechanisms enabled civil society organisations and individuals to participate in constitution-building processes, including Constitutional Commissions (June–July 2001), the Constituent Assembly Public Hearings

100 Constitution-drafting and the first elections

(October–November 2001) and the Public Consultations on the drafted Constitution (February–March 2002).[12] Although itself accused of not being sufficiently inclusive or participatory, the United Nations Transitional Administration in East Timor (UNTAET) directed the Constituent Assembly to give due consideration in its deliberations 'to the results of the consultations conducted by any duly constituted Constitutional Commission or Commissions'.[13] However, there were no specific guidelines about how consultations should operate, what levels of consultation were required or how the consultative reports should be incorporated into the Constitution.[14]

Civil society organisations, such as *Yayasan HAK*, *La'o Hamutuk* and the NGO Forum, themselves provided mechanisms of community consultation, participation and civic education throughout the constitution-building processes.[15] As the previous chapter argued, strong civil societies are important sites for establishing and maintaining active political participation.[16] Lovell argues that 'civil society is a particular type of pluralism' because it encompasses diverse associations among organisations that hold distinctive and/or common interests.[17] Within a plural democracy, organisations within civil society can attain political power within the public sphere by setting agendas, shaping opinions, lobbying governments and participating in political discussions and debates. Civil society organisations in East Timor held similar interests in ensuring sufficient consultation in the constitution-building process. Civil society organisations can reflect the ideological diversity and sociological pluralism that characterise modern political communities as they seek to legitimise themselves as 'grass-roots' representatives of various community interests.

According to Linz and Stepan, one of the key conditions for effective democracy includes the presence of a 'lively and free civil society'.[18] Civil society in East Timor sought to facilitate inclusion in the constitution-building processes by contributing to political debate, providing representation and advocacy, establishing civic education sessions and creating channels of communication across different levels of society.[19] The relationship between state-building processes and civil society was twofold: societal involvement assisted in building a democracy in East Timor, which simultaneously strengthened and expanded civil society itself. In East Timor's political transition, these dynamics were reflected in the large degree of overlap between the social and political realms.

East Timor's constitution-drafting took place within a context of existing power relationships, alliances and tensions that shaped constitution-drafting processes.[20] The Constitution was written within a context of a 'contest for power' among political leaders, characterised by contrasting ideas about the nature of democracy held by various East Timorese political actors and members of civil society.[21] Concerns were raised by civil society organisations and members of minor political parties regarding the responsiveness of the Constituent Assembly when the constitution that emerged from the initial drafting processes closely resembled an earlier FRETILIN draft.[22] Political divisions between FRETILIN and Xanana Gusmão reappeared during the period of constitution-drafting, providing the blueprint for their political relations following East Timor's

Constitution-drafting and the first elections 101

achievement of independence. The search for political influence and power was part of these processes, especially as the Constituent Assembly was also provided the option by the UNTAET to form East Timor's first government after the achievement of full independence.[23]

Ultimately, the second phase of political transition in East Timor oversaw the transition from the UNTAET as the key institutional designers to the Constituent Assembly. Arguments about representation shift to whether the elected East Timorese officials were appropriately consultative with the public and civil society organisations, reflecting the differences between procedural and deliberative models in democratic theory. While there were opportunities for people to share their views, the processes were not as consultative as they might have been. Nevertheless, the constitution was a product of elected East Timorese leaders that reflected the views and the values of the independence movement. This is significant for the legitimacy of the document as a foundational structure of the new state.

Building East Timor's Constitution

The context of international state-building presented a number of challenges to drafting the Constitution, primarily because 'imposed constitutions' are less likely to be durable and provide political stability, particularly if they outline institutions and values that do not correspond with citizenry expectations.[24] There was a risk that the UNTAET would use constitution-building to institute modern 'Western' state structures that clashed with existing paradigms of authority and compliance. 'Imposed' constitutions can have negative effects on the democratic transition if constitution-building processes contravene self-determination rights and the people feel that the document is 'foreign'.[25]

A complex balance needed to be struck in ensuring international standards were met in East Timor without disregarding local political contexts and existing social structures.[26] While an internationally supported new constitution must broadly conform to dominant international norms around democratic organisation and liberal rights, international law also recognises the importance of self-determination in the drafting of new constitutions. For instance, Article 25 of the International Covenant on Civil and Political Rights declares that citizens have the right to participate 'directly in the conduct of public affairs when they choose or change their constitution'.[27] As Zaum argues, international norms regarding the relationships between states and societies provide a framework for sovereign authority.[28] As the basis for establishing internal sovereignty in new states, constitutions establish legal principles to enable local participation in developing structures and mechanisms of political decision-making.

As a 'constitution' embodies more than its written content, the processes underpinning its establishment foster the norms and values required for 'constitutionalism' and democratic stability. Constitutionalism refers to 'the institutions, practices, customs, and norms that guide and legitimate the exercise of public power'.[29] A widespread belief in the validity of the constitution acts as a

102   *Constitution-drafting and the first elections*

structural mechanism insofar as it develops new ways of thinking about political authority over time.[30] In new states with new constitutions, constitutionalism involves changes in the way that people exercise political power.[31] Hence, constitutionalism requires more than simply writing the document, it also entails fostering perceptions of its political legitimacy. Constitution-drafting processes provide an initial site of democratic deliberation and collaboration and establish patterns of political engagement between political and social actors. Canvassing views through citizen participation and deliberative practices assists in drafting a constitution that is inclusive of diverse views and supports democratic plurality.[32] The legitimacy of the constitution is contingent upon people believing that they have produced it themselves (even if, realistically, it is a product of political elites), as the right to create instruments of political order belong to a sovereign nation in democratic states.[33]

The processes of constitution-drafting also reveal beliefs about the nature of political authority and the relationships between important sites of political influence in the social and political realms.[34] These processes often contribute to a re-articulation of nationhood, as constitution-drafting provides 'an important 'official' contribution to the development of an independent political culture'.[35] Constitutions can represent the aspirations of people and assist the institutionalisation of political values by embodying values about political organisations, insofar as they 'express guiding national principles'.[36] Deliberative participatory mechanisms enable public discourse, which shapes the narratives of national identity and the values that are reflected in the constitution.

According to Putnam, participatory structures are forces of 'social capital' that work to bind people to the social institutions that they create.[37] For a constitution to become legitimate and authoritative, widespread participation was required for a sense of public ownership, to engender a widespread belief in its legitimacy within society and to foster 'goodwill' among people toward their constitution.[38] This feeling of ownership assists in the institutionalisation of, and habituation to, the constitution, and the laws and frameworks contained within it because democratic legitimacy must arise from the collective decisions of equal citizens.[39] Civil society organisations in East Timor, such as *La'o Hamutuk*, pressed for inclusive and deliberative mechanisms of decision-making and constitution-drafting in order to enable society to 'feel a sense of ownership over the country's constitution and political structures'.[40] Surveys of the East Timorese population by the National Democratic Institute conducted in March 2001 also reported an 'outright rejection' of the idea that foreigners should be involved in developing the constitution.[41]

To satisfy the 'local ownership' criterion, constitutions must be drafted by a democratically elected body of citizens in an exercise of self-determination rather than an 'outside' or international actor.[42] While the ideal of 'local ownership' demands 'that all have a voice in the constitutional process', constitutions built within a context of international state-building can result in local ownership being the end, but not necessarily the means.[43] The UNTAET recognised that the Constitution could not be perceived by the East Timorese as 'imposed'.[44] One

Constitution-drafting and the first elections 103

rationale for improving efforts at 'local ownership' is that the principle of sovereignty implies that social, political, economic and cultural infrastructure should be controlled and determined domestically without outside interference.[45] In effect, self-determination underpins the belief that citizens of the state (or future state) are in the best position to write an appropriate constitution for their political community, irrespective of their levels of legal or political expertise.

Several models of constitution-drafting were discussed by various actors, including the National Council of Timorese Resistance (CNRT) and the UNTAET. In August 1999, the CNRT advocated the establishment of a special convention comprised of all social and political groups, which would appoint a team of legal professionals to assist in drafting the Constitution.[46] Later, in a conference at Tibar from 29 May to 2 June 2000, the CNRT reversed its position and decided that additionally, a constitutional working party should be formed to draft the constitution.[47] The CNRT stressed the importance of mechanisms that involved public participation.[48] However, at the same conference, the Political Affairs department of the UNTAET announced a vision of constitution-building whereby members of the public would elect the Constituent Assembly to draft the constitution.[49] At the CNRT National Congress in August 2000, the UNTAET offered participants a choice between two models of constitution-building: the Political Affairs Unit's model of a Constituent Assembly; or, the selection of an unelected, independent constitutional commission followed by a referendum on the draft constitution held in conjunction with first elections.[50]

In collaboration with the National Council, the UNTAET decided against the 'conservative' approach to constitution-building whereby experts in politics and law draft the Constitution; instead, it opted for a democratic system where representatives are elected specifically to write it.[51] The National Council decided to forgo an independent commission on the basis that decisions about the nature of the Constitution and East Timor's future state identity should be drafted by representatives of the public rather than appointed officials. Members viewed this as necessary for engendering self-determination in constitution-drafting.[52]

After a two-month consultation period with constitutional and electoral experts, the UNTAET decided that an assembly of elected officials would operate as constitution-drafters.[53] The consultations covered issues such as the type of electoral system, the number of members required in the Constituent Assembly, and the period of time necessary for drafting the Constitution.[54] Using elections to establish constituent assemblies has a number of antecedents, including in Cambodia.[55] Under the Paris Peace Accords (PPA), Cambodians elected a 120-member constituent assembly in 1993 to draft a new constitution which then turned itself into a unicameral national assembly.[56] An annex in the PPA provided a number of guidelines for drafting the Constitution including the protection of a large range of human rights and the requirement that Cambodia would establish a plural liberal-democratic system of government.[57]

The National Council adopted the UNTAET Regulation 2001/2 on 16 March 2001, which outlined the responsibilities of an elected Constituent Assembly to draft the Constitution over 90 days.[58] This resolution mandated the Constituent

Assembly to ensure the protection of basic human rights to conscience, expression, association and freedom from discrimination during the election period.[59] These were the only conditions imposed upon the Constituent Assembly by the UNTAET relating to the content of the Constitution. As Figure 4.1 demonstrates, the National Council and Cabinet was disestablished before the election of the Constituent Assembly (which subsequently became the Second Transitional Government).[60] The first set of elections were required to be free, fair, secret and universal following commonly accepted practices of democratic elections according to international law.[61] Certain conditions such as freedom of speech and assembly, security of individuals and social inclusion had to be met for constitution-building processes to be considered sufficiently 'democratic'.[62] These rules for constitution-drafting highlight the importance of the Constitution being constructed through democratic procedures conducted by local actors for its future political validity.

Civil society and the constitution-building

Civil society organisations contributed to the debates about how constitution-drafting processes should occur. For example, FONGTIL argued at the International Donors Conference in Canberra in June 2001 that they represented the

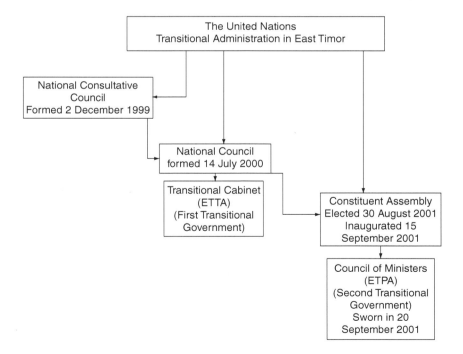

Figure 4.1 Structure of transitional governments.

Constitution-drafting and the first elections 105

first opportunity to establish a political culture within a new state previously unfamiliar with self-governance. The organisation argued that fundamental decisions would be made regarding the type of state East Timor would become during the constitution-building period, pointing out that these processes would embed citizens' political collaboration and participation in East Timor's political fabric.[63] Constitution-building represented an opportunity for East Timor's leaders, particularly members of FRETILIN (as the political party with the most support) to meet the expectations set throughout the independence movement about establishing a multi-party plural democracy.[64]

Civil society organisations argued that constitution-building should entail consultative and inclusive processes that canvassed different views from organisations and individuals in society. Groups, such as *Yayasan HAK*, FONGTIL and *La'o Hamutuk*, believed that the East Timorese Constitution should reflect the 'needs, hopes and aspirations of the Timorese people'.[65] In an August 2001 bulletin of *La'o Hamutuk*, Aderito Soares stated:

> Just as important as the constitution's substance is the process of drawing up the actual document. It is through this process that the citizenry comes to feel a sense of ownership over the country's constitution and its political institutions. Also, assuming that this process is sufficiently inclusive and participatory, it will help to lay the basis for a tolerant, democratic and vibrant political culture.[66]

This reflects a belief that sharing public 'authorship' assists people in understanding, respecting and supporting the Constitution, and creates inclusive democratic structures that can represent their interests and aspirations.[67] Public authorship can occur through free deliberation, rational dialogue and consensus, which Habermas perceives as essential to the project of building a democratic civil society based upon the 'justified consent' of citizens.[68]

Many civil society organisations in East Timor argued that democratic political participation entailed more than voting in elections, and that the establishment of a representative Constituent Assembly alone did not allow sufficient opportunities for citizenry involvement in constitution-building processes.[69] For instance, the Catholic Church contended that all major civil society organisations and interest groups must approve of the Constitution in order for it to be a genuinely representative and inclusive document.[70] Joaquim Fonesca of *Yayasan HAK* agreed, arguing that 'it is important that the constitution is not only owned by the elite, but also by ordinary men and women. It is important that all the Timorese are involved enough in the process so that we can call it a People's Constitution'.[71] A 'legitimate' process relied upon the East Timorese having opportunities to have their visions 'included' in its creation. These organisations advocated the development of deliberative mechanisms of citizenry participation, conforming to a participatory, social democratic vision of statehood rather than a procedural model. It appears that the East Timorese public agreed: surveys conducted by the National Democratic Institute of the population in March 2001

106   *Constitution-drafting and the first elections*

indicated that 85 per cent of those surveyed considered public participation to be important in constitution-drafting.[72]

In Cambodia, for instance, Marks described the process of constitution-building as 'disappointing'. The Constitution as a document might present a 'reasonable blueprint for democratic governance' if the context in which it was drafted is not taken into account. However, the process was undermined by 'unstable' power sharing arrangements between key parties and elites, and ongoing violence and intimidation.[73] The Constitution was largely a product of FUNCINPEC, which might be defended on the basis that they achieved the highest percentage of votes, but a democratic constitution-process requires more than just the participation of elected elites. Marks suggests that the UNTAC was 'too sensitive to the sovereignty issues' and did not press for greater political participation of citizens and there was no requirement that the public participate in the processes of constitution-drafting.[74] While the emerging civil society was important for providing information and education about human rights and democracy, Marks reports that 'there was precious little participation from either NGOs or members of the [constituent] assembly in the formulation of the Constitution'.[75] The process of constitution-drafting was ultimately a 'highly-secretive' 'manifestation of intervention from above because the drafting process was not transparent and civil society was given few opportunities to be heard'.[76] This has impacted upon the Constitution's subsequent roles in restraining state power and protecting key civil and political rights as the elite's unwillingness to consider public opinion served as 'an anti-democratic precedent'.[77] These issues around the nature of democratic participation and representation during constitution-building also came to the fore in East Timor.

The FONGTIL argued that 'Constitutional Commissions' were needed to be established as 'a formal and effective mechanism for consultation throughout East Timor'.[78] Under the proposal, Constitutional Commissions would conduct genuine, widespread consultation and assist in building a democratic political culture. Each district would hold meetings and provide opportunities for consultation and education and assist the future Constituent Assembly in developing an understanding of the visions of statehood held among the East Timorese population.

In March 2001, *Yayasan HAK* member Aniceto Guterres Lopes formally submitted the proposal to the National Council for the establishment of Constitutional Commissions, which gained support from Xanana Gusmão and the CNRT.[79] On 27 March 2001, the Standing Committee on Political Affairs in the National Council defeated a draft resolution to establish Constitutional Commissions with five votes in favour, seven against and eight abstaining.[80] A FRETILIN representative, Cipriana Pereira, accused Guterres Lopes of manoeuvring against the political parties by casting doubt over the Constituent Assembly's capacities to fully represent the people.[81] The majority of the Assembly members considered themselves as 'sufficient representatives of East Timorese public opinion'.[82] In a joint press conference with SRSG Sérgio Vieira de Mello, Chief Minister of the Constituent Assembly, Mari Alkatiri, stated that 'democracy is not managed by consensus ... people sometimes think that all matters dealing with democracy

Constitution-drafting and the first elections 107

should be dealt through consensus. Consensus is sometimes against democracy because the majority has won but only a minority do not agree'.[83] These examples reflect constructed binaries between democratic mass participation and the obligations of an elected leadership to make decisions on behalf of constituents.

Gusmão left the National Council over its failure to establish Constitutional Commissions, criticising the slow pace of establishing civic education programs, and refusing to be involved 'in a politically irresponsible process'.[84] The NGO forum appealed to the United Nations Security Council, arguing that it was necessary to establish Constitutional Commissions as formal mechanisms of inclusive dialogue between members of the East Timorese community and the Constituent Assembly.[85] The UNTAET ultimately overturned the National Council's decision by implementing the directive in Regulation 2001/2 that the Commissions be held.[86] The Transitional Administration was interested in promoting social inclusion given that this is an important indicator of democratic constitution-building processes.[87] Constitutional Commissions ran from 18 June 2001 until late July of the same year.[88] In this example, it was the UNTAET that compelled the East Timorese leadership to expand mechanisms for political participation and inclusion.

The Transitional Administrator, Sérgio Vieira de Mello, set up Constitutional Commissions in the 13 districts 'to gather results of village-led consultations conducted by NGOs'.[89] Each Constitutional Commission was composed of between five and seven East Timorese members appointed by the Transitional Administrator, selected often from civil society organisations, who were employed to inform citizens of the Constitutional Commissions and facilitate public hearings.[90] The Constitutional Commissions consulted with people and civil society organisations in each of the 65 sub-districts, led community discussions and collated the opinions of the public in relation to the Constitution.[91] Two hundred and five meetings were held in less than two months and the UN reported that over 36,000 views were consulted.[92] On 16 August 2001, the reports from the 13 districts were handed over to de Mello.[93]

Despite the large number of people consulted during the Constitutional Commissions, East Timorese civil society organisations continued to press for further opportunities for people to participate in constitutional development. In contrast, Nicholson argues that during this time the Constitutional Commissions consulted significantly with the East Timorese community and were generally inclusive and participatory.[94] These Commissions represented deliberative models of inclusion because they created public space for political dialogue.[95] While a participatory process for constitution-building does not necessarily lead to consensus on all issues, social inclusion matters because people need to feel their constitution reflects their visions of statehood and common political values.[96]

In a post-conflict society partly fragmented by social and political differences, such as East Timor, tolerance for opposing views and dissent are necessary for reconciliation and building democratic culture. Majoritarian systems in plural societies can encourage divisions along social and political lines, particularly when beliefs, values and interests sit in tension.[97] The UNTAET considered the

108   *Constitution-drafting and the first elections*

Constitutional Commissions an important part of constitution-making, which is evident in its overturning of the National Council's decision not to hold them. Deliberative structures can give voice to different minority groups or vulnerable members of a plural society. Ideas of plural democracy stand in contrast with notions of the 'general will', which tends to imply that interests are fairly homogeneous within a 'nation-state'.

Electing the Constituent Assembly

On 30 August 2001, the first democratic elections were held in East Timor. These established the Constituent Assembly comprising 88 elected officials responsible for drafting the Constitution. The elections were held in accordance with the UNTAET regulation 2001/2, with 75 national seats distributed through the 'party-list' Proportional Representation (PR) electoral system, and 13 district seats allocated to the party with the highest number of votes.[98] Of all eligible East Timorese participants, 91.3 per cent voted, a significant number given the criticisms that many East Timorese remained ill-informed about the elections despite the efforts of civil society organisations to provide civic education.[99]

The UNTAET's civic education program to inform the East Timorese about voting processes was criticised by Soares and Baltazar as providing insufficient information and knowledge to the public, and focusing more on how to vote rather than explaining the purpose of the ballot.[100] The National Democratic Institute report in March 2001 found a lack of knowledge among people about how the Constitution would be written and the role of community in its development, but people did have a feeling it should represent the Timorese and their values.[101] This lack of knowledge was compounded by an insufficient distribution of civic education materials including radio and newspapers outside of Dili.[102] Baltazar notes that there was only time for basic voter education and, as such, 'only the political elite had access to all the information during the entire transitional process'.[103] Errors were made by voters due to the similarities between flags and symbols of the different parties.[104] The Catholic Church undertook its own program of civic education, 'including promoting principles which should guide the election of political candidates'.[105] The NGO Forum and civil society organisations also undertook campaigns of community engagement by disseminating information and conducting workshops.[106]

During the 2001 Constituent Assembly elections, the political parties had 'developed and adhered to the Pact of National Unity, which included a commitment to defend multiparty democracy, respect the rights of all legally established parties, and support nonviolent discourse and interaction between political parties'.[107] The Independent Electoral Commission was established to run the elections, and the Carter Centre Observation team found it 'functioned in a participatory and inclusive way, working with all parties and conducting effective voter education campaigns'.[108] While more opportunities might have been presented to East Timorese in running the elections, generally the vote met all international standards of free and fair elections.[109] Ultimately, the elections were

Constitution-drafting and the first elections   109

a success insofar as the high voter turnout indicated the lack of intimidation and accurately reflected the will of the people.

In contrast, international efforts in assisting Cambodia's first democratic elections in 1993 were more problematic for a number of reasons. While there were limited examples of violence prior to the elections or during the campaign period in East Timor, international democracy promoters in Cambodia struggled to contain violence.[110] Cambodian elites were, at times, reluctant to play by the rules and were keen to subvert the process. In East Timor, the National Unity Pact was generally respected, with a limited number of examples where political discourse contravened the pact.[111]

Led by Mari Alkatiri, FRETILIN achieved the highest number of votes, attaining 55 of 88 seats (62 per cent of available seats), but only 54 per cent of the total vote.[112] *Partido Democrata* (PD), a party led by former student activist, Fernando de Araújo, directed its focus to the younger generation, followed with seven nationally elected seats (8.7 per cent of vote).[113] A FRETILIN breakaway party, the *Associação Social Democrática Timorense* (ASDT), led by key independence leader Francisco Xavier do Amaral, attained 7.8 per cent of the vote and won six national seats and one district seat.[114] The *Partido Social Democrata* (PSD), an offshoot of the UDT party led by Mário Carrascalão, won 8.1 per cent of the vote and six seats.[115] For FRETILIN to achieve the two-thirds majority to pass the Constitution through the assembly, they recruited the support of smaller parties, including the more conservative parties such as the ASDT and *Partido Democratia Cristao* (PDC) with two seats.[116] Table 4.1 demonstrates the broad popularity of FRETILIN across many of the districts. It shows it had strongest support in the Eastern districts of Lautem, Baucau and Viqueque, which has long been considered FRETILIN heartland.[117] Support for FRETILIN was weakest in the middle districts of Aileu, Ermera and Ainaro.

Table 4.1 Election results by district[1]

District	% of vote	FRETILIN	ASDT	PD	PSD
Lautem	6.5	62.8	0.3	10.4	10.1
Viqueque	7.8	75.0	0.6	3.9	3.5
Baucau	12.3	82.0	0.4	2.4	3.6
Manatuto	4.4	47.6	11.7	11.0	11.7
Dili	18.4	54.6	10.7	5.9	4.8
Manufahi	4.6	54.6	21.9	4.7	3.5
Aileu	3.9	21.2	52.3	5.2	1.5
Ermera	10.4	31.9	4.4	20.7	20.0
Ainaro	5.4	27.6	15.2	8.4	6.2
Liquiça	5.7	72.4	2.6	3.9	4.9
Bobonaro	8.5	57.4	4.4	12.7	11.2
Covalima	5.9	61.4	4.6	18.6	6.1
Oecussi	6.3	38.6	1.8	7.6	23.5

Note

1 Fox, 'A District Analysis of the East Timor Elections 2001–2002', 18.

110 *Constitution-drafting and the first elections*

The Proportional Representation (PR) electoral system entailed parties sharing power according to the proportion of the vote that each one received (see also Chapter 5). This system was responsible for the large number of parties represented in the Constituent Assembly as the non-FRETILIN votes were spread across a range of parties. This type of electoral system was selected by the Political Affairs Unit of the UNTAET in consultation with constitutional and electoral experts.[118] It was also preferred by the Transitional Administrator, Sérgio Vieira de Mello, because he wanted to avoid 'the tyranny of the majority', on the understanding that an electoral majority does not necessarily support plural democracy or protect minority groups.[119] The district seats also ensured a component of geographically based seat allocation, whereby elected members represented people within the regions rather than being responsible for the political party to which they belonged. Proportional Representation allowed a range of different groups to be represented in the Constituent Assembly. While PR generally promotes multi-party representation, FRETILIN were the dominant political party.[120]

Drafting the Constitution

Throughout the transition period, civil society organisations sought to avoid an 'imposed' constitution from either domestic political leaders or the UNTAET by lobbying for deliberative mechanisms. Following the elections, these organisations, including the NGO Forum, were concerned that the Constituent Assembly, headed by FRETILIN, would unilaterally impose a constitution upon society without due consideration for community consultation.[121] They argued that restricting opportunities for the East Timorese to assist in building a sustainable democratic order would adversely impact the legitimacy of the Constitution and the political institutions it would establish.[122]

In July 2001, the National Council was dissolved to be replaced by the Constituent Assembly.[123] On 15 September 2001, the Constituent Assembly was inaugurated and the reports from the Constitutional Commissions of the 13 districts were presented to it the first time it convened on 17 September.[124] Three days later, a 24-member National Council of Ministers was selected by Sérgio Vieira de Mello and became the East Timor Public Administration (ETPA), replacing the Transitional Cabinet (ETTA) as the Second Transitional Government.[125]

Five parties submitted draft texts as the basis for discussing the new Constitution: perhaps unsurprisingly given the balance of power, the Constituent Assembly adopted the FRETILIN draft that was established at a party congress in Melbourne in 1998.[126] Four thematic committees were established within the Assembly to work on the draft, hold public hearings and report to the Plenary Sessions of the Constituent Assembly, which were also open to the public.[127] Across October and November 2001, many people attended the debates, which were also broadcast live on radio, and 'the public interest was considerable'.[128] A Systematisation and Harmonisation Committee was established and charged

Constitution-drafting and the first elections   111

with preparing a draft for a Plenary Session, which 'considered the whole draft constitution clause by clause'.[129] The structure of the Constitution was approved on 30 November 2001.[130]

Although extensive reports from the Constitutional Commissions were given to the Constituent Assembly, Regan argues that almost no reference was made to them during their deliberations in the Constituent Assembly.[131] Others, such as Baltazar, agree that the results were not adequately incorporated into the drafting process: 'the Thematic Commissions of the CA [Constituent Assembly] did not discuss the reports, which were meant to feed the CA with the opinions of the people or the future Constitution during the debates'.[132] Political leaders were perceived as serving their own interests rather than genuinely responding to community concerns. In response to criticisms from civil society organisations, FRETILIN leaders argued that the Consultation Commissions lacked legitimacy because they were not elected by the public, which again reflected a procedural model of political participation.[133] The UNTAET Regulation 2001/2 gave the Constituent Assembly three months to draft the Constitution from its first sitting, however on 15 December the Constituent Assembly voted to extend its deliberations until 25 January.[134] On 9 February 2001, the draft Constitution was approved by the Constituent Assembly.[135]

Following the approval of the FRETILIN draft, the Constituent Assembly consented to holding public consultations and debates on the draft.[136] Minor parties in the Constituent Assembly proposed that public consultations be held for a month between March and April 2002. Ultimately, the Constituent Assembly approved the one-week consultation period proposed by FRETILIN, beginning in February 2002.[137] The Constituent Assembly held a number of public hearings, inviting civil society organisations, such as the FONGTIL, to participate; however, these organisations complained that their advice and opinions were not taken seriously.[138] These complaints were expressed in bulletins such as *La'o Hamutuk*, in press releases and in letters to the United Nations Security Council.[139]

On 25 February, the public consultations began and the draft was subject to public scrutiny until 2 March, with the Plenary receiving the reports two days later.[140] At the time, the Vice-President of the Constituent Assembly, Arlindo Marcal, said 'our main task is to listen to the people ... we are open to other opinions and criticisms provided the criticism is constructive'.[141] Drafts were translated from Portuguese into Indonesian, Tetum and English, but some districts such as Lautem only received Portuguese versions.[142]

While the constitution-building processes in East Timor had its critics in civil society organisations, Nicholson argued that the processes were peaceful, open and democratic, commencing from a national vote for self-determination and entailing extensive community consultation.[143] Similarly, the Carter Centre report in 2004 noted that:

> [a]ssembly leaders [had] stated their intent that the constitution accurately reflect the desires of the East Timorese people. Individual citizens were

112 *Constitution-drafting and the first elections*

provided the opportunity to voice their aspirations and opinions directly to members of the Constituent Assembly by writing letters to the Assembly and the Assembly president. Leaders of civil society, members of government, and others often wrote. This process served as a mechanism for input from civil society, the government, and the international community.[144]

The consultations provided the East Timorese with an opportunity to give feedback and comment on any concerns, although some 'attendees expressed frustration with the limited nature of the public consultations'.[145] The criticisms of the lack of consultation by civil society organisations were driven by high expectations that there would be a greater role for people and society in drafting the Constitution. *Yayasan HAK* argued that limited debate opportunities and civic education leading up to the elections meant that the results of the election could not properly represent the voices of the people during the drafting of the Constitution.[146] Many civil society organisations were disillusioned with the shortcomings of procedural democracy, whereby elections are the dominant mechanisms for political participation.

Their criticisms indicate that they envisaged democracy as involving genuine and widespread opportunities to consult at grass-roots level. A variety of ideas and interests concerning features of constitutions, such as civil rights (including rights of women and children), national identity, language, wealth redistribution and so on, existed in East Timorese society. A *Yayasan HAK* press release stated in September 2001 that it was 'imperative that the Constituent Assembly provides further opportunity to connect people with the decision-making process, rather than attempt to encompass the aspiration of their diverse electorate'.[147] These activities of civil society organisations, however, meant that the Constituent Assembly could not neglect the views of the East Timorese, which is evident in the consultations on the draft and the open public hearings. Nevertheless, many civil society organisations consistently pressed for more public consultation, and in so doing contributed to the bourgeoning democratic public sphere in East Timor through activism, debate and holding leaders to account.

Evaluating East Timor's constitution-drafting processes

One way of measuring the impact of community consultation on the written Constitution is to examine the changes to the draft that were adopted by the Constituent Assembly following the public consultations in March and April 2002. Contentious issues in the Constitution included language, independence day, marriage and family.[148] Baltazar argues that the Constitution did not reflect the expectations of the people on many issues, which underscored the various complaints of civil society organisations.[149] After the draft consultation commissions, 45 amendments were recommended for revision. In a report written after the Assembly's approval of the Constitution, Lutz stated that 'observers suspected that the Assembly did not intend to make any significant changes to the constitutional draft, and ultimately they did not'.[150] Eight of the recommendations

Constitution-drafting and the first elections 113

emerged from East Timorese individuals and 13 were from civil society organisations. Of these recommendations, four revisions were ultimately accepted and they were nearly all from institutions rather than individuals.[151]

However, measuring the revisions made to the Constitution does not tell the complete story about the democratic responsiveness of the Constituent Assembly. Lutz argued that many of the changes suggested by people were quite conservative, including demands for a constitutionally mandated belief in God and the inclusion of the Catholic Church in government.[152] She commented that 'it is perhaps to the Assembly's credit that they were not swayed by public opinion on such critical issues to a democracy such as participation in public office, freedom of religion, or the separation of Church and State'.[153] Lutz's observation suggests there are risks involved in public participation in political decision-making, particularly if demands contradict democratic practice. However, consultation was useful in establishing the popularity of a presidential or semi-presidential system of government, and people demonstrated a willingness to institute human rights norms more generally within the Constitution.[154] The potential difficulty with widespread participation and inclusion, then, is that non-democratic ideals may be valued by people who have limited experience with democracy, although Lutz suggests the East Timorese were generally more politically sophisticated than what this analysis suggests.[155]

The Constitution produced by the Constituent Assembly closely resembles the Constitution written by FRETILIN in 1998, which does indicate that public consultation during the constitution-drafting period had little impact on the final document.[156] The FRETILIN draft was heavily based on Mozambique's Constitution, itself an abridged version of the Portuguese Constitution.[157] Commentators such as Soares raised serious concerns about the power of FRETILIN in the drafting process, however FRETILIN did not have the numbers or influence that they thought they would.[158] The commentary tended to criticise the Constitution as purely a product of FRETILIN. For instance, Soares criticised it for exerting too much influence and creating an imbalance within the constitution-drafting processes.[159] Similarly, Regan contended that the use of a Constituent Assembly to draft the Constitution suited FRETILIN because they were the major political party and were keen to consolidate their power.[160] Kingsbury argued that FRETILIN co-opted political legitimacy in East Timor, claiming that they provided unity and representation despite the presence of other parties.[161] FRETILIN's dominant role in constitution-drafting, however, was not entirely unreasonable given its centrality in establishing and maintaining East Timor's resistance movement. It is important to acknowledge that East Timor's Constitution also resembled the Magna Carta adopted by the CNRT in 1998. The resultant Constitution was a product of the visions created during the independence movement. The main difficulty was less about 'the interference of international actors than a rather authoritarian tendency within the Timorese leadership'.[162] This 'authoritarian' streak within FRETILIN would arise more forcefully following East Timor's transition to independence (examined further in Chapter 5).

114   *Constitution-drafting and the first elections*

While it is reasonable to expect collaboration among diverse social and political organisations during constitution-building, the fact that FRETILIN achieved a fair majority in the elections should not be disregarded. This election result did lend FRETILIN the political legitimacy necessary for taking a leading role in constitution-drafting. There were also arguments that the views of small parties in the Constituent Assembly were not taken into account and that it was largely seen by the East Timorese as a 'one-party' draft.[163] It is important to consider, however, that FRETILIN did not have the two-thirds outright majority required to pass the draft, and was thus required to consult with smaller parties.

Members of opposition groups, such as Social Democrat Lucia Lobato, criticised the Constitution on the basis that they did not believe it represented the will of the people.[164] In some regards these are fair criticisms, given the seeming lack of attention paid to the Constitutional Commission reports by the Constituent Assembly. Political parties said that the process had produced a 'FRETILIN constitution' and the majority of other parties voted against it.[165] As Garrison notes, this could be problematic for democracy if groups feel that they could resort to force rather than play by FRETILIN's constitutional rules.[166] While this is a valid point, it should not be overlooked that in a new democracy, even a constitution developed from the most inclusive and participatory processes may fail to establish constitutionalism and rule of law. East Timor's Constitution was ultimately a local product, insofar as it was not imposed upon them by the international community. The use of deliberative mechanisms before and during the drafting period reflects East Timor's orientation towards democratic processes advocated by 'new constitutionalism'.

Civil society organisations were viewed by the UNTAET as important collaborators in building a national civic education framework, which included the training of civic educators, disseminating mass information through media to the public and other 'civil society initiatives'.[167] According to a UN report of the Secretary-General in May 2001, the UNTAET acknowledged and supported the role of non-governmental organisations (NGOs) and Constitutional Commissions by facilitating public participation in the development of the Constitution.[168] On the other hand, civil society organisations criticised the level of influence of political parties in the processes of drafting the Constitution, as social organisations were forced to voice opposition through political parties rather than having a channel or forum for serious discussion.[169] In the context of democratic theory, this is a somewhat problematic argument since it is politicians that possess electoral legitimacy: civil society organisations, on the other hand, are not formally elected by the public.

Despite this, it is important to avoid conflating 'participation' with voting in elections: although political participation can be a vague concept, popular participation emphasises collective efforts to increase the population's control over the distribution of resources and political institutions.[170] According to Kaufman, all representative democracies have weaknesses and more inclusive forms of organisation and decision-making can deepen democracy.[171] Organisations within civil society promoted a model of democracy in East Timor that extended

Constitution-drafting and the first elections 115

participation beyond formal elections to incorporate deliberative mechanisms for direct participation and collaboration. Ultimately, civil society organisations were not satisfied with explanations by FRETILIN that the elections provided sufficient opportunity for the East Timorese to participate. Aredito Soares, in the *La'o Hamutuk Bulletin* in August 2001, contended that East Timor's constitutional processes were unlikely to engender trust in law and political institutions among East Timor, given that these had previously been instruments of repression.[172]

Discontent over constitution-drafting processes was largely directed towards political 'elites' by people and civil society activists, who appealed to international actors to ensure greater political participation for the people of East Timor. Importantly, however, many of the new political elites were civil society activists themselves during the independence movement. The dynamics of constitution-building reflect the risky business of transition wherein democratically elected leaders are required to share power and consult widely. A National Democratic Institute survey reported a widespread reluctance of people in the districts to leave the role of constitution-building to Dili-based elites.[173] There was also a sense that the East Timorese were feeling left out of the constitution-building process, particularly at the beginning.[174] According to Chesterman, 'many ordinary Timorese expressed doubt about the need for political parties'.[175] Elite politics was seen by some, including Bishop Carlos Belo of the Roman Catholic Church, to be dominated by the upper class in society, which consisted of influential families and focused on personalities.[176]

Tensions between social and political actors were partly driven by their different visions about the nature of democratic engagement and the relationships between the social and political spheres. According to *Yayasan HAK*:

> [f]or hundreds of years, the East Timorese people have been excluded from democratic governance and control of their own affairs. This cannot be reversed by people exercising their right to vote. Avenues for participation and an ability to have active input in the decision-making processes are vital to ensure that the East Timorese people have a voice in governance which they have been denied so long.[177]

This indicates a belief that democracy comprises more than its procedural elements, such as voting, as deliberation and consultation are also viewed as essential to constitution-building and democratic processes more generally. Social democracy is hence interpreted as deliberative democracy, extending beyond the procedural and relying upon civil society as an important site of political influence and advocacy. In this sense, connecting the social and political realms is integral to producing a stable and durable political order, the foundation of which is a constitution. On 22 March 2002, East Timor's Constitution was adopted with 72 in favour, 14 against, one abstention and one absence.[178] East Timor's Constituent Assembly elected to transform itself into East Timor's first government.

116 *Constitution-drafting and the first elections*

East Timor became an independent democratic state on May 2002, attaining UN membership the following September.[179] In his inauguration speech, first President Xanana Gusmão's emphasised the importance of social, economic, cultural and scientific development for all people, as well as tolerance and respect for human rights that is consonant with democratic pluralism. He told citizens that the occasion of independence demanded of all people the:

> disciplina para fortalecer a nossa capacidade, tolerância para fortalecer a nossa democracia, reconciliação para fortalecer a nossa unidade, dentro dos valores da justiça e dos direitos humanos [discipline to strengthen our capacity, tolerance to strengthen our democracy, reconciliation to strengthen our unity within the values of justice and human rights].[180]

This was a performative act that reinforced the independence movement's vision of East Timorese statehood and the values embedded in the Constitution. The following chapters examine East Timor's pursuit of democracy, human rights and justice in further detail.

Conclusion

Dialogue between community and political actors plays an important role in legitimising structures such as the Constitution because it provides opportunities for the document to encompass or incorporate the diverse beliefs and aspirations of the people. Widespread acceptance of structures underpins their legitimacy, which is crucial for their institutionalisation and beneficial in regards to establishing democratic relationships between citizens and the state.[181] Building a plural, consensus-oriented democracy can embed the accommodation of diversity within the culture and institutions of the state. These issues intersect with questions about the different relationships between civil society (itself encompassing diverse actors, power dynamics and networks) and newly constituted political leaders.

Most observers of East Timor's constitution-building exercise agreed that international influence should be limited to organising the process.[182] Engendering self-governance within a people through consultation and collaboration is a valuable source of democratic internal sovereignty and 'local ownership' of state structures. Moreover, direct consultation with the public can provide governments with a meaningful claim to be an 'embodiment of the will of the people'.[183] Feldman suggests that 'autonomy and self-determination function as crucial parts of the very phenomenon of democratic constitutionalism itself'.[184] Enabling self-determination through participation in the processes of constitution-making was important for the future role of the Constitution as it 'must be understood as locally produced to acquire legitimacy'.[185] This legitimacy can be built through inclusive and responsive constitution-building processes where people believe they have contributed to the construction of the new state's primary legal document.

Constitution-drafting and the first elections   117

Deliberative mechanisms in constitution-drafting matter for ensuring constitutional provisions are known and accepted by citizens and political leaders, which is more likely to produce a 'self-enforcing' constitution.[186] In plural post-conflict societies, such as East Timor, the goal of constitution-building is to seek a 'workable' formula that will be sustainable based upon a 'conversation, conducted by all concerned, open to new entrants and issues'.[187] A constitution that is 'imposed', on the other hand, is less likely to engender the types of attachment required to ensure its endurance.[188]

The NGOs examined in this chapter, including *La'o Hamutuk, Yayasan HAK* and the NGO Forum, were invested in encouraging dialogue between political leaders and citizens across East Timor and in gaining a level of political influence. They encouraged political actors to take seriously the views and visions of individuals within the community. Civil society organisations sought to hold the Constituent Assembly to account, and influence the constitution-building process to ensure they could support a plural model of social democracy characterised by extensive citizenry participation.

The processes of East Timorese constitution-building suggest that criticisms around a lack of community engagement stemmed primarily from the reluctance of East Timorese leaders to consult rather than from heavy handed intervention of the UNTAET. The extent to which East Timor's Constitution reflects the aspirations of the East Timorese was questioned by those who criticised the commanding influence of FRETILIN in the drafting processes. Through their criticisms of the Constituent Assembly, civil society organisations simultaneously claimed a privileged position informed by their own vested interests. Ultimately, these contests over participation reflected the different models of majoritarian or electoral democracy on the one hand, and deliberative, participatory democracy on the other. Consultation mechanisms were included within constitution-building processes, although the drafting of the Constitution itself was subject to contests over political power in the new state. While civil society organisations were dissatisfied with levels of consultation, their criticisms and contributions to constructive political debates in the public sphere, in addition to their efforts at civic education, assisted in developing a political culture based upon democratic behaviours in East Timor.

Notes

1 Garrison, *The Role of Constitution-Building Processes in Democratization*, 29.
2 Smith, 'East Timor: Elections in the World's Newest Nation', 149. See also Coehlo, *Dua Kali Merdeka*, 112–113.
3 Habermas, 'The European Nation-State', 400.
4 Martin, 'Protest in a Liberal-Democracy', 13–24.
5 Linz and Stepan, *Problems of Democratic Transition and Consolidation*, 8.
6 Habermas, *Legitimation Crisis*, 45 and Weber, *From Max Weber*, 215.
7 Harmer and Frith, '"Walking Together" Toward Independence?', 244.
8 Linz and Stepan, *Problems of Democratic Transition and Consolidation*, 6.
9 Hart, *Democratic Constitution Making*, 4.
10 Ibid., 3.
11 Cohen, 'Democracy and Liberty', 187.

118 Constitution-drafting and the first elections

12 Garrison, *The Role of Constitution-Building Processes in Democratization*, 29.
13 United Nations Transitional Administration in East Timor, *On the Elections of a Constituent Assembly to Prepare a Constitution for an Independent and Democratic East Timor*, Section 2:4.
14 Brandt, *Constitutional Assistance in Post-Conflict Countries*, 8.
15 East Timor NGO Forum, *The Constitutional Process in East Timor;* La'o Hamutuk, *The La'o Hamutuk Bulletin* 2, no. 5, (August 2001) and Yayasan HAK, *A People's Constitution for East Timor.*
16 Hart, *Democratic Constitution Making*, 1.
17 Lovell, 'Promoting Democracy', 337.
18 Linz and Stepan, *Problems of Democratic Transition and Consolidation*, 7.
19 Carter Centre, *East Timor Political and Election Observation Project*, 46.
20 Chesterman, *You, the People*, 135–136.
21 Garrison, *The Role of Constitution-Building Processes in Democratization*, 2.
22 Goldstone, 'UNTAET with Hindsight', 90.
23 United Nations Transitional Administration in East Timor, *On the Elections of a Constituent Assembly to Prepare a Constitution for an Independent and Democratic East Timor.*
24 Chesterman, 'Imposed Constitutions, Imposed Constitutionalism and Ownership', 954 and Feldman, 'Imposed Constitutionalism', 880.
25 Saul, 'Local Ownership of Post-Conflict Reconstruction in International Law', 166.
26 Charlesworth, 'The Constitution of East Timor', 329.
27 Hart, *Democratic Constitution Making*, 6 and United Nations General Assembly, *International Covenant on Civil and Political Rights*, Article 25.
28 Zaum, *The Sovereign Paradox*, 231.
29 Feldman, 'Imposed Constitutionalism', 882.
30 Chesterman, 'Imposed Constitutions, Imposed Constitutionalism and Ownership', 949 and 954.
31 Ibid., 949.
32 Aucoin and Brandt, 'East Timor's Constitutional Passage to Independence', 245.
33 Chesterman, 'Imposed Constitutions, Imposed Constitutionalism and Ownership', 947; Dann and Al-Ali, 'The Internationalized *Pouvoir Constituant*', 426; Feldman, 'Imposed Constitutionalism', 880 and Hart, *Democratic Constitution Making*, 4.
34 Hart, ibid., 4.
35 Leach, 'Valorising the Resistance', 43.
36 Hart, *Democratic Constitution Making*, 4 and Ginsberg, Elkins and Melton, 'The Lifespan of Written Constitutions', 1.
37 Putnam, *Making Democracy Work.*
38 Saul, 'Local Ownership of Post-Conflict Reconstruction in International Law', 166.
39 Linz and Stepan, *Problems of Democratic Transition and Consolidation*, 6 and Cohen, 'Democracy and Liberty', 185.
40 Aderito Soares cited in La'o Hamutuk, *The La'o Hamutuk Bulletin* 2, no. 5 (August 2001), 16.
41 Della-Giacoma, *Timor Loro Sa'e is Our Nation*, 4.
42 Feldman, 'Imposed Constitutionalism'.
43 Chesterman, *You, the People*, 248.
44 Dann and Al-Ali, 'The Internationalized *Pouvoir Constituant*', 426.
45 Saul, 'Local Ownership of Post-Conflict Reconstruction in International Law', 173.
46 Aucoin and Brandt, 'East Timor's Constitutional Passage to Independence', 250–251.
47 Ibid., 251 and Baltazar, 'An Overview of the Constitution Drafting Process in East Timor', 2. Baltazar reports that the CNRT's decision to advocate for an elected body was made in the political transition calendar that was produced by Xanana Gusmão on 12 December 2000.

Constitution-drafting and the first elections 119

48 Aucoin and Brandt, ibid.
49 Ibid., 252.
50 Ibid., 251.
51 Nicholson, 'Observation on the New Constitution of East Timor', 204.
52 Ibid.
53 Baltazar, 'An Overview of the Constitution Drafting Process in East Timor', 3.
54 Ibid.
55 See for example Samuels, 'Post-War Constitution Building'.
56 United Nations, *Agreements on a Comprehensive Political Settlement of the Cambodia Conflict*, Part 1. See also Marks, 'The Process of Creating a New Constitution in Cambodia', 213 and Gallup, 'Cambodia's Electoral System', 31.
57 United Nations, ibid., Annex 5.
58 United Nations Transitional Administration in East Timor, *On the Elections of a Constituent Assembly to Prepare a Constitution for an Independent and Democratic East Timor*, Section 2:3.
59 Ibid., Section 1:1–2.
60 On the UNTAET's structure, see Sanches, *Mengenal Pemerintahan Timor-Leste*, 30–32.
61 United Nations Transitional Administration in East Timor, *On the Elections of a Constituent Assembly to Prepare a Constitution for an Independent and Democratic East Timor*, Section 1:2.
62 Garrison, *The Role of Constitution-Building Processes in Democratization*, 11.
63 East Timor National NGO Forum, *The Constitutional Process in East Timor*.
64 Della-Giacoma, *Timor Loro Sa'e is Our Nation*, iii and 1.
65 Joaquim Fonesca cited in Yayasan HAK, *A People's Constitution for East Timor*. See also Aucoin and Brandt, 'East Timor's Constitutional Passage to Independence', 245.
66 Aderito Soares cited in La'o Hamutuk, *The La'o Hamutuk Bulletin* 2, no. 5 (August 2001), 16.
67 Aucoin and Brandt, 'East Timor's Constitutional Passage to Independence', 245–246 and Hart, *Democratic Constitution Making*, 3.
68 Habermas, 'Constitutional Democracy', 766–781.
69 East Timor National NGO Forum, *The Constitutional Process in East Timor*; Joaquim Fonesca cited in Yayasan HAK, *A People's Constitution for East Timor*; La'o Hamutuk, *The La'o Hamutuk Bulletin* 2, no. 3 (June 2001), 10 and La'o Hamutuk, *The La'o Hamutuk Bulletin* 2, no. 5, (August 2001), 16.
70 La'o Hamutuk, *The La'o Hamutuk Bulletin* 2, no. 5, (August 2001), 16.
71 Joaquim Fonesca cited in Yayasan HAK, *A People's Constitution for East Timor*.
72 Della-Giacoma, *Timor Loro Sa'e is Our Nation*, 1 and 3.
73 Marks, 'The Process of Creating a New Constitution in Cambodia', 223 and Brandt, *Constitutional Assistance in Post-Conflict Countries*, 11.
74 Marks, ibid., 217 and Brandt, ibid., 11.
75 Marks, ibid., 220.
76 Marks, ibid., 234 and Brandt, *Constitutional Assistance in Post-Conflict Countries*, 12.
77 Brandt, ibid., 12.
78 East Timor National NGO Forum, *Letter to Members of the United Nations Security Council*.
79 Aucoin and Brandt, 'East Timor's Constitutional Passage to Independence', 258–259.
80 La'o Hamutuk, *East Timor: National Council Rejects Bill on Constitutional Commission*; United Nations Security Council, *Interim Report of the Secretary-General on the United Nations Transitional Administration in East Timor*, 1 and United Nations Transitional Administration in East Timor, *National Council Defeats Constitution Committees*.

120 *Constitution-drafting and the first elections*

81 Vanaja, 'East Timor: Tensions Rise as Elections Nears'.
82 Carter Centre, *East Timor Political and Election Observation Project*, 44.
83 See United Nations Transitional Administration in East Timor, *Alkatiri/deMello Press Conference*.
84 Ibid. and United Nations Security Council, *Interim Report of the Secretary-General on the United Nations Transitional Administration in East Timor*.
85 East Timor National NGO Forum, *Letter to Members of the United Nations Security Council* and La'o Hamutuk, *The La'o Hamutuk Bulletin* 2, no. 3 (June 2001), 8.
86 Brandt, *Constitutional Assistance in Post-Conflict Countries*, 8.
87 Garrison, *The Role of Constitution-Building Processes in Democratization*, 11.
88 Regan, 'Constitution Making in East Timor', 38.
89 Vanaja, 'East Timor: Tensions Rise as Elections Nears' and Baltazar, 'An Overview of the Constitution Drafting Process in East Timor', 3.
90 Baltazar, ibid., 4.
91 Regan, 'Constitution Making in East Timor', 38.
92 Ibid.; Baltazar, 'An Overview of the Constitution Drafting Process in East Timor', 4 and United Nations Security Council, *Report of the Secretary-General on the United Nations Transitional Administration in East Timor*, S/2001/983. Garrison and Baltazar suggest it was over 38,000. See Garrison, *The Role of Constitution-Building Processes in Democratization*, 19.
93 Regan, 'Constitution Making in East Timor'.
94 Nicholson, 'Observation on the New Constitution of East Timor', 203.
95 Rosenberg, 'An Introduction', 9.
96 For more on the importance of inclusion, political debate and communication for deliberative democracy see Young, *Inclusion and Democracy*.
97 Rosenberg, 'An Introduction', 2.
98 United Nations Transitional Administration in East Timor, *On the Elections of a Constituent Assembly to Prepare a Constitution for an Independent and Democratic East Timor*, Sections 36 and 37.
99 Baltazar, 'An Overview of the Constitution Drafting Process in East Timor', 5.
100 Ibid. and Soares, 'Election in East Timor', 10–11.
101 Della-Giacoma, *Timor Loro Sa'e is Our Nation*, 4.
102 Ibid., 8.
103 Baltazar, 'An Overview of the Constitution Drafting Process in East Timor', 5.
104 Soares, 'Election in East Timor', 11.
105 Walsh, 'East Timor's Political Parties and Groupings', 28.
106 The East Timor NGO Forum, *Letter to Members of the United Nations Security Council*.
107 Carter Centre, *East Timor Political and Election Observation Project*, 34.
108 Ibid., 27–28.
109 Ibid., 11.
110 The Carter Centre report stated: 'the limited incidences of violence during both elections contributed to a relatively calm pre-election environment, campaign period, and election-day environment'. Ibid., 34.
111 Ibid., 11–12, 34.
112 Fox, 'A District Analysis of the East Timor Elections 2001–2002', 18 and McWilliam and Bexley, 'Performing Politics', 75.
113 Fox, ibid., 18–19.
114 Ibid. and Garrison, *The Role of Constitution-Building Processes in Democratization*, 18. A third FRETILIN breakaway party, the *Partido Socialista de Timor* (PST), won 1.8 per cent of the national vote and 1 seat.
115 Garrison, ibid.
116 Soares, 'The Challenges of Drafting a Constitution', 26.
117 McWilliam and Bexley, 'Performing Politics', 75.

Constitution-drafting and the first elections   121

118 Baltazar, 'An Overview of the Constitution Drafting Process in East Timor', 3.
119 Matsuno, 'The UN Transitional Administration and Democracy Building in Timor-Leste', 60–61.
120 Baltazar, 'An Overview of the Constitution Drafting Process in East Timor', 3.
121 Soares, 'The Challenges of Drafting a Constitution', 25.
122 Garrison, *The Role of Constitution-Building Processes in Democratization*, 3.
123 Matsuno, 'The UN Transitional Administration and Democracy Building in Timor-Leste', 61.
124 Nicholson, 'Observation on the New Constitution of East Timor', 203 and United Nations Transitional Administration in East Timor, *Swearing-In of Constituent Assembly Members*.
125 Garrison, *The Role of Constitution-Building Processes in Democratization*, 29; Matsuno, 'The UN Transitional Administration and Democracy Building in Timor-Leste', 60; Tjandraningsih, *East Timor Announces Cabinet Lineup* and United Nations Transitional Administration in East Timor, *East Timorese Government Sworn-In*.
126 Baltazar, 'An Overview of the Constitution Drafting Process in East Timor', 5 and Garrison, ibid., 20.
127 Baltazar, ibid.; Garrison, ibid. and Nicholson, 'Observation on the New Constitution of East Timor', 204.
128 Nicholson, ibid.
129 Ibid.
130 Garrison, *The Role of Constitution-Building Processes in Democratization*, 29.
131 Regan, 'Constitution Making in East Timor', 38.
132 Baltazar, 'An Overview of the Constitution Drafting Process in East Timor', 4.
133 Ibid., 6 and Carter Centre, *East Timor Political and Election Observation Project*, 44.
134 Brandt, *Constitutional Assistance in Post-Conflict Countries*, 16 and United Nations Transitional Administration in East Timor, *On the Elections of a Constituent Assembly to Prepare a Constitution for an Independent and Democratic East Timor*.
135 Garrison, *The Role of Constitution-Building Processes in Democratization*, 29.
136 Nicholson, 'Observation on the New Constitution of East Timor', 204.
137 Baltazar, 'An Overview of the Constitution Drafting Process in East Timor', 6 and Carter Centre, *East Timor Political and Election Observation Project*, 44.
138 Baltazar, ibid., 6.
139 See for example East Timor National NGO Forum, *Letter to Members of the United Nations Security Council*, and La'o Hamutuk, *The La'o Hamutuk Bulletin* 2, no. 5 (August 2001), 16.
140 Constituent Assembly Secretariat, *Press Release*; Nicholson, 'Observation on the New Constitution of East Timor', 204 and Carter Centre, *East Timor Political and Election Observation Project*, 44.
141 Arlindo Marcal cited in Constituent Assembly Secretariat, ibid.
142 Garrison, 'The Role of Constitution-Building Processes in Democratization', 6–7 and Carter Centre, *East Timor Political and Election Observation Project*, 44.
143 Nicholson, 'Observation on the New Constitution of East Timor', 204.
144 Carter Centre, *East Timor Political and Election Observation Project*, 44.
145 Ibid., 45.
146 Yayasan HAK, *East Timor: Elections in the Context of Nation-Building Press Release*.
147 Ibid.
148 Baltazar, 'An Overview of the Constitution Drafting Process in East Timor', 6.
149 Ibid., 7.
150 Lutz, *Constitutionalism as Public Culture in East Timor* and Carter Centre, *East Timor Political and Election Observation Project*, 45.
151 Baltazar, 'An Overview of the Constitution Drafting Process in East Timor', 6.

122 *Constitution-drafting and the first elections*

152 Lutz, *Constitutionalism as Public Culture in East Timor.*
153 Ibid.
154 Ibid.
155 Ibid.
156 Charlesworth, 'The Constitution of East Timor', 328.
157 In some passages, the East Timor Constitution replicates Mozambique's word-for-word. See Jolliffe, 'East Timor Approves Draft Constitution'; Della-Giacoma, *Timor Loro Sa'e is Our Nation*, 4; Regan, 'Constitution Making in East Timor', 39 and Soares, 'The Challenges of Drafting a Constitution', 29.
158 Soares, ibid., 32–33.
159 Ibid.
160 Regan, 'Constitution Making in East Timor', 38.
161 Kingsbury, *East Timor: The Price of Liberty*, 110.
162 Ibid., 434.
163 Soares, 'The Challenges of Drafting a Constitution', 25.
164 Jolliffe, 'East Timor Approves Draft Constitution'.
165 Garrison, 'The Role of Constitution-Building Processes in Democratization', 22.
166 Ibid.
167 United Nations Security Council, *Interim Report of the Secretary-General on the United Nations Transitional Administration in East Timor*, 1.
168 Ibid.
169 Garrison, 'The Role of Constitution-Building Processes in Democratization', 13.
170 Kaufman, 'Community Power, Grassroots Democracy, and the Transformation of Social Life', 6–7.
171 Ibid., 11.
172 Aderito Soares cited in La'o Hamutuk, *The La'o Hamutuk Bulletin* 2, no. 5 (August 2001), 16.
173 Della-Giacoma, *Timor Loro Sa'e is Our Nation*, 4.
174 Ibid.
175 Chesterman, 'East Timor in Transition', 63.
176 Walsh, 'East Timor's Political Parties and Groupings', 27–28.
177 Yayasan HAK, *East Timor: Elections in the Context of Nation-Building Press Release.*
178 United Nations Transitional Administration in East Timor, *East Timor Assembly Signs into Force First Constitution.*
179 Ibid., 17.
180 Gusmão, *Xanana Gusmão e os Primeiros 10 anos da Construção do Estado Timorense*, 32.
181 Ottaway, 'Rebuilding State Institutions in Collapsed States', 1004.
182 Dann and Al-Ali, 'The Internationalized *Pouvior Constituant*', 432.
183 Saul, 'Local Ownership of Post-Conflict Reconstruction in International Law', 172.
184 Feldman, 'Imposed Constitutionalism', 889.
185 Ibid., 859.
186 Ginsberg, Elkins and Melton, 'The Lifespan of Written Constitutions', 8.
187 Hart, *Democratic Constitution Making*, 3–4.
188 Feldman, 'Imposed Constitutionalism'.

5 Institutions, leaders and elections

The success of East Timor's political transition relied upon the development of institutions articulated in the Constitution.[1] Institutions entail systems of stable operational rules that 'define and defend values, norms, interests, identities and beliefs'.[2] They are created through regular and consistent activities, and once established, have a 'quasi-independent quality and sense of self or culture'.[3] Constitutions matter for fostering democratic civil culture, setting appropriate patterns of behaviour and distributing political power to prevent authoritarianism or the emergence of other non-democratic structures and behaviours. As such, participatory and inclusive dynamics of constitutional-building were important for supporting constitutional legitimacy and establishing patterns of political behaviour necessary for the 'habituation' of state-based political institutions.

East Timor's Constitution established rules regarding elections and the electoral system, articulated the parameters of legitimate activity and demarcated political power and responsibilities between the President, government, national parliament and courts within a semi-presidential system of governance. In so doing, East Timor's elected Constituent Assembly sought to create an independent social democracy that would uphold rule of law and self-determination, provide social justice and economic development, and guarantee the human rights and freedoms of its people. In two crucial decisions, East Timor's constitution-drafters chose a semi-presidential administrative system and Proportional Representation (PR) electoral system. These particular choices have consequences for forms of political participation and representation, and can determine whether a consensus- or majoritarian-oriented pattern of democracy is likely to emerge.

According to some perspectives, international state-building encouraged gaps between modern and traditional forms of governance that resulted in state-based institutions that were unable to 'penetrate and reframe ... many communities in Timor-Leste'.[4] However, this reflects a tendency to underplay the important roles played by East Timorese elites in designing East Timor's institutional framework, and the enduring vision of social democracy supported by East Timor's civil society before and after the independence referendum. East Timor's elections since 2001 have experienced a high degree of voter turnout and have been largely free from violence and intimidation, which represents a significant step

124 *Institutions, leaders and elections*

in developing a democratic political culture in a territory marked by historical hostility between political parties.[5]

Upon independence, resistance leader Xanana Gusmão became East Timor's first President after he attained an 'overwhelming majority' of votes in the presidential elections.[6] The first Government of East Timor was formed by FRETILIN and there was a distinct risk that FRETILIN could become a dominant party. 'Dominant', 'one-party' or 'hegemonic' regimes have been problematic in other post-colonial states, including Cambodia which displays a form of 'competitive authoritarianism' in which elections are used to provide legitimacy to a non-democratic regime, government is not sufficiently accountable, responsible or responsive to constituents and civil liberties are curtailed. A similar form of one-party dominance of FRETILIN could have been detrimental to East Timor's plural multi-party democracy; however, the analysis of the 2007 and 2012 elections in this chapter demonstrates that it avoided a one-party regime and competitive authoritarianism.

Semi-presidentialism in East Timor

Institutional design is important for providing a constitutional system of 'checks and balances' and ensuring no one organ of the state becomes too powerful.[7] As institutions derive their authority from citizens, the scope of their power and decision-making capacities is limited by the Constitution. The choice between presidential or parliamentary systems can influence the relationships between the executive and legislature and impact on the likelihood of democratic transition and consolidation.[8] Benjamin Reilly, for instance, argues that parliamentary democracies are three times more likely to survive than presidential systems. Internationally, the 15 transitioning states that retained their democratic institutions in the 1980s employed parliamentary systems, whereas all new presidential democracies from the same period experienced a reverse wave.[9] Most established democracies employ a parliamentary system in which legislative and executive powers are invested in the parliament, in contrast to presidential systems in which legislative powers belong to parliament and executive powers to the office of the President.[10]

Creating a political structure that could avoid establishing patterns of authoritarianism was paramount. As Mackie explains, power structures that are highly centralised and focused on key individuals have proven problematic in other post-colonial states and were particularly unsuitable for East Timor where the presence of charismatic and prominent independence leaders, such as Xanana Gusmão and Mari Alkatiri, was predicted to lead to complex power struggles between political elites.[11] For example, in Cambodia, contests between multiple centres of charismatic leadership, including long-time Prime Minister Hun Sen, Norodom Ranariddh and Sam Rainsy, have ultimately undermined Cambodian democracy as political authority remains largely viewed as a supreme right.

Roberts notes that in Cambodia, power has always been exercised by a centralised executive, and power-sharing, consensus and legitimate opposition is

Institutions, leaders and elections 125

'antithetical to absolutist traditions'.[12] In practical terms, in Cambodia's constitutional monarchy, power has been largely vested in the executive branch while the legislature and judiciary has remained under-institutionalised.[13] The 'power sharing' arrangement between Hun Sen's CCP and Norodom Ranariddh's FUNCINPEC that was negotiated after the CPP refused to accept the 1993 election result ultimately 'erupted' into political violence in July 1997.[14] The resultant military *coup* confirmed the rollback of democracy in Cambodia, and Hun Sen has since centralised his authority through entrenched, hierarchically-organised patronage networks, and the capacities of the bicameral parliament to provide a check on executive power have progressively weakened.[15] Consequently, Hun Sen has enjoyed three decades of nearly uninterrupted rule in Cambodia, and electoral outcomes have not displayed the uncertainty that democracies ideally exhibit.

East Timor's constitutional designers selected a 'power-sharing' system of semi-presidentialism that contains features of both parliamentary and presidential systems.[16] A semi-presidential system exists if the Constitution combines three elements: the President is elected; the President holds 'considerable' powers; and a government encompassing a prime minister and a cabinet of ministers possesses executive power.[17] Table 5.1 describes the different arms of East Timor's state. According to Guedes, East Timor's decision to implement semi-presidentialism was underpinned by a perception that adding two systems of government together creates 'a new, greater, whole'.[18] The day-to-day functioning resembles a parliamentary system with an assembly and political parties, but has a national leader who is independent from the legislature and executive. This system features two distinct sets of elections, parliamentary and presidential, designed to prevent the 'winner-takes-all' attitude of pure presidential systems.[19]

East Timor's Constitution grants the President limited powers.[20] The President is responsible for promulgating statutes, approving agreements and ratifying international treaties, is notionally the Supreme Commander of the Defence Force, and has veto rights. The President has no constitutional right to make laws and, as such, can be interpreted as a 'figurehead' President. Many of the key responsibilities of the President are only enacted following authorisation from the executive, placing constraints on the effective power of the President.

The Council of Ministers comprises the Prime Minister, the Deputy Prime Ministers and Ministers, and holds executive power in East Timor as the Government. The Government holds the power to enact legislation regarding its own organisation and matters of the state, and holds rights to make and enact decree laws without reference to Parliament.[21] Problematically, the Prime Minister is permitted to select Cabinet Ministers who have not been elected by the public.[22] Given the wide-range of law-making capacities possessed by Cabinet, this does not correspond comfortably with democratic principles of representation and accountability.

Table 5.2 also demonstrates the legislature's responsibility for making laws on domestic and foreign policy and the budget, and authorising the Government

Table 5.1 Structure of government

Type of institution	Nature of institution in East Timor	Key features
Head of State	Office of the President	• Council of State • Superior Council for Defence and Security
Executive	Government	• Prime Minister • Cabinet of Ministers
Legislature	National Parliament	• Unicameral • minimum 52 and maximum 65 elected representatives
Judiciary	Courts	• Superior Council of the Judiciary • Supreme Court (yet to be formed as of 2015) • Court of Appeals • District Courts – Dili, Baucau, Suai and Oecussi • High Administrative, Tax and Audit Court • Military Courts • Maritime and Arbitration Courts • Office of the Prosecutor General • Superior Council for Public Prosecution • Office of the *Provedor de Direitos Humanos e Justiça*/Ombudsman for Human Rights and Justice

Table 5.2 Organs of government and constitutional competencies

Institution	Head of state	Executive	Legislature
Governmental Body	President	Prime Minister and Cabinet (government)	Unicameral Parliament
Key Constitutional Competencies	Section 85–88: Promulgate statutes and ratifying international treaties and conventions; Exercise competencies inherent in the functions of Supreme Commander of the Defence Force; Exercise the right of veto; To appoint and swear in the Prime Minister; To declare the state of siege or the state of emergency following authorisation of the National Parliament; To declare war and make peace following a Government proposal, after consultation with the Council of State and the Supreme Council of Defence and Security, under authorisation of the National Parliament.	Section 115–117: Define national policy; Guarantee rights and freedoms of citizens; Ensure public order; Prepare Budget; Submit and draft resolutions to the National Parliament; Council of Ministers: Defines the general guidelines of the government policy; Approve bills and draft resolutions.	Section 95–98: It is incumbent upon the National Parliament to make laws on: Domestic and foreign policy; The borders of the Democratic Republic of East Timor; Rights, freedoms and guarantees; The electoral law and the referendum system; Political parties and associations; The suspension of constitutional guarantees and the declaration of the state of siege and the state of emergency; The defence and security policy; The tax policy; The budget system.

128 *Institutions, leaders and elections*

to make laws. The Constitution states '[t]he National Parliament is the organ of sovereignty of the Democratic Republic of East Timor that represents all Timorese citizens and is vested with legislative supervisory and political decision making powers'.[23] This suggests constitution-drafters considered the legislature the primary representative body of the state and so invested it with legal and political decision-making competencies. National Parliament was to consist of a minimum of 52 and a maximum of 65 representatives, each with a set term of office of five years.

There are a number of advantages with a semi-presidential system. The powers of the President are more limited than in the full presidential system, which is focused on a contest between individual candidates. This power-distribution model can encourage consensus-oriented forms of democracy insofar as political leaders are required to negotiate.[24] Parliamentary systems can promote checks and balances because the executive is at least partly dependent upon the legislature and the President can provide a site of unity and accountability without a significant amount of sovereign power being invested in an individual.[25] The choice of a semi-presidential system was likely influenced by a desire to have a figurehead, and signifies the charismatic legitimacy of former independence leaders in East Timorese politics.[26]

However, a power-sharing system like semi-presidentialism also has the potential to encourage 'political infighting' between the dual power centres of Prime Minister and President.[27,28] In post-conflict states, the question of how to best balance power between the executive and legislative arms of the state is crucial in the design of the institutional framework.[29] While East Timor's President has limited oversight capacities in regard to the activities of the government, s/he possesses a constitutional right to veto a bill if they have a substantive reason to do so, in which case the statute must be reappraised by Parliament. If the legislation is passed by an absolute majority (two-thirds), then the President must pass the statute.[30] While East Timor's Constitution curtails both the legislative powers of the President and rights to hold the Cabinet to account, the President may dismiss the Prime Minister and dissolve Parliament in case of serious institutional crisis (for instance, if the budget is not passed in two consecutive attempts).[31]

Feijó writes that one of the key differences between 'premier-presidential' and 'president-parliamentary' forms of semi-presidentialism is that in president-parliamentary systems, the President is constitutionally permitted to dismiss the government. This bestows more power upon the President than in premier-parliamentary forms.[32] The distinction is important, as 'no premier-presidential democracy has ever been replaced by an authoritarian regime'.[33] Whether East Timor is a president-parliamentary type is debatable: while the President does possess rights to dismiss parliament in institutional crisis under the Constitution, much of the literature infers that East Timor is a 'premier-presidential' form of semi-presidentialism. In practice, the right to dismiss the Prime Minister 'assumes an ambiguous position in the president's arsenal of political competencies'.[34] Hence, Feijó argues its necessary to look beyond a strict hermeneutical

Institutions, leaders and elections 129

analysis of the constitutional text by employing a political analysis of presidential activity, which indicate that East Timor's Presidents have thus far held a 'restrained view' of the constitutional right to dismiss the Prime Minister.[35]

As Reilly notes, presidentialism has been a popular choice in new democracies in Asia because a President can be accountable to voters, act as a unifying figure and allow voters a choice for President and legislature.[36] In East Timor, the presidential role is largely positioned as ceremonial, with the Constitution declaring the role of the President as 'the symbol and guarantor of national independence and unity of the state and of the smooth functioning of democratic institutions'.[37] East Timor's three Presidents, Xanana Gusmão, José Ramos-Horta and Taur Matan Ruak, all possess charismatic legitimacy by virtue of their roles in the resistance and independence movement. This legitimacy heightened the authority and influence of the presidential office despite constitutional limitations.

Semi-presidentialism following transition: contests and crisis (2002–2006)

A semi-presidential system in East Timor could have resulted in a less personalised system of government with an emphasis on power-sharing and consensus rather than majority rule.[38] The first opportunity to test this came with the withdrawal of the UNTAET in 2002. The East Timorese went to the polls to elect a President on 14 April 2002, and although conducted under the UNTAET's authority, efforts to 'Timorise' transition enabled far greater participation of East Timorese in running the elections than the earlier vote for the Constituent Assembly.[39] Xanana Gusmão was the overwhelming favourite, and would have run unopposed if not for Francisco Xavier do Amaral (Timorese Social Democratic Association, ASDT), who declared he was running on democratic principles 'by providing the electorate with a choice'.[40] While officially running as an independent, Gusmão was supported by nine parties.[41] Similar to the Constituent Assembly elections, both presidential candidates committed to a Pact of National Unity ensuring free and fair elections.[42]

Gusmão and do Amaral were praised by the Carter Centre for their civil conduct during their campaigns, which assisted in limiting violence and providing a relatively calm environment before, during and after the elections.[43] Despite allegations that FRETILIN's Mari Alkatiri attempted to encourage voters to submit blank ballots (reflecting the historically tense relationship between Gusmão and FRETILIN), only 3.6 per cent of ballots cast were invalid, and a relatively high 86.3 per cent of eligible voters turned out. In an unsurprising victory, Gusmão attained 301,634 votes (82.68 per cent) while 63,146 votes (17.31 per cent) chose do Amaral.[44] Gusmão won 12 of 13 districts, while do Amaral carried Aileu, which had also supported ASDT in the Constituent Assembly elections.[45] Upon independence on 20 May 2002, the Constituent Assembly transformed itself into the first National Parliament of the Democratic Republic of Timor-Leste. Gusmão was sworn in as East Timor's first President, with Alkatiri becoming East Timor's first Prime Minister.

130 *Institutions, leaders and elections*

Following independence, Shoesmith suggested that the dual leadership system was a destabilising force; while Prime Minister Alkatiri sought to centralise state power, the President's priority 'was 'democratic accountability in a pluralist party system'.[46] Certainly, the first administration of East Timor was characterised in part by the tense balance-of-power between two long-standing rivals.[47] As an independent, President Gusmão assumed the role of a 'moderating power', which Feijó argues is consistent with a 'premier-presidential' form of semi-presidentialism.[48] Constitutionally, law-making responsibilities are held by both Government and the Parliament, however power-sharing arrangements are weighted largely in favour of the executive.[49] A 2006 World Bank report advised East Timor to shift the balance of power by strengthening other key institutions, especially parliament, in order to deter the development of a strong authoritarian state.[50] This was sound advice: between 2002–2006, while Parliament passed an average of 11 laws per year, FRETILIN's Cabinet of Ministers enacted over 80.[51]

In spite of the strong impetus towards democracy, the FRETILIN Government was 'tempted to introduce laws ... that flout[ed] democratic principles'.[52] Their desire to retain popular support and establish political dominance, as demonstrated during the constitution-drafting processes, was instrumental in their attempts to restrict civic space after independence. As Simonsen notes, there was 'a pattern of confrontational and self-preservatory' behaviour by the first Government that was detrimental to the development of democratic policies.[53] Tensions emerged between the democratic aspirations articulated in East Timor's Constitution and FRETILIN's pursuit of dominance. The 'authoritarian tendencies' of FRETILIN highlighted the weaknesses of East Timor's Constitution as it invested too much power in the executive, including unelected Cabinet members, thereby undermining the representative nature of the democratic system.[54,55]

There were several examples of the FRETILIN government attempting to force through legislation, signalling a 'Mozambique-style oppression of opposition and freedom of speech'.[56] In 2006, FRETILIN attempted to re-introduce the Penal Code, a defamation Act from the Indonesian era that would have curtailed political freedom of speech by instituting harsh penalties for defamation of political leaders. This Act was 'seen within opposition circles as intended to silence opposition in the country prior to the 2007 legislative and presidential elections'.[57] Alkatiri also attempted to boycott *Suara Timore Lorosae*, the biggest newspaper in East Timor.[58] Siapno reports these laws would have been 'wide-ranging, arbitrarily applied, and elastic', essentially curtailing citizens' democratic rights to freedom of opposition, speech and expression, which are requisite conditions for the functioning of a democratic system.[59] The Act was ultimately vetoed by President Gusmão.[60]

Simonsen argues the Alkatiri government 'on numerous occasions acted to alienate non-FRETILIN actors in a way that the country ... [could] ill afford'.[61] Personal leadership style was a significant factor in FRETILIN's attempts to institute a strong executive. During the Alkatiri administration, contests between leaders and political parties were largely shaped by their past relationships

Institutions, leaders and elections 131

during the independence movement, in particular between the moderate (under Xanana Gusmão) and leftist FRETILIN under Mari Alkatiri.[62] Leadership contests in fragile states can affect the workings of key democratic institutions; in East Timor, the executive branch sought to limit the influence of President Gusmão. It is worth bearing in mind that transitioning states with weak legislatures and strong executives tend to score lower on Freedom House rankings for political rights and civil liberties as the parliament has limited capacities to provide an adequate check on the power of the executive.[63]

This initial risk period in East Timor's new democracy highlights the importance of the behaviours, activities and values of elites. The need for elites to support the democratisation project is well recognised in the transitional literature. In 'competitive authoritarian' regimes, democratic mechanisms might be in place, but key players can manipulate political processes to create a façade of democracy. Levitsky and Way identify a number of regimes, including Cambodia's, that have 'elections without democracy'; that is, where civil liberties are limited, civil society and media constrained, systems of patronage, electoral 'irregularities' and fraud subvert the will of the people and campaigns of violence and intimidation undermine the legitimacy of electoral processes.[64] Cambodian elections in 2013 were reported to demonstrate serious voting irregularities, intimidation of opposition and suppression of civil liberties and press freedoms.[65] It is the political activities and motivations of elected leaders and party elites that constrain or enable the capacities of state institutions to make democracy work.

In East Timor, authoritarian tendencies within FRETILIN's leadership were put to an end in 2006 during a political crisis. On 17 May 2002, United Nations Security Council Resolution 1410 (2002) had replaced the UNTAET with the United Nations Mission of Support in East Timor (UNMISET) to assist the new state with 'core administrative functions', law and order and maintenance of internal and external security.[66] The UNMISET was replaced on 20 May 2005 by the significantly smaller United Nations Office in Timor-Leste (UNOTIL), which meant East Timor became responsible for ensuring its own internal security operations.[67]

A security crisis emerged when members of the 'Petitioners Group', comprising 591 national army soldiers (of 1,400), protested against perceived positive discrimination towards ex-Falintil soldiers from the East in February 2006.[68] After refusing to return to their barracks, the petitioners were fired for desertion by the Alkatiri government.[69,70] Divisions between *Lorosa'e* (Easterners) and *Loromonu* (Westerners) intensified as youth gangs and martial arts groups committed acts of violence.[71] The 2006 United Nations Independent Special Commission of Inquiry for Timor-Leste found that a divisive speech made by Xanana Gusmão contributed to the tensions between East and West, which were exacerbated when Alkatiri ordered troops to shoot at the protesters on 28 March 2006.[72] East Timorese police were unable to control the ensuing violence. Over 400 members of the East Timorese military took up arms in April 2006 to protest the firings and demand an investigation into claims of discrimination, leading to violent clashes with government troops and police in Dili.[73]

132   Institutions, leaders and elections

In late May, nine people died and 27 were wounded after members of the military opened fire on the central police compound.[74] Over 1,600 houses were destroyed and 150,000 people displaced during the riots.[75]

The UN Commission of Inquiry highlighted the shortcomings of East Timor's security institutions and the decisions made by key actors within them, including the Chief of the Defence Force, future President Taur Matan Ruak.[76] Trindade suggests that:

> the East Timorese hierarchical social structure only allows room for one leader whom they follow and obey. Having two leaders, without clear roles and proper traditional legitimacy, has divided society and resulted in violent disputes between members ... the 2006 crisis may have resulted from the fact that wrong leaders were installed at the national level from 2002 to 2006 without proper local legitimacy.[77]

For Trindade, traditional legitimacy is perceived as 'proper' as elections are so 'alien' they cannot provide leaders with rational-legal legitimacy, hence the crisis is explained through a prism of legitimacy deficit.[78] This perspective, however, tends to emphasise democracy's 'foreignness' in spite of the long-standing aspirations for democratic rights and freedoms. There is a risk period in new democracies when independence fails to rapidly translate into the attainment of the full suite of promised individual socio economic rights due to the political and practical realities of governing a low-income, developing state. The protests were 'a lightning rod' for a 'range of disaffected groups with grievances over the high level of unemployment and other concerns about the lack of democratic responsiveness of the Alkatiri administration'.[79] The riots can hence be interpreted as an expression of frustration that the social democratic aspirations of the independence movement were not immediately realisable.[80]

The riots were partly a method of resistance to the measures taken by FRETILIN to shore up its political position by instituting undemocratic laws and violating key civil rights of citizens. While East Timor supported the establishment of a democracy, the presence of political violence in 2006 implies that rule of law had not yet consolidated, democratic behaviours were not inculcated and there remained a lack of trust in political elites and structures. The FRETILIN government was empowered by an institutional design weighted in favour of the executive and it turned increasingly authoritarian in order to quell the political unrest.[81]

During and after the riots, concerns were raised about the capacities of East Timor to ensure effective governance. Much of the rhetoric pointed to the possibility of East Timor becoming a failed state unable to control affairs within their sovereign jurisdiction.[82] These claims now appear premature, and overlooked the centuries it took for Western democracies to consolidate institutions and limit political violence.[83] While it was clear that East Timor's security challenges were impeding its abilities to make its independence 'real', this also indicates that the international community withdrew before East Timor's security institutions were sufficiently developed. On 26 May 2006, international

Institutions, leaders and elections   133

assistance from Australia, New Zealand and Portugal in the form of the International Stabilisation Force (ISF) was provided at the request of the government to improve the security situation.[84] On 31 May, employing his constitutional powers under Section 85, President Gusmão declared a state of emergency and took control of East Timor's security institutions.[85]

On 11 June 2006, East Timorese leaders requested assistance from the United Nations, and on 25 August, UN Security Council Resolution 1704 (2006) established the United Nations Integrated Mission in Timor-Leste (UNMIT).[86] The new mission comprised peace-keeping, peacebuilding, humanitarian and development actors. The mandate mainly focused on security, humanitarian assistance, assisting with institutional strengthening and 'enhancing a culture of democratic governance'.[87] The language emphasised 'support' and 'assistance', presumably in an attempt to avoid charges of neo-colonialism, even though the request for international assistance was made through an exercise of sovereign authority. On 20 June, President Gusmão requested the Prime Minister to stand down amid claims that Alkatiri knew his Interior Minister Rogerio Lobato had illegally provided weapons to civilians, threatening his own resignation two days later if Alkatiri did not comply.[88] Although constitutionally permitted to dismiss the Prime Minister, President Gusmão behaved as though East Timor's Constitution had established a 'premier-presidential' subtype of semi-presidentialism by refusing to implement this power.[89] Alkatiri resigned on 26 June, replaced by Foreign Minister José Ramos-Horta, who was sworn in two weeks later as interim Prime Minister.[90] Priority was given to restoring public order, with the East Timorese leadership engaging in 'national dialogue and political reconciliation', including a dialogue commission in November 2006 and a peace ceremony on 10 December. The government-led '*Simu-Malu*' community dialogue addressed social fragmentation and led to a reduction in violence, indicating the significance of regaining the support of the general population.[91]

The uneven dynamics between the executive and legislature during the first administration impacted upon East Timor's capacity to consolidate and maintain democratic structures. Local specifics mattered for political relationships and stability, as highly diverse groups – including resistance veterans, members of the East Timorese diaspora and civil society actors – competed for power and influence. It also reflects the power of FRETILIN in establishing the Constitution and the particular choices the party made in order to enhance their authority following the achievement of independence. Although the Constitution has a strong democratic and human rights focus, it was also skewed in favour of FRETILIN, who, prior to the 2006 crisis, had expected to become the dominant political party in East Timor's independent democracy.

The electoral system

The type of electoral system matters for the establishment and consolidation of political parties and the balance of power between them. Majoritarian electoral systems tend to see a strong two-party political system develop, while Proportional

134 *Institutions, leaders and elections*

Representation (PR) systems are more likely to produce a broader range of small parties representing diverse interests. According to Mackie, democracy 'is hardly meaningful without strongly rooted political parties that will extend political participation in public policy deliberations beyond the formalities of elections and parliamentary debates down to the grass-roots level'.[92] Popular loyalty to political parties is important for interest aggregation as well as for consolidating 'the ways in which political behaviour comes to be normally channelled'.[93] Healthy competition between political parties is important for limiting the dominance of a single party.

Elections are described in East Timor's Constitution as the 'organised expression of the popular will', consistent with a Schumpeterian process-oriented view. Regular elections give citizens the power to accept or reject representatives, and validate the rights of the elected to make political decisions on behalf of the nation.[94] Hence, a critical component in assessing the health of a democracy is whether peaceful transfers of power occur that accurately reflect election results, and the open possibility that government can and will change. As Gill points out, democratisation cannot occur without liberalisation: that is, individual civil and political liberties, free media and civil society, freedom from violence and intimidation must be protected, and debate, information sharing and contestation freely permitted.[95]

Section 47 of the Constitution outlines 'that every citizen has the right to vote and to be elected'.[96] Voting is described in the Constitution as a 'civic duty', and active and direct political participation is cited as necessary for consolidating democratic processes.[97] East Timor's Constitution prescribes that members of Parliament and the President be elected through regular and secret ballots every five years, with presidential elections being held separately.[98] All people older than 17 hold an equal vote in East Timorese democracy, which is essential because all people hold equal rights to self-determination.[99] These electoral features are consistent with the expectations of democratic institutions held by East Timorese independence leaders.

Representative structures are designed to protect the rights and freedoms of people and promote responsibility and consultation: if politicians seek to return to office, they must represent the interests of their constituents and avoid implementing programs citizens oppose.[100] Regular elections promote ownership and allow citizens a sense of political self-determination, which is important to protecting freedoms and rights as policies and laws can have far-reaching impacts on the social and economic circumstances of people. Liberal-democratic theorists have long argued that individuals are the best judge of their own interests, and the role of governments is to safeguard rights and liberties so they can pursue 'the good life'.[101] This assumes a basic level of political consciousness among people, and a belief in rationality. The relationship between states and citizens is central here as the power of the government is justified by their capacity to protect the rights of citizens.

East Timor employs a 'party list' Proportional Representation (PR) electoral system for electing Parliament as outlined in Section 65:4 of the Constitution

Institutions, leaders and elections 135

and Law No. 6/2006.[102] The PR system works on the principle that the number of seats accorded to a political party are proportional to the percentage of votes that the party attained, as citizens vote for parties, not individuals. In East Timor's plurinominal 'party-list' PR system, the entire country is considered a single constituency: political parties list their candidates and seats are filled from the party list. In contrast, majoritarian electoral systems require a simple majority of the votes for an individual to be elected to a seat.[103] While PR systems tend to produce a 'fairer' reflection of the votes cast, majoritarian systems tend to assure a one-party executive.[104]

Table 5.3 highlights the strengths and weaknesses of each system in relation to key democratic norms of representation, accountability, equality, effectiveness and participation. One of the advantages of a PR system is that it is inclusive: it allows representation of a plurality of interests in the legislature and encourages the development of a 'multi-party' democracy. It can enable smaller parties to be represented in parliament, which is beneficial for new states such as East Timor, given that 'the inclusion of all significant groups in the parliament can be an important condition for democratic consolidation'.[105] Proportional Representation systems can improve national unity by allowing minorities to gain a seat in parliament. As Reynolds and Carey note, even small parties should be able 'to win a measure of representation ... for the assembly to reflect the diversity of society'.[106,107] Table 5.3 demonstrates how the electoral systems are likely to impact upon key democratic indicators.

Majoritarian electoral systems tend to produce two dominant political parties as the 50 per cent threshold makes it difficult for smaller parties to win seats. In two-party systems, there is a tendency to alternate between the two dominant parties, who have roughly similar chances of winning government power. Often the party that is in power, after receiving a majority of the votes, is able to rule by itself and implement its programs without compromising or bargaining with other parties (as is necessary in coalition governments). This suggests that majoritarian electoral systems produce more stable governance, even if PR systems are considered more reflective of the distribution of preferences within the voting population.

Regan criticised the decision to implement a PR electoral system in East Timor, predicting it would probably entrench the power of FRETILIN.[108] This position views PR as potentially consolidating the power of a dominant party by encouraging the creation of many small but ineffective parties incapable of forming government in their own right. In Cambodia, for instance, the PR system – originally mandated under the Paris Peace Accords and subsequently enacted through electoral law in 1998 – has entrenched the CCP's grip on power. Although the CCP has not always achieved over 50 per cent of the vote in elections (for instance, they attained 49 per cent in 2013), no other party or coalition has a large enough support base to provide substantial opposition, or to challenge the CCP's complex network of patronage, control over state machinery and military support.[109]

However, PR systems do have the capacity to produce coalition governments and consensus-oriented forms of democracy, whereas majoritarianism tends to

Table 5.3 Choosing an electoral system

Democratic norms	Representation	Accountability	Equality	Participation	Effectiveness
PR	Enables greater access to parliament for interest and minority groups. Representation is not based on geography and local interests, which could lead to alienation of rural population.	No members of parliament representing distinct geographic areas, thus no local member for citizens to hold to account.	More likely to enable smaller parties to represent in parliament. Can enable a diverse range of people to access political office.	Enhances participation by increasing potential for small parties to have a voice. More likely to be consensus-driven than adversarial.	Tend to lead to coalition governments, which can create instability and deadlocked parliaments. Can lead to national unity and stability by allowing minorities to gain seats in parliament.
Majoritarian	Each region has an elected representative. Tends to lead to two major powers which can alienate special interest groups.	Citizens can hold local representatives to account.	System tends to favour 'majority' group.	Can enable participation at a 'grassroots' level. Can limit participation of minorities and special interest groups. Can create an adversarial rather than consensus-driven environment.	Tends to create stable two-party systems with strong governments. Can create disunity if minority groups experience disadvantage.

Institutions, leaders and elections   137

produce a more adversarial system.[110] Roberts suggests that ideals of consensus and comprise do not sit comfortably with Cambodia's culture of all-or-nothing approaches to political rule, and that this dynamic should have been recognised prior to mandating PR in the PPA.[111] In PR, political parties are encouraged to negotiate and co-operate in the design of policy and legislation, although it can also produce deadlocked parliaments and unstable government coalitions.[112] As the following section highlights, the evidence that PR systems produce consensus-driven politics is mixed in East Timor as multi-party political competition has retained its position as a primary – and necessary – feature of democratic politics.

2007 elections

Following the violence in 2006, the 2007 elections 'held out hope of a new beginning' as the East Timorese shared an optimistic belief that elections would provide a democratic fix to social problems.[113] With the UNMIT's assistance, East Timor successfully conducted one parliamentary and two presidential elections in 2007. The first round of presidential elections was held on 9 April 2007 amid relatively peaceful conditions.[114] Many of the candidates were former leaders of the independence movement, including José Ramos-Horta (running as an independent), Fernando 'Lasama' de Araújo (Democratic Party, PD), Francisco 'Lú Olo' Guterres (FRETILIN) and João Carrascalão (Timorese Democratic Union, UDT).[115] Incumbent Xanana Gusmão did not run, but his opponent from the 2002 presidential elections, Francisco Xavier do Amaral (ASDT), did.

As set out in Law No. 7/2006, electing the President is rather straightforward compared with the PR system.[116] In the first round of voting, the candidate with over 50 per cent of the vote becomes President. If no candidate achieves a 50 per cent majority, a second round is held between the two candidates who attained the highest number of votes, and the candidate who attains over 50 per cent of the vote becomes President.[117] A total of 81.79 per cent of enrolled East Timorese voters participated in the first round of the presidential elections.[118] FRETILIN representative Francisco 'Lú Olo' Guterres achieved the highest percentage of votes with 27.89 per cent, followed by José Ramos-Horta with 21.8 per cent.[119] Lú Olo proved most popular in the three Eastern districts, Baucau, Lautem and Viqueque, in which FRETILIN retained strong support.[120] In the other nine districts, however, support for Lú Olo was significantly lower: his next best result was just over 20 per cent in two seats. Meanwhile, Ramos-Horta was popular in central-north districts, including Dili.[121]

The second round of elections were held one month later, on 9 May 2007, recording 81 per cent of the 524,073 registered voters in East Timor.[122] As expected, Lú Olo again achieved a majority in the three Eastern districts of Baucau, Lautem and Viqueque.[123] However, his vote only increased by 2.93 per cent nationally to 30.82 per cent (127,342).[124] In contrast, most citizens who voted for other candidates in the first round funnelled their votes to José Ramos-Horta, lifting his vote by 47.37 per cent to 69.18 per cent of votes (285,835).[125]

138 *Institutions, leaders and elections*

Given the crisis of 2006, the peaceful 2007 presidential elections and transfer of power represented an overwhelming democratic success.[126]

On 30 June 2007, the Democratic Republic of Timor-Leste held its first set of parliamentary elections. Similar to the independence ballot in 1999 and the elections for the Constituent Assembly in 2001, the East Timorese once again demonstrated their 'general enthusiasm for democratic politics' and the atmosphere before and during the vote was generally calm and peaceful.[127] The National Electoral Commission (CNE) received only 83 complaints across East Timor, with 29 sent to the Office of the Public Prosecutor. Many of these complaints were submitted by political parties against other political parties.[128] Of 529,189 total registered voters, 426,210 turned out to vote in 708 polling booths which formal records represented as 80.5 per cent of eligible voters.[129] However, Leach suggests that there was some doubling up of voter registrations, lifting the actual participation rate to the low 90 per cent range, a significant figure compared with other democracies.[130] Each party submitted a list of 65 candidates and 25 alternative candidates, meaning a total of 910 candidates were listed, a large number for a population totalling just over one million people.[131] Due to electoral Law 6/2006 stipulating that parties must meet a 3 per cent threshold, 14 political parties contested the elections but only 9 parties obtained at least one of the 65 seats on offer.[132] Consequently, only 91.09 per cent of voters were actually represented by a member in parliament.

The results confirmed predictions that East Timor's PR electoral systems would encourage multiple parties and require a coalition government. Fears of a shift toward authoritarianism were allayed as FRETILIN haemorrhaged votes in 2007, receiving less than one third of votes compared to 54.7 per cent in 2001 (Table 5.4). This drop was largely due to widespread dissatisfaction over issues such as political corruption, the 'petitioners' issues and restrictions on civil freedoms, which had earlier culminated in the 2006 riots.[133] This percentage translated into 21 parliamentary seats using the *d'Hondt* system of highest averages, which was not sufficient for FRETILIN to form government outright.[134] Prior to the election, FRETILIN had hoped to retain power: however the newly constructed *Conselho Nacional de Reconstrução do Timor/* National Congress for the Reconstruction of Timor-Leste (CNRT) party, a rebadged version of the National Council for Timorese Resistance, was not far behind FRETILIN with 24.1 per cent of votes.[135] Led by former President Xanana Gusmão, CNRT formed the Alliance for Parliamentary Majority (AMP) coalition with the Coalition of the East Timorese Social Democratic Association and the Social Democratic Party (ASDT-PSD, 16 per cent) and the Democratic Party (11.3 per cent, up from 8.7 per cent in 2001) in order to secure a majority.[136] Later, UNDERTIM – a political party that refused to recognise the Constitution and regards the East Timorese state 'as an illegitimate expression of the independence struggle' – also joined the AMP, taking the coalition to five parties.[137] Of the 65 seats available, 18 were accorded to female politicians, which represented just over the legislated quota threshold of 1 in 4.[138]

Table 5.4 East Timor parliamentary election results, 2007

Party	Eligible votes (%)	Eligible votes (#)	Seats
UNDERTIM (*Unidade Nacional Democrática da Resistência*/National Democratic Unity of Timorese Resistance)	3.19	13,247	2
CNRT (*Congresso Nacional Para a Reconstrução de Timor-Leste*/National Congress for the Reconstruction of Timor-Leste)	24.10	100,175	18
PR (*Partido Republikanu*/Republican Party)	1.06	4,408	0
PDRT (*Partido Democrática Republica de Timor*/Democratic Republic of Timor-Leste Party)	1.86	7,718	0
PDC (*Partido Democrática Cristão*/Christian Democratic Party)	1.03	4,300	0
UDT (*União Democrática Timorense*/Timorese Democratic Union)	0.90	3,753	0
PD (*Partido Democrático*/Democratic Party)	11.30	46,946	8
PMD (*Partido Milénio Democrático*/Millennium Democratic Party)	0.69	2,878	0
PST (*Partido Socialista de Timor*/Socialist Party of Timor)	0.96	3,982	0
ASDT (*Associação Social-Democrata Timorense*/Timorese Social-Democratic Association) – PSD (*Partido Social Democrata*/Social Democratic Party) Coalition	15.73	65,358	11
KOTA (*Klibur Oan Timor Asuwain*) – PPT (*Partido do Povo de Timor*/People's Part of Timor)	3.20	13,294	2
FRETILIN (*Frente Revolucionária de Timor-Leste Independente*/Revolutionary Front for an Independent Timor-Leste)	29.02	120,592	21
PNT (*Partido Nacionalista Timorense*/Timorese Nationalist Party)	2.42	10,057	0
PUN (*Partido Unidada Nacional*/National Unity Party)	4.55	18,896	3
Total		415,604	65

140 *Institutions, leaders and elections*

The 2007 parliamentary elections highlighted the importance of personalities and experience in East Timorese politics, and leaders were legitimised in terms of their credentials in the independence movement. Similar to the formation of political parties in 1974, it was difficult to differentiate the parties according to policy or ideology as many adhered 'to the broad social democratic and human rights goals of the 1998 National Council for Timorese Resistance *Magna Carta*'.[139] The new party, CNRT, which ultimately led the AMP coalition, relied heavily on the charismatic legitimacy of independence leader Xanana Gusmão. McWilliam and Bexley report that leading up to the elections, the CNRT focused on promoting Gusmão as both a resistance hero and statesman.[140] Similarly, FRETILIN President Francisco 'Lú Olo' Guterres was portrayed as a resistance hero, and PD leader Fernando 'La Sama' de Araújo's position as the leader of the clandestine youth organisation RENETIL was emphasised.[141] Smaller parties used their roles in the independence movement to gain votes, including ASDT, whose support rested upon the authority of Francisco Xavier do Amaral, the inaugural President of the first Democratic Republic of Timor-Leste in 1975.[142] Geographic voting patterns highlighted two significant trends: the importance of resistant movement allegiances to the 2007 elections, and the divisions between East and West that partly drove the 2006 political crisis. Citizens in the East – long considered FRETILIN heartland – continued to show strong support for FRETILIN, and it subsequently achieved a majority in Viqueque and Baucau, and nearly half of all votes cast in Lautem. To vote otherwise was perceived by many voters as an act of betrayal.[143] Conversely, the Western districts of Bobonaro, Covalima and Liquiça oversaw a heavy decline in FRETILIN's vote from 2001.

The formation of a coalition government did not immediately lead to a consensus-driven parliament. Under East Timor's Constitution, the newly elected President, José Ramos Horta, possessed extended constitutional powers to nominate a government in circumstances where a clear majority was not achieved by any party.[144] On 10 July, FRETILIN leader Mari Alkatiri supported an inclusive government, and reports by Leach suggest that some ground was made regarding the 'government of national unity'.[145] Ramos-Horta gave the parties until 25 July to agree on the composition of government, but by the time parliament was sworn in on 30 July, there was still no government.[146] Citing the defeat of a FRETILIN candidate by PD member Fernando 'La Sama' de Araújo as President of Parliament, and the overall balance-of-power, President Ramos-Horta announced on 3 August that he would request the CNRT to form government on 6 August.[147] On 8 August, Xanana Gusmão was sworn in as Prime Minister.

Section 106:1 of East Timor's Constitution states:

> '[t]he Prime Minister shall be designated by the political party or alliance of political parties with parliamentary majority and shall be appointed by the President of the Republic, after consultation with the political parties sitting in the National Parliament'.[148]

Institutions, leaders and elections 141

In opposition, FRETILIN argued they should have been approached first, as they attained the highest percentage of the vote, and declared the new Government unconstitutional and illegitimate.[149] FRETILIN's central committee threatened to boycott parliament and supported a 'civil uprising'.[150] Leach predicted the Court of Appeal would 'favour President Ramos-Horta's interpretation, as Proportional Representation systems normally require parliamentary alliances to guarantee majorities, and political stability'; however, this was not tested as FRETILIN did not mount a legal challenge.[151] The 2007 parliamentary election result in East Timor highlighted some of the difficulties that can occur in multi-party systems where clear majorities are unusual and government must be negotiated.

Following the result, a number of FRETILIN supporters participated in political violence by burning down houses, and a small number of deaths were recorded.[152] Post-election violence was recorded in Eastern districts, with around 150 houses burnt, as a manifestation of the disappointment felt by many FRETILIN supporters.[153] In Dili, the International Stabilisation Force managed to contain any political violence within several days.[154] By October, the violence had subsided and the AMP was able to implement relatively stable government. The issue of who would govern was ultimately resolved within the parameters of the Constitution, which was a positive sign for rule of law. However, political violence re-appeared in East Timor in February 2008 when a renegade group of petitioners headed by Alfredo Reinado shot President Ramos-Horta three times and attempted to ambush Prime Minister Gusmão's house.[155] While Ramos-Horta survived the attack and soon resumed his position as President, the pursuit of the rebel group, alongside various unresolved issues stemming from the 2006 crisis, distracted the new AMP government for much of 2008.[156]

Writing soon after the 2007 election, McWilliam and Bexley observed that 'the efforts to create a stable, democratic and prosperous East Timor ... [were] frequently undermined by regressive and destructive oppositional political agendas'.[157] In some ways this observation was quite prescient, as internal spats between the AMP over its five-year period of government appeared, at times, to threaten the durability of government. In 2008, Francisco Xavier do Amaral suggested he would withdraw the ASDT from the AMP, but ultimately continued to support it.[158] Deputy Prime Minister and PSD member Mário Carrascalão resigned in 2010, and threats were made by Foreign Minister Zacarais da Costa to resign in the same year. Shoesmith laid the blame at Gusmão's feet, arguing that AMP's internal divisions were 'provoked by a prime minister who is impatient with his coalition partners'.[159] This is problematic in some respects: for example, in offering further evidence to his claim that Xanana Gusmão was actively campaigning against the PSD, Shoesmith states that Justice Minister Lucia Lobato 'claimed in July 2011 that the prime minister was moving against her as well'.[160] However, journalist José Antonio Belo exposed mobile phone text messages sent by Lobato in 2008 as evidence of corrupt deal making.

An anti-corruption commission was established in 2009 to deal with the collusion, corruption and nepotism allegations that threatened to engulf the AMP (and Gusmão himself, who was implicated in a multi-million dollar contract

142 *Institutions, leaders and elections*

awarded to a company part-owned by his daughter). It had its first success with Lobato's guilty verdict and five-year sentence.[161] In light of this context, it appears appropriate that a prime minister would 'move against' members of parliament making corrupt deals. The Anti-Corruption Commission was necessary for dealing with corruption, which was almost inevitably going to be an issue in a small, fragile new democracy relying significantly upon oil and gas profits. Corruption, clientelism and graft are well recognised as undermining democratic development in other Southeast Asian states. Corruption continues to represent a significant risk to democratic consolidation: reports in late November 2014 emerged of Xanana Gusmão's protection of potentially corrupt Finance Minister Emilia Pires and the parliamentary sacking of independent members of the judiciary.[162]

While Shoesmith argues that multi-party politics generally fails to provide effective government or democratic representation in new, post-colonial states, he concedes that during the period of the AMP administration, East Timor was 'at least a partial success in sustaining competitive, multi-party politics'.[163] More optimistically, United Nations Secretary-General bi-annual reports on the United Nations Integrated Mission in Timor-Leste over the five-year period of the AMP government emphasised the efforts of political leaders, particularly President Ramos-Horta, in creating community dialogues that enhanced reconciliation. The reports consistently contained references to the good work of FRETILIN in its role as opposition, despite its persistent descriptions of the AMP as an unconstitutional 'de facto' government.[164]

Elections in 2012

The United Nations Secretary-General reports from 2009, 2010 and 2011 consistently pointed to the relative political stability and calm in East Timor following the assassination attempts in early 2008.[165] Even by December 2008, 87 per cent of the 1,120 surveyed in a country-wide opinion poll reported 'feeling safer in their communities compared to 2006', and by October 2009, the UN Secretary-General reported that 'substantial progress' had been made on the issue of internally displaced people from the 2006 crisis.[166] Hence, the successes of the AMP government included increasing security across Timor-Leste, which corresponded with 'improvements across a range of human development indicators'.[167] However, there were still fears among the public regarding unemployed youth and gang violence, particularly in Dili.[168] The 2012 parliamentary elections were a key test of democratic consolidation in East Timor, as these were the second set of elections following independence, and, crucially, the first in which East Timorese actors – led by the CNE and Technical Secretariat for Electoral Administration (STAE) – would in effect single-handedly coordinate the technical aspects of electoral processes. International actors, such as UNMIT, possessed a supporting role and were mainly responsible for responding to any major violations and monitoring electoral processes to ensure international legitimacy of the ballot.[169]

Institutions, leaders and elections 143

On 17 March 2012, the first round of presidential elections were held. Thirteen candidates were listed on the ballot, and similar to 2007, many of them were key players in the independence movement.[170] They included Fernando 'La Sama' de Araújo (PD), José Luis Guterres (former exiled FRETILIN representative during the independence movement, now representing FRETILIN splinter group FRENTI-Mudança), incumbent José Ramos-Horta and Francisco Xavier do Amaral, who had contested all three parliamentary elections in East Timor (he died before the first round). FRETILIN's President Francisco 'Lú Olo' Guterres, who lost the second round of presidential elections in 2007, also contested the presidential election, alongside a new candidate, the former resistance leader José Maria de Vasconcelos, better known as Taur Matan Ruak. He had been the last Commander of the FALINTIL from 1998, and served as the Commander of FALINTIL-*Forças de Defesa de Timor-Leste* following independence. He had previously been identified by the United Nations as 'having illegally distributed guns to civilians'.[171] While he was once close to FRETILIN, and retained his popularity among FRETILIN supporters, he was supported by CNRT and Prime Minister Xanana Gusmão.

A total of 489,933 East Timorese turned out to vote in the first round of the elections, representing 78.20 per cent of the voting population.[172] Similar to 2007, Lú Olo achieved the highest number of votes in the first round with 28.76 per cent.[173] Not far behind was Taur Matan Ruak with 25.71 per cent, a result that was partly due to his endorsement by Xanana Gusmão.[174] The incumbent, José Ramos-Horta, and PD leader, La Sama, were third and fourth with over 17 per cent each, disqualifying them from the second round. The rest of the field polled quite low, with many attaining less than 1 per cent of the vote.[175]

As neither Lú Olo nor Taur Matan Ruak achieved a minimum 50 per cent of all votes, a second round of elections was held on 16 April 2012. A slightly lower number of voters turned out for the second round, with the official record showing a 73.12 per cent turnout, although a number of 'eligible' voters were actually deceased, rendering participation rates more likely around 80 per cent.[176] Once again, past allegiances played a determining role in the results of the first round of presidential elections. The number of votes attained by Lú Olo in the second round – 38.77 per cent nationally (174,879) – was higher than in the second round of the 2007 presidential elections (30.82 per cent).[177] In the East, Lú Olo achieved a majority of votes in Baucau and Viqueque, and over 49 per cent in Lautem.[178] Taur Matan Ruak, on the other hand, achieved over 70 per cent of the vote in three districts, and over 60 per cent in five districts, achieving an overall vote of 61.23 per cent nationally.[179] At least two international observer group noted that the 2012 elections 'very substantially met internationally recognised standards for free and fair elections at the venues observed' and confirmed East Timor's capacities to run elections independently.[180] The atmosphere was reported by the UNMIT Human Rights and Transitional Justice Section as mostly calm, although there were some reports of intimidation.[181] On 20 May 2012, the same day that East Timor celebrated its ten-year anniversary as a sovereign democratic state, Taur Matan Ruak was sworn in as its third President.

144 *Institutions, leaders and elections*

The two rounds of presidential elections were 'generally well-conducted and peaceful', largely because political leaders 'sent out the right signals' regarding appropriate democratic behaviour.[182] For instance, long-time rivals Xanana Gusmão and Mari Alkatiri had improved their political relationship in the year leading to the elections.[183] Furthermore, on 10 February, the CNE launched the 'Pact for Peaceful Elections 2012', which ran until 28 February, which included consultations in all 13 districts involving representatives of political parties, members of civil society organisations, traditional leaders, *suco* council members and representatives from security institutions.[184] On the last day, members of the political parties signed an agreement committing themselves to encouraging peace and stability in East Timor during the election campaign. As the European Union Election Observation Mission suggested, political stability and increased familiarity with electoral processes was conducive to the institutionalisation of democratic political culture in East Timor.[185]

Leading up to the parliamentary elections, key campaign issues included infrastructure development, arguments around fiscal responsibility versus public spending of gas and oil revenues, corruption, and, importantly for a fledgling social democracy, wealth distribution and social welfare. While some observers inferred that the CNRT attempted to use its incumbency as an unfair advantage through government spending program such as the elderly and veterans pension scheme, this actually reflects the purpose of elections. By investing heavily in the 'widely popular cash transfer scheme' to the elderly and veterans, the AMP attempted to demonstrate their social democratic credentials to the East Timorese population. According to a report by the United Nations Secretary-General, both the presidential and parliamentary campaigns activities involved rallies, door-to-door campaigns and community dialogues, all of which took place in 'a calm environment, with no serious campaign-related security incidents', partly because candidates frequently appealed for peace and stability.[186]

The parliamentary elections were held on 7 July 2012, with 75.2 per cent of East Timorese eligible citizens turning out to vote, a relatively high percentage given this was the third election for the year.[187] Twenty-one political parties or coalitions contested the parliamentary elections, although the two main contenders were CNRT and FRETILIN, and many of the other parties were not expected to achieve above the 3 per cent threshold.[188] As the Table 5.5 below indicates, in the 2012 parliamentary elections, CNRT improved its percentage of the vote from 24.1 to 36.66, and FRETILIN also improved by less than 1 per cent to 29.87. In contrast to the 2007 parliamentary elections, CNRT achieved the highest number of votes of any party, including FRETILIN. Only two other parties, PD and the new splinter party FRENTI-Mudança, achieved above the 3 per cent threshold necessary to attain seats, whereas in 2007, nine political parties achieved above this threshold. This could be explained by an increase in the number of parties contesting the vote: while 14 parties and coalitions participated in 2007, there were 21 options in 2012, which meant votes were more thinly spread across minor parties. Using the *d'Hondt* method of seat distribution, these percentages translated into 30 seats for the CNRT, 25 for FRETILIN, eight for PD and two for FRENTI-Mudança.

Table 5.5 Parliamentary election results, July 2012

Party	Votes (%)	Votes (#)	Seats
UDT (*União Democrática Timorense*/Timorese Democratic Union)	1.13	5,332	
PR (*Partido Republikanu*/Republican Party)	0.91	4,270	
PDN (*Partido Desenvolvimento Nacional*/National Development Party)	1.99	9,386	
AD (Democratic Alliance): KOTA (Klibur Oan Timor Asuwain/Association of Timorese Heroes) – Trabhalista	0.56	2,622	
PUN (*Partido Unidada Nacional*/National Unity Party)	0.68	3,191	
PD (*Partido Democrático*/Democratic Party)	10.31	48,581	8
PTD (*Partido Timorense Democrática*/Democratic Timorese Party)	0.54	2,561	
PSD (*Partido Social Democrata*/Social Democratic Party)	2.15	10,158	
FRENTI-Mudança (*Frente de Reconstrução Nacional de Timor-Leste-Mudança*/Front of National Reconstruction of Timor-Leste)	3.11	14,648	2
KHUNTO (*Partido Kmanek Haburas Unidade Nacional Timor*/Timor National Unity Better Growing Party)	2.97	13,998	
CNRT (*Congresso Nacional Para a Reconstrução de Timor-Leste*/National Congress for the Reconstruction of Timor-Leste)	36.66	172,831	30
FRETILIN (*Frente Revolucionária de Timor-Leste Independente*/Revolutionary Front for an Independent Timor-Leste)	29.87	140,789	25
PDP (*Partidu Ba Dezenolvimentu Populár*/People's Development Party)	0.40	1,904	
Bloko Proklamador	0.66	3,125	
ASDT (*Associação Social-Democrata Timorense*/Timorese Social-Democratic Association)	1.80	8,487	
PST (*Partido Socialista de Timor*/Socialist Party of Timor)	2.41	11,379	
PDC (*Partido Democrática Cristão*/Christian Democratic Party)	0.19	887	
PDL (*Partido Democrático Liberal*/Democratic Liberal Party)	0.47	2,222	
APMT (*Associação Popular Monarquia Timorense*/Timorese Monarchy Popular Association)	0.84	3,968	
UNDERTIM (*Unidade Nacional Democrática da Resistência*/National Democratic Unity of Timorese Resistance)	1.49	7,041	
PLPA-PDRT (*Partido Liberta Povu Aileba*/Aileba People's Liberty Party – *Partido Democratica Republica de Timor*/Democratic Republic of Timor-Leste Party)	0.85	4,012	
TOTAL		471,389 (75.2% of registered voters)	65

146   *Institutions, leaders and elections*

Following the election, there was a week of uncertainty 'where any of several permutations' – including a CNRT-FRETILIN coalition – seemed possible.[189] According to East Timorese newspaper *Tempo Semanal*, Alkatiri approached Gusmão about the possibility of FRETILIN forming a coalition government with the CNRT.[190] In response, Gusmão announced at a CNRT national conference in Dili on 15 July that he would rather the CNRT be strong in opposition than form a coalition with FRETILIN, indicating a belief that opposition is crucial for democracy.[191] Even though they failed to achieve the stand-alone majority that they sought, the 2012 parliamentary elections constituted a win for the CNRT as they negotiated a new coalition government with previous partners PD, as well as the new FRENTI-Mudança. The formation of the new governing alliance – named *Bloku Governu Koligasaun*/Government Coalition Bloc (BGK) – did not come with the same opposition by FRETILIN, who had consistently referred to the AMP as an 'unconstitutional' or 'de facto government', primarily because the CNRT attained the highest number of votes. Following the announcement of the BGK, some FRETILIN members engaged in rioting, damaging 63 cars and seven houses, and one person was killed in Hera, just outside of Dili.[192] There were initial concerns that some East Timorese would not accept the validity of the vote. New President Taur Matan Ruak declared: "There is no justification to use violence as a measure to resolve issues. There are political and democratic means to find a way to move forward".[193] These concerns were put aside as normality restored within a matter of days, which highlighted East Timor's improved security capacities and the general recognition that the elections were free and fair.[194] On 8 August 2012, the fifth constitutional government of East Timor was sworn in, with Xanana Gusmão once again becoming Prime Minister of East Timor and PD leader Fernando 'La Sama' de Araújo taking the role of Deputy Prime Minister.[195]

The election constituted a loss for some of the CNRT's former coalition partners, whose votes were subsumed by the CNRT. Three of the four parties that formed the AMP with the CNRT in 2007 achieved no seats in the 2012 parliamentary elections. The citizens who had elected these parties in 2007 appear to have shifted their vote to the CNRT, establishing a new balance of power in East Timor. Shoesmith's fears that East Timor's PR system and the potential for multi-party politics would hinder East Timor's democratisation proved unfounded in the 2012 parliamentary elections, as only four parties achieved above the 3 per cent of the national vote necessary to be accorded a seat. Perhaps surprisingly, given the nature of the PR system, the 2012 elections resulted in East Timor's power-balance resembling a majoritarian two-party system, with CNRT and FRETILIN the dominant parties, followed by PD as a minor but influential third force.

There were no security related incidents recorded on the day of the election and any complaints were dealt with appropriately.[196] Atmosphere on the day was calm, which was due to: first, the recognition by political leaders that peaceful elections would be necessary for the withdrawal of the UN and ISF; second, a zero-tolerance security policy; and, third, the Code of Conduct for Political

Parties and Political Coalitions that most parties signed on 28 February (those who did not were formed after the code was signed).[197] The STAE and CNE had 'considerably strengthened since the 2007 elections', and only minor irregularities in polling operations were recorded.[198] Grass-roots dialogue and civic participation programs, including 45 democratic governance forums held between January and September 2012, also assisted in ensuring peaceful elections.[199] Given these were the first elections conducted by East Timorese state-based bodies, it is premature to judge the consolidation of East Timor democracy; however, there were several positive signs regarding East Timor's democratic transition. These include the consistently high participation rates and voting, the general acceptance of the election results, the success of the electoral management bodies (the STAE and CNE), the normalisation of electoral processes and the management of government formation through constitutional channels. More generally, the United Nations Secretary-General reports that political progress has been made in promoting citizens' constitutional rights and guarantees, including those that assist the advancement of civil society, ensuring constitutional checks and balances, and establishing an 'overarching anti-corruption legal framework', which did assist East Timor in meeting some of the benchmarks relating to transparent governance.[200]

A potential problem emerging from the 2012 election was that nearly 20 per cent of the voting population were not represented in parliament because a large majority of parties did not reach the 3 per cent threshold. The PR system can be problematic because voters do not directly elect district representatives that they can hold accountable, thus creating social distance between representatives and constituents. In majoritarian systems, on the other hand, there are clear links between citizens and their district representatives, as they choose individuals rather than parties. Dionisio Soares argues that 'this is not a system that comes naturally to the East Timorese people and deprives many of them of the opportunity of having elected members representing the particular region of East Timor from which they come'.[201] Proportional Representation systems 'provide little geographic link between voters and their representatives, and thus create difficulties in terms of accountability and responsiveness between elected politicians and the electorate'.[202] Current efforts to decentralise are anticipated to improve representation and have been justified on the basis that local government is 'about making democracy work by enhancing the capacity of the citizens to participate in decision-making processes'.[203]

As the 2007 and 2012 elections demonstrated in East Timor, Proportional Representation electoral systems tend to lead to a more consensus-oriented form of democracy due to the need to form coalitions. Power has been shared between several parties who are forced to produce a consensus.[204] According to Mackie, it is perhaps 'preferable [in East Timor] to create a consensus-oriented pattern of government, as far as possible, rather than a conflictual one'.[205] The strong sense of authority assumed by Gusmão at times restricted consensus-oriented decision-making during the AMP government. This reflected the impact that personalities, behaviour and leadership – established and embedded over the decades of

148 *Institutions, leaders and elections*

campaigning for independence – have on the development and efficacy of political institutions. Political institutions can only work to produce democratic outcomes if they are supported by political leaders and the public. While coalition governments can be problematic and unstable, and may find it difficult to pass legislation, power-sharing arrangements offer benefits in terms of representation, compromise and negotiation, which has been especially useful for balancing the potential dominance of FRETILIN.[206]

The elections further confirmed Xanana Gusmão's assumed charismatic and traditional authority, as the 2012 election campaigns once again appealed to East Timor's military traditions and the status of leaders during the independence and resistance movements.[207] Gusmão's success across three sets of elections also provided him and the CNRT with rational-legal authority. In fact, the International Crisis Group actually listed 'resistance credentials' as a primary campaign issue in the 2012 elections.[208] In a move that reflects consensus rather than adversarial politics, in 2015 Gusmão handed over the Prime Ministership to opposition FRETILIN member and former East Timorese student resistance fighter, Dr Rui Maria de Araújo.[209]

In his swearing-in speech of the sixth constitutional government on 16 February 2015, de Araújo emphasised the importance of 'governing in dialogue' with civil society. He encouraged new forms of consensus government to overcome problems of democratic contest and promised he 'would put the interests of the people above any other partisan interests'.[210] Other representatives of the current East Timorese government have spoken about the need to 'govern in dialogue', and on the international stage has promoted 'infrastructures of peace' that build trust through national consultation and ownership. [211] Minister Agio Pereira argued in an article in *Tempo Semanal* that consensus democracy promotes checks and balances and 'enhances the balance of power through the lens of mutual trust' that is missing in what he describes as 'belligerent democracy'.[212] The 'Dili consensus' that emerged from an international conference hosted by East Timor in 2012 advocated a 'new' development agenda based on priorities formed through 'country-led consultative processes' and sustained political leadership and commitment to realising goals of good governance.[213] The long-term dependence upon Gusmão's leadership suggests that generational change will provide a crucial test to state-based consolidation, and time will tell whether consensus-driven democracy persists in East Timor.

Conclusion

While the Democratic Republic of Timor-Leste has faced significant social, political and economic challenges, there have also been positive signs for the consolidation of democracy. Following both the 2007 and 2012 elections, politicians demonstrated respect for the 2002 Constitution. Linz and Stepan argue that consolidation of democracy (and institutions) occurs when it is largely recognised as the 'only game in town'.[214] There are several indicators that democratic consolidation has occurred: first, the absence of attempts to overthrow governments; second, the

Institutions, leaders and elections 149

overwhelming majority believe political change must occur within democratic frameworks; and third, political conflict is resolved according to established norms. In the ten years since East Timor's achievement of sovereign democratic independence, the new state has faced difficulties in the form of social and political disorder during the 2006 riots and the attempted assassination attempts in 2008. The 2012 elections provided some positive signals in regards to democratic consolidation, including the relative lack of political violence, the effective operation of electoral processes, the supremacy of the Constitution and the protection of citizen's civil and political rights during elections.

East Timor's fledgling democracy has faced institutional weaknesses in terms of the separation of powers and the distribution of responsibilities. Although the National Parliament holds 'a clear mandate and a working organisational system', Shoesmith argues that the division of responsibilities between the distinct state apparatuses has left the executive with too much power and the legislature with not enough.[215] Following independence, East Timor's national Parliament experienced difficulties keeping a check on the powers of the executive, for a variety of reasons, including a lack of legal and political advisors to provide advice to Ministers, as well as the constitutional rights of the executive to enact decree laws that do not have the approval of Parliament.[216] An effective balance of power is necessary for preventing authoritarianism as a weak parliament negatively impacts on the accountability, transparency and representation necessary for a healthy democratic political system.

Notes

1 Mackie, 'Future Political Structures and Institutions in East Timor', 195.
2 March and Olsen, *Rediscovering Institutions*, 17.
3 Kingsbury, *East Timor: The Price of Liberty*, 110.
4 Grenfell, 'Governance, Violence and Crises in Timor-Leste', 87.
5 Carter Centre, *East Timor Political and Election Observation Project*, 26 and 31.
6 Ibid., 17.
7 World Bank, *Strengthening the Institutions*, 2.
8 Mackie, 'Future Political Structures and Institutions in East Timor', 195 and Shoesmith, 'Legislative-Executive Relations in Timor-Leste', 70.
9 Reilly, *Government Structure and Electoral Systems*, 5.
10 Guedes, 'Power-Sharing in the Tropics and the Ubiquitous "Presidential Drift"', 131–133.
11 Mackie, 'Future Political Structures and Institutions in East Timor', 194.
12 Roberts, *Political Transition in Cambodia 1991–99*, 35 and 44.
13 Ibid., 32 and Peou, *International Democracy Assistance for Peacebuilding*, 87 and 88.
14 Un, 'Patronage Politics and Hybrid Democracy', 209.
15 Ibid., 218.
16 Mackie, 'Future Political Structures and Institutions in East Timor', 194; Regan, 'Constitution Making in East Timor', 40 and Reilly, *Government Structure and Electoral Systems*, 1.
17 Duverger, 'A New Political System Model', 166.
18 Ibid.
19 Mackie, 'Future Political Structures and Institutions in East Timor', 200–201.
20 Shoesmith, 'Timor-Leste: Divided Leadership in a Semi-Presidential System', 232.

150   *Institutions, leaders and elections*

21 Constituent Assembly, *Constitution*, Section 96. See also Sanches, *Mengenal Pemerintahan Timor-Leste*, 29.
22 Shoesmith, 'Remaking the State in Timor-Leste', 7–8.
23 Constituent Assembly, *Constitution*, Section 92.
24 Mackie, 'Future Political Structures and Institutions in East Timor', 194 and 200.
25 Reilly, *Government Structure and Electoral Systems*, 2.
26 Mackie, 'Future Political Structures and Institutions in East Timor', 199.
27 Guedes, 'Power-Sharing in the Tropics and the Ubiquitous 'Presidential Drift', 134.
28 Shoesmith, 'Timor-Leste: Divided Leadership in a Semi-Presidential System', 232.
29 Mackie, 'Future Political Structures and Institutions in East Timor', 194.
30 Constituent Assembly, *Constitution*, Section 88:2.
31 Ibid., Section 86:f–g.
32 Feijó, 'Semi-Presidentialism, Moderating Power and Inclusive Governance', 2.
33 Ibid.
34 Ibid., 8.
35 Ibid., 7.
36 Reilly, *Government Structure and Electoral Systems*, 2–3.
37 Constituent Assembly, *Constitution*, Section 74:1.
38 Mackie, 'Future Political Structures and Institutions in East Timor', 200–201.
39 Carter Centre, *East Timor Political and Election Observation Project*, 19. On the structure of successive East Timorese governments (in Indonesian), see Sanches, *Mengenal Pemerintahan Timor-Leste*, 31–50.
40 Smith, 'East Timor: Elections in the World's Newest Nation', 154.
41 Carter Centre, *East Timor Political and Election Observation Project*, 32.
42 Ibid.
43 Ibid., 34.
44 Ibid., 40.
45 Smith, 'East Timor: Elections in the World's Newest Nation', 155.
46 Shoesmith, 'Timor-Leste: Divided Leadership in a Semi-Presidential System', 232.
47 Shoesmith, 'Remaking the State in Timor-Leste', 1.
48 Feijó, 'Semi-Presidentialism, Moderating Power and Inclusive Governance', 11.
49 World Bank, *Strengthening the Institutions of Governance in Timor-Leste.*
50 Ibid.
51 Shoesmith, 'Remaking the State in Timor-Leste', 8.
52 Ibid., 2.
53 Simonsen, 'The Authoritarian Temptation in East Timor', 577.
54 Shoesmith, 'Legislative-Executive Relations in Timor-Leste', 71.
55 Shoesmith, 'Remaking the State in Timor-Leste', 2.
56 Siapno, 'Timor-Leste: On a Path of Authoritarianism?', 325. See also Kingsbury, 'Political Developments', 20.
57 Siapno, ibid., 326.
58 Simonsen, 'The Authoritarian Temptation in East Timor', 583.
59 Siapno, 'Timor-Leste: On a Path of Authoritarianism?', 326.
60 Shoesmith, 'Remaking the State in Timor-Leste', 9.
61 Simonson, 'The Authoritarian Temptation in East Timor', 580–581.
62 Shoesmith, 'Legislative-Executive Relations in Timor-Leste', 242–243.
63 Shoesmith, 'Remaking the State in Timor-Leste', 3.
64 Levitsky and Way, *Competitive Authoritarianism.*
65 Um, 'Cambodia in 2013', 100.
66 United Nations Security Council, *Resolution 1410 (2002)*, 1.
67 United Nations Security Council, *Security Council Establishes One-Year Political Mission in Timor-Leste Unanimously Adopting Resolution 1599 (2005).*
68 Matsuno, 'Analysing Timor-Leste Electoral Politics from a Socio-Economic Perspective', 334.

Institutions, leaders and elections   151

69 Kingsbury, 'Political Developments', 21.
70 Ibid.; Kingsbury and Leach, 'Introduction', 5; Sahin, 'Building the State in Timor-Leste', 266 and Simonsen, 'The Authoritarian Temptation in East Timor', 576.
71 Leach, 'The 2007 Presidential and Parliamentary Elections in Timor-Leste', 220.
72 Kingsbury, 'Political Developments', 21 and United Nations Independent Special Commission of Inquiry for Timor-Leste, *Report of the United Nations Independent Special Commission of Inquiry for Timor-Leste.*
73 Sahin, 'Building the State in Timor-Leste', 266.
74 See United Nations Independent Special Commission of Inquiry for Timor-Leste, *Report of the United Nations Independent Special Commission of Inquiry for Timor-Leste.*
75 McWilliam and Bexley, 'Performing Politics', 68.
76 United Nations Independent Special Commission of Inquiry for Timor-Leste, *Report of the United Nations Independent Special Commission of Inquiry for Timor-Leste.*
77 Trindade, 'Reconciling Conflicting Paradigms', 172.
78 Ibid.
79 Kingsbury and Leach, 'Introduction', 6.
80 McWilliam and Bexley, 'Performing Politics', 79.
81 Kingsbury, *East Timor: The Price of Liberty*, 186 and 190.
82 See Cotton, 'The Crisis of the Timor-Leste', 13–21.
83 Kingsbury, 'Timor-Leste: The Harsh Reality After Independence', 370.
84 Simonsen, 'The Authoritarian Temptation in East Timor', 576.
85 Ibid. See also Constituent Assembly, *Constitution*, Section 85: g.
86 United Nations Security Council, *Report of the Secretary-General on the United Nations Integrated Mission in Timor-Leste (for the period 9 August 2006 to 26 January 2007)*, 1. See also Butler, 'Ten Years After'.
87 United Nations Security Council, *Resolution 1704.*
88 Leach, 'The 2007 Presidential and Parliamentary Elections in Timor-Leste', 220.
89 Feijó, 'Semi-Presidentialism, Moderating Power and Inclusive Governance', 9.
90 Ibid.
91 United Nations Security Council, *Report of the Secretary-General on the United Nations Integrated Mission in Timor-Leste (for the period 9 August 2006 to 26 January 2007)*, 2.
92 Mackie, 'Future Political Structures and Institutions in East Timor', 171 and 196.
93 Ibid.
94 Schumpeter, *Capitalism, Socialism and Democracy*, 269.
95 Gill, *The Dynamics of Democratization*, 46–47.
96 Constituent Assembly, *Constitution*, Section 47.
97 Ibid., Section 48 and 63.
98 Ibid., Section 75.
99 Ibid., Section 63:2 and Democratic Republic of Timor-Leste National Parliament, *Law on the Election of the National Parliament*, Article 4:1.
100 Dahl, *Democracy and its Critics*, 95.
101 Held, *Models of Democracy*, 262.
102 Constituent Assembly, *Constitution*, Section 65:4 and Democratic Republic of Timor-Leste National Parliament, *Law on the Election of the National Parliament*, Articles 9, 11 and 12.
103 Lijphart, 'Constitutional Choices for New Democracies', 75.
104 Mackie, 'Future Political Structures and Institutions in East Timor', 199.
105 Reilly, *Government Structure and Electoral Systems*, 7.
106 Reynolds and Carey, 'The Impact of Election Systems', 37.
107 Lijphart, 'Constitutional Choices for New Democracies, 75.
108 Regan, 'Constitution Making in East Timor', 40.
109 Um, 'Cambodia in 2013', 102.

152 *Institutions, leaders and elections*

110 See Lijphart, 'Constitutional Choices for New Democracies'.
111 Roberts, *Political Transition in Cambodia 1991–99*, 36 and 44.
112 Mackie, 'Future Political Structures and Institutions in East Timor', 201.
113 McWilliam and Bexley, 'Performing Politics', 68.
114 United Nations Security Council, *Report of the Secretary-General on the United Nations Integrated Mission in Timor-Leste (for the period 27 January 2007 to 20 August 2007)*.
115 Comissão Nacional de Eleições, *Elisaun Prezidente 2007 República Democrática de Timor-Leste Total Votus Kandidatus Eleisaun Prezidente 2007 Nivel Nacional*, 1.
116 Democratic Republic of Timor-Leste National Parliament, *Law on the Election of the President of the Republic*.
117 Ibid., 4.
118 Comissão Nacional de Eleições, *Elisaun Prezidente 2007 República Democrática de Timor-Leste Total Votus Kandidatus Eleisaun Prezidente 2007 Nivel Nacional*, 1.
119 Scheiner, *First Round Presidential, by District, CNE Final Results*.
120 Ibid. and Comissão Nacional de Eleições, *Elisaun Prezidente 2007 República Democrática de Timor-Leste: Acta Final Apuramentu Nacional*, 1.
121 Comissão Nacional de Eleições, ibid.
122 Leach, 'The 2007 Presidential and Parliamentary Elections in Timor-Leste', 224.
123 Comissão Nacional de Eleições, *Elisaun Prezidente 2007 República Democrática de Timor-Leste Total Votus Kandidatus Eleisaun Prezidente 2007 Nivel Nacional*, 1.
124 Ibid.
125 Ibid.
126 United Nations Security Council, *Report of the Secretary-General on the United Nations Integrated Mission in Timor-Leste (for the period 27 January 2007 to 20 August 2007)*.
127 McWilliam and Bexley, 'Performing Politics', 66
128 Leach, 'The 2007 Presidential and Parliamentary Elections in Timor-Leste', 226 and Commisão Nacional de Eleições, *National Provision Results from the 30 June 2007 Parliamentary Elections*.
129 Commisão Nacional de Eleições, ibid.
130 Leach, 'The 2007 Presidential and Parliamentary Elections in Timor-Leste', 223.
131 Democratic Republic of Timor-Leste National Parliament, *Law on the Election of the National Parliament*.
132 Ibid.
133 Kingsbury, 'East Timor's Political Crisis', 40.
134 See Democratic Republic of Timor-Leste National Parliament, *Law on the Election of the National Parliament* and Democratic Republic of Timor-Leste, *1st Amendment to Law No. 6/2006*.
135 McWilliam and Bexley, 'Performing Politics', 66.
136 Ibid, 77.
137 Leach, 'The 2007 Presidential and Parliamentary Elections in Timor-Leste', 225.
138 Ibid., 226 and Democratic Republic of Timor-Leste, *2nd Amendment to Law No. 6/2006*, Article 12.
139 Helen Hill cited in Leach, 'The 2007 Presidential and Parliamentary Elections in Timor-Leste', 230.
140 McWilliam and Bexley, 'Performing Politics', 69.
141 Ibid.
142 Ibid.
143 Ibid., 76.
144 Constituent Assembly, *Constitution*, Section 106:1 and Feijó, 'Semi-Presidentialism, Moderating Power and Inclusive Governance', 7.
145 Leach, 'The 2007 Presidential and Parliamentary Elections in Timor-Leste', 227–228.

Institutions, leaders and elections   153

146 Ibid.
147 Ibid.
148 Constituent Assembly, *Constitution*, Section 106:1.
149 European Union Election Observation Mission, *Timor-Leste*, 8.
150 McWilliam and Bexley, 'Performing Politics', 78.
151 Leach, 'The 2007 Presidential and Parliamentary Elections in Timor-Leste', 228.
152 Kingsbury, 'East Timor's Political Crisis', 41.
153 McWilliam and Bexley, 'Performing Politics', 78.
154 Ibid., 78 and Leach, 'The 2007 Presidential and Parliamentary Elections in Timor-Leste', 228.
155 Leach, ibid., 231.
156 United Nations Security Council, *Report of the Secretary-General on the United Nations Integrated Mission in Timor-Leste (for the period 9 July 2008 to 20 January 2009)*, 2.
157 McWilliam and Bexley, 'Performing Politics', 78.
158 Shoesmith, 'Timor-Leste: On the Road to Peace and Prosperity', 325.
159 Shoesmith, 'Is Small Beautiful?', 35.
160 Ibid., 45.
161 Gunn, 'Timor-Leste in 2009: Cup Half Full or Half Empty?', 236. See Democratic Republic of Timor-Leste National Parliament, *Law on the Anti-Corruption Commission* and United Nations Security Council, *Report of the Secretary-General on the United Nations Integrated Mission in Timor-Leste (for the period from 21 January to 20 September 2010)*, 2.
162 Allard, 'Timor PM Protecting "Corrupt" Cabinet Ministers'.
163 Shoesmith, 'Is Small Beautiful?' 35.
164 United Nations Security Council, *Report of the Secretary-General on the United Nations Integrated Mission in Timor-Leste (for the period from 21 January 2009 to 23 September 2009)*, 3.
165 United Nations Security Council, *Report of the Secretary-General on the United Nations Integrated Mission in Timor-Leste (for the period from 9 July 2008 to 20 January 2009)*, 1; United Nations Security Council, *Report of the Secretary-General on the United Nations Integrated Mission in Timor-Leste (for the period from 21 January to 23 September 2009)*, 1; United Nations Security Council, *Report of the Secretary-General on the United Nations Integrated Mission in Timor-Leste (for the period from 24 September 2009 to 20 January 2010)*, 1; United Nations Security Council, *Report of the Secretary-General on the United Nations Integrated Mission in Timor-Leste (for the period from 21 January 2010 to 20 September 2010)*, 1; United Nations Security Council, *Report of the Secretary-General on the United Nations Integrated Mission in Timor-Leste (for the period from 21 September 2010 to 7 January 2011)*, 1; United Nations Security Council, *Report of the Secretary-General on the United Nations Integrated Mission in Timor-Leste (for the period from 8 January 2011 to 20 September 2011)*, 1 and United Nations Security Council, *Report of the Secretary-General on the United Nations Integrated Mission in Timor-Leste (for the period from 20 September 2011 to 6 January 2012)*, 1.
166 Sahin, 'Timor-Leste in 2009', 345.
167 Kingsbury, 'Timor-Leste in 2012', 312.
168 International Crisis Group, *Timor-Leste's Elections*, 1.
169 Ibid.
170 International Foundation for Electoral Systems, *Election Guide Democratic Republic of Timor-Leste Election for President.*
171 Kingsbury, 'Timor-Leste in 2012', 369.
172 Democratic Governance Support Unit of United Nations Integrated Mission in Timor-Leste, *Compendium of the 2012 Elections in Timor-Leste*, 23.
173 Ibid.

154 *Institutions, leaders and elections*

174 Ibid.
175 Ibid.
176 Ibid., 26 and Kingsbury, 'Timor-Leste in 2012', 313.
177 Democratic Governance Support Unit of United Nations Integrated Mission in Timor-Leste, *Compendium of the 2012 Elections in Timor-Leste*, 26.
178 Ibid.
179 Ibid.
180 Ibid., 34.
181 Ibid., 38.
182 European Union Election Observation Mission, *Timor-Leste* and International Crisis Group, *Timor-Leste's Elections*, 2.
183 International Crisis Group, ibid., 6.
184 Democratic Governance Support Unit of United Nations Integrated Mission in Timor-Leste, *Compendium of the 2012 Elections in Timor-Leste*, 9.
185 European Union Election Observation Mission, *Timor-Leste*, 3.
186 United Nations Security Council, *Report of the Secretary-General on the United Nations Integrated Mission in Timor-Leste (for the period from 7 January to 20 September 2012)*, 2.
187 La'o Hamutuk, *Seats Resulting from Parliamentary Elections.*
188 European Union Election Observation Mission, *Timor-Leste*, 3.
189 Ibid.
190 Tempo Semanal, *Alkatiri seeks Transitional Council for Old Generation.*
191 Tempo Semanal, *Xanana Prefers CNRT to be the Opposition.*
192 Tempo Semanal, *Taur Concern with the Violance* [sic].
193 Ibid.
194 Kingsbury, 'Timor-Leste in 2012', 315.
195 Tempo Semanal, *East Timorese Fifth Government.*
196 United Nations Security Council, *Report of the Secretary-General on the United Nations Integrated Mission in Timor-Leste (for the period from 7 January to 20 September 2012)*, 2.
197 European Union Election Observation Mission, *Timor-Leste*, 4 and 15. This is also based on my personal observation of the elections as an international observer in Dili.
198 Ibid., 3 and 5.
199 United Nations Security Council, *Report of the Secretary-General on the United Nations Integrated Mission in Timor-Leste (for the period from 7 January to 20 September 2012)*, 4.
200 United Nations Security Council, *Report of the Secretary-General on the United Nations Integrated Mission in Timor-Leste (for the period from 7 January to 20 September 2012)*, 5.
201 Soares, 'The Challenges of Drafting a Constitution', 31.
202 Reilly, *Government Structures and Electoral Systems*, 9.
203 Pereira, *Working Together with Timor-Leste.* On decentralisation, see also Sanches, *Mengenal Pemerintahan Timor-Leste*, 67 and 113 and Farram, ed., *Locating Democracy.*
204 Lijphart, 'Constitutional Choices for New Democracies', 81.
205 Mackie, 'Future Political Structures and Institutions in East Timor', 196 and 199.
206 Ibid., 201–202.
207 Kingsbury, 'Timor-Leste in 2012', 305.
208 International Crisis Group, *Timor-Leste's Elections*, 6.
209 Minister of State and of the Presidency of the Council of Ministers and Official Spokesperson for the Government of Timor-Leste, *President of the Republic announces the new Prime Minister of Timor-Leste is to be Dr. Rui Maria de Araújo.*
210 de Araújo, *Speech by His Excellency the Prime Minister Dr Rui Maria de Araújo on the Occasion of the Swearing-In of the Sixth Constitutional Government*, 2 and 12.

Institutions, leaders and elections   155

211 United Nations Development Programme, *Sustaining Human Progress: Reducing Vulnerabilities and Building Resilience*, 108 and 119. See Gusmão, *Strategies for the Future*, 207.
212 Pereira, 'Timor-Leste Transforming Belligerent Democracy into Consensus Democracy'.
213 Democratic Republic of Timor-Leste, *The Dili Consensus*, Dili, 28 February 2012.
214 Linz and Stepan, *Problems of Democratic Transition and Consolidation*, 5.
215 Shoesmith, 'Legislature-Executive Relations in Timor-Leste', 72.
216 Ibid, 79.

6 Social democratic citizenship

Citizenship is a legal and political status that bestows upon individuals membership into a political community and articulates the rights and responsibilities that states and citizens hold in relation to each other. Citizenship is simultaneously 'an inclusionary process involving some re-allocation of resources and an exclusionary process of building identities on the basis of common or imagined solidarity'.[1] It contributes to state-based identity formation by establishing the basis of national unity through commonly shared rights and promoting a particular vision of legitimate statehood to the broader international community.[2] Constitutions provide the basis for citizenship by defining the parameters of acceptable state activities, and can hence provide valuable insights into how constitution-drafters envisaged the relationship between states and citizens.[3]

East Timor's Constitution provides a rights-based model of citizenship that emphasises the obligations of the state to provide citizens access to certain socio-economic goods. The extensive allocation of socio-economic rights conforms to the pursuit of social democracy during the independence movement, which was based upon the belief that the state has an economic responsibility to (re-)allocate resources to provide social protections for vulnerable citizens. However, these social democratic conceptions of liberal citizenship sit in tension with the global economic order.[4] While international institutions, such as the International Monetary Fund and World Bank, have ostensibly embraced 'inclusive growth' through development, contemporary strategies have largely retained the 'neoliberal plus' agenda of the post-Washington Consensus.[5]

The Constitution established East Timor's values and aspirations for different types of rights including political, legal, socio-economic and cultural rights. Those fundamental human rights enshrined in the Constitution include, among others, the right to self-determination, rights to life (including adequate food, water and shelter), freedom of movement, freedom from arbitrary detention, cruelty and torture, the right to fair trial and freedom of opinion and expression.[6] These multi-layered citizenship rights, encompassing human, political, socio-economic and cultural components, reflect East Timor's vision of a fair, prosperous and equitable independent social democracy supported by political order.

Following independence, key strategic planning documents produced by East Timorese governments demonstrated consistency regarding the pursuit of civil,

Social democratic citizenship   157

political and socio-economic rights.[7] Based on widespread community consultation, these documents reinforce East Timor's social democratic citizenship model and the goals of poverty alleviation and meeting socio-economic needs. According to Xanana Gusmão, East Timor's Constitution should be reflected in the policies, the activities and the efforts of leadership and governance, which should be based on human rights.[8] This chapter examines the extent to which governments have attempted to convert these political visions into reality. While the Constitution provides the basis for a social democratic state identity, this is only meaningful if citizenship rights are supported by substantive policies and budgetary choices. Since independence, progress in key human development indicators has been mixed, and government policies and budget decisions have not always conformed to the rhetoric around rights and opportunities. Overall, however, welfare policies have been pursued by successive East Timorese governments, including the creation of a social safety net to expand vulnerable citizens' access to fundamental socio-economic rights.

Constitutional citizenship rights

As Chapter 1 demonstrated, human rights were firmly embedded in the political claims to self-determination made by leaders of the independence movement. The CNRT's 1998 Magna Carta was envisaged as a basis for a future constitution. It was significantly influenced by international humanitarian law, and the United Nations Charter was considered 'an integral part of the Constitution of a future independent East Timor'.[9] In a number of speeches, José Ramos-Horta rejected the idea that human rights are purely a 'Western' concept.[10] He argued that human rights referred to:

> the actual lives of people, people who do not wish to be tortured, people who do not wish to be arrested for no reason, or to be locked up without trial, without legal processes ... these human rights are actually universal rights, not an exclusive property of some Western Christian civilization.[11]

Building the Constitution provided an opportunity to legally and symbolically enshrine the values of the independence movement and construct a state identity in accordance with democratic conceptions of the purpose and functions of states in relation to their citizens.

Prior to constitution-drafting, on 7–8 August 2000, the UNTAET Human Rights Unit and the East Timor Jurists Association held a human rights workshop in Dili titled 'Human Rights and the Future of East Timor'. The workshop included East Timorese law graduates, human rights activists, domestic civil society organisations (such as *Yayasan HAK* and the NGO Forum) and international representatives.[12] The purpose of the workshop was to assist East Timor in translating the extensive list of rights in the Magna Carta into tangible policies, and provide opportunities for different organisations to discuss the steps required to ensure rights standards in East Timor.

158 *Social democratic citizenship*

In the same month, the CNRT National Congress endorsed human rights by taking:

> 'into account the many long years of pain and suffering resulting from the denial of our basic rights and freedoms as a people … [and acknowledged the abuses] were essentially the outcome of an oppressive system and policies which legitimised and institutionalised the violation of human rights and fostered impunity and the abuse of power'.[13]

The National Congress recognised that ensuring the prevention of rights violations into the future required building 'a new society which embraces human rights as the basis of democracy, good governance, the rule of law and sustainable economic and social development for all the citizens of East Timor, especially the disadvantaged and minorities'.[14] The nature of state responsibilities in relation to protecting and preserving human rights, and the limitations placed on the capacities of state agencies to violate fundamental rights, reflects the history of rights violations perpetrated by Indonesia.

The Constitution broadly reflects the views of the East Timorese political elite. At the Human Rights and the Future of East Timor Workshop in 2000, one of the basic principles outlined was that the Constitution 'should uphold the full range of civil, political, economic, social and cultural rights for all East Timorese and include guarantees for the protection of these rights'.[15] It also recommended that '[a]ll East Timorese should enjoy equal rights and equal opportunity, including women, children and minorities. There should be no discrimination in East Timor on the basis of ethnic origin, religion, gender, age, political ideology, or on the basis of being a refugee or victim'.[16] Both the Magna Carta and the workshop paid particular attention to 'vulnerable' members of the community, including women, children, the elderly, the disabled and cultural and religious minorities. Overall, political leaders and civil society members largely agreed that social citizenship rights were essential for facilitating socio-economic prosperity. In a democratic state, poverty should not disadvantage people in the legal system or be an obstacle for appropriate legal representation. According to Reverend Arlindo Marcal and Maria Olandina Alves, presenters at the Human Rights Workshop, the law can often impact more heavily on the poor than the rich.[17] Subsequently, they argued that the new state should establish programs to ensure the poor are represented in court, and that accused, vulnerable groups and minorities would have legal protections.

In August 2000, the CNRT National Congress endorsed the recommendations of the workshop, including specific provisions such as non-discrimination and equality, freedom of expression, association and assembly, and economic, social and cultural rights.[18] It committed the CNRT to ensuring that civil, political, economic, social and cultural rights were 'enshrined as an integral part of East Timor's new Constitution and that the Constitution includes guarantees for the protection of these rights for all the citizens of East Timor'.[19] The nature and range of these citizenship rights reflected the aspirations of the CNRT, the

Social democratic citizenship 159

UNTAET and other organisations, such as the East Timor Jurists Association, concerning the responsibilities of the East Timorese state towards its citizens.

The Constitution presents the Democratic Republic of Timor-Leste as a rights-based, independent social democracy. Section 1 positions East Timor as 'a democratic, sovereign, independent and unitary State based on the rule of law, the will of the people and respect for the dignity of the human person'.[20] Like the Magna Carta, it requires that fundamental rights be interpreted in accordance with the 1948 Universal Declaration of Human Rights.[21]

José Ramos-Horta described East Timor's Constitution as 'one of the most progressive in the world' because it 'enshrines a host of progressive social, economic and cultural rights'.[22] The Constitution institutes an extensive range of rights and guarantees, including basic human rights, political, legal, socio-economic and cultural rights.[23] It extends the responsibilities of the state to ensure 'negative' liberties by emphasising 'positive' rights: indeed, the lengthiest section of the Constitution is the Bill of Rights, titled 'Part II Fundamental Rights, Duties, Freedoms and Guarantees', which articulates the social, political, cultural and economic rights bestowed upon citizens in 45 sections.[24] These rights loosely resemble Marshall's theory on modern citizenship, in which rights are divided into three broad components: civil, political and social.[25] Civil and political rights are necessary for achieving individual freedoms, including the right to own property and to access the justice system, and to participate in political life, including the right to vote. East Timor's Constitution also guarantees particular cultural rights, ensuring citizenship rights are inclusive of a diverse range of state-encompassed identities.

Social citizenship rights range from economic welfare and security to the right to share in the full social heritage and 'live the life of a civilized being'.[26] Social rights are connected with social services and education, which, Marshall argues, evolved with the development of 'welfare' states in the twentieth century.[27] Social citizenship rights are underpinned by a belief that citizens are entitled to services such as education, health and a basic income, which are provided through the redistribution of wealth and income through progressive taxation.[28] Socio-economic rights, such as the right to education, social security and health, are embedded in East Timor's Constitution, most notably in Sections 50–61 headed 'Economic, Social and Cultural Rights and Duties'.[29] These rights reflect a belief that the purpose of welfare is to limit the negative effects of class inequalities in capitalist societies and assist citizens' access to 'positive' civil and political rights. Marshall recognised that poverty limits the capacities of individuals to access civil and political rights. While constitutional equality may be accorded in theory, poor citizens will only achieve access to the full suite of rights if financial and social barriers are removed by the state.[30] In the presence of widespread poverty, social citizenship rights can offer 'social protection' for the most vulnerable and disadvantaged members of the community.

As Figure 6.1 reflects, East Timor's Constitution provides multi-faceted citizenship rights to support its vision of an 'ideal' society. Political and legal equality and equal voting rights have been consolidated within international law,

Table 6.1 Constitutional rights in East Timor

Types of rights	Key rights, freedoms, protections and guarantees	Section	Corresponding international law rights documents
Human Rights	Right to life (including no death penalty); Human life 'inviolable'; Rights to freedom, security and integrity; Freedom from torture; Freedom from cruel, inhuman and degrading treatment.	29 29 30 30:4 30:4	Section 23 of East Timor's Constitution guarantees that fundamental rights will be interpreted in accordance with the Universal Declaration of Human Rights.
Civil, political and legal rights	Equal right to vote; Legal and political equality – exercise same rights and duties; No discrimination on basis of sex, religion and so forth; Freedom of speech (and no censorship); Freedom of press and mass media; Freedom of association; Right to assemble (unarmed); Right to form and participate in political parties; Right to access courts and legal representation; Freedom from unlawful trial and indefinite sentences; Assumed innocence before proven guilty.	47 16 16 40 41 43 42 46 33 31 34	International Covenant on Civil and Political Rights (1966)
Socio-economic and cultural rights	Right to free basic and universal education; Right to free health care and medical assistance through a national health service; Right to social security; Right to vocational training; Special protections for youth; Special protections for senior citizens; Special protections for disabled citizens; Right to preserve, protect and value culture.	59 57 56 19:2 19 20 21 59	International Covenant on Social, Economic and Cultural Rights (1966)

Social democratic citizenship 161

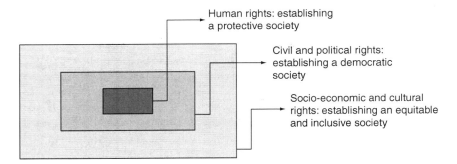

Figure 6.1 Types of citizenship rights in East Timor.

whereby equality provides men and women with equal access to the enjoyment of other civil and political rights.[31] They feature in East Timor's Constitution as they are essential to the creation of an independent democratic state. Equal legal and political rights are necessary for the functioning of democratic states because they are 'founded on the primacy of the law and the exercise of human rights ... no one is above the law and all are equal before the law'.[32] For example, the Constitution asserts that 'access to courts is guaranteed to all for the defence of their legally protected rights and interests. Justice shall not be denied for insufficient economic means'.[33]

Socio-economic rights (along with democratic rights and freedoms) contribute to the development of a prosperous, 'civilised' society, and to the vision of state identity as equitable and inclusive. Welfare or 'subsistence' rights allow disadvantaged citizens to access opportunities that might otherwise be denied, and attempts to ensure an adequate standard of living. While building East Timor's Constitution provided elites with an opportunity to establish a new political culture and institutions, individual rights prescribed under international law contrast in some instances with traditional understandings of social roles in East Timor.[34] In one example, tensions emerged during the constitution-drafting processes between traditional understandings of gender roles and universal citizenship rights. Alldèn notes that customary laws have tended to favour men over women, who have been largely regarded as inferior.[35] Women are viewed as 'primarily responsible for housework and child-rearing' and their social roles most often located within the domestic sphere.[36] A Gender and Constitutional Working Group developed a Charter for Women's Rights, which 'sought the prohibition of all forms of discrimination and the adoption of positive measures to promote equality'.[37] The Charter, published in *La'o Hamutuk*, included policies of non-discrimination on the basis of gender in access to political positions and laws against domestic violence, a significant problem in East Timorese society.[38]

The Constitution guarantees gender equality, with women and men holding the 'same rights and duties in all areas of family, political, economic, social and

162 *Social democratic citizenship*

cultural rights'.[39] Some within East Timor continue to view 'women's rights' as inconsistent with East Timorese culture and social practices. For example, Dionisio Babo Soares argued that gender rights 'were approved unanimously [by the Constituent Assembly] despite fears that traditional groups might refuse to back them, since women and children have a unique place in traditional customary law'.[40] While fears continue to exist around the upheaval of traditional social roles and norms (including among some East Timorese politicians), Hilary Charlesworth suggests many East Timorese women 'were disappointed with the minimal impact that they had on drafting the Constitution'.[41] Contests over rights in the Constitution were contests over identity as East Timorese constitution-drafters created a state built upon political values that were not always compatible with existing social paradigms. Democratic state-making requires changing public attitudes in areas where customary law or social mores clash with new state-based law and forms part of the ongoing challenge of democratic consolidation.

Citizenship in the Democratic Republic of Timor-Leste

Since independence, East Timorese governments have conducted consultations and dialogues in order to identify the needs and aspirations of citizens, and in so doing promoted nation-building through participation in political decision-making. In 2002, 38,293 East Timorese participated in the 980 community consultations conducted across 498 *sukus* by the Civil Society Consultative Commission on Development, which would ultimately form the basis of the 2002 'Our Nation, Our Vision' document.[42] The document provided the basis for a 'national vision' about East Timor's development that would shape the National Development Plan.

Both the 'Our Nation, Our Vision' document and the National Development Plan highlighted a general belief that the state was responsible for providing social citizenship rights, including education and health, and for ensuring housing and housing materials for the poor.[43] The vision included improved living standards for all people and fair distribution of income.[44] The popularity of a fair distribution of income points to the egalitarian social democratic traditions evident throughout the independence movement. Development goals included the reduction of poverty among women and men and the establishment of 'a social security net to reduce the burden on those who are unable to work/ help themselves'.[45]

According to Xanana Gusmão, 'the vision which sprang from people's participation in the planning process encapsulates all that is fundamental to development – peace, security, freedom, tolerance, equity, improved health, education, access to jobs and food security'.[46] The National Development Plan emphasised the provision of social citizenship rights as a central part in its economic policy:

> [t]he economical policy that the Government is proposing to implement shall always have as its centre of attention the life conditions of the Timorese and as

Social democratic citizenship 163

objective the improvement of those conditions.... Public resources have to be used in accordance with policies in favour of the poor and the creation of a social security network for the more vulnerable groups.[47]

This vision incorporated a belief that redistributing wealth and income can support social services and assist the well-being and life opportunities of vulnerable citizens.

The East Timorese population positioned education as the top priority and largely considered the government as responsible for building more schools, increasing teacher numbers, providing teacher training and assisting children in poverty to access primary education.[48] The 'Our Nation, Our Vision' document states 'we want to be well-educated and highly-productive. We want education for all, particularly the poor, the disabled, the elderly and women so they become literate and skilled, to help build our country'.[49] The National Development Plan emphasised access to free education as essential for state-building and creating a prosperous democracy.[50] Education goals included increasing the literacy rate and the numbers of students pursuing higher education and vocational and technical training.[51] Rights to education were seen to promote the capacities of people to develop meaningful careers, raising the skill-base of the population across different fields, and potentially contributing to a rise in living standards across the whole of society.[52] Hence, the provision of socio-economic rights was not just important for social justice or welfare, but also linked to inclusive development and economic growth.

Following the 2002 National Development Plan, several government documents reinforced East Timor's commitment to providing socio-economic rights and 'social protection', including the IV Constitutional Government Program in 2007 and the Strategic Development Plan in 2011.[53] The IV Constitutional Government Programme was developed by the AMP Government with the promise to 'respect and promote the citizen's freedom and equality rights, promoting the values of civil and human rights and the values of tolerance and respect'.[54] The program vowed to use public resources 'in accordance with policies in favour of the poor and the creation of a social security network for the more vulnerable groups'.[55] It was envisioned that this would assist in reducing 'social inequalities' and exclusion: the program stated that 'the Government is going to carry out *social policies*, because it is the State duty to safeguard the welfare of the population [emphasis in original]'.[56] It also suggested that social services, including the age pension, should 'offer a set of programs directed at the needy population and aiming at the development and promotion of human dignity'.[57] This belief in the obligations of governments to ensure citizens' capacities to access rights is represented through the positioning of the social security system as a key national priority.

East Timor's 2011 Strategic Development Plan was also concerned with delivering universal social services, such as education and health, although it also focused significantly on infrastructure and development projects, such as building roads and improving access to clean water, electricity and sanitation.[58]

164 *Social democratic citizenship*

The Strategic Development Plan stated: 'the true wealth of any nation is in the strength of its people. Maximising the overall health, education and quality of life of the Timorese people is central to building a fair and progressive nation'.[59] It also outlined the aim to have a universal social security system in place to guarantee all East Timorese workers a pension after retirement, and to provide a social safety net for vulnerable families alongside a 'comprehensive' assistance program for veterans of the resistance movement.[60]

The IV Constitutional Government Programme again considered universal education as a central investment in the future of East Timor, with the AMP government promising to promote free primary schooling and the expansion of technical-professional schooling.[61] The Strategic Development Plan similarly linked 'social capital' to building a healthy and educated society 'to address the social needs of our people and promote human development'.[62] Human development was mutually intertwined with the goals of social and economic development, as access to education and employment was viewed as the 'stepping stones that lead to economic independence'.[63] These government program indicate that the social citizenship rights espoused during the independence movement retained their currency within the visions of statehood held by East Timorese people and their political leaders.

Ongoing international aid and UN assistance was also a factor in East Timor's continuing commitment to the preservation of human rights. East Timor's first Prime Minister, Mari Alkatiri, argued that the National Development Plan represented the desire of the government to satisfy, and be accountable to, the people of East Timor and external agency requirements.[64] In 2008, 2009 and 2010, a series of international compacts were drawn up between the United Nations Integrated Mission in Timor-Leste and East Timor's Government, and included civil society organisations and international agencies.[65] In the compacts, 'Social Protection and Services, including Health' were listed as the fourth national priority in 2008 and 2009.[66] The compact for 2010 listed 'Access to Social Justice' and 'Social Services and Decentralised Service Delivery' as key national priorities.[67] During this period, the United Nations Development Assistance Framework (UNDAF) 2009–2013 also positioned peace and security as the central goal in East Timor, suggesting that this relied upon achieving three subsidiary aims: democratisation and social cohesion, including deepening statebuilding, security and justice; poverty reduction and facilitating sustainable livelihoods; and advancing basic social services, such as education, health, nutrition, water, sanitation, social welfare and social protection.[68] This reflects dominant ideals of 'good governance' in which effective sovereignty requires states to manage public resources in such ways as to provide particular public goods to citizens. Meeting the expectations of citizens regarding their social rights and alleviating circumstances of poverty can also help engender political order and legitimacy of the democratic regime.

Both the National Development Plan and Strategic Development Plan, which incorporated the views of the East Timorese, recognised socio-economic rights as pathways for inclusive economic development. As noted in the Strategic

Social democratic citizenship 165

Development Plan, meeting commitments to provide socio-economic rights 'poses many financial, social and cultural challenges for Timor-Leste, but we recognise that one of the features of a strong, cohesive and progressive nation is its capacity to protect the rights and interests of its most vulnerable citizens'.[69] In East Timor, the rights-based model of citizenship articulated the 'positive' and 'negative' freedoms deemed necessary for democratic politics and social justice, including the provision of life opportunities for all citizens supported by a guaranteed minimum standard of living.[70]

Actualising social citizenship rights

Within East Timor's Constitution, the provision of rights is contingent upon state capacities, acknowledging the financial demands of social welfare and poverty reduction strategies.[71] The capacity of East Timor to enact its social democratic agenda has been hampered by economic realities, and since independence, the provision of socio-economic rights has often been dependent upon the assistance of IGOs and NGOs.[72] But while the adoption of neo-liberal 'free market' policies have been conditions of aid and debt relief in many developing states since in the 1980s, East Timor's economy – the world's most 'petroleum dependent' – is heavily reliant upon state revenues from oil and gas reserves.[73] The government plays a substantial role in providing public services, allocating resources, building infrastructure and promoting economic growth. Increased government spending has resulted in economic expansion since 2008, including 12.8 per cent growth in 2009.[74]

While strategic plans have clearly prioritised the key areas of health, education and socio-economic security, infrastructure projects largely dominated the budgets of the AMP government (2007–2012). The policies of the AMP government are particularly significant as it came to power at the time when oil and gas reserves began providing the state with large revenues.[75] The AMP government had significantly more money to spend, which is useful for assessing whether policy and budget choices have matched the vision outlined in policy documents.

While economic growth has contributed to the progress made in a range of socio-economic and human development indicators, East Timor's progress towards socio-economic development can be described as mixed. Optimistically, the United Nations Development Programme states: 'since independence in 2002, Timor-Leste has increased life expectancy, reduced child mortality, boosted school enrolment and reduced illiteracy'.[76] In her report for the United Nations, Special Rapporteur Magdalena Sepúlveda Carmona linked success with the role of the state, arguing that '[t]he challenge of constructing the country has, in many ways, been tackled with significant success by the State, which has demonstrated a strong commitment to democracy and determination to improve the lives and livelihoods of all Timorese'.[77] In 2013, East Timor was considered by the Human Development Index (HDI) as having medium human development ranked at 128 from 187 states.[78] East Timor's human development indicator has

166 *Social democratic citizenship*

steadily improved from 0.465 (adjusted for comparative purposes) to 0.620 in 2013, placing it ahead of the Southeast Asian states of Cambodia and Laos, and the Pacific island states of Vanuatu, Papua New Guinea and Solomon Islands.[79] East Timor's annual HDI growth from 2000–2013 was calculated at 2.25, which reflects greater progress over ten years than any other state in the medium development band.

In terms of income, East Timor is considered a lower middle-income country with the World Bank calculating the Gross National Income per capita at $7,670 (PPP) in 2012.[80] Somewhat ambitiously, the AMP and BGK governments have aimed to transform East Timor into an upper middle-income state by 2030 encompassing a 'healthy, well-educated and safe population'.[81] Achieving the Millennium Development Goals in relation to poverty would require East Timor to lower the percentage of people living under $1 a day (PPP) to 14 per cent by 2015, a figure that represents approximately half the population living in conditions of extreme poverty in 2001 (36 per cent). By 2007, the extreme poverty rate had increased by 13 per cent to 49 per cent.[82] This was driven partly by the 2006 governance crisis, which set back the modest economic gains that had been made during the 2002–2005 period.[83] As a result of the crisis, East Timor's non-oil economy contracted, resulting in higher unemployment levels and a restriction in social welfare services.[84] Additionally, the AMP government was forced to prioritise urgent humanitarian challenges, such as the 150,000 people that became internally displaced following the widespread riots.[85]

In 2007, the per capita income was estimated at 20 per cent lower than in 2002, when East Timor achieved independence.[86] According to the World Bank's 2009 projections, at least 41 per cent of the population lived below the poverty line, which was roughly similar to figures for the transition period in 2001.[87] In 2013, it was estimated that 37.4 per cent of the East Timorese population lived on less than $1.25 (PPP) per day (defined by the World Bank as extreme poverty).[88] The Multidimensional Poverty Index similarly suggests that around 38.7 per cent of people are living in severe poverty, but that a significant 68.1 per cent of people experience multi-dimensional poverty.[89]

Problematically, the poverty rates demonstrate that high rates of economic growth and government spending may not have made a considerable difference to the lives of many East Timorese. Ambitious goals of 'inclusive growth' that reflect the orthodox international development paradigm appear to have only had a limited impact upon the numbers of East Timorese living in conditions of severe poverty. One of the key components of social democracy is the redistribution of wealth and income to ensure the equalising of access to positive rights and life opportunities. The extent of inequality in East Timor is contested. Development has been inequitable in East Timor's social democracy as the benefits have not been 'reaching the poorest sectors of society, particularly rural populations'.[90] Seventy-one per cent of people living in Dili fall within the highest wealth quintile, whereas 75 per cent of the rural population 'suffer disproportionately from poverty and disadvantage'.[91] This could be viewed as a result of underinvestment in agricultural sectors and inequitable distribution of resources

Social democratic citizenship   167

across the 13 East Timorese districts, but can also be more broadly identified as a result of budgeting measures that have prioritized infrastructure ahead of other social democratic aims.[92]

On the other hand, the World Bank's Gini index, which ranks income inequalities, places East Timor at 34, with 0 being most perfectly equal and 100 being most unequal. The data suggests that at a global level, East Timor is more egalitarian than many other developed and developing states. In his 2014 analysis of Timor-Leste's pursuit of 'inclusive opportunity', Craig Sugden also found that 'pro-poor' public policies were 'heading in the right direction' and opportunity distribution 'typically moved in favour of the poorer Timorese' to enhance inclusion and progress in developmental goals.[93] These public policies included cash payments to those people displaced by the 2006 crisis, the development of a public safety net and providing grants to villages.[94] The lowered poverty rate can be partly explained by the oil and petroleum revenue than began flowing into the state in 2007, in addition to government policies that have provided cash transfers to some of the states' most vulnerable citizens.

According to the United Nations Development Programme, well-designed cash transfers schemes can contribute to poverty reduction and integrate with other services and programs.[95] The AMP government provided 'pensions, lump sum payments and scholarships' to vulnerable citizens, particularly former resistance fighters who continue to hold a somewhat privileged status in the eyes of successive East Timorese governments.[96] In the AMP government's 'Goodbye Conflict, Welcome Development' document, produced to highlight the key achievements of the government, five out of seven of the self-identified successes related to welfare or humanitarian assistance. For instance, the document stated that East Timor's 'national heroes, the Combatants for National Liberation, were living in situation of extreme poverty and without dignity. *We began a bold program to acknowledge these heroes and provide support to address their suffering* [emphasis in original text]'.[97] On 19 June 2008, Decree Law 19/2008 established a non-contributory pension designed to provide monthly support allowances for the elderly (over 60) and disabled (over 18 and unable to work) of US$20 a month.[98] A non-contributory distribution model – whereby new generations contribute to the retirement funds of the older generation – was selected as it was viewed as more 'sympathetic' than a capitalisation model (in which workers contribute to their own pension during their working lives).[99]

The 'Goodbye Conflict, Welcome Development' document credits the AMP government with introducing 'social justice measures, including pensions to … vulnerable groups including women and children'.[100] Here, the document reflects a key belief underpinning social democratic politics that one of the best ways for a state to pursue its core objective of internal sovereignty is through the promotion of rational-legal stability, order and domestic security, which itself is reliant upon providing people with basic socio-economic rights. In other words, providing meaningful access to socio-economic rights can counteract social violence that can arise from conditions of poverty and deprivation.

168 *Social democratic citizenship*

By achieving access to first order rights such as water, food, shelter and so forth, as well as improving access to second order rights such as universal health and education, the state can work to secure its legitimacy in the eyes of the populace. According to the 'Goodbye Conflict, Welcome Development' document, the AMP government began pilot projects for building houses to provide 'decent housing and access to water, sanitation, electricity, health, education and markets'.[101] An Economic Stabilisation Fund in 2008 was put in place by the AMP government 'to regulate the price of rice, cement and other staple goods', an example of government intervention in the economy to enhance food security.[102] The AMP government also implemented a program for distributing daily meals for 300,000 children in basic education in order to curb the incidence of malnutrition.[103]

Despite these policies, East Timor remains a long way from meeting several Millennium Development Goals, including those pertaining to food insecurity and chronic malnutrition.[104] This is despite the efforts of the government to increase food security with the assistance of the World Food Programme through the Ministry of Health's mother and child maternal program, the Ministry of Education's school feeding program and the food for work/asset program.[105] To deal with ongoing food insecurity, on 1 October 2012, the Secretariat of State for Professional Training and Employment launched a pilot program on conditional cash transfers targeting 5,000 food insecure households in Bobonaro district.[106] According to the Special Rapporteur's report, there also remains a significant lack of access to water and sanitation, which limits East Timor's capacities to achieve the goal of halving the proportion of the population without access to clean water or sanitation: 43 per cent of households have no access to clean water.[107]

Positively, some important gains have been made in the area of health since independence. According to 'Goodbye Conflict, Welcome Development', leprosy has been eliminated as a public health problem, tuberculosis prevalence was reduced from 450 out of 100,000 people to 124 and malaria was reduced from 200 per 1,000 in 2003 to just 30 in 2010.[108] East Timor also achieved the Millennium Development Goals of reducing child mortality (from 125 per 1,000 live births in 2003 to 55 in 2012) and is on track to improve maternal health.[109] A United Nations Secretary-General report from October 2010 attributed the decline in infant and under-five mortality rates to the 'efforts of the Ministry of Health through its national reproductive health and family planning strategy'.[110] The government attempted to improve citizens' access to rights relating to health through the implementation of the SISCA (Integrated Community Health Services) system, 'in which village communities work together with local health clinic staff to promote and deliver a basic health package (combating infectious diseases, improving nutrition, maternal and child health, and family planning)'.[111] Over 550,000 people accessed the system in the 477 SISCA posts spread across East Timor.[112] Although gains have been met in some health areas, significant challenges remain, particularly as the health and well-being of a population is directly affected by rates of poverty, hunger and malnutrition, all

Social democratic citizenship 169

of which remain high in East Timor. For instance, the nutritional status of children remains a concern: in 2011, 53 per cent of children under the age of five were reported by the United Nations as stunted.[113]

As mentioned previously, there is a broad consensus among the East Timorese people that education is vital for state-building: in a 2002 Civil Society Consultation involving 38,293 Timorese, 70 per cent elected education 'as the most important area requiring improvement, both for their own livelihoods and for the country's development'.[114] Significant improvements have been made in this area since independence. According to the United Nations Human Development Report 2011, while net enrolments in primary education dropped from 65 per cent in 2001 to 63 per cent in 2007 (most likely as a result of the mass displacements caused by 2006 crisis), enrolments increased to 83.2 per cent in 2009.[115] The AMP government claimed an enrolment rate of 88 per cent, with a 91 per cent enrolment rate in basic education representing 'a significant improvement'. By contrast, in the same time period the rates of secondary enrolments were markedly lower at 11.7 per cent (the AMP government claimed 22 per cent).[116] While recent figures from international organisations reveal an overall enrolment rate at 71 per cent, there are a range of complicating factors, such as a high dropout rate (around 70 per cent), students starting when they are too old and students taking too many years to complete (11.2 years for primary education).[117] Other issues include stunted growth due to malnutrition, low rates of pre-school attendance (1 in 10) and gender imbalance: girls drop out of high school earlier than boys.[118] In terms of adult education, 58 per cent were classified by the UNDP as illiterate, although the 'Goodbye Conflict, Welcome Progress' claimed that the National Literacy Campaign had resulted in the eradication of illiteracy in Ataúro, Oecussi, Manatuto, Manufahi, Lautém, Aileu and Viqueque, with 173,000 people no longer illiterate.[119]

Social democratic policies emphasising education, health and welfare are necessary for achieving equitable distribution of income and alleviating conditions of poverty in Timor-Leste. While budget sustainability is a concern in resource-rich, low-income states, neo-liberal policies centred upon small government, minimal state intervention in the economy and limited wealth distribution are inappropriate given the reliance of East Timor's economy on petroleum revenues. According to 2011 Human Development Report, '[p]olicies to address levels of poverty cannot rely solely on the "trickle down" effect of petroleum wealth, but as shown by the experiences of countries in the Southeast Asian region, policies and programs must be put in place to ensure that growth is inclusive'.[120] In East Timor, cash transfers, food subsidization policies and labour schemes have meant that the relatively high rate of economic growth has had a positive impact on poverty.[121]

Providing socio-economic rights and developing economic growth while relying heavily on finite natural resources is a major challenge for East Timor and concerns have been identified about the potential to lapse into a 'resource curse'.[122] The AMP government was accused by some of risking emptying the petroleum fund by 2020 through its spending on infrastructure and social welfare

170 *Social democratic citizenship*

policies such as cash transfers.[123] Similarly, *La'o Hamutuk* critiqued the 2012 budget by pointing out that East Timor was the 'world leader in budget escalation': the 2012 budget was projected as 28 per cent larger than in 2011.[124] The proposed budget for 2012 consisted of US$1,763 billion in spending, although was later reduced to US$1,674 million.[125] However, the United Nations Development Programme suggests that East Timor's policies to avoid the resource curse have been largely overlooked by these commentators.[126] Furthermore, justifying budgetary constraint when nearly half the population is living in conditions of multidimensional poverty is problematic. As the state is viewed as responsible for dealing with widespread deprivations, fulfilling the expectations of citizens regarding progress and human rights contributes to enhancing democratic consolidation and political stability.

The 2011 UNDP Timor-Leste Development Report recognised the role of the AMP government in 'improving public safety and security, enhancing social protection, addressing the problems faced by youth, tackling unemployment, improving social service delivery, and promoting clean and effective government'.[127] Problematically, the United Nations Special Rapporteur notes that although the State budget has increased since 2007, 'there has been a gradual decline in the percentage allocated to social services, including health and education services, as well as to agriculture'.[128] For instance, the 2012 budget had 6.3 per cent of state expenditures allocated to education and only 2.9 per cent for health, which is significantly less than in other developing countries.[129] Civil society organization *La'o Hamatuk* criticised the 2012 budget as lacking 'sufficient attention to Timor-Leste's human resources which are the foundation of economic development, as well as essential to our people's quality of life'.[130] A similar point is made in the Timor-Leste Human Development Report 2011, which notes that education was only allocated 10 per cent of the budget in 2009 (less than in 2011), compared with other developing states in Southeast Asia, such as Thailand and Malaysia, where 20 per cent or more is allocated to education.[131] The Special Rapporteur called upon government to 'reassess the allocation of its resources, to ensure that social services are sufficiently financed to facilitate the progressive realization of economic, social and cultural rights for all Timorese in a sustainable manner'.[132]

In 2012, East Timor devoted more resources to defence than health, and the majority of the defence spending was allocated to the military, which deals predominantly with external defence, than to the police force, which is responsible for internal security.[133] Devoting resources to socio-economic areas is more likely to prove effective for East Timor's security challenges – which are overwhelmingly internal in nature – than prioritising military projects, which may be popular in the domestic political sphere but are somewhat redundant: the international support East Timor receives suggests their external security is unlikely to be threatened by other states.[134] The AMP government has also allocated a greater percentage of budget spending to big infrastructure projects instead of directly investing in the East Timorese people, which somewhat undermined its social democratic credentials.[135] The government produced a 'Citizen's Guide to the Budget' in 2012 which outlined the distribution of the US$1,674 million

Social democratic citizenship 171

budget, emphasising infrastructure, improving service delivery and poverty reduction.[136] The guide outlined that infrastructure was allocated US$800 million, the Ministry of Social Solidarity was allocated US$128 million, education US$95 million and only US$48 million allocated to health.[137] This continued the AMP's prioritization of 'capital and development' since 2007.[138] While the citizen's guide argued that spending on goods and services had increased, including cash transfers to 'needy and deserving groups', this corresponded with an increase in the size of the budget, and hence the percentage of the budget allocated to health and education had actually decreased.[139] This follows a consistent spending pattern from independence: the World Bank identifies that the spending on health (as a percentage of overall Gross National Product) had decreased from 8.6 per cent in 2006 to 5.1 per cent in 2011.[140]

While spending on goods and services was significantly lower than infrastructure, several commentators have suggested that the AMP government took advantage of the oil and gas reserves, driving a huge expansion in public spending during the 2012 election campaign, particularly in 'generous' cash transfer schemes, subsidized rice, cash-for-work schemes'.[141] The International Crisis Group attributed this increased spending to the prominence of social welfare as a campaign issue and the huge popularity of the cash transfer scheme among the East Timorese.[142] While poverty clearly remains a significant challenge, and the distribution of wealth was a significant campaign issue, the International Crisis Group argued there were few 'real' policies proposals on improving the welfare of the *oma ki'ik* (little people).[143]

An election budget is a tool that an incumbent government can use to attempt to maintain and gain votes, which offers one reason why incumbency is considered an electoral advantage. In the AMP government's 2012 budget, Dili, Viqueque, Covalima and Baucau were allocated the most money of the districts, which is noteworthy as three of those districts routinely favour FRETILIN.[144] Shoesmith criticised Prime Minister Xanana Gusmáo in particular for using the Petroleum Fund to establish the CNRT 'as the dominant actors in a multi-party system' as part of a 'strategy' for CNRT to be re-elected and govern in its own right.[145] However, this is why democracies hold regular elections: if political parties are not responsive to voters, and fail to care about their re-election, then they may not sufficiently represent the 'will of the people'. The use of cash-transfer schemes (which were actually introduced in 2008) reflects the popularity of social democratic policies designed to assist the most vulnerable members of community, which is hardly surprising given the majority of East Timorese voters experience socio-economic rights deprivations.

In any case, in 2013 the new BGK government appeared to heed the calls from civil society organisations and commentators for reduced spending.[146] The 2013 budget, passed on 18 February and promulgated as Law No. 02/2013 on 1 March 2013 by new President Taur Matan Ruak, totalled US$1,647 million, with US$783 million allocated to infrastructure, and electricity the highest priority with US$283 million, compared with US$39 million to social security, US$69 million to health, and US$139 million to education.[147] The BGK has continued

172 *Social democratic citizenship*

to endorse the 2011 SDP, including high levels of spending on infrastructure 'deriving overwhelmingly from the country's Petroleum Fund'.[148] The Programme of the Fifth Constitutional Government (2012–2017) reiterated early documents of the AMP government, stating:

> our vision is that of a Nation that is prosperous, healthy, educated and skilled, with broad access to essential goods and services, and where production and employment in all sectors corresponds to that of an emerging economy. Our goal is to create opportunities for all, in a fair and inclusive manner, to enable the growth of a dynamic and innovating economy.[149]

The program of the Fifth Constitutional Government also suggested that the social and economic policies of the government 'have sought to reduce poverty among our people, to consolidate the security and stability of the Nation and to build and strengthen State institutions', again drawing a link between political order and the delivery of human security.[150] It 'recognises that the true wealth of any nation is in the strength of its people. Maximising the overall health, education and quality of life of the Timorese people is central to building a fair and progressive society'.[151] Further, the government suggests that '[a]ssisting the poor and vulnerable members of our society is an important Government obligation. Subsidies, transfer payments and in kind support to our most vulnerable people help alleviate poverty, but are mostly an issue of social justice'.[152] These statements reflect the social democratic vision of previous governments and the independence movement.

The budget allocations suggest that the practical priorities of the state do not necessarily conform to the rhetoric, particularly given the proposed low budget allocation to health, which is of concern given the continuing high incidence of poverty and poverty-related diseases in East Timor. However, despite ongoing challenges, since independence East Timor can be considered a relatively successful case of development when compared with other post-colonial, post-conflict states.[153] According to the World Bank 'on average post-conflict countries take between 15 and 30 years – a full generation – to transition out of fragility and to build resilience. It is against this backdrop that social and economic development in Timor-Leste can be seen as remarkable'.[154] Some improvements have clearly been made in terms of human development indicators and Millennium Development Goals, although progress was made with considerable assistance of IGOS and NGOs. Progress in key socio-economic indicators correlates with an overall increase of security and stability in East Timor since 2008 (alongside other factors such as the introduction of the International Stabilisation Force and Security Sector Reform).

East Timor has demonstrated a commitment to institutionalizing social democratic policies, including welfare and social security, food security, universal access to health and education services, gender equality and the protection of children's rights. Both the AMP and BGK governments viewed socio-economic development as integral to securing peace in East Timor. However, it is concerning that the BGK government continues to prioritise infrastructure projects over

Social democratic citizenship 173

basic social services as many East Timorese are still yet to achieve basic socio-economic rights outlined in the Constitution. In his 2012 speech to parliament on the new government's program, Prime Minister Xanana Gusmão stated that:

> [t]he development of social capital means placing people above all other interests. Valuing the Timorese, which are the true wealth of the Nation, means building a fair and developed Nation. We vow to improve the quality of – and access to – health, education, professional training, information, social justice and culture.[155]

Yet, the UNDP suggests that states making significant progress on Millennium Development Goals spend approximately 28 per cent of their budget on education and health.[156] This is much higher than the commitments set out by the BGK government in the 2013 budget. Providing socio-economic rights through wealth and income redistribution, government policies and social security is necessary for both citizens' capacities to access to their citizenship rights and democratic consolidation more generally. While including socio-economic rights as instruments of the state is fundamentally important, these rights can only be rendered meaningful if they are supported by a budget that appropriately resources health, education and social welfare sectors.

Conclusion

An independent democracy requires particular rights to be afforded to citizens, including civil, political and social rights. Democratic political order is based on a popular belief in the legitimacy of institutions, which is contingent upon citizens' perceptions of their validity and suitability and the extent of their willing compliance. The capacities of East Timor to build a fair, democratic and equitable state depend upon people's perceptions of key state institutions as just and fair. Legitimate institutions that support functional internal sovereignty require the support of the majority of the population. For East Timor, citizenship rights were important for fostering democratic political order through popular support rather than coercion or violence, because this was one of the key promises of independence.

The progressive list of citizenship rights reflects the 'radical social-democratic tradition with a direct lineage to the Portuguese revolution of 1974'.[157] The CNRT's Magna Carta produced in 1998 provided the basis of the Constitution's Bill of Rights, which illustrates the continuity in the goals to establish a social democratic system of governance based upon social citizenship rights. East Timor's Constitution highlights the aspirations of the leaders of the new state insofar as it provided the blueprint for the new type of relationship between state and society.

One of the key challenges for the East Timorese state is addressing widespread socio-economic deprivation.[158] Socio-economic and cultural citizenship rights are important for providing people with a measure of protection, and their presence in East Timor's Bill of Rights demonstrates a commitment to building a social

174 *Social democratic citizenship*

democratic political model in East Timor. Distributive rights, understood as socio-economic rights arising from the redistribution of wealth, underpinned the establishment of citizenship in contemporary East Timor. The 2002 National Development Plan and 2011 Strategic Development Plan both demonstrate continuity in the belief that the state is responsible for ensuring a minimum standard of living and improving life opportunities of citizens by providing the social citizenship rights necessary to be 'free'. The analysis of budgetary spending has demonstrated a recent preference for big infrastructure projects and defence spending which has led to a decrease in the percentage of budgetary spending on the key social areas of health and education. In spite of this, policies consistent with a welfare state, including cash transfers and pensions for vulnerable community members, have been instituted by the state. The extent to which a prosperous and fair society is developed, and the promises of the independence movement fulfilled, is likely to impact upon the democratic consolidation in the future.

Notes

1 Turner, 'The Erosion of Citizenship', 192.
2 Miller, *Citizenship and National Identity*, 82–83 and Pierson, *The Modern State*, 128 and 134.
3 Sunstein, *Designing Democracy*, 7.
4 Leach, 'Valorising the Resistance', 46.
5 See Saad-Filho, *Growth, Poverty and Inequality*.
6 Constituent Assembly, *Constitution*.
7 This is conceded by Morison. See Morison, 'Democratisation and Timor-Leste after UNTAET', 180 and 183.
8 Translated from Portuguese: 'constituição da republica democrática de timor-leste, devem esta reflectidas nas políticas, nas acções e nos esforcos de liderança e a governação deve ter por base os dereitos humanos'. A number of speeches reflect the importance of human rights. See for example the 2002 speech by Xanana Gusmao titled 'Por Ocasião dos Celabraçoões Do Dia Internacional dos Direitos Humanos' in Gusmão, *A Construção da Nação Timorense Desafios e Oportunidades*, 78 and the 2004 speech 'A Tendêencia dos Movimentos Pela Paz Mundial – A Experiêcia de Timor-Leste' in Gusmão, *Xanana Gusmão e os Primeiros 10 anos da Construção do Estado Timorense*, 99–100.
9 National Council of Timorese Resistance, *Magna Carta concerning Freedoms, Rights, Duties and Guarantees for the People of East Timor*.
10 Ramos-Horta, *Towards a Peaceful Solution in East Timor*, 43.
11 Ramos-Horta, 'Human Rights, Democracy and Rule of Law', 2.
12 The East Timor Jurist Association comprised around 100 East Timorese law graduates, para-legals and human rights activists. See Walsh, *The Human Rights and Future of East Timor Workshop*.
13 National Council of Timorese Resistance National Congress, *Draft Resolution on Human Rights*.
14 Ibid.
15 Walsh, *The Human Rights and Future of East Timor Workshop*.
16 Ibid.
17 Ibid.
18 National Council of Timorese Resistance National Congress, *Draft Resolution on Human Rights*.
19 Ibid.

Social democratic citizenship   175

20 Constituent Assembly, *Constitution*, Section 1.
21 Ibid., Section 23.
22 Leach, 'Valorising the Resistance', 46.
23 Nicholson, 'Observation on the New Constitution of East Timor', 205.
24 Constituent Assembly, *Constitution*.
25 Marshall, 'Citizenship and Social Class', 8.
26 Ibid. See also Heater, *Citizenship*, 101.
27 Marshall, ibid., 28 and Heater, *What is Citizenship?*, 10.
28 John Rawls for example argues that institutions can only be just if they could ensure a minimum standard of welfare, whereby the poorest and most disadvantaged members of society would be raised above this minimum standard by distributing rights and duties, and benefits and burdens. See Rawls, *A Theory of Justice.*
29 Constituent Assembly, *Constitution*.
30 Marshall, 'Citizenship and Social Class', 21–22.
31 See United Nations General Assembly, *Universal Declaration of Human Rights*, Articles 1 and 2 and United Nations General Assembly, *International Covenant on Civil Rights and Political Rights*, Article 2.
32 Inter-Parliamentary Union, *Universal Declaration on Democracy.*
33 Constituent Assembly, *Constitution*, Section 26.
34 The relationships between cultural identity and concepts of rights and justice have been much debated by scholars. See Reilly, 'Political Engineering in the Asia-Pacific', 58–72.
35 Alldèn, 'Internalising the Culture of Human Rights', 1–2.
36 Ibid, 4.
37 Chesterman, *You, the People*, 332. See also East Timor Planning Commission, *East Timor 2020*, 25–26.
38 See Charlesworth and Wood, 'Women and Human Rights'; Retbøll, 'The Women of East Timor', 27–28 and Alldèn, 'Internalising the Culture of Human Rights', 1.
39 Constituent Assembly, *Constitution*, Section 17.
40 Soares, 'Nahe Biti', 27.
41 Charlesworth, 'The Constitution of East Timor', 332. See Niner, 'Between Earth and Heaven', 243.
42 East Timor Planning Commission, *East Timor 2020*, 2, 4 and 5 and East Timor Planning Commission, *National Development Plan.*
43 East Timor Planning Commission, *East Timor 2020*, 25.
44 East Timor Planning Commission, *National Development Plan*, xviii and 8.
45 Ibid., 20.
46 Cited in Ibid., xvi.
47 Ibid., 7.
48 Ibid., 5–6.
49 East Timor Planning Commission, *East Timor 2020*, 6.
50 Ibid., 20.
51 Ibid., 9.
52 Ibid., 9, 20 and 29. See also Government of Democratic Republic of Timor-Leste, *Strategic Development Plan*, 27.
53 Government of Democratic Republic of Timor-Leste, *IV Constitutional Government Program 2007–2012* and Government of Democratic Republic of Timor-Leste, *Strategic Development Plan.*
54 East Timor Planning Commission, *National Development Plan*, 5.
55 Ibid., 7.
56 Ibid., 9.
57 Ibid.
58 José Ramos-Horta cited in Government of Democratic Republic of Timor-Leste, *Strategic Development Plan*, 7.

176   *Social democratic citizenship*

59   Ibid., 16.
60   Ibid., 54. The AMP government began paying veterans, disabled and elderly pensions after they came to power in 2007. Approximately 16 per cent of East Timor's 2011 budget was allocated to social protection, and included US$58.8 million for paying pensions to veterans and US$30.2 million for other social vulnerable groups. See Ministry of Finance, *State Budget 2011: Budget Overview Book One*, 3 and 14.
61   East Timor Planning Commission, *National Development Plan*, 9.
62   Government of Democratic Republic of Timor-Leste, *Strategic Development Plan*, 13.
63   Ibid., 46.
64   East Timor Planning Commission, *East Timor 2020*, xvii.
65   United Nations Integrated Mission in Timor-Leste, *International Compact* and Prime Minister and Cabinet of the Government of Timor-Leste, *Prime Minister Hails Compact as a Platform for Unity*.
66   United Nations Integrated Mission in Timor-Leste, ibid.
67   Ibid.
68   United Nations Development Assistance Framework, *UNDAF 2009–2013: Democratic Republic of Timor-Leste*, 5 and 10–12.
69   Government of Democratic Republic of Timor-Leste, *Strategic Development Plan*, 46.
70   Rawls, *A Theory of Justice*.
71   Constituent Assembly, *Constitution*, Sections 56: 2 and 57: 3.
72   See Hughes, *Dependent Communities*, 6–7.
73   Shoesmith, 'Timor-Leste: On the Road to Peace and Prosperity', 324.
74   Global Finance, *Timor-Leste Country Report*.
75   European Union Election Observation Mission, *Timor-Leste: Final Report Parliamentary Election 2012*, 7.
76   United Nations Development Programme, *United Nations Development Programme: About Timor-Leste*.
77   Carmona, *Report of the Special Rapporteur on Extreme Poverty and Human Rights Mission to Timor-Leste*, 6.
78   United Nations Development Programme, *Human Development Report 2013* and United Nations Development Programme, *Human Development Report 2011*, 126.
79   United Nations Development Programme, *Timor-Leste*, Table 2, 166.
80   World Bank, *World Development Indicators 2013*, 24. PPP refers to Purchasing Power Parity and is used by economists to compare relative values across diverse currencies.
81   Government of Democratic Republic of Timor-Leste, *'Goodbye Conflict, Welcome Development'*, 3; Government of Democratic Republic of Timor-Leste, *IV Constitutional Government Program 2007–2012*, 7 and Government of Democratic Republic of Timor-Leste, *Strategic Development Plan*.
82   Government of Democratic Republic of Timor-Leste, *'Goodbye Conflict, Welcome Development'*.
83   United Nations Development Programme, *Human Development Report 2011*, 14.
84   Ibid.
85   United Nations Security Council, *Report of the Secretary-General on the United Nations Integrated Mission in Timor-Leste (for the period from 24 September to 20 January 2010)*, 5.
86   Ibid.
87   Ibid., 5 and Carmona, *Report of the Special Rapporteur on Extreme Poverty and Human Rights Mission to Timor-Leste*, 5. See also United Nations Security Council, *Report of the Secretary-General on the United Nations Integrated Mission in Timor-Leste (for the period from 21 January to 20 September 2010)*, 11.
88   Government of Democratic Republic of Timor-Leste, *IV Constitutional Government Program 2007–2012*, 15 and Kingsbury, 'Timor-Leste in 2012', 311.
89   Oxford Poverty and Human Development Initiative, *OPHI Country Briefing January 2015: Timor-Leste*, 1.

Social democratic citizenship 177

90 Carmona, *Report of the Special Rapporteur on Extreme Poverty and Human Rights Mission to Timor-Leste*, 7.
91 Ibid., 5.
92 Ibid., 6.
93 Sugden, 'Timor-Leste's Pursuit of Inclusive Opportunity', 1 and 8.
94 Ibid., 10.
95 United Nations Development Programme, *Timor-Leste Human Development Report 2011*.
96 Government of Democratic Republic of Timor-Leste, *'Goodbye Conflict, Welcome Development'*. See also Gusmão, *Strategies for the Future*, 209.
97 Ibid., 2.
98 Ibid. and Pension Watch, *Country Fact Sheet: Timor-Leste*.
99 Government of Democratic Republic of Timor-Leste, *Which Social Security for Timor-Leste?*
100 Government of Democratic Republic of Timor-Leste *'Goodbye Conflict, Welcome Development'*.
101 Ibid.
102 Ibid.
103 Ibid.
104 Ibid.
105 United Nations Security Council, *Report of the Secretary-General on the United Nations Integrated Mission in Timor-Leste (for the period from 21 January to 20 September 2010)*, S/2010/522, 13 October 2010, 13.
106 United Nations Security Council, *Report of the Secretary-General on the United Nations Integrated Mission in Timor-Leste (for the period from 20 September 2011 to 6 January 2012)*, 12.
107 Carmona, *Report of the Special Rapporteur on Extreme Poverty and Human Rights Mission to Timor-Leste*, 5.
108 Government of Democratic Republic of Timor-Leste, *'Goodbye Conflict, Welcome Development'*.
109 United Nations Development Programme, *Timor-Leste: Country Profile.*
110 United Nations Security Council, *Report of the Secretary-General on the United Nations Integrated Mission in Timor-Leste (for the period from 21 January to 20 September 2010)*, S/2010/522, 13 October 2010, 12.
111 United Nations Development Programme, *Timor-Leste Human Development Report 2011*.
112 Government of Democratic Republic of Timor-Leste, *'Goodbye Conflict, Welcome Development'*.
113 United Nations Security Council, *Report of the Secretary-General on the United Nations Integrated Mission in Timor-Leste (for the period from 21 September 2010 to 7 January 2011)*.
114 United Nations Development Programme, *Timor-Leste Human Development Report 2011*, 47.
115 Ibid., 22.
116 United Nations Development Programme, *Timor-Leste: Country Profile.*
117 Ibid.
118 Government of Democratic Republic of Timor-Leste, *IV Constitutional Government Program 2007–2012*, 14.
119 Government of Democratic Republic of Timor-Leste, *'Goodbye Conflict, Welcome Development'*.
120 United Nations Development Programme, *Human Development Report 2013*, 7.
121 From 2007–2009, for example, Government funded labour schemes employed 40,000 Timorese annually, and the 2009 *Pakote Referendum* infrastructure development program created 64,000 short-term jobs in the rural sector. See ibid., 5.

178 *Social democratic citizenship*

122 Shoesmith, 'Timor-Leste: On the Road to Peace and Prosperity', 328 and Kingsbury, 'Timor-Leste in 2012', 310.
123 Petroleum Economist, *Going for Broke*.
124 La'o Hamutuk, *RDTL General State Budget for 2012*.
125 Ibid.
126 United Nations Development Programme, *Timor-Leste Human Development Report 2011*, 7.
127 Ibid., 4.
128 Carmona, *Report of the Special Rapporteur on Extreme Poverty and Human Rights Mission to Timor-Leste*, 8.
129 La'o Hamutuk, *RDTL General State Budget for 2012*.
130 Ibid.
131 United Nations Development Programme, *Timor-Leste Human Development Report 2011*, 46.
132 Carmona, *Report of the Special Rapporteur on Extreme Poverty and Human Rights Mission to Timor-Leste*, 8.
133 La'o Hamutuk, *RDTL General State Budget for 2012*.
134 Strating, 'East Timor's Emerging National Security Agenda', 185–210.
135 According to the citizen's guide, the biggest area of spending under infrastructure was on electricity. See Democratic Republic of Timor-Leste, '*Goodbye Conflict, Welcome Development*', 5 and 6.
136 Ibid., 4.
137 Ibid., 5.
138 Ibid., 4.
139 Ibid., 4.
140 World Bank, *Health Expenditure, total (% of GDP)*.
141 International Crisis Group, *Timor-Leste's Elections*, 5 and Gunn, 'Timor-Leste in 2009', 237–238.
142 International Crisis Group, ibid., 7.
143 Ibid.
144 Ibid., 6.
145 Shoesmith, 'Is Small Beautiful?', 48.
146 Author Unknown, 'No Clean Sweep', *The Economist*.
147 La'o Hamutuk, *RDTL General State Budget for 2013*, and Democratic Republic of Timor-Leste National Parliament, *General State Budget for 2013*.
148 Kingsbury, 'Timor-Leste in 2012', 308.
149 Government of Democratic Republic of Timor-Leste, *IV Constitutional Government Program 2007–2012*, 6.
150 Ibid., 6.
151 Ibid., 10.
152 Ibid., 20.
153 Ibid., 6.
154 World Bank, *Timor-Leste Overview*.
155 Tempo Semanal, *PM Xanana Present to TL Parliament the Programs of Government*, Dili, 12 September 2012.
156 United Nations Development Programme, *Timor-Leste Human Development Report 2011*, 122.
157 Leach, 'Valorising the Resistance', 46.
158 East Timor Planning Commission, *East Timor 2020 – Our Vision, Our Future*, 2.

7 Transitional justice and social democracy

While the ideal 'modern' state relies upon formal institutions and office-bearers possessing 'rational-legal' authority, this can pose challenges for new states if 'traditional' or 'customary' forms of authority clash with centralised, state-based structures.[1] Achieving the democratic ideals of rule of law and political equality promised by modern democratic statehood requires bringing customary and localised legal orders and conflict resolution structures under the auspices of centralised state-based laws. In East Timor, this is particularly important as local justice mechanisms operated autonomously from Portuguese and Indonesian rule and continue to possess 'traditional' legitimacy among the population.[2]

O'Donnell argues that democratic accountabilities run vertically as elected officials are answerable to citizens through elections, and horizontally as powers and responsibilities are separated across political institutions in a system of checks and balances.[3] Rule of law requires that no individuals are considered 'above the law', that citizens are free from arbitrary rules that violate constitutional citizenship rights and that due limits are placed on the power of state institutions.[4] An independent judiciary acts as an arbiter of rule of law by ensuring that laws are properly applied and preventing improper abuses of power by individuals in formal offices or state agencies. Facilitating a 'human rights' culture requires judicial institutions that can both protect and be seen to protect citizens from violations of constitutionally guaranteed human, civil and socio-economic rights.

Just as importantly for rule of law and political order, judicial institutions need to be seen by the population as effectively fulfilling the functions of adjudication and enforcement of state-based law. Broadly speaking, the legitimacy of democratic procedures, rules and norms – even in the face of challenges – rests upon popular consent as it is derived from 'an intrinsic value commitment rooted in the political culture at all levels of society'.[5] Constitutionalism relies upon a widespread belief in the validity of the Constitution as the foundation for a state-based legal system. In transitional contexts, this involves citizens changing the way they perceive the legitimate exercise of public power.[6] Simultaneously, perceptions are shaped by whether or not the judicial system fulfils the promises of statehood and the rights-bearing status of citizens.

Following the 1999 independence referendum, the United Nations Transitional Administration in East Timor (UNTAET) faced significant challenges in

180   *Transitional justice and social democracy*

re-building the judiciary to restore political order. The destruction of buildings and the lack of transport, communication and 'governmental superstructure' necessitated the UNTAET re-building the justice system virtually from scratch.[7] The UNTAET's task was more extensive than previous judiciary-building operations in Cambodia, Bosnia and Kosovo.[8] Strohmeyer reported that 'not a single judge, prosecutor or attorney was left, the court buildings were destroyed or stripped of any useful materials, including the electrical wiring, legal libraries were removed or dislocated, the prisons were emptied'.[9] Much of the legal office equipment, law books, case files and so forth was destroyed.[10] In addition to re-building physical infrastructure, a significant training program was also necessary: by the time the UNTAET arrived in East Timor, there were less than ten lawyers left in the territory, all inexperienced.[11] To assist the UNTAET find East Timorese with legal experience, the INTERFET dropped leaflets across the territory from planes.[12]

The UNTAET also faced a major challenge in pursuing justice for past crimes and violations of human rights in East Timor. 'Transitional justice' refers to temporary justice mechanisms instituted during periods of political instability with the aim of promoting democratisation and a culture of human rights.[13] The United Nations Security Council Resolution 1272 that established the UNTAET obliged the new body to ensure that 'those [persons] responsible for such violence be brought to justice' and 'bear individual responsibility' for their past crimes'.[14] The Serious Crimes process began under the UNTAET regime in June 2000. Not long after the establishment of the Serious Crimes process in East Timor, in August 2001, Indonesia created an ad hoc Human Rights Court on East Timor in Jakarta to prosecute crimes committed in East Timor. Ongoing impunity for perpetrators of past human rights violations represents an ongoing challenge for the East Timorese state as many civil society organisations emphasise the failures of retributive justice to support democratic consolidation and rule of law.

Working in parallel with the Serious Crimes Process was the Commission for Reception, Truth and Reconciliation/*Comissão de Acolhimento, Verdade e Reconciliação de Timor* (CAVR) mandated both by the UNTAET Regulation No. 2001/10 in July 2001 and Section 162 of East Timor's Constitution.[15] Truth and Reconciliation Commissions reflect restorative approaches to transitional justice and are generally employed to ease political transition across different orders.[16] One of the key functions is to help new political orders establish a culture of human rights.[17] The CAVR was responsible for recording human rights abuses since 1975 and promote community reconciliation in dealing with low-level offences.[18] The resultant CAVR's *Chega!* report (released in 2005) was based upon widespread community participation and deliberation. In emphasising the importance of socio-economic rights and reparations, the CAVR processes also reflected restitutive approaches to transitional justice.[19]

Since independence, East Timor has been challenged by issues of impunity. However, restorative and restitutive justice approaches fostered largely by CAVR processes appear to have assisted with both reconciliation and rule of law in East Timor. The state has remained focused on issues of socio-economic rights and social justice, which is consistent with the independence movement's vision of building a social democracy in East Timor.

Models of transitional justice

While there are several different forms of 'transitional justice', it is commonly split into 'retributive' and 'restorative' approaches. Retributive approaches to justice focus predominantly upon punishment and accountability.[20] According to Samuel Huntington, advocates of retributive justice in post-transition contexts emphasise a moral obligation to victims to hold perpetrators of rights abuses to account.[21] Retributive justice supports rule of law by ensuring no one is seen as above the law, and assists internal sovereignty in preventing impunity, which undermines deterrence. State institutions, such as the police or military, successfully preventing prosecutions for past crimes undermines political equality. A retributive justice approach suggests that instilling a human rights culture in a new state, such as East Timor, requires all citizens understanding that human rights violations will be punished through an independent and robust judicial system. Prosecution is hence necessary for asserting 'the supremacy of democratic values and norms' and instilling trust in the new legal system.[22]

In contrast, restorative justice emphasises constructive relationships between community members and judicial institutions, and the collective engagement among people in addressing wrongdoings.[23] Restorative justice is intertwined with the political objective of reconciliation as both encourage parties in conflict to come together to resolve issues and can aim to heal the pain of victims and re-integrate community members.[24] Those who advocate reconciliation often do so on the basis that it encourages negotiation, engagement and dialogue that is often found in customary systems of conflict resolution. It enables groups to set aside past divisions, allows agreement on no retribution for past crimes and, importantly, takes pressure off a weak and under-institutionalised formal judiciary system. Reconciliation recognises that many people may share guilt in crimes committed and building a stable democracy requires finding common ground and fostering national unity.[25]

A third 'restitutive' approach, based on reparations and social justice, can also be observed in East Timor's transitional justice model. According to Lambourne, incorporating restitutive justice mechanisms alongside retributive and restorative approaches can assist in alleviating conflict in transitional contexts, which she perceives as primarily arising from social and economic rights deprivations.[26] Similarly, La Plante suggests that politically motivated violence arises from socio-economic problems, and, as such, the concept of social justice should be incorporated in the practices of transitional justice.[27] There are several ways transitional justice mechanisms can support and enhance the achievement of social justice. First, the processes can involve the identification of social, cultural and economic rights violations, in addition to civil and political rights, and can assist in addressing underlying social structural causes for violence. Second,

182   *Transitional justice and social democracy*

justice bodies can make recommendations and assist in embedding a culture of socio-economic rights by pursuing their protection as a pathway to community reconciliation.[28] Restitutive justice can also be considered a restorative mechanism insofar as reparations may enable the re-establishment (as far as possible) of the socio-economic situation of the beneficiary prior to the rights violation.[29] Restitutive justice is important in the context of East Timor's development of social democracy. The inclusion of social justice in East Timor's transitional justice mechanisms was underpinned by a belief that violations of socio-economic rights were as significant as crimes against civil and political rights.

The challenge for East Timor following the independence ballot was 'to find the right balance between justice and reconciliation in a society that holds the principle of forgiveness at the core of its culture'.[30] According to Kingston, East Timor's leaders 'opted for reconciliation and restorative justice while seeking a healing process in advocating good governance and alleviating pressing socio-economic needs', which highlights the different responsibilities of the state.[31] While retributive and restorative approaches may be considered overlapping and mutually dependent, restorative and reconciliatory justice models can provide greater opportunities for integrating local customary processes than formal retributive justice mechanisms. In the context of East Timor's pursuit of transitional justice, many civil society organisations argued that reconciliation and restorative justice would not be possible without the state holding perpetrators of past human rights violations to account. Customary forms of justice were incorporated into state-based reconciliation mechanisms to reconcile tensions between different forms of legitimacy authority. These attempts are significant given that local authority structures continue to guide collective life within most *sukus* (villages).[32] The implementation of 'grass-roots', participatory justice mechanisms in the CAVR process, involving active roles for citizens and civil society organisations, indicate the importance of public deliberation in facilitating 'local ownership' of state institutions.

Pursuing retributive justice

Transitional justice mechanisms in East Timor have largely concerned the violence that occurred around the time of the 1999 referendum. The 'Operation Clean Sweep' campaign consisted of destroying physical infrastructure, including private homes, shops, government offices, schools and medical clinics, and other crucial infrastructure, such as water, electricity, and telecommunications facilities.[33] Approximately 2,000 people were killed and 400,000 people forced to flee their homes, and crimes against humanity were perpetrated, including torture, bodily mutilation and rape.[34] On 15 September 1999, United Nations Security Council Resolution 1264 expressed concerns at the 'systematic, widespread and flagrant violations of international humanitarian and human rights law', called upon their immediate end and demanded that those responsible for such acts be brought to justice.[35] While UN Security Council Resolution 1272 did not explicitly declare the UNTAET responsible for providing justice for

Transitional justice and social democracy   183

human rights violations, by early 2000 it was clear that the UN Legal Office would be required to pursue retributive justice and establish domestic courts.[36] As Katzenstein points out, public trust in East Timor's judiciary would depend upon the capacities of the legal system to prosecute these crimes.[37]

In January 2000, a UN-sponsored International Commission of Inquiry was instituted to examine possibilities for pursuing justice for rights violations committed in 1999, and ultimately recommended the creation of an international tribunal.[38] United Nations Secretary-General Kofi Annan emphasised the responsibilities of the international community in investigating and punishing those responsible for rights violations and to 'help safeguard the rights of the people of East Timor, promote reconciliation, [and] ensure future social and political stability'.[39] The report suggested that finding the truth and bringing those responsible for human rights crimes to justice would be 'fundamental for the future social and political stability of East Timor'.[40] An internationally administered tribunal was preferred as the likely implication of senior Indonesian TNI members would make it difficult to secure convictions in Indonesian courts, and East Timor did not have the resources to operate such an extensive tribunal.

Indonesia rejected the proposals, and instead, assured the international community of its commitment to pursuing justice by signing a Memorandum of Understanding with the UNTAET in April 2000, which included provisions for sharing evidence, facilitating the participation of witnesses and extraditing accused perpetrators.[41] Indonesia also committed to establishing its own human rights tribunal to investigate and prosecute crimes committed in East Timor. These promises successfully prevented the creation of an international tribunal: international NGO Human Rights Watch suggested that United Nations Secretary-General Kofi Annan accepted Indonesian President Abdurrahman Wahid's 'unambiguous' assurances that Indonesia would uphold rule of law.[42] The decision to not introduce an international tribunal was influenced by the extremely costly and slow processes that occurred in other ad hoc courts, such as those for Yugoslavia and Rwanda.[43]

In the absence of an international tribunal, the UNTAET decided to establish a 'hybrid' tribunal composed of international and domestic personnel, based on a realistic assessment of East Timor's capacities to independently operate a tribunal of the size and scope required. The UNTAET Regulation 2000/11, promulgated on 6 March 2000, mandated the creation of the judiciary, composed of Districts Courts and one Court of Appeal, following consultation with the National Consultative Council.[44]

Linton suggests the establishment of a hybrid tribunal system was based on discussions regarding Cambodia's model.[45] Hybrid tribunals offer UN authority, funding and resources but can simultaneously enable local participation and training.[46] This worked against the Extraordinary Chambers in the Courts of Cambodia: while it had more Cambodian than international judges, the hybrid courts suffered from a lack of public trust due to perceptions of the incompetence and corruption of national judges, which was then compounded by the

184   *Transitional justice and social democracy*

small number of prosecutions.[47] Nevertheless, 'local ownership' over judicial processes can assist in building capacity and East Timorese legal professionals would have an active role in prosecuting past crimes. While the UNTAET consulted with the National Consultative Council on the hybrid tribunals, the UNTAET was criticised over the lack of broad local participation.[48] Technically, the Serious Crimes project was part of the East Timor Transitional Authority (ETTA), however Linton suggests that it was dominated by international personnel.[49] There was little evidence of the UNTAET carrying out extensive research or consultation with civil society on how best to address the atrocities in an East Timorese context.[50]

The District Court of Dili was given exclusive jurisdiction over serious crimes committed in the period between 1 January 1999 and 25 October 1999, defined as genocide, war crimes, crimes against humanity, murder, sexual offences and torture.[51] On 6 June 2000, the UNTAET established the Special Panels in the District Court of Dili to hear serious crimes, comprising one East Timorese and two international judges.[52] The panels would have universal jurisdiction with regard to serious criminal offences committed in the mandated timeframe, regardless of whether it was committed by an East Timorese citizen.[53] Reflecting the state-building context, the Rome statute designed for the International Criminal Court was adapted, meaning that the panels were to defer to the principle and norms of international law in issues not covered by the 'law of East Timor'.[54,55] The two Special Panels first commenced their work on January 2001.[56]

Meanwhile, in Indonesia, the National Human Rights Commission (KOMASHAM) established the Commission for Human Rights Violations in East Timor (KPP-HAM) on 22 September 1999 to investigate crimes in East Timor.[57] The resultant report (released only as an executive summary on 31 January 2000, the same day as the UN Commission of Inquiry) found 'widespread collaboration between Indonesian military and police and pro-autonomy militia', and identified high-ranking officials as responsible for crimes against humanity.[58] It made the same recommendation as the UN Commission of Inquiry that an international tribunal was necessary for trying crimes committed in East Timor in 1999.[59] In November 2000, amid substantial international pressure, the Indonesian Parliament passed legislation to create an ad hoc Human Rights Court in Jakarta, which started operations in August 2001.[60]

By August 2002, significant international criticism of Indonesia's ad hoc courts had emerged, including from the High Commissioner of the Human Rights Commission, Mary Robinson.[61] Civil society reports criticised 'sham prosecutions' in Indonesia, arguing that the influence of the Indonesian military distorted judicial processes and they highlighted the lack of political will in prosecuting those implicated in human rights violations in East Timor.[62]

These criticisms were largely driven by the verdicts of the first ad hoc court: by the end of 2002, only two individuals had been convicted, both East Timorese.[63] Former Governor of East Timor, Abilio Soares, had been charged with crimes against humanity, including '*failing to prevent* his subordinates from carrying out the attack on the Liquiça church [my emphasis]' in which at least 22

Transitional justice and social democracy 185

East Timorese were killed.[64] The language used suggested a passive role for Soares despite his senior leadership. In 2004, the ad hoc Court handed down guilty verdicts for 12 accused perpetrators, however these verdicts were overturned on appeal in May 2005 in a closed court.[65] This move was 'widely condemned' by international, East Timorese and Indonesian civil society organisations.[66] In 2009, *La'o Hamutuk* reported that of the 18 people indicted for failing to prevent crimes against humanity, 12 were acquitted at first instance.[67] Of the six convicted, all had their convictions overturned by the Appeals court despite 'considerable' evidence against Indonesian officials.[68]

A 2005 UN Commission of Experts report commissioned by the United Nations Security Council argued that the ad hoc courts were 'manifestly inadequate'.[69] The failure to indict high-level military officers, such as General Wiranto, pointed to a team of prosecutors 'not ... eager to succeed' and unreasonable mandate limitations: only crimes in three of East Timor's 13 districts were investigated, and only during the months of April and September 1999.[70] Consequently, international NGOs, such as the Justice System Monitoring Programme (JSMP) and Amnesty International, regarded Indonesia's trials 'as a whitewash' and highly 'unsatisfactory ... with not a single member of the security forces held to account'.[71] As the UN Commission of Experts report suggests, the ad hoc court failed to investigate and prosecute crimes in a 'credible manner' and the process did not hold those who bore 'the greatest responsibility for serious violations' to account.[72] Indonesia's promises to the international community that it would prosecute those responsible for human rights violations were not kept.[73] Ultimately, Indonesia's ad hoc courts did little to contribute to retributive justice of crimes committed in East Timor in 1999.

In contrast, East Timor's hybrid court was considered by the UN Commission of Experts as a genuine attempt to achieve justice; however, inadequate personnel, training and resources stifled East Timor's capacities to punish many of the implicated senior Indonesian officials.[74] There was also a lack of clarity regarding the purpose of the hybrid tribunal and whether it was designed for retributive justice or national reconciliation.[75] Cohen also suggests that 'ownership' of the process was also problematic as its hybrid nature led to an avoidance of responsibility on both of sides.[76] While the hybrid tribunal achieved a high number of indictments – of approximately 1,400 murders, a total of 572 were captured in indictments – it faced significant challenges in bringing indictees to court, particularly Indonesian officials.[77] This was partly due to the lack of funds and the 'inadequate capacity-building programs', which had created problems for the Serious Crimes processes in East Timor.[78]

For all of East Timor's judicial shortcomings, the most substantial obstacle to achieving justice was Indonesia's unwillingness to extradite those individuals indicted for war crimes or crimes against humanity. The Memorandum of Understanding signed by Indonesia and the UNTAET did not result in extraditions, and many of those most responsible for crimes against humanity during 1999 remained shielded by Indonesia. According to ETAN, by January 2008, 76 per cent of indictees continued to enjoy sanctuary in Indonesia.[79] Of those convicted,

186   *Transitional justice and social democracy*

many were 'low level Timorese functionaries'.[80] East Timor's Serious Crimes process, while achieving a notable degree of accountability, struggled to meet the 1272 UNTAET Resolution directive to 'bring to justice those who bore "greatest responsibility"'.[81] Kingston argues that 'not only did the big fish get away, even the designated scapegoats ... walked'.[82]

The impunity of many high- and middle-ranking Indonesian officials and East Timorese militia members undermined East Timor's pursuit of retributive justice during transition. While Indonesia was reluctant to pursue perpetrators, the lack of political will of the East Timor leadership and the United Nations to pressure Indonesia was evident.[83] General Wiranto, for instance, continued to pursue a career in Indonesian politics, partaking in high-profile campaigns for President in 2004 and Vice-President in 2009.[84] East Timor, in balancing its internal and external interests, has prioritised reconciliation with Indonesia ahead of substantive justice, which is problematic for the development of rule of law in both states.[85]

Civil society organisations argued that the Serious Crimes process 'unequivocally failed' to fulfil its mandate.[86] The Serious Crimes process did not prosecute or punish those who bore the most responsibility, and therefore failed to achieve retributive justice in most cases. The failure of both the Serious Crimes process in East Timor and the Indonesian ad hoc tribunal to prosecute those individuals most responsible for human rights violations was viewed as problematic for democratic consolidation, rule of law and creating a human rights culture.[87] Refusing to allow impunity for past crimes can demonstrate the commitment of the state to guarantee the citizenship rights embedded in the new Constitution.

The development of the rational-legal authority of the state – that is, its capacity to command willing compliance of citizens – can be restricted if individuals believe they can commit crimes without the likelihood of punishment. In a study by Piers Piguo for the International Center for Transitional Justice in 2003, most of the East Timorese surveyed emphasised the retributive aspects of the legal system, such as the application of law and punishment, when asked to explain the concept of justice.[88] Almost all participants placed importance on holding perpetrators of rights violations to account through prosecution.[89] Meeting those expectations is important for the capacities of state-based transitional justice mechanisms to assist the development of political order.

Civil society organisations also targeted Indonesia, the international community and complicit states as responsible for ensuring the achievement of retributive justice in East Timor. This obligation was partly based on East Timor's lack of 'institutional capacity', but was also derived from the May 5 Agreements that had created an environment in which widespread human rights abuses could occur. The International Center for Transitional Justice called upon Indonesia to end the impunity and recognise its 'legal and moral authority to the people of Timor-Leste'.[90] Other states, such as New Zealand, Australia and the United States, also came under attack from civil society organisations for reneging on their international responsibilities.[91]

The UN Commission of Experts report on the Serious Crimes process looked more positively at its participatory aspects, suggesting that it 'significantly

Transitional justice and social democracy   187

contributed to strengthening respect for rule of law in Timor-Leste... encouraged the community to participate in the process of reconciliation and justice ... [and] has also discouraged private retributive and vengeful attacks'.[92] The report also commended the Special Crimes process for presenting a broader perspective.[93] The Serious Crimes Unit terminated its investigations on 30 November 2004 and filed last indictments on 17 December 2004. By the completion of the Serious Crimes process in May 2005, 35 trials were held and 48 people convicted.[94] Nearly 400 people were indicted, with 339 accused individuals residing outside East Timorese jurisdiction, and a total of 514 investigative files remained open.[95] In April 2005, Amnesty International stated that 'responsibility remains with the Security Council to ensure that justice is delivered'.[96] Additionally, civil society organisations have pointed out that no judicial processes have been established for the crimes committed before 1999.[97]

In August 2006, the United Nations Integrated Mission in Timor-Leste (UNMIT) instated the Serious Crimes Investigation Team (SCIT) through Security Council Resolution 1704 (2006), however its remit was limited to an investigative function, with indictments lying exclusively in the hands of the Office of the Prosecutor-General.[98] The SCIT also conducted valuable community outreach activities in nearly all of the sub-districts of Timor-Leste to assist people understand their legal rights, the importance of justice and rule of law and the role of the SCIT.[99] While nearly all of the remaining cases were investigated by the time UNMIT completed its mission at the end of 2012, with the exception of 61 cases, the national justice sector had 'very limited expertise to prosecute, defend, and adjudicate these cases'.[100] Hence, impunity has continued to challenge East Timorese democracy since independence.

Pursuing restorative justice

Truth and Reconciliation Commissions fall into the category of 'National Human Rights Institutions' and often involve 'thematic investigations' which seek to identify and redress serious and widespread rights abuses and provide recommendations for avoiding similar violations in the future.[101] On 13 July 2001, the UNTAET regulation 2001/10 established East Timor's Commission for Reception, Truth and Reconciliation (CAVR).[102] The purpose of the CAVR was to identify, analyse and provide recommendations for the range of human rights violations that occurred during Indonesia's occupation and the post-referendum violence.[103] The CAVR is consistent with a global trend towards establishing reconciliation mechanisms during political transitions to 'promote democratic reforms in post-conflict society'.[104] While there have been a number of these commissions held in states across the globe, no other Southeast Asian state had established a truth and reconciliation commission.[105]

Truth and reconciliation commissions are official investigations into past patterns of abuses.[106] Stahn suggests there are many reasons why truth and reconciliation commissions have been instituted within states undergoing democratic transition, such as East Timor. First, truth commissions focus on causes of

188   *Transitional justice and social democracy*

violence, and 'can amass a more comprehensive and diversified record of past injustices than individual trials'.[107] Second, they can provide a platform for the voices of victims that would otherwise be silenced.[108] Third, they render justice by formally acknowledging the rights violations.[109] Truth commissions support retributive justice measures as they can deal with a large number of rights violations and combine traditional justice mechanisms, such as arbitration and mediation, which can alleviate pressures on the formal judicial system.[110,111] Reconciliation has become a rights-based political objective favoured by the international community, and an important tool in establishing a human rights culture in transitioning states.

The United Nations Security Council Resolution 1272 stressed the importance of a truth and reconciliation commission in East Timor to address human rights abuses and make recommendations for the new state. The UNTAET was mandated to provide 'institutions responsible for administering justice, including for past violations'.[112] It became responsible for dealing with past human rights abuses as well as instituting a rights culture in the new state. East Timorese human rights organisations, international experts, and local representatives (including the CNRT) assisted in planning the commission. The commission itself was mandated by the UNTAET's Human Rights Unit 'by a legal act of the United Nations' which had previously 'never gone so far as to act formally as the founding authority of such an institution'.[113]

Reconciliation was declared a top priority by key East Timorese political leaders.[114] Xanana Gusmão argued in a speech before the referendum on 30 August 1999 that reconciliation was fundamental to East Timor's development, national unity and political stability, and that forgiveness was necessary for even those who had 'committed the most reprehensible acts'.[115] He argued that 'regardless of past political positions, all citizens are called upon to embrace the need for harmony, and to show forgiveness and tolerance towards their brothers for the sake of our national interests'.[116] He continued by suggesting that the East Timorese nation would 'be greater if each and everyone of us is able to forgive.... For Timor's future to be one of joy and prosperity, we must be united around our nation'.[117] In May 2000, Gusmão advocated the Truth and Reconciliation Commission as a 'solution to coping with the past'.[118] Gusmão inferred a link between reconciliation and strengthening nationhood and democracy in East Timor, perceiving reconciliation as a mechanism for enabling the restoration of justice following past rights abuses and preventing them in the future. East Timor Member of Parliament Fernanda Borges also argued that reconciliation had the potential to enable national unity and allow consolidation of democratic processes and institutions.[119]

The 2000 UN Commission of Inquiry recommended that the United Nations establish an independent and international body responsible for conducting investigations of the human rights violations, identifying the persons responsible, ensuring reparations and considering issues of truth and reconciliation.[120] A number of workshops held from June to August 2000 involving the UNTAET's Human Rights Unit, key leaders and civil society organisations also

Transitional justice and social democracy   189

recommended the creation of a human rights commission.[121,122] The CNRT National Congress endorsed the recommendations, claiming an 'imperative need for justice, truth and reconciliation in East Timor'.[123] Commission 3 of the National Congress argued that future policies should seek to establish 'universal values that lead to the formation of a modern, more dignified, more humane and just society'.[124] The CNRT congress unanimously voted for the formation of a Steering Committee for Resettlement and National Reconciliation, including international and East Timorese actors, such as the CNRT, NGOs, women's groups, youth organisations, representatives of the Roman Catholic Church, the UNTAET and members of the UN Human Rights Commission.[125] The Steering Committee sought and received assistance from the Human Rights Unit of the UNTAET in establishing their vision of a truth and reconciliation commission in East Timor.[126] It was also responsible for determining whether the people of East Timor accepted the idea of a truth and reconciliation commission.[127]

By late 2000, human rights activists had turned their attention to past crimes, and began to address the issues of developing respect for rule of law and human rights in East Timor.[128] From September 2000 until January 2001, the Steering Committee held consultations and public hearings in East Timor's 13 districts at sub-district and village levels.[129] They consulted political parties, jurists and human rights NGOs, and, according to the CAVR's *Chega!* report, found 'overwhelming community support for a truth and reconciliation commission'.[130] On 13 December 2000, the East Timor Transitional Authority (ETTA) agreed to establish a Truth and Reconciliation Commission and by 28 February the following year it had endorsed a draft regulation of the CAVR.[131] Two months later, the National Council endorsed the draft.[132]

Human rights activists in East Timor had concerns 'for the potential for violence to re-ignite particularly in the context of the virtually complete impunity enjoyed by perpetrators of crime'.[133] As Philpott asserts, 'truth'-seeking justice mechanisms framed in terms of national reconciliation can be problematic in transitional post-conflict states if they oversimplify the past and provide substantial advantages to some groups in authoring or shaping national historiography.[134] The Steering Committee was aware that valuable lessons could be learnt from the past but also that the process could be co-opted by groups pursuing revenge or political power.[135]

There were other concerns among human rights activists that the CAVR would detract from retributive forms of justice.[136] Kingston, for example, described the CAVR process as 'soft peddling' justice, which the political leadership believed made more sense and would 'better serve the people'.[137] Domestic and international civil society organisations, such as *La'o Hamutuk* and Amnesty International, were also concerned that the CAVR would prevent the persecution of serious crimes through courts and establishing an international war crimes tribunal.[138] In an editorial in June 2000, *La'o Hamutuk* suggested that 'reconciliation cannot take place in East Timor without an effective process to realize justice'.[139]

However, the Commission was conceived by others as a way of 'developing a culture of respect for human rights and the rule of law' in a society that had

190   *Transitional justice and social democracy*

long demanded action on human rights violations.[140] In June 2000, Aniceto Guterres Lopes, the director of East Timorese human rights organisation *Yayasan HAK*, argued that reconciliation was necessary for building an effective democratic state.[141] In *La'o Hamutuk*, he wrote that East Timor's independence:

> must result in a new society that is free from a past full of oppression, human rights violations and injustice. It must be a society that inspires the entire population to respect the law, human rights, democracy and social justice.... Only by coming to terms with these problems will we be able to create a base to develop a new society consistent with people's hopes.[142]

Guterres Lopes suggested that the Commission for Reception, Truth and Reconciliation could assist in developing an effective and stable democratic state based upon principles of human rights and rule of law.[143] The vision of statehood articulated by Guterres Lopes reflects the aspirations of a rights-based democracy underpinned by principles of social justice.

The Steering Committee drafted legislation over three months with legal assistance from the UNTAET and the INGO International Centre for Transitional Justice.[144] This legislation was passed by East Timor's National Council with 30 votes in favour of the regulation, one against and one abstention.[145] After a month of deliberations, on 13 June 2001 a final draft was approved and forwarded to the Transitional Administrator Sérgio Vieira de Mello.[146] One week later, the National Council approved the creation of the CAVR, and on 13 July 2001, the UNTAET regulation 2001/10 established the CAVR with the purposes of promoting national reconciliation after years of conflict.[147] The Chair of the CAVR, Aniceto Guterres Lopes described its mission as establishing 'accountability in order to deepen and strengthen the prospects for peace, democracy, the rule of law and human rights in our new nation'.[148] Community consultations with the justice sector, grass-roots organisations, Catholic Church and village elders were undertaken by the CAVR to embed the processes with local legitimacy.[149]

During transition, the UNTAET and local political leaders encouraged community leaders to engage in grass-roots reconciliation processes that were similar with informal mechanisms of traditional justice.[150] The CAVR corresponded to traditional notions of reconciliation – called *Badame*, or 'road to peace' in Tetum – and CAVR processes incorporated elements of *nahe biti* ('rolling out the mat') dispute resolution.[151,152] *Nahe biti* is underpinned by two key principles: a willingness to come together and the voluntary confession of culpability. Restitution can include a fine or volunteer work.[153] While each *suku* interprets *nahe biti* differently, it generally begins with arbitration and mediation between relevant families with the aim of achieving consensus and resolution.[154] These forms of grass-roots reconciliation, which relied heavily upon community meetings, discussion and consensus with the aim of continuing peace and *rohan* (harmony in life), were embedded in the CAVR processes.[155] In October 2001, a *La'o Hamutuk* editorial suggested that the CAVR would assist in 'restoring the dignity of victims ... [and] making the truth public'.[156]

Transitional justice and social democracy 191

The provision for a Truth and Reconciliation Commission was made in Article 162 of East Timor's Constitution, which entrenched the 'reconciliation policies' aimed at bringing about justice without 'revenge, resentment or hatred'.[157] Seven National Commissioners were elected by a panel consisting of political and civil society organisations.[158] On 21 January 2002, five men and two women were sworn in as National Commissioners, alongside Regional Commissioners.[159] Key principles of the Commission were established, including 'promoting international, universal human rights standards in Timor-Leste', with human rights violations at the centre of its work.[160] The Commission noted that 'consulting directly with a wide and representative cross-section of East Timorese society was important to establish and maintain the legitimacy of the Commission'.[161] This recognised that elite-driven reconciliation (i.e. between political parties) would not be sufficient in achieving community reconciliation; rather, significant involvement of individuals at the grass-roots level was crucial for legitimacy.

The Commission had three main areas of responsibility, all concerning human rights: truth seeking in relation to human rights abuses committed in East Timor throughout the Indonesian occupation; community reconciliation; and recommendations to government.[162] The first objective, truth-seeking, included determining the truth about 'context, causes, antecedents, motives and perspectives which led to the violence, whether they were part of a systemic pattern of abuse, [and] the identity of persons, authorities, institutions and organisations involved in the violations'.[163] It involved recording summaries of oral statements and histories, conducting surveys and holding community meetings.[164] The Commission collected 7,824 statements, and a coalition of NGOs assisted in collecting an additional 91 statements from East Timorese in West Timor.[165] Dozens of East Timorese were trained as statement takers and conducted open-ended interviews in which deponents were permitted to 'narrate their stories at length'.[166] In so doing, these processes gave a voice to victims and an opportunity to participate in the national 'truth-seeking' agenda.[167] While the CAVR itself could not prosecute crimes, the statement-taking methodology reflects principles of reconciliatory and community-based justice found in East Timor's local customary law.

The second major function of the Commission was to encourage community reconciliation. One of the central means for achieving this end was the implementation of public hearings at community and national levels.[168] The open community forums allowed victims the opportunity to speak openly about their experiences, and restore their dignity through the 'acknowledgement of their struggle'.[169] The national commissions were broadcast across East Timor, and while also a truth-seeking venture, the main purpose was to 'assist national reconciliation and promote the rights of victims'.[170] Reconciliation also entailed facilitating 'the acceptance and re-integration into East Timorese society of persons accused of having committed less serious crimes'.[171] These functions were indicative of the broader goals of producing a human rights culture and encouraging post-conflict stability and social order.[172] Further, the 'reception' component of the CAVR name was designed to limit fears of reprisals.[173]

192 *Transitional justice and social democracy*

The use of customary legal mechanisms was significant in embedding legitimacy in the process through the broad public acceptance. The central plank of the CAVR processes were the Community Reconciliation Process (CRP), which sought to resolve 'less serious' crimes committed between 1974 and 1999.[174] They began with voluntary statements by perpetrators, which could then be followed by a hearing.[175] The CRP drew heavily upon *nahe biti* as they included elements of 'local spiritual practices, confession and forgiveness' and incorporated local leaders such as *lia-nian* (leader of the *uma lisan* or sacred house).[176] Acts of reconciliation acted as a 'stabilising force' by employing local practices that already possessed widespread community acceptance of the process.[177] Panels of between three and five local leaders presided over hearings, which permitted community-specific spiritual or traditional practices.[178] For example, the summoning of ancestors as witnesses to the *nahe biti* ritual prior to hearings made the process binding in the eyes of many East Timorese, with the failure to accept the outcome largely viewed as having 'serious consequences'.[179] Victims were permitted to question the perpetrator and reveal the impact of the crime on their lives.[180] Similar to customary law, perpetrators were encouraged to confess and apologise to their victims and the general community as a way of restoring social order and harmony.[181] More than 1,400 perpetrators successfully completed the CRP, and an estimated 40,000 people participated in the process.[182] According to the *Chega!* report, these hearings became defining events within communities.[183]

While predominantly focusing on reconciliation and restorative justice, the Commission provided an opportunity to hold individuals to account for their actions, and it was envisaged that this form of national dialogue could assist East Timor in ensuring past mistakes would not occur again. According to *La'o Hamutuk*, the Commission could play a role in preventing the recurrence of human rights violations.[184] Reconciliation was the political aim designed to scaffold a democratic civic nation among the East Timorese through shared sufferings of the past and a desire to prevent atrocities from re-occurring. In one study of the CAVR, Grenfell examined the ways in which the CAVR was a nation-building project as it connected and mobilised local communities around a national project.[185]

Pursuing restitutive justice

The CAVR encouraged 'restitutive' justice in the CRP as perpetrators were required to undertake negotiated 'acts of reconciliation' in order to be reaccepted into the community, a process that resembled the customary institution of *kasu sala*.[186] The compensatory acts were not necessarily monetary, but also included an apology, community service or the donation of animals.[187] These acts reflected the varied customary dispute resolutions undertaken in East Timorese communities, where crimes committed are viewed as disrupting social order. Customary dispute resolutions in East Timor generally involve negotiation between actors regarding the methods by which the perpetrators can repair the damage

Transitional justice and social democracy 193

and highlights the impacts of the violation on community and social order.[188] The *Chega!* report argues that incorporating these customary processes was beneficial for maintaining peace and security in instances where individual cases might have provoked reprisals.[189]

On 31 October 2005, the final report of the Commission, *Chega!* (Portuguese for 'enough!'), was presented to President Xanana Gusmão, providing a comprehensive history of violence between pro-autonomy and pro-independence groups.[190] However, he did not hand the report to Parliament until 28 November 2005 because he concerned about the report's impact upon East Timor's relations with Indonesia.[191] The report recommended that Indonesia should 'be encouraged to contribute to the achievement of justice by (a) transferring those indicted who reside in Indonesia to renewed Panels, and (b) strengthening the independence and efficiency of its judicial system'.[192] The report also recommended re-establishing the Serious Crimes Unit and Special Panels in Timor-Leste to prepare indictments for the Indonesian military officers identified in the report.[193]

However, many of the other recommendations focused on developing a human rights culture in East Timor and providing for retributive, restorative and restitutive justice measures to address ongoing issues of reconciliation, impunity and reparations. The 'restitutive' approach of the CAVR was evident in its advocacy of social democratic policies based on principles of distributive justice. The CAVR recommended that East Timor's government develop and implement 'policies that ensure that the fruits of development are enjoyed equitably, reaching the most isolated communities, benefiting and involving men and women, children, the elderly and the disabled, and providing opportunities to those who are most disadvantaged'.[194] The report also focused on ensuring the development of a robust civil sphere, recommending that East Timor government 'open two-way communication' in 'the interests of promoting participation and accountability', and support civil society organisations through consultation, policy dialogue, financial assistance and training.[195]

The CAVR regarded reparations as essential to East Timor's human rights framework, emphasising compensation and restitution in its recommendations.[196] Generally speaking, the objective of social justice 'is to bring each person up to the accepted minimum standard of living by providing him [*sic*] with the necessary goods and services'.[197] Lambourne advocates 'transformational' justice rather than transitional justice, which she argues entails a 'long-term sustainable process embedded in society and adoption of psychosocial, political and economic, as well as legal, perspectives on justice'.[198] In East Timor's case, transformational justice involved building the social, economic and political structures necessary for consolidating an effective democracy. Restitutive justice in transformational models can assist in alleviating the underlying causes of conflict, namely poverty, and provide rights protection as a foundation that will 'ensure ongoing respect for human rights and rule of law'.[199]

The first step to achieving social justice in a transitional setting relates to recognising the socio-economic rights of citizens and including these in truth and

194   *Transitional justice and social democracy*

reconciliation commissions. This was reflected in the CAVR's specific focus on violations of socio-economic rights – as defined by the International Covenant on Economic, Social and Cultural Rights – in Chapter 7:9.[200] The second step requires restitution for violations or deprivations of these rights. In the discourse of social democracy, this requires making recognised, universal positive rights meaningful through reparations that compensate victims of socio-economic rights violations. This is distinct from state-based social justice, which focuses on wealth redistribution through progressive taxation, and was examined in Chapter 6. Rather, social justice in a transformational justice context requires reparations through collective or individual acts of redress for violations of socio-economic rights. This was partly achieved through the CRP processes, which included fines and community service as a way of restituting socio-economic rights violations.

The third step entails recommendations in relation to those responsible for protecting and guaranteeing socio-economic rights of the East Timorese in the future. The CAVR recommended that the East Timorese state implement a National Reparations program, including material components such as the delivery of social services to individuals and medical and psycho-social care, and symbolic measures, incorporating memorialisation and commemoration ceremonies.[201] The *Chega!* report notes that victims 'overwhelmingly' sought accountability on behalf of the perpetrator, in addition to the 'simple assistance to enable them and their children to participate on an even footing in the new democratic Timor-Leste'.[202] Here, the CAVR's advice to the East Timorese state to minimise the disadvantages of being a victim of crime correspond with principles of social justice. The collective National Reparations Programme would seek to honour, rehabilitate and empower 'vulnerable' victims of rights abuses, and commemorate the key events of the period between 25 April 1974 and 25 October 1999, in addition to promoting civic education on human rights.[203] In contrast, the Individual Reparations Program would assist vulnerable victims though the provision of health, mental health and rehabilitation services, education subsidies for children and vocational training.[204] While the CAVR recognised the importance of reparations for social justice, it is not clear that either the AMP or BGK governments are or were inclined to turn these recommendations into policy. In February 2013, Parliament began debating draft laws to establish a national reparations scheme and a public memory institution, however the debates were postposed for the third time since June 2010.

The CAVR suggested that the responsibility of financing the National Reparations program should not be borne by individual perpetrators, but by the East Timorese state, through a fixed allocation in the national budget, and other states in the international community, including Indonesia.[206] On the recommendation that Indonesia contribute to restitutive justice in East Timor, Nevins argued that 'reparations must go beyond the immediate conflict so that those persons, groups or institutions whose privilege in part derived from East Timor's victimization also provide amends. Such an approach embraces the notion that reconciliation and redistributive justice are inextricably linked'.[207] Reparations, as a form of

Transitional justice and social democracy 195

restitutive justice, are central to reconciliation and promoting socio-political order based on common conceptions of social justice and the legitimacy of formal institutions. These steps contribute to the capacities of the state, through transitional justice mechanisms, to meaningfully protect and improve access to basic socio-economic rights. Repairing rights violations is central in instituting a culture of human rights in which they are not just guaranteed on paper or in rhetoric but possess substance and value in the 'real world'. Following the submission of the report, grass-roots reconciliation processes continued in the form of dialogues including *nahe biti* principles.[208] These initiatives stemmed primarily from church and community leaders and NGOs and were attempts to deal with a significant range of ongoing justice issues.

In moving the focus away from 'eye for an eye' ideals of justice, East Timor's political leadership has instead shifted the focus to social justice.[209] For Xanana Gusmão, distributing scarce resources in a way that deals with the 'more pressing and all-too-evident needs of the Timorese' was more important than prosecuting rights violations.[210] He linked the prioritisation of socio-economic challenges with the promises of self-determination, arguing that East Timor could 'best honor that struggle and those sacrifices by building a better democracy here, improving governance and providing better services to the people'.[211] José Ramos-Horta was criticised by civil society groups for several rounds of Presidential amnesty that they argued violated constitutional separation of powers.[212]

However, civil society organisations have continued to advocate extensively for retributive justice, and have held East Timor, Indonesia and the broader international community responsible for failing to prevent impunity.[213] The failures of East Timor, Indonesia and the international community to prosecute crimes against humanity has consequences for East Timor's rule of law and institutional stability, particularly as people's expectations about bringing 'high level inductees' to justice have not been met by the state.[214] NGOs such as Human Rights Watch, Timor-Leste National Alliance for an International Tribunal and the Australian Coalition for Transitional Justice in East Timor linked the 2006 crisis with a cultural of impunity that meant people believed they could 'get away with murder'.[215] The 2006 UN Commission of Inquiry also suggested that the crisis was an 'expression of deep-rooted problems inherent in fragile State institutions and a weak rule of law'.[216]

Despite these calls, political leaders have prioritised reconciliation ahead of the laws of the land, including Xanana Gusmão who has argued: 'não há justiça sem prévia reconciliação [there is no justice without prior reconciliation]'.[217] These reconciliation efforts were also extended to Indonesia. In December 2004, the joint establishment of the Indonesia–Timor-Leste Commission of Truth and Friendship (CTF) was announced.[218] As I have argued elsewhere, the CTF addressed international priorities and further compromised efforts to achieve substantive justice as it was not able to recommend prosecution.[219] Both states acknowledged that it was designed to block progress on the 2005 Commission of Experts recommendation that an international tribunal be established if East

196 *Transitional justice and social democracy*

Timor and Indonesia did not commit to prosecuting perpetrators within six months.[220] The final report 'From Memory to Hope', submitted to East Timor's Parliament on 9 October 2008, acknowledged the institutional responsibility of Indonesian military, police and personnel in the rights violations following the 1999 referendum.[221] However, this has failed to address issues of impunity in both states: for instance, the JSMP considered the CTF as offering protection to high ranking officials by promoting a façade of closure.[222]

However, Lambourne points out that when the East Timorese are asked about justice, many speak about the need for healthcare, safe drinking water, help with school fees and so forth, and suggests that the state was responsible for reducing poverty as part of the reconciliation and justice process.[223] LaPlante suggests that 'if economic and social *inequalities* go unaddressed and the grievances of the poor and marginalized go unheard, we are left only with uncertain guarantees of non-repetition. It is like treating the symptoms while leaving the underlying illness to fester'.[224] Poverty and deprivation can contribute to the emergence of social violence and disorder, which undermines rule of law and the legitimacy of democratic structures. Alleviating the impact of socio-economic deprivations and 'targeting the causes through distributive justice are important for transitional justice to contribute to peace-building'.[225]

Conclusion

Since independence, East Timorese governments have faced the intimidating challenge of balancing multiple and competing agendas, including the establishment of formal judicial institutions and rule of law, the investigation and prosecution of past crimes against humanity, the pursuit of reconciliation within East Timorese society and with Indonesia, and the provision of collective and individual reparations. According to Stahn, East Timor's model of transitional justice and reconciliation reflected 'a sophisticated approach to addressing past human rights tragedies while meeting the practical realities of a transitional process'.[226] Nevins also suggests that the CAVR process held 'significant moral authority' and that the *Chega!* was a valuable report.[227] The principles of reconciliatory justice corresponded with entrenching and enforcing a human rights culture and seeking 'punishment' for past rights violations as part of a vision of a 'just' state. Leaders such as Ramos-Horta argued that East Timor 'needed to foster a culture of forgiveness to move forward'.[228] The CAVR has contributed to building a 'just' state identity that articulates and seeks to protect 'positive' rights of citizens, which is important for a stable society in which 'everyone accepts and knows that the others accept the same principles of justice'.[229]

The success of the reconciliation model of transitional justice in East Timor remains contested among relevant political actors, civil society organisations and academics.[230] Discontent about East Timor's transitional justice has been driven by the reality that only perpetrators of small crimes have been held responsible for their role in the 1999 crisis.[231] East Timor's vision of statehood has consistently supported human rights and democracy as a means of establishing a free,

Transitional justice and social democracy 197

prosperous and equitable society. However it remains the case that those most responsible for the rights violations have largely avoided prosecution as the East Timorese government has had little choice but to abandon the pursuit of these individuals.[232] The failure to achieve 'genuine' justice was damaging for East Timor's capacity to institute rule of law, evidenced by the 2006 political crisis.

However, the conflation of retributive justice with 'genuine' justice tends to marginalise alternative forms of transitional justice implemented by East Timor. The CAVR provided a restorative justice mechanism, reconciling a formal state-based structure with elements of customary justice and enabling widespread participation of individuals and civil society organisations. The CRP's provided restitutive justice based on ideals of in social justice, again reflecting the social democratic vision of statehood.

Notes

1 Weber, *From Max Weber*, 328.
2 Hohe and Nixon, *Reconciling Justice.*
3 O'Donnell, 'Delegative Democracy', 165.
4 Rosenfeld, 'The Rule of Law and the Legitimacy of Constitutional Democracy', 1307.
5 Diamond, Linz and Lipset, 'Introduction', 9–10.
6 Chesterman, 'Imposed Constitutions, Imposed Constitutionalism and Ownership', 949 and 954.
7 Reiger and Wierda, *The Serious Crimes Process in Timor-Leste*, 11 and Strohmeyer, 'Collapse and Reconstruction of a Judicial System, 47.
8 Strohmeyer, Ibid., 261.
9 Ibid., 266
10 Ibid., 268.
11 Ibid., 263.
12 Ibid., 264.
13 Anderlini, Conaway and Kays, 'Transitional Justice and Reconciliation', 1.
14 United Nations Security Council, *Resolution 1272.*
15 CAVR, *Chega!*, Chapter 3, 10.
16 Gorjão, 'The East Timorese Commission for Reception, Truth and Reconciliation', 144.
17 Laplante, 'Transitional Justice and Peace Building', 333.
18 Ibid.
19 CAVR, *Chega!*, Chapter 7:9, 2.
20 Anderlini, Conaway and Kays, 'Transitional Justice and Reconciliation', 1–2.
21 Ibid., 2 and Huntington, *The Third Wave*, 213–214. See Gorjão, 'The East Timorese Commission for Reception, Truth and Reconciliation', 146.
22 Huntington, ibid.
23 Anderlini, Conaway and Kays, 'Transitional Justice and Reconciliation', 2.
24 Ibid. and Soares, *'Nahe Biti'*, 21.
25 Huntington, *The Third Wave*, 213–214 and Gorjão, 'The East Timorese Commission for Reception, Truth and Reconciliation', 146–147.
26 Lambourne, 'Transitional Justice and Peacebuilding after Mass Violence', 34.
27 Laplante, 'Transitional Justice and Peace Building', 332–333.
28 Nevins, 'Restitution over Coffee', 677–701.
29 CAVR, *Chega!*, Chapter 11, 37.
30 Strohmeyer, 'Building a New Judiciary for East Timor ', 279.

198   *Transitional justice and social democracy*

31 Kingston, 'Balancing Justice and Reconciliation in East Timor', 273.
32 Tilman, 'Customary Social Order and Authority in the Contemporary East Timorese Village', 192.
33 Robinson, *East Timor 1999 Crimes against Humanity*, 1; Beauvais, 'Benevolent Despotism', 1103; CAVR, *Chega!*, Chapter 3, 145 and United Nations Office of the Commissioner of Human Rights, *Report of the Commission of Inquiry on East Timor to Secretary-General*.
34 Robinson, ibid., 1 and Beauvais, ibid., 1103.
35 United Nations Security Council, *Resolution 1264*.
36 Katzenstein, 'Hybrid Tribunals', 250.
37 Ibid.
38 United Nations Office of the Commissioner of Human Rights, *Report of the Commission of Inquiry on East Timor to Secretary-General*, Section 4.
39 Ibid., 1.
40 Ibid., Section 155.
41 Human Rights Watch, *Justice Denied in East Timor* and TAPOL, *International Tribunal Proposal for East Timor Welcomed*.
42 Bowman, 'Letting the Big Fish Get Away', 380 and Kingston, 'Balancing Justice and Reconciliation in East Timor', 273.
43 Kingston, ibid., 276–277 and Reiger and Weirda, *The Serious Crimes Process in Timor-Leste*, 8.
44 United Nations Transitional Administration in East Timor, *On the Organization of Courts in East Timor*, 1.
45 Linton, 'Cambodia, East Timor and Sierra Leone', 203–204.
46 Kingston, 'Balancing Justice and Reconciliation in East Timor', 277.
47 Stensrud, 'New Dilemmas in Transitional Justice', 10–11 and 13.
48 Katzenstein, 'Hybrid Tribunals', 246.
49 Linton, 'Cambodia, East Timor and Sierra Leone', 205.
50 Ibid., 213 and Reiger and Wierda, *The Serious Crimes Process in Timor-Leste*, 12.
51 Ibid., 4.
52 United Nations Transitional Administration in East Timor, *On the Establishment of Panels with Exclusive Jurisdiction over Serious Criminal Offences*, 1.
53 Ibid., Section 2.2, 2.
54 Ibid.; Cohen, '"Hybrid" Justice in East Timor, Sierra Leone, and Cambodia', 8; Katzenstein, 'Hybrid Tribunals', 251 and Linton, 'Cambodia, East Timor and Sierra Leone', 214.
55 United Nations Transitional Administration in East Timor, *On the Establishment of Panels with Exclusive Jurisdiction over Serious Criminal Offences*, Section 3.1, 3 and Cohen, ibid., 8.
56 Human Rights Watch, *Justice Denied in East Timor*.
57 Commission for Human Rights Violations in East Timor (KPP-HAM), *Executive Summary on the Investigation of Human Rights Violations in East Timor*.
58 Ibid.; Reiger and Wierda, *The Serious Crimes Process in Timor-Leste*, 8–9 and La'o Hamutuk, *Justice for Timor-Leste Remains an Unfulfilled International Obligation*, 2.
59 Bowman, 'Letting the Big Fish Get Away', 380.
60 Human Rights Watch, *Justice Denied in East Timor*.
61 Ibid.
62 Ibid.
63 For further analysis see Purdey, 'Legal Responses to Violence in Post-Soeharto Indonesia', 521–522.
64 Human Rights Watch, *Justice Denied in East Timor*.
65 Purdey, 'Legal Responses to Violence in Post-Soeharto Indonesia', 522.
66 Ibid.

Transitional justice and social democracy 199

67 La'o Hamutuk, *Justice for Timor-Leste Remains an Unfulfilled International Obligation*, 4.
68 Ibid.; Human Rights Watch, *UN Security Council Must Ensure Justice* and United Nations Commission of Experts, *Report to the Secretary-General of the Commission of Experts to Review the Prosecution of Serious Violations of Human Rights in Timor-Leste (then East Timor) in 1999*, 6.
69 United Nations Commission of Experts, ibid.
70 Ibid.
71 Amnesty International, *Justice For Timor-Leste*; East Timor and Indonesia Action Network, *Truth Known, East Timorese Need Justice* and Judicial System Monitoring Program, '*Truth and Friendship Commission*'.
72 United Nations Commission of Experts, *Report to the Secretary-General of the Commission of Experts to Review the Prosecution of Serious Violations of Human Rights in Timor-Leste (then East Timor) in 1999*, 6.
73 Kingston, 'Balancing Justice and Reconciliation in East Timor', 273.
74 Ibid., 271; Reiger and Wierda, *The Serious Crimes Process in Timor-Leste*, 29 and United Nations Commission of Experts, *Report to the Secretary-General of the Commission of Experts to Review the Prosecution of Serious Violations of Human Rights in Timor-Leste (then East Timor) in 1999*, 4.
75 Linton, 'Cambodia, East Timor and Sierra Leone', 217.
76 Cohen, '"Hybrid" Justice in East Timor, Sierra Leone, and Cambodia', 10.
77 Ibid., 9 and La'o Hamutuk, *Justice for Timor-Leste Remains an Unfulfilled International Obligation*, 4.
78 Kingston, 'Balancing Justice and Reconciliation in East Timor', 277.
79 East Timor and Indonesia Action Network, *Truth Known, East Timorese Need Justice* and East Timor and Indonesia Action Network, *ETAN Renews Call for Meaningful Justice for Victims of Indonesian Occupation.*
80 Judicial System Monitoring Program, '*Truth and Friendship Commission'.*
81 Ibid. and Human Rights Watch, *East Timor: UN Security Council Must Ensure Justice.*
82 Kingston, 'Balancing Justice and Reconciliation', 274.
83 See Strating, 'The Indonesia-Timor-Leste Commission of Truth and Friendship'.
84 Author Unknown, 'Wiranto Officially Runs for President'.
85 Strating, 'The Indonesia-Timor-Leste Commission of Truth and Friendship'.
86 Kingston, 'Balancing Justice and Reconciliation', 273.
87 Scheiner, *Statement to the Alternative Public Hearing against the Truth and Friendship Commission.*
88 Piguo, *Crying Without Tears*, 27.
89 Ibid., 34.
90 International Center for Transitional Justice, *Truth Commission Report Reveals Shocking Brutality, Calls for End to Impunity.*
91 East Timor and Indonesia Action Network, *East Timor Truth Commission Report Must be Released.*
92 United Nations Commission of Experts, *Report to the Secretary-General of the Commission of Experts to Review the Prosecution of Serious Violations of Human Rights in Timor-Leste (then East Timor) in 1999*, 5.
93 Ibid., 4.
94 Cohen, '"Hybrid" Justice in East Timor, Sierra Leone, and Cambodia', 9 and Reiger and Wierda, *The Serious Crimes Process in Timor-Leste*, 3.
95 Cohen, ibid., Reiger and Wierda, ibid. and United Nations Commission of Experts, *Report to the Secretary-General of the Commission of Experts to Review the Prosecution of Serious Violations of Human Rights in Timor-Leste (then East Timor) in 1999*, 4.
96 Amnesty International, *Justice For Timor-Leste.*

200 *Transitional justice and social democracy*

97 East Timor and Indonesia Action Network, *Truth Known, East Timorese Need Justice;* East Timor and Indonesia Action Network, *On Anniversary of East Timor Church Massacre UN Must Take Responsibility for Justice* and East Timor and Indonesia Action Network, *Indonesia Must Confront its Past, Accept Responsibility and Deliver Justice for Timor Atrocities.*

98 United Nations Integrated Mission in Timor-Leste, *Serious Crimes Investigation Team.*

99 United Nations Integrated Mission in Timor-Leste, *Serious Crimes Investigation Team Newsletter.*

100 International Center for Transitional Justice, *Impunity in Timor-Leste: Can the Serious Crimes Investigation Team Make a Difference?;* Amnesty International USA, *Annual Report: Timor-Leste 2013* and United Nations News Centre, *UN to Stay Engaged in Timor-Leste after Peacekeeping Mission Ends.*

101 Renshaw, Byrnes and Durbach, 'Human Rights Protection in the Pacific', 120.

102 United Nations Transitional Administration in East Timor, *On the Establishment of a Commission for Reception, Truth and Reconciliation in East Timor* and Hohe and Nixon, *Reconciling Justice,* 53.

103 See United Nations Transitional Administration in East Timor, ibid., Section 3:1 and Philpott, 'Post-Colonial Troubles', 253.

104 Stahn, 'Accommodating Individual Criminal Responsibility and National Reconciliation', 953.

105 CAVR, *Chega!,* Chapter 1, 47.

106 Cited in Roosa, 'How Does a Truth Commission Find out What the Truth Is?', 570.

107 Stahn, 'Accommodating Individual Criminal Responsibility and National Reconciliation', 954.

108 Ibid.

109 Ibid.

110 Vieira, *The CAVR and the 2006 Displacement Crisis in Timor-Leste,* 7.

111 Ibid.

112 United Nations Security Council, *Resolution 1272,* S/RES/1272, 25 October 1999, Section 1 and 2 and CAVR, *Chega!,* Chapter 1, 3.

113 Stahn, 'Accommodating Individual Criminal Responsibility and National Reconciliation', 956.

114 See Zifcak, 'Restorative Justice in Timor-Leste', 51 and Gorjão, 'The East Timorese Commission for Reception, Truth and Reconciliation', 149.

115 Gusmão, 'Reconciliation, Unity and National Development in the Framework of the Transition Towards Independence', 1–2.

116 Ibid., 1.

117 Ibid., 1 and Gusmão, *Timor Lives! Speeches of Freedom and Independence,* 79.

118 Gorjão, 'The East Timorese Commission for Reception, Truth and Reconciliation', 150.

119 Borges, 'CAVR Implementation', 3.

120 United Nations Office of the Commissioner of Human Rights, *Report of the Commission of Inquiry on East Timor to Secretary-General,* United Nations General Assembly, Section 152.

121 CAVR, *Chega!,* Chapter 1, 3–4.

122 Walsh, *The Human Rights and Future of East Timor Workshop.*

123 National Council of Timorese Resistance National Congress, *Draft Resolution on Human Rights* and CAVR, *Chega!,* Chapter 1, 3.

124 CAVR, ibid., Chapter 1, 10.

125 Ibid.

126 Ibid.

127 Ibid., Chapter 1, 4.

128 Ibid., Chapter 1, 3.

Transitional justice and social democracy 201

129 Ibid., Chapter 1, 11.
130 Ibid.
131 Stahn, 'Accommodating Individual Criminal Responsibility and National Reconciliation', 956.
132 Gorjão, 'The East Timorese Commission for Reception, Truth and Reconciliation', 151.
133 CAVR, *Chega!*, Chapter 1, 11.
134 Philpott, 'Post-Colonial Troubles', 252.
135 CAVR, *Chega!*, Chapter 1, 11.
136 A 'truth and reconciliation mechanism ideally complements judicial processes'. See Linton, 'Cambodia, East Timor and Sierra Leone', 204 and 223–224.
137 Kingston, 'Balancing Justice and Reconciliation in East Timor', 271.
138 East Timor NGO Forum, *Expression of Concern at Xanana's Statement Regarding an International Tribunal.*
139 La'o Hamutuk, *The La'o Hamutuk Bulletin* 1, no. 1 (21 June 2000): 6.
140 CAVR, *Chega!*, Chapter 1, 3.
141 La'o Hamutuk, *The La'o Hamutuk Bulletin* 1, no. 1 (21 June 2000): 2–3.
142 Ibid.
143 Ibid.
144 CAVR, *Chega!*, Chapter 1, 12–13.
145 Ibid., Chapter 1, 13.
146 Ibid.
147 United Nations, *East Timor National Council Sets Up Truth Commission to Probe Rights Violations*; Linton, 'Cambodia, East Timor and Sierra Leone', 223; United Nations Security Council, *Progress Report of the Secretary-General on the United Nations Transitional Administration in East Timor*, 6 and United Nations Transitional Administration in East Timor, *On the Establishment of a Commission for Reception, Truth and Reconciliation in East Timor.*
148 Grenfell, 'Reconstituting the Nation', 19.
149 CAVR, *Chega!*, Chapter 1, 12 and 18.
150 Soares, *'Nahe Biti'*, 31.
151 Gusmão, *Xanana Gusmão e os Primeiros 10 anos da Construção do Estado Timorense*, 38 and Nordquist, 'Reconciliation as a Political Concept', 219.
152 Ibid., 15 and 23 and Tilman, 'Customary Social Order and Authority in the Contemporary East Timorese Village', 194.
153 Soares, *'Nahe Biti'*, 25–27.
154 Tilman, 'Customary Social Order and Authority in the Contemporary East Timorese Village', 194.
155 Soares, *'Nahe Biti'.*
156 La'o Hamutuk, *The La'o Hamutuk Bulletin* 2, no. 6 and 7 (October 2001), 8.
157 Gusmão, *Timor Lives!*, 80.
158 CAVR, *Chega!*, Chapter 1, 14.
159 Ibid., Chapter 1, 14 and 18–19.
160 Ibid., Chapter 1, 18.
161 Ibid., Chapter 1, 14.
162 Ibid., 8 and Stahn, 'Accommodating Individual Criminal Responsibility and National Reconciliation', 953.
163 See CAVR, *Chega!*, Chapter 1, 8–9.
164 Roosa, 'How Does a Truth Commission Find out What the Truth Is?', 570.
165 CAVR, *Chega!*, Chapter 1, 26.
166 Roosa, 'How Does a Truth Commission Find out What the Truth Is?', 571–573.
167 Ibid., 572.
168 CAVR, *Chega!*, Chapter 1, 28–29.
169 Ibid., 28.
170 Ibid., 29.

202　*Transitional justice and social democracy*

171　Stahn, 'Accommodating Individual Criminal Responsibility and National Reconciliation', 953.
172　La'o Hamutuk, *The La'o Hamutuk Bulletin* 2, no. 6 and 7 (October 2001), 8.
173　Vieira, *The CAVR and the 2006 Displacement Crisis in Timor-Leste*, 16.
174　CAVR, *Chega!*, Chapter 1, 32–33.
175　Vieira, *The CAVR and the 2006 Displacement Crisis in Timor-Leste*, 7.
176　Ibid.; CAVR, *Chega!*, Chapter 1, 33 and Lambourne, 'Transitional Justice and Peacebuilding after Mass Violence', 37.
177　Stahn, 'Accommodating Individual Criminal Responsibility and National Reconciliation', 957.
178　CAVR, *Chega!*, Chapter 1, 33.
179　Vieira, *The CAVR and the 2006 Displacement Crisis in Timor-Leste*, 8.
180　Ibid. and CAVR, *Chega!*, Chapter 1, 33.
181　CAVR, ibid.
182　Ibid., Chapter 11, 29 and Grenfell, 'Reconstituting the Nation', 20–21.
183　CAVR, ibid., Chapter 1, 33.
184　La'o Hamutuk, *The La'o Hamutuk Bulletin* 2, no. 6 and 7 (October 2001), 8.
185　Grenfell, 'Reconstituting the Nation', 21.
186　CAVR, *Chega!*, Chapter 1, 33 and Chapter 11, 38.
187　Vieira, *The CAVR and the 2006 Displacement Crisis in Timor-Leste*, 8.
188　Hohe and Nixon, *Reconciling Justice.*
189　CAVR, *Chega!*, Chapter 1, 33–34.
190　Ibid., Chapter 1, 49.
191　Human Rights First, *Timor-Leste Should Release Truth Commission Report Without Delay.*
192　CAVR, *Chega!*, Chapter 11, 26.
193　Ibid., Chapter 11, 25.
194　Ibid., Chapter 11, 7.
195　Ibid., Chapter 11, 9, 15.
196　Ibid., Chapter 11, 36.
197　Miller, 'Democracy and Social Justice', 18.
198　Lambourne, 'Transitional Justice and Peacebuilding after Mass Violence', 30.
199　Ibid., 34.
200　CAVR, *Chega!*, Chapter 7:9.
201　Ibid., Chapter 11, 40.
202　Ibid., Chapter 11, 37.
203　Lipscomb, 'Beyond the Truth'.
204　Ibid.
205　Democratic Republic of Timor-Leste National Parliament, *Framework of the National Reparations Programme.*
206　CAVR, *Chega!*, Chapter 11, 42.
207　Nevins, 'Restitution over Coffee', 686.
208　Vieira, *The CAVR and the 2006 Displacement Crisis in Timor-Leste*, 12.
209　Gusmão, *Xanana Gusmão e os Primeiros 10 anos da Construção do Estado Timorense*, 44, 47–48 and 51.
210　Kingston, 'Balancing Justice and Reconciliation', 289 and 295.
211　Cited in ibid., 282 and 285.
212　Judicial System Monitoring Program, *Competency of the President to Grant Pardons;* La'o Hamutuk, *Letter to UN Security Council on Justice and Impunity in East Timor* and Amnesty International, *Timor-Leste: Justice in the Shadow.*
213　See for example La'o Hamutuk, *Justice for Timor-Leste Remains an Unfulfilled International Obligation*, 2.
214　Gorjão, 'The East Timorese Commission for Reception, Truth and Reconciliation', 155 and Jolliffe cited in Kingston, 'Balancing Justice and Reconciliation', 281.

215 Timor-Leste National Alliance for an International Tribunal, Australian Coalition for Transitional Justice in East Timor and International Federation for East Timor, *Joint Letter to Kofi Annan on Commission for Reception, Truth and Reconciliation Report.*

216 United Nations Independent Special Commission of Inquiry for Timor-Leste, *Report of the United Nations Independent Special Commission of Inquiry for Timor-Leste*, 74.

217 Gusmão, *Xanana Gusmão e os Primeiros 10 anos da Construção do Estado Timor-ense*, 38 and 90.

218 Commission of Truth and Friendship, *From Memory to Hope*, ii and Republic of Indonesia and Democratic Republic of Timor-Leste, *Terms of Reference for The Commission of Truth and Friendship.*

219 See Strating, 'The Indonesia-Timor-Leste Commission of Truth and Friendship'.

220 See for example TAPOL, Amnesty International, Human Rights Watch and Progressio, *Timor-Leste: Letter to Parliament Honoring Report of the Commission for Reception, Truth and Reconciliation.*

221 Indonesia Human Rights Committee, *Call for Action on Truth and Reconciliation Report;* East Timor and Indonesia Action Network, *ETAN Renews Call for Meaningful Justice for Victims of Indonesian Occupation;* TAPOL, *Though Limited by its Mandate, the CTF Revealed a Great Deal* and Hirst, *Too Much Friendship Too Little Truth*, 8.

222 Judicial System Monitoring Program, *Justice Not Served by Truth and Friendship Commission.*

223 Lambourne, 'Transitional Justice and Peacebuilding after Mass Violence', 43–44.

224 Laplante, 'Transitional Justice and Peace Building', 333.

225 Lambourne, 'Transitional Justice and Peacebuilding after Mass Violence', 42.

226 Stahn, 'Accommodating Individual Criminal Responsibility and National Reconciliation', 965.

227 Nevins, 'The CAVR: Justice and Reconciliation in a Time of "Impoverished Political Possibilities"', 594.

228 See Michelmore, 'Ramos-Horta Cuts Jail Terms for Militia'.

229 Rawls, *A Theory of Justice*, 4–5.

230 While NGOs, such as the ANTI, also argue that the 'CAVR did not achieve genuine justice', it did play an important role in establishing a just and orderly state. See Jenkins, 'A Truth Commission for East Timor', 238.

231 Kingston, 'Balancing Justice and Reconciliation', 271.

232 Philpott, 'Post-Colonial Troubles', 250 and Strating, 'The Indonesia-Timor-Leste Commission of Truth and Friendship'.

Conclusion

> Para mantermos a democracia e os Direitos Humanos fundamentais, pelos quais lutamos durante tanto tempo, precisamos de construir um sistema justo e efectivo de lei e ordem, justiça e boa governação [To maintain democracy and fundamental human rights, for which we fought for so long, we need to build a fair and effective system of law and order, justice and good governance].
>
> (Xanana Gusmão)[1]

East Timor remains in the process of consolidating democracy. While facing a number of socio-economic and political challenges, East Timor increasingly looks like a successful example of international democratic assistance. In a radio interview in 2012, World Bank Country Manager in East Timor, Luis Constantino, stated:

> [w]hat they've accomplished in 10 years is absolutely impressive. I mean 10 years ago the country was completely destroyed. And right now they were able to cut infant and child mortality by half, they have gains in health and education ... there's been a lot of progress compared to what we usually achieve [in] post-conflict countries.[2]

Presidential and parliamentary elections that took place in East Timor in 2007 were relatively peaceful, and over 90 per cent of voters took part, reflecting an ongoing willingness to participate in democratic processes.[3,4] Free and fair local government elections were held in 2009, and national presidential and parliamentary elections in 2012, each undertaken in conditions of relative stability characterised by almost no violence.[5] The successful implementation of these elections highlights a level of acceptance of core democratic processes.[6] While it began life as one of the world's poorest and most dependent states, it is now in a new phase of independence borne from the withdrawal of the United Nations Integrated Mission in East Timor in December 2012.

According to Linz and Stepan, consolidation occurs when democracy is 'deeply internalized in social, institutional, and even psychological life'.[7] Normative support for democratic political institutions can ensure their long-term

Conclusion 205

viability and prevent the re-emergence of authoritarianism. For Rotberg, states fail when 'governments lose legitimacy, and the very nature of the particular nation-state itself becomes illegitimate'.[8] Citizenry support for democratic ideals is, and will continue to be, essential for the institutionalisation and habituation of democratic norms and behaviours in East Timor. As a new generation of leaders emerges, it will become clearer whether East Timor is capable of sustaining and enhancing democratic governance.

Diamond usefully points out that the best ways of developing a democratic civic culture that supports democratisation is through direct experience, however imperfect the structures may be. Direct experience with democratic models of governance significantly influences political attitudes and values, more than socio-economic conditions, levels of development and the performance of regimes. Developing an autonomous and robust political society is hence a condition for democratisation, and the presence of both a free and lively civil society is important for the development of a democratic political culture.[9] A flourishing civil society permits and encourages individuals to participate and engage in politics and is an essential requirement for democratic consolidation. The relationship between civil society and democratisation in contemporary East Timor is one that requires further scholarly attention.

Prior to independence, civil society organisations were crucial for East Timor's achievement of a ballot for independence. They applied pressure on governments, raised awareness and provided reliable information of the human rights situation in East Timor. As Figure 8.1 below illustrates, the establishment of the East Timorese nation began within civil society, which encompassed the independence and resistance movements, clandestine organisations and 'political' parties such as FRETILIN and the Timorese Democratic Union (UDT). The Carnation Revolution in Portugal in 1974 created an opportunity for the fledgling East Timorese civil society, and its new leaders, to claim political independence, and enabled the development of the resistance movement following Indonesia's annexation of East Timorese territory in December 1975. These twin processes of seeking independence and resisting occupation established the East Timorese nation and facilitated the pursuit of democratic independence.

The pressure applied to Indonesia from the international community ultimately forced the new Habibie government in Indonesia to grant a referendum in 1999. East Timor's independence was the product of a fortuitous mix of international and domestic factors which coincided to enable a regime change in Indonesia and a subsequent policy shift. East Timor's claims to independence were embedded in the broader pro-democracy movements across Indonesia which ultimately removed Suharto and provided a catalyst for the chain of events that led to East Timor's referendum on independence. In this way, East Timor's pursuit of democratic independence corresponded with the broader pro-democracy movement that occurred across Indonesia.

The aspirations of the independence movement contributed to the establishment and maintenance of democracy in East Timor. As March and Olsen assert, 'it seems clear that no system can function without general acceptance of the

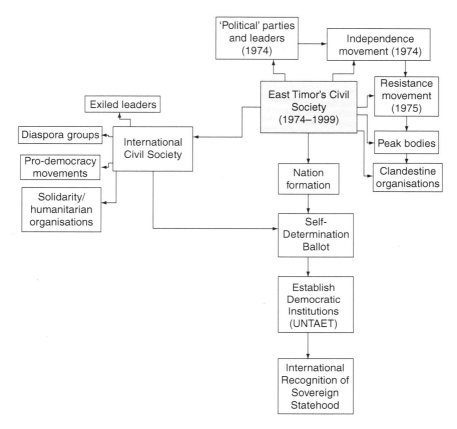

Figure 8.1 Evolution of East Timor's political society.

rules of the game'.[10] East Timor's pursuit of democratic independence reveals a coherent relationship between self-determination and democracy insofar as a commitment to ongoing self-determination *via* political participation is deemed necessary for international recognition of external self-determination rights. By committing themselves to democracy, the East Timorese independence movement and its supporters recognised the international legitimacy of democracy. It would, however, be an oversimplification to think that ideas of democracy and human rights were used solely as a tool for achieving independence. Rather, independence was necessary for instituting a social democratic government, a goal that was apparent from 1974 with the construction of the UDT and the Timorese Social Democratic Association (ASDT, later FRETILIN).

Depending on the context at the time, assessments of East Timor's politics since the referendum have tended to be polarising, ranging from criticising the slow pace of 'timorisation' during the state-building period,[11] crediting the UNTAET with the success of East Timor's transition following independence,[12]

Conclusion 207

fearing the rise of authoritarianism,[13] and blaming the UNTAET for creating a failed state during the 2006 crisis and aftermath.[14] East Timor was not experiencing an authority vacuum like that of Somalia in the 1990s.[15] Concerns about state failure reflect overly high expectations that new states will quickly acquire all of the features of positive sovereignty and 'good governance', despite the violent and protracted history of state-making in the West.[16] Following the 2006 political crisis, East Timor required international assistance to establish peace and security in its territory, pointing to a contemporary model of international intervention of 'supported' sovereignty during periods of risk.

The social realm is important for understanding East Timor's social democratic state and its capacities to consolidate new institutions. The vision of the independence movement has largely been carried out in the development of the Constitution, key political and judicial institutions and citizenship rights and responsibilities. Continuity in the ways that East Timorese leaders and people viewed the roles of the state, and its relationships to individuals and society, is reflected in the democratic and liberal nature of key political structures. These structures appear to be viewed by the majority of citizens as 'the most appropriate way to govern collective life'.[17]

In his swearing-in speech as East Timor's Prime Minister, Dr Rui Maria de Araúo paid tribute to the 'older brothers' of the independence movement stating: 'they started a new struggle, and that is building the foundations of our State. They built our democratic institutions and they identified the essence of democratic values in Timor-Leste: peace, reconciliation, solidarity, pluralism, tolerance and dialogue'.[18] He also confirmed the sixth constitutional government's commitment to creating 'a welfare regime', acknowledging the importance of social justice for supporting vulnerable citizens and veterans and 'honouring the ideal of freedom for which our grandparents, parents and older siblings fought'.[19]

East Timorese leaders shaped their institutional parameters and forged a new state identity through constitution-drafting, a process they used to establish East Timor as a liberal, multi-party, social democracy in accordance with the aspirations of the independence movement. By outlining the key democratic institutions of the state, the rights and responsibilities of citizens and state and social justice mechanisms in the Constitution, political leaders provided a vision of the relationship between state and society. This commitment to upholding these standards reflect a desire to protect and preserve democratic structures, which will work to aid democratic consolidation.

Notes

1 In a speech titled 'A Tendência dos Movimentos Pela Paz Mundial – A Experiênca de Timor-Leste' delivered in Seoul on June 14 2004. See Gusmão, *Xanana Gusmão e os Primeiros 10 anos da Construção do Estado Timorense*, 100.
2 Everingham, 'East Timor, 10 Years On', *ABC Radio 744 AM.*
3 Guterres, 'Timor-Leste: A Year of Democratic Elections', 359 and Kingsbury, 'East Timor's Political Crisis', 40–41.

208   Conclusion

4 Kingsbury, *East Timor: The Price of Liberty*, 183.
5 Sahin, 'Timor-Leste in 2009', 345.
6 Guterres, 'Timor-Leste: A Year of Democratic Elections', 360.
7 Linz and Stepan, *Problems of Democratic Transition and Consolidation*, 5.
8 Rotberg, 'Failed States, Collapsed States, Weak States', 1.
9 Linz and Stepan, *Problems of Democratic Transition and Consolidation*, 7.
10 March and Olsen, *Rediscovering Institutions*, 155.
11 Beauvais, 'Benevolent Despotism' and Suhrke, 'Peacekeepers as Nation-Builders', 2.
12 Stahn, 'The United Nations Transitional Administrations in Kosovo and East Timor', 109; Gorjão, 'The Legacy and Lessons of the United Nations Transitional Administration in East Timor', 313; Goldstone, 'UNTAET with Hindsight', 85 and 95; Morrow and White, 'The United Nations in Transitional East Timor', 1–47; Steele, 'Nation Building in East Timor', 86 and Diamond, 'Promoting Democracy in Post-Conflict and Failed States', 98.
13 Siapno, 'Timor-Leste: On a Path of Authoritarianism?', 338.
14 See Cotton, 'Timor-Leste and the Discourse of State Failure', 456.
15 See Rotberg, 'Failed States, Collapsed States, Weak States', 9.
16 Ayoob, 'Inequality and Theorizing in International Relations', 40 and Benzing, 'Midwifing a New State', 370.
17 Linz and Stepan, *Problems of Democratic Transition and Consolidation*, 6.
18 de Araújo, *Speech by His Excellency the Prime Minister Dr Rui Maria de Araújo on the Occasion of the Swearing-In of the Sixth Constitutional Government.*
19 Ibid.

Bibliography

Books and periodicals

Almond, Gabriel and Sidney Verba. *The Civic Culture: Political Attitudes and Democracy in Five Nations*. Newbury Park, California: Sage Publications, 1989.

Alagappa, Muthiah. 'Introduction'. In *Political Legitimacy in Southeast Asia: The Quest for Moral Authority*, edited by Muthiah Alagappa, 1–10. Stanford: Stanford University Press, 1995.

Alatas, Ali. *Pebble in the Shoe: the Diplomatic Struggle for East Timor*. Jakarta: Aksara Karunia, 2006.

Alldèn, Susanne. 'Internalising the Culture of Human Rights: Securing Women's Rights in Post-Conflict East Timor'. *Asia-Pacific Journal on Human Rights and the Law* 1 (2007): 1–23.

Ambrosio, Thomas. 'East Timor Independence: The Changing Nature of International Pressure'. In *Transforming East Asian Domestic and International Politics: The Impact of Economy and Globalization*, edited by Robert W. Compton Jr, 115–137. Aldershot: Ashgate, 2002.

Anderlini, Sanam Naraghi, Camille Conaway and Lisa Kays. 'Transitional Justice and Reconciliation'. In *Inclusive Security, Sustainable Peace: A Toolkit for Advocacy and Action*. International Alert: Women Waging Peace, November 2004.

Anderson, Tim. 'Timor Leste: The Second Australian Intervention'. *Journal of Australian Political Economy* 58 (2006): 62–93.

Anheier, Helmut. *Civil Society: Measurement, Evaluation, Policy*. Sterling, VA: Earthscan, 2004.

Anwar, Dewi Fortuna. 'Implementasi Kebijakan Luar Negeri dan Pertahanan Australia terhadap Indonesia: Studi Kasus Timor Timur (1996–2001)'. In *Indonesia dalam kebijakan luar negeri dan pertahanan Australia 1996–2001*, edited by Ganewati Wuryandari, 99–128. Jakarta: Pusat Penelitian Politik, Lembaga Ilmu Pengetahuan Indonesia, 2001.

Aucoin, Louis and Michele Brandt. 'East Timor's Constitutional Passage to Independence'. In *Framing the State in Times of Transition: Case Studies in Constitution Making*, edited by Laurel Miller, 245–274. Washington: United States Institute of Peace Press, 2010.

Ayoob, Mohammed. 'Inequality and Theorizing in International Relations: The Case for Subaltern Realism'. *International Studies Review* 4, no. 3 (Autumn 2002): 27–48.

Ayoob, Mohammed. 'State-Making, State-Breaking and State Failure: Explaining the Roots of 'Third World' Insecurity'. In *Between Development and Destruction: An*

210 *Bibliography*

Enquiry into the Causes of Conflict in Post-Colonial States, edited by Luc Van de Goor, Kumar Rupesinghe and Paul Sciavone, 67–89. Hampshire: Macmillan, 1996.

Ballard, John. *Triumph of Self-Determination: Operation Stabilise and United Nations Peacemaking in East Timor*. Connecticut: Praeger Security International, 2004.

Baltazar, Alipio. 'An Overview of the Constitution Drafting Process in East Timor'. *East Timor Law Journal* 9 (2004).

Barnett, Michael and Christoph Zürcher. 'The Peacebuilder's Contract: How External Statebuilding Reinforces Weak Statehood'. In *The Dilemmas of Statebuilding: Confronting the Contradictions of Postwar Peace Operations*, edited by Roland Paris and Timothy Sisk, 23–52. New York: Routledge, 2009.

Bartu, Peter. 'The Militia, the Military, and the People of the Bobonaro District'. In *Guns and Ballot Boxes: East Timor's Vote for Independence*, edited by Damien Kingsbury, 81–98. Clayton: Monash Asia Institute, 2000.

Beauvais, Joel. 'Benevolent Despotism: A Critique of UN State-building in East Timor'. *New York University Journal of International Law and Politics* 33 (2001–2002): 1101–1178.

Bellamy, Alex. 'Kosovo and the Advent of Sovereignty as Responsibility'. In *Kosovo, Intervention and Statebuilding: The International Community and the Transition to Independence*, edited by Aidan Hehir, 38–59. Oxon: Routledge, 2010.

Benzing, Markus. 'Midwifing a New State: The United Nations in East Timor'. *Max Planck Yearbook of United Nations Law* 9 (2005): 295–372.

Bickerton, Christopher. 'State-Building: Exporting State Failure'. *Arena Journal* 32 (2009): 101–123.

Binchy, William. 'The Constitution of Timor-Leste in Comparative Perspective'. In *Timor-Leste: Challenges for Justice and Human Rights in the Shadow of the Past*, edited by William Binchy, 261–289. Dublin: Clarus Press, 2009.

Bogandy, Armin von., Stefan Häußler, Felix Hanschmann and Raphael Utz. 'State-Building, Nation-Building, and Constitutional Politics in Post-Conflict Situations: Conceptual Clarifications and an Appraisal of Different Approaches'. *Max Planck Yearbook of United Nations Law* 9 (2005): 579–613.

Borgerhoff, Andre. 'The Double-Task: Nation- and State-Building in Timor-Leste'. *European Journal of East Asian Studies* 5, no. 1 (2006): 101–130.

Borges, Fernanda. 'CAVR Implementation: The Key to Transforming the Country and East Timorese Society'. In *Democratic Governance in Timor-Leste: Reconciling the Local and the National*, edited by David Mearns and Steven Farram, 3–9. Darwin: Charles Darwin University Press, 2008.

Bowman, Herbert. 'Letting the Big Fish Get Away: The United Nations Justice Effort in East Timor'. *Emory International Law Review* 18 (2004): 371–400.

Brown, M. Anne. 'Local Identity and Local Authority: Culture and Local Government in Timor-Leste'. In *Locating Democracy: Representation, Elections and Governance in Timor-Leste*, edited by Steven Farram, 42–51. Darwin: Charles Darwin University Press, 2010.

Brown, M. Anne. 'The Nation-Building Agenda in Timor-Leste'. In *Security, Development and Nation-Building in Timor-Leste: a Cross-Sectoral Assessment*, edited by Vandra Harris and Andrew Goldsmith, 17–37. Oxon: Routledge, 2011.

Brunnstrom, Cecilia. 'Another Invasion: Lessons from International Support to East Timorese NGOs'. *Development in Practice* 13, no. 4 (2003): 310–321.

Buchanan, Allan. *Justice, Legitimacy and Self-Determination: Moral Foundations for International Law*. Oxford: Oxford University Press, 2004.

Bibliography 211

Burchill, Scott. 'East Timor, Australia and Indonesia'. In *Guns and Ballot Boxes: East Timor's Vote for Independence*, edited by Damien Kingsbury, 169–184. Clayton: Monash Asia Institute, 2000.

Butler, Michael. 'Ten Years After: (Re) Assessing Neo-Trusteeship and UN State-building in Timor-Leste'. *International Studies Perspectives* 13 (2012): 85–104.

Case, William. 'Low-Quality Democracy and Varied Authoritarianism: Elites and Regimes in Southeast Asia Today'. *The Pacific Review* 22, no. 3 (2009): 255–269.

Cassese, Antonio. *Self-Determination of Peoples: A Legal Reappraisal*. Cambridge: Cambridge University Press, 1999.

Castellino, Joshua and Jeremie Gilbert. 'Self-Determination and Indigenous Peoples and Minorities'. *Macquarie Law Journal* 3 (2003): 155–178.

Cerna, Christina. 'Universal Democracy: An International Legal Right or the Pipe Dream of the West?' *New York Journal of International Law and Policy* 27 (1995): 289–329.

Chandler, David. *Empire in Denial: The Politics of Statebuilding*. London: Pluto Press, 2006.

Chandler, David. 'Great Power Responsibility and "Failed States": Strengthening Sovereignty?' In *Facets and Practices of Statebuilding*, edited by Julia Raue and Patrick Sutter, 15–30. Leiden: Martinus Nijhoff Publishers, 2009.

Charlesworth, Hilary. 'The Constitution of East Timor'. *International Journal of Constitutional Law* 1, no. 2 (2003): 325–334.

Charlesworth, Hilary and Mary Wood. 'Women and Human Rights in the Rebuilding of East Timor'. *Nordic Journal of International Law* 71 (2002): 325–348.

Chesterman, Simon. 'East Timor in Transition: Self-determination, State-building and the United Nations'. *International Peacekeeping* 9, no. 1 (Spring 2002): 45–76.

Chesterman, Simon. 'Imposed Constitutions, Imposed Constitutionalism and Ownership'. *Connecticut Law Review* 37 (2004–2005): 947–954.

Chesterman, Simon. *You, the People: The United Nations, Transitional Administration, and State-Building*. Oxford: Oxford University Press, 2005.

Coelho, Avelino. *Dua Kali Merdeka: Esai Sejarah Politik Timor-Leste*. Yogyakarta: Djaman Baroe, 2012.

Chopra, Jarat. 'The UN's Kingdom of East Timor'. *Survival* 42, no. 3 (Autumn 2000): 27–39.

Chopra, Jarat. 'Building State Failure in East Timor'. *Development and Change* 33, no. 5 (2002): 979–1000.

Chopra, Jarat and Tanja Hohe. 'Participatory Intervention'. *Global Governance* 10 (2004): 289–305.

Cogen, Marc and Eric de Brabandere. 'Democratic Governance and Post-Conflict Reconstruction'. *Leiden Journal of International Law* 20 (2007): 669–693.

Cohen, David. '"Hybrid" Justice in East Timor, Sierra Leone, and Cambodia: "Lessons Learned" and Prospects for the Future'. *Stanford Journal of International Law* 43 (2007): 1–38.

Cohen, Joshua. 'Democracy and Liberty'. In *Deliberative Democracy*, edited by Jon Elster, 185–231. Cambridge: Cambridge University Press, 1998.

Cooper, Robert. *The Breaking of Nations: Order and Chaos in the Twenty-First Century*. London: Atlantic Monthly Press, 2003.

Copp, David. 'The Idea of a Legitimate State'. *Philosophy and Public Affairs* 28, no. 1 (1999): 3–45.

Cotton, James. *East Timor, Australia and Regional Order: Intervention and its Aftermath in Southeast Asia*. London and New York: RoutledgeCurzon, 2004.

212 Bibliography

Cotton, James. 'The Crisis of the Timor-Leste State in Comparative Perspective'. In *The Crisis in Timor-Leste: Understanding the Past, Imagining the Future*, edited by Dennis Shoesmith, 13–21. Darwin: Charles Darwin University Press, 2007.

Cotton, James. 'Timor-Leste and the Discourse of State Failure'. *Australian Journal of International Affairs* 61, no. 4 (2007): 455–470.

Crawford, James. *The Creation of States in International Law*. 2nd edn. Oxford: Clarendon Press, 2006.

Croissant, Aurel. 'The Perils and Promises of Democratization Through United Nations Transitional Authority – Lessons from Cambodia and East Timor'. *Democratization* 15, no. 3 (2008): 649–648.

Croissant, Aurel and Jeffrey Haynes. 'Inequalities and Democracy in Southeast Asia'. *Democratization* 21, no. 5 (2014): 775–779.

Crook, Richard and James Manor. *Democracy and Decentralisation in South Asia and West Africa: Participation, Accountability and Performance.* New York: Cambridge University Press, 1998.

Crouch, Harold. 'The TNI and East Timor Policy'. In *Out of the Ashes: The Destruction and Reconstruction of East Timor*, edited by James J. Fox and Dionisio B. Soares, 141–167. Canberra: Australian National University Press, 2003.

Crouch, Harold. *Political Reform in Indonesia After Soeharto*. Singapore: Institute of Southeast Asian Studies, 2010.

Cummins, Deborah. 'Democracy or Democrazy? Local Experiences of Democratization in Timor-Leste'. *Democratization* 17, no. 5 (2010): 899–919.

Dahl, Robert. *Polyarchy: Participation and Opposition.* Michigan: Yale University Press, 1971.

Dahl, Robert. *Democracy and its Critics.* Michigan: Yale University Press, 1989.

Dann, Philipp and Zaid Al-Ali. 'The Internationalized *Pouvoir Constituant* – Constitution-Making Under External Influence in Iraq, Sudan and East Timor'. *Max Planck Yearbook of United Nations Law* 10 (2006): 423–463.

Diamond, Larry. 'Cause and Effect'. In *Political Culture and Democracy in Developing Countries*, edited by Larry Diamond, 229–249. Colorado: Lynne Rienner, 1994.

Diamond, Larry. 'Introduction: Political Culture and Democracy'. In *Political Culture and Democracy in Developing Countries*, edited by Larry Diamond, 1–28. Colorado: Lynne Rienner Publishers, 1994.

Diamond, Larry. *Developing Democracy: Toward Consolidation*. Baltimore: The Johns Hopkins University Press, 1999.

Diamond, Larry. 'Promoting Democracy in Post-Conflict and Failed States: Lessons and Challenges'. *Taiwan Journal of Democracy* 2, no. 2 (2005): 93–116.

Diamond, Larry, Juan Linz and Seymour Lipset. 'Introduction: What Makes for Democracy', *Politics in Developing Countries*. 2nd edn, edited by Larry Diamond, Juan Linz and Seymour Lipset, 1–16. Lynne Rienner Publisher: Boulder, Colorado, 1995.

Di Palma, Giuseppe. *To Craft Democracies: An Essay on Democratic Transitions*. Berkeley: University of California Press, 1990.

do Amaral, Xavier. *Nao ha duvida de que a Indonesia invadiu um pais livre neutro, pacifico, soberano, independente e nao-alinhado.* Maputo: Representacao Permanente da FRETILIN em Maputo, 1975.

do Reis Lobato, Nicolau. *Fretilin e a liberdade do povo em marcha: discursos.* Lisbon: Edicoes Comite, 28 November 1979.

Dobbins, James and Laurel Miller. 'Overcoming Obstacles to Peace'. *Survival: Global Politics and Strategy* 55, no. 1 (2013): 103–120.

Bibliography 213

Downie, Sue. 'UNTAET: State-building and Peace-Building'. In *East Timor: Beyond Independence*, edited by Damien Kingsbury and Michael Leach, 29–42. Clayton: Monash University Press, 2007.

Dunn, James. *Timor: A People Betrayed*. Milton, Queensland: The Jacaranda Press, 1983.

Dunn, James. *A Rough Passage to Independence*. Double Bay, New South Wales: Longueville Books, 2003.

Duverger, Maurice. 'A New Political System Model: Semi-Presidential Government'. *European Journal of Political Research* 8, no. 2 (1980): 166–187.

Eisenstadt, Shmuel. 'Public Spheres and Civil Society in Selected Pre-Modern Societies: Some Comparative Observations'. *Comparative Sociology* 5, no. 1 (2006): 1–31.

Emmerson, Donald K. 'Minding the Gap Between Democracy and Governance'. *Journal of Democracy* 23, no. 2 (2012): 62–73.

Engel, Rebecca. 'Reaching for Stability: Strengthening Civil Society-Donor Partnerships in East Timor'. *Journal of International Affairs* 57, no. 1 (Fall 2003): 169–181.

Eurich, Hanja. *Factors of Success in Mission Communication Strategies in Post-Conflict Settings: Critical Assessment of the UN Mission in East Timor and Nepal*. Berlin: Logos Verlag Berlin GmbH, 2010.

Falk, Richard. 'The East Timor Ordeal: International Law and its Limits'. In *Bitter Flowers, Sweet Flowers: East Timor, Indonesia and the World Community*, edited by Richard Tanter, Mark Selden and Stephen Shalom, 149–161. Annandale, New South Wales: Pluto Press Australia, 2001.

Fan, Hua. 'The Missing Link between Self-Determination and Democracy: The Case of East Timor'. *Northwestern Journal of International Human Rights* 6, no. 1 (2007): 176–195.

Farram, Steven, ed. *Locating Democracy: Representation, Elections and Governance in Timor-Leste*. Darwin: Charles Darwin University Press, 2010.

Fearon, James and David Laitin. 'Neo-Trusteeship and the Problem of Weak States'. *International Security* 28, no. 4 (2004): 5–43.

Federer, Juan. *The UN in East Timor: Building Timor-Leste, a Fragile State*. Darwin: Charles Darwin University Press, 2005.

Feijó, Rui. 'Semi-Presidentialism, Moderating Power and Inclusive Governance: The Experience of Timor-Leste in Consolidating Democracy'. *Democratization* (2012): 1–12.

Feldman, Noah. 'Imposed Constitutionalism'. *Connecticut Law Review* 37 (2004–2005): 857–889.

Fernandes, Clinton. *Reluctant Saviours: Australia, Indonesia and the Independence of East Timor*. Melbourne: Scribe Publications, 2004.

Fernandes, Clinton. *The Independence of East Timor: Multi-Dimensional Perspectives – Occupation, Resistance, and International Political Activism*. Brighton: Sussex Academic Press, 2011.

Fox, Gregory and Brad Roth. 'Democracy and International Law'. *Review of International Studies* 27 (2001): 327–352.

Fox, James. 'A District Analysis of the East Timor Elections 2001–2002'. In *Elections and Constitution Making in East Timor*, edited by Dionisio B. Soares, Michael Maley, James J. Fox and Anthony Regan, 15–23. Canberra: Pandanus Books, 2003.

Franck, Thomas. 'The Emerging Right of Democratic Governance'. *American Journal of International Law* 86 (1992): 46–91.

Franck, Thomas and Paul Hoffman. 'The Right of Self-Determination in Very Small Places'. *New York University Journal of International Law and Politics* 8, (1975/1976): 332–386.

214   *Bibliography*

FRETILIN. *East Timor, Indonesia's Vietnam.* Dili: Department of External Relations of FRETILIN, 1977.

FRETILIN. *What is Fretilin?* Sydney: Campaign for Independent East Timor, 1974.

Fukuyama, Francis. *The End of History and the Last Man.* New York: Free Press, 1992.

Fukuyama, Francis. *State-Building: Governance and World Order in the Twenty-First Century.* Ithaca: Cornell University Press, 2004.

Gallup, Jeffrey. 'Cambodia's Electoral System: A Window of Opportunity for Reform'. In *Electoral Politics in Southeast and East Asia*, edited by Aurel Croissant, 25–73. Singapore: Freidrich Ebert Foundation, 2002.

Gellner, Ernest. *Conditions of Liberty: Civil Society and Its Rivals.* London: Hamish Hamilton, 1994.

Gill, Graeme. *The Dynamics of Democratization: Elites, Civil Society and the Transition Process.* London: Palgrave Macmillan, 2000.

Goldstone, Anthony. 'UNTAET with Hindsight: The Peculiarities of Politics in an Incomplete State'. *Global Governance* 10 (2004): 83–98.

Gorjão, Paulo. 'The East Timorese Commission for Reception, Truth and Reconciliation: Chronicle of a Foretold Failure?' *Civil Wars* 4, no. 2 (2001): 142–162.

Gorjão, Paulo. 'The Legacy and Lessons of the United Nations Transitional Administration in East Timor'. *Contemporary Southeast Asia* 24, no. 2 (2002): 313–336.

Grenfell, Damien. 'Reconstituting the Nation: Reconciliation and National Consciousness in Timor-Leste'. In *Occasional Series in Criminal Justice and International Studies,* 18–33. Melbourne: RMIT publishing, 2006.

Grenfell, Damien. 'Governance, Violence and Crises in Timor-Leste: *Estadu Seidauk Mai*'. In *Democratic Governance in Timor-Leste: Reconciling the Local and the National*, edited by David Mearns and Steven Farram, 85–97. Darwin: Charles Darwin University Press, 2008.

Gunn, Geoffrey. 'Timor-Leste in 2009: Cup Half Full or Half Empty?' *Asian Survey* 50, no. 1 (2010): 235–240.

Gusmão, Martinho. *Timor Lorosae: perjalanan menuju dekolonisasi hati-diri.* Malang: Dioma, 2003.

Gusmão, Xanana. 'Reconciliation, Unity and National Development in the Framework of the Transition Toward Independence'. In *Guns and Ballot Boxes: East Timor's Vote for Independence*, edited by Damien Kingsbury, 1–9. Clayton: Monash Asia Institute, 2000.

Gusmão, Xanana. *To Resist is to Win! With Selected Letters and Speeches.* Edited by Sarah Niner. Richmond, Victoria: Aurora Books, 2000.

Gusmão, Xanana. *A Construção da Nação Timorense Desafios e Oportunidades.* Lisbon: Lidel, 2004.

Gusmão, Xanana. *Timor Lives! Speeches of Freedom and Independence.* Alexandria, New South Wales: Longueville Media, 2005.

Gusmão, Xanana. *Strategies for the Future.* Double Bay, New South Wales: Longueville Books, 2012.

Gusmão, Xanana. *Xanana Gusmão e os Primeiros 10 anos da Construção do Estado Timorense.* Portugal: Porto Editora, 2012.

Guterres, Jose. 'Opening Address at the Conference, Darwin, Australia, 7 February 2008'. In *Democratic Governance in Timor-Leste: Reconciling the Local and the National*, edited by David Mearns and Steven Farram, ix–xii. Darwin: Charles Darwin University Press, 2008.

Guterres, Jose. 'Timor-Leste: A Year of Democratic Elections'. *Southeast Asian Affairs* (2008): 359–372.

Bibliography 215

Habermas, Jurgen. *Legitimation Crisis.* London: Heinemann Educational, 1976.

Habermas, Jurgen. 'The European Nation-State: On the Past and Future of Sovereignty and Citizenship'. In *Mapping the Nation,* edited by Gopal Balakrishnan. London: Verso, 1996: 281–294.

Habermas, Jurgen. 'Constitutional Democracy: A Paradoxical Union of Contradictory Principles?' *Political Theory* 29, no. 6, (December 2001): 766–781.

Hadenius, Axel and Jan Teorell. 'Pathways from Authoritarianism', *Journal of Democracy* 18, no. 1 (2007): 143–157.

Hadiwinata, Bob Sugeng. 'Sejarah Perbatasan Indonesia-Timor-Leste'. In *Keamanan di perbatasan Indonesia-Timor Leste: Sumber Ancaman Dan Kebijakan Pengelolaannya,* edited by Ganewati Wuryandari, 55–76. Jakarta: P2P-LIP, Yogyakarta, Pustaka Pelajar, 2009.

Hainsworth, Paul and Stephen McCloskey, eds. *The East Timor Question: The Struggle for Independence From Indonesia.* London: I.B. Tauris Publishers, 2000.

Halperin, Morton. 'Guaranteeing Democracy'. *Foreign Policy* 91, Summer (1993): 105–122.

Hannum, Hurst. *Autonomy, Sovereignty, and Self-Determination: the Accommodation of Conflicting Rights.* Philadephia: University of Philadelphia Press, 1990.

Harmer, Andrew and Robert Frith. ' "Walking Together" Toward Independence? A Civil Society Perspective on the United Nations Administration in East Timor, 1999–2002'. *Global Governance* 15, no. 2 (April–June 2009): 239–258.

Harris, Vandra and Andrew Goldsmith. 'The Struggle for Independence Was Just the Beginning'. In *Security, Development and Nation-Building in Timor-Leste: A Cross-Sectoral Assessment,* edited by Vandra Harris and Andrew Goldsmith, 3–16. Oxon: Routledge, 2011.

Heater, Derek. *What is Citizenship?* Cambridge: Polity Press, 1999.

Heater, Derek. *Citizenship: The Civic Ideal in World History, Politics and Education,* 3rd edn. Manchester: Manchester University Press, 2004.

Held, David. *Models of Democracy.* Stanford: Stanford University Press, 1987.

Helman, Gerard and Stephen Ratner. 'Saving Failed States'. *Foreign Policy* 89 (1992–1993): 3–20.

Hohe, Tanja. 'The Clash of Paradigms: International Administration and Local Political Legitimacy in East Timor'. *Contemporary Southeast Asia* 24, no. 3 (December 2002): 569–589.

Hill, Helen. *Stirrings of Nationalism in East Timor, Fretilin 1974–1978: the Origins, Ideologies and Strategies of a Nationalist Movement.* Otford, New South Wales: Otford Press, 2002.

Holsti, Kaveli. *The State, War, and the State of the War.* Cambridge: Cambridge University Press, 1996.

Hooper, James and Paul Williams. 'Earned Sovereignty: The Political Dimension'. *Denver Journal of International Law and Policy* 31, no. 3 (2002–2003): 355–372.

Hughes, Caroline. *Dependent Communities: Aid and Politics in Cambodia and East Timor.* Ithaca: Cornell Southeast Asia Program, 2009.

Hunt, Janet. 'Building a New Society: NGOs in East Timor'. *New Community Quarterly* 2, no. 1 (2004): 16–23.

Huntington, Samuel. *The Third Wave: Democratization in the Late Twentieth Century.* Oklahoma: University of Oklahoma Press, 1991.

Huntington, Samuel. 'After Twenty Years: The Future of the Third Wave'. *Journal of Democracy,* no. 4 (1997): 3–12.

216   *Bibliography*

Huntley, Wade and Peter Hayes. 'East Timor and Asian Security'. In *Bitter Flowers, Sweet Flowers: East Timor, Indonesia and the World Community*, edited by Richard Tanter, Mark Selden and Stephen Shalom, 173–185. Annandale: Pluto Press Australia, 2001.

Hurd, Ian. 'Legitimacy and Authority in International Politics'. *International Organizations* 53, no. 2 (1999): 379–408.

Jackson, Robert. 'Boundaries and International Society'. *International Society and the Development of International Relations Theory*, edited by Barbara Robertson, 156–172. London and New York: Continuum, 2002.

Jackson, Robert. 'Quasi-States, Dual Regimes, and Neo-Classical Theory: International Jurisprudence and the Third World'. *International Organization* 41, no. 4 (Autumn 1987): 519–549.

Jackson, Robert. *Quasi-States: Sovereignty, International Relations and the Third World*. Cambridge: Cambridge University Press, 1990.

Jenkins, Catherine. 'A Truth Commission for East Timor: Lessons from South Africa?' *Journal of Conflict and Security Law* 7, no. 2 (2002): 233–251.

Jolliffe, Jill. *East Timor: Nationalism and Colonialism*. St Lucia, Queensland: University of Queensland Press, 1978.

Jolliffe, Jill. 'Psychosocial Healing as a Prerequisite to Good Governance in East Timor'. In *Democratic Governance in East Timor: Reconciling the Local and the National*, edited by David Mearns and Steven Farram, 10–20. Darwin: Charles Darwin University Press, 2008.

Kartasasmita, Sabana. *East Timor: A Quest for a Solution.* Singapore: Crescent Design Associates, 1998.

Katzenstein, Suzanne. 'Hybrid Tribunals: Searching for Justice in East Timor'. *Harvard Human Rights Journal* 16 (2003): 246–278.

Kaufman, Michael. 'Community Power, Grassroots Democracy, and the Transformation of Social Life'. In *Community Power and Grassroots Democracy: The Transformation of Social Life*, edited by Michael Kaufman and Haroldo Dilla Alfonso, 1–26. London and New Jersey: Zed Books, 1997.

Kiernan, Ben. *Genocide and Resistance in Southeast Asia: Documentation, Denial and Justice in Cambodia and East Timor*. New Jersey: Transaction Publishers, 2008.

Kingsbury, Damien. 'East Timor to 1999'. In *Guns and Ballot Boxes: East Timor's Vote for Independence*, edited by Damien Kingsbury, 17–27. Clayton, Melbourne: Monash Asia Institute, 2000.

Kingsbury, Damien. 'The TNI and the Militias'. In *Guns and Ballot Boxes: East Timor's Vote for Independence*, edited by Damien Kingsbury, 69–80. Clayton, Melbourne: Monash Asia Institute, 2000.

Kingsbury, Damien, 'Political Developments'. In *East Timor: Beyond Independence*, edited by Damien Kingsbury and Michael Leach, 19–28. Clayton, Melbourne: Monash University Press, 2007.

Kingsbury, Damien. 'Timor-Leste: The Harsh Reality after Independence'. *Southeast Asian Affairs* (2007): 363–377.

Kingsbury, Damien. 'East Timor's Political Crisis: Origins and Resolution'. In *Democratic Governance in Timor-Leste: Reconciling the Local and the National*, edited by David Mearns and Steven Farram, 33–51. Darwin: Charles Darwin University Press, 2008.

Kingsbury, Damien. *East Timor: The Price of Liberty.* New York: Palgrave Macmillan, 2009.

Bibliography   217

Kingsbury, Damien. 'Post-Colonial States, Ethnic Minorities and Separatist Conflicts: Case Studies from Southeast and South Asia'. *Ethnic and Racial Studies* 34, no. 5 (2011): 762–778.

Kingsbury, Damien. 'Timor-Leste in 2012: The Harsh Reality of Independence'. *Southeast Asian Affairs* (2013): 305–322.

Kingsbury, Damien and Michael Leach. 'Introduction'. In *East Timor: Beyond Independence*, edited by Damien Kingsbury and Michael Leach, 1–18. Clayton, Melbourne: Monash University Press, 2007.

Kingston, Jeffrey. 'Balancing Justice and Reconciliation in East Timor'. *Critical Asian Studies* 38, no. 3 (2006): 271–302.

Kondoch, Boris. 'The United Nations Administration of East Timor'. *Journal of Conflict and Security Law* 6, no. 2 (2001): 245–265.

Krause, Jill and Neil Renwick. 'Introduction'. In *Identities in International Relations*, edited by Jill Krause and Neil Renwick, x–xv. Hampshire: Macmillan Press, 1996.

Krasner, Stephen. *Sovereignty: Organized Hypocrisy*. New Jersey: Princeton University Press, 1999.

Krasner, Stephen. *Power, the State, and Sovereignty: Essays on International Relations*. New Jersey: Routledge, 2009.

Kraser, Stephen and Carlos Pascual. 'Addressing State Failure'. *Foreign Affairs* 84, (2005): 153–163.

Krieger, Heike. *East Timor and the International Community: Basic Documents*. Cambridge: Cambridge University Press, 1997.

Kuntari, C. M. Rien. 'Timor Timur Satu Menit Terakhir: Catatan Seorang Wartawan'. Bundung: Mizan, 2008.

Lambourne, Wendy. 'Transitional Justice and Peacebuilding after Mass Violence'. *The International Journal of Transitional Justice* 3 (2009): 28–48.

Laplante, Lisa. 'Transitional Justice and Peace Building: Diagnosing and Addressing the Socioeconomic Roots of Violence through a Human Rights Framework'. *The International Journal of Transitional Justice* 2 (2008): 331–355.

Leach, Michael. 'Valorising the Resistance: National Identity and Collective Memory in East Timor's Constitution'. *Social Alternatives* 21, no. 3 (Winter 2002): 43–47.

Leach, Michael. 'The 2007 Presidential and Parliamentary Elections in Timor-Leste'. *Australian Journal of History-Politics* 55, no. 2 (June 2009): 219–232.

Lemay-Hébert, Nicolas. 'Statebuilding without Nation-building? Legitimacy, State Failure and the Limits of the Institutionalist Approach'. *Journal of Intervention and Statebuilding* 3, no. 1 (2009): 21–45.

Lemay-Hébert, Nicolas. 'The Empty-Shell Approach: The Setup Process of International Administrations in Timor-Leste and Kosovo, Its Consequences and Lesson'. *International Studies Perspectives* 12 (2011): 190–211.

Levitsky, Stephen and Lucan Way. *Competitive Authoritarianism: Hybrid Regimes Since the Cold War*. New York: Cambridge University Press, 2010.

Lijphart, Arend. 'Constitutional Choices for New Democracies'. *Journal of Democracy* 2, no. 1 (1991): 72–84.

Lijphart, Arend. *Patterns of Democracy: Government Forms and Performance in Thirty-Six Countries*. New Haven and London: Yale University Press, 1999.

Linton, Suzannah. 'Cambodia, East Timor and Sierra Leone: Experiments in International Justice'. *Criminal Law Forum* 12 (2001): 185–246.

Linz, Juan. 'Democracy Today: An Agenda for Students of Democracy'. *Scandinavian Political Studies* 20, no. 2 (1997): 115–134.

218 *Bibliography*

Linz, Juan and Alfred Stepan. *Problems of Democratic Transition and Consolidation*. Baltimore: John Hopkins University Press, 1996.

Lipset, Seymour. *Political Man and the Social Bases of Politics*. Baltimore: Johns Hopkins University Press, 1981.

Lloyd, Grayson. 'The Diplomacy on East Timor: Indonesia, the United Nations and the International Community'. In *Out of the Ashes: Destruction and Reconstruction of East Timor*, edited by James J. Fox and Dionisio B. Soares, 79–105. South Australia: Crawford House Publishing, 2000.

Lovell, David. 'Promoting Democracy: The Challenge of Creating a Civil Society'. *Comparative Sociology* 6 (2007): 324–343.

Mackie, James. 'Future Political Structures and Institutions in East Timor'. *East Timor, Development Challenges for the World's Newest Nation*, edited by Helen Hill and Jose Saldanha, 193–206. Singapore: Institute of Southeast Asian Studies, 2001.

Manning, Chris and Peter Van Diermen, eds. *Indonesia di Tengah Transisi: Aspek-Aspect Sosial Reformasi dan Krisis.* Yogyakarta: LKiS, 2000.

Manor, James. 'Democratisation with Inclusion: Political Reforms and People's Empowerment at the Grassroots'. *Journal of Human Development* 5, no. 1 (March 2004): 5–29.

March, James and Johan Olsen. *Rediscovering Institutions: The Organizational Basis of Politics*. New York: The Free Press, 1989.

Marker, Jamsheed. *East Timor: A Memoir of the Negotiations for Independence*, Jefferson: MacFarland, 2003.

Marks, Stephen. 'The Process of Creating a New Constitution in Cambodia'. In *Framing the State in Times of Transition*, edited by Laurel Miller, 207–244. Washington DC, United State Institute of Peace, 2010.

Marshall, T.H. 'Citizenship and Social Class'. In *Citizenship and Social Class*, edited by T.H. Marshall and Tom Bottomore, 3–49. London: Pluto Press, 1992.

Martin, Brian. 'Protest in a Liberal-Democracy'. *Philosophy and Social Action* 20, no. 2 (January–June 1994): 13–24.

Martin, Ian. *Self-Determination in East Timor: the United Nations, the Ballot, and International Intervention.* Boulder: Lynne Rienner Publishers, 2001.

Martinkus, John. *A Dirty Little War.* New South Wales: Random House, 2001.

Mashad, Dhurorudin. 'Indonesia menjawab tantangan global'. In *Politik luar negeri Indonesia di tengah pusaran politik internasional*, edited by Ganewati Wuryandari, 170–213. Jakarta and Yogyakarta: P2P-LIPI and Pustaka Pelajar, 2011.

Matsuno, Aksuno. 'The UN Transitional Administration and Democracy Building in Timor-Leste'. In *Democratic Governance in Timor-Leste: Reconciling the Local and the National*, edited by David Mearns and Steven Farram, 52–70. Darwin: Charles Darwin University Press, 2008.

McWilliam, Andrew. 'East and West in Timor-Leste: Is There an Ethnic Divide?' In *The Crisis in Timor-Leste: Understanding the Past, Imagining the Future*, edited by Dennis Shoesmith, 37–43. Darwin: Charles Darwin University Press, 2007.

McWilliam, Andrew. 'Customary Governance in Timor-Leste'. In *Democratic Governance in Timor-Leste: Reconciling the Local and the National*, edited by David Mearns and Steven Farram, 129–142. Darwin: Charles Darwin University Press, 2008.

McWilliam, Andrew and Angie Bexley. 'Performing Politics: The 2007 Parliamentary Elections in Timor Leste'. *The Asia Pacific Journal of Anthropology* 9, no. 1 (2008): 66–82.

Mearns, David. *Looking Both Ways: Models for Justice in East Timor*. Australia: Australian Legal Resources International, 2002.

Bibliography 219

Mearns, David. 'Masking the Pain: Nation-Building and 'Local Anaesthetic' in Timor-Leste'. *The Crisis in Timor-Leste: Understanding the Past, Imagining the Future*, edited by Dennis Shoesmith, 45–50. Darwin: Charles Darwin University Press, 2007.

Mearns, David. 'Imagining East Timor Again: The Ideas of a 'National Identity' and 'Democratic Governance' in Timor-Leste'. In *Democratic Governance in Timor-Leste: Reconciling the Local and the National*, edited by David Mearns and Steven Farram, xiii–xxv. Darwin: Charles Darwin University Press, 2008.

Meyer, Thomas and Lewis Hinchman. *The Theory of Social Democracy*. Cambridge: Polity, 1997.

Migdal, Joel. *Weak Societies and Strong States*. Princeton: Princeton University Press, 1988.

Migdal, Joel. 'Integration and Disintegration: An Approach to Society-Formation'. In *Between Development and Destruction: An Enquiry into the Causes of Conflict in Post-Colonial States*, edited by Luc Van de Goor, Kumar Rupesinghe and Paul Sciavone, 91–106. Hampshire: Macmillan, 1996.

Migdal, Joel. 'State Building and the Non-Nation-State'. *Journal of International Affairs* 8, no. 1 (Fall 2004): 17–46.

Miller, David. 'Democracy and Social Justice'. *British Journal of Political Science* 18, no. 1 (1978): 1–19.

Miller, David. *Citizenship and National Identity*. Malden: Polity Press, 2000.

Miller, Russell. 'Self-Determination in International Law and the Demise of Democracy?' *Columbia Journal of International Law* 41 (2003): 601–648.

Milliken, Jennifer and Keith Krause. 'State Failure, State Collapse, and State Reconstruction: Concepts, Lessons and Strategies'. *Development and Change* 33, no. 5 (2002): 753–774.

Molnar, Andrea. *Timor-Leste: Politics, History, and Culture*. London and New York: Routledge, 2010.

Morrow, Jonathon and Rachel White. 'The United Nations in Transitional East Timor: International Standards and the Reality of Governance'. *Australian Year Book of International Law* 22, no. 1 (2002): 1–47.

Munir, S. H. 'Kekarasan Negara: Pemicu Disintegrasi Bangsa'. In *Indonesia di Tengah Transisi*, edited by George Aditjondro and Kusnanto Anggoro, 25–31. Jakarta: Propatria, 2000.

Nevins, Joseph. 'Restitution over Coffee: Truth, Reconciliation, and Environmental Violence in East Timor'. *Political Geography* 22 (2003): 677–701.

Nevins, Joseph. 'The CAVR: Justice and Reconciliation in a Time of "Impoverished Political Possibilities"'. *Pacific Affairs* 80, no. 4 (2007/2008): 593–602.

Nicholson, Graham. 'Observation on the New Constitution of East Timor'. *Alternative Law Journal*, no. 5 (October 2002): 203–206.

Nicol, Bill. *Timor: The Stillborn Nation*. Camberwell, Victoria: Visa, 1978.

Niner, Sara. 'A Long Journey of Resistance: The Origins and Struggle of CRNT'. In *Bitter Flowers, Sweet Flowers: East Timor, Indonesia and the World Community*, edited by Richard Tanter, Mark Selden and Stephen Shalom, 15–30. Sydney: Pluto Press Australia, 2001.

Niner, Sara. 'Martyrs, Heroes and Warriors: The Leadership of East Timor'. In *East Timor: Beyond Independence*, edited by Damien Kingsbury and Michael Leach, 113–128. Clayton, Melbourne: Monash University Press, 2007.

Niner, Sara. *Xanana: Leader of the Struggle for Independent Timor-Leste*. North Melbourne: Australian Scholarly Publishing, 2009.

220 Bibliography

Niner, Sara. 'Between Earth and Heaven: The politics of gender. 'In *The Politics of Timor-Leste: Democratic Consolidation after Intervention*, edited by Michael Leach and Damien Kingsbury, 239–258. Ithaca, NY: Cornell, 2014.

Nordquist, Kjell Åke. 'Reconciliation as a Political Concept: Some Observations and Remarks'. In *Multidisciplinary Perspectives on Peace and Conflict Research: A View from Europe*, edited by Francisco Ferrándiz and Antonius Robben, 197–222. Bilbao: University of Duesto, 2007.

O'Donnell, Guillermo. 'Delegative Democracy'. *Counterpoints: Selected Essays on Authoritarianism and Democratization*, edited by Guillermo O'Donnell, 159–174. Notre Dame: University of Notre Dame Press, 1999.

Onuf, Nicholas. 'The Constitution of International Society'. *European Journal of International Law* 5, (1994): 14.

Ottaway, Marina. 'Nation-Building'. *Foreign Policy* 132 (September/October 2002): 16–22.

Ottaway, Marina. 'Rebuilding State Institutions in Collapsed States'. *Development and Change* 33, no. 5 (2002): 1001–1023.

Patrick, Ian. 'East Timor Emerging from Conflict: The Role of Local NGOs and International Assistance'. *Disasters* 25, no. 1 (2001): 48–66.

Paris, Roland. 'Saving Liberal Peacebuilding'. *Review of International Studies* 36, (2010): 337–365.

Paris, Roland and Timothy Sisk. 'Introduction: Understanding the Contradictions of Postwar Statebuilding'. In *The Dilemmas of Statebuilding: Confronting the Contradictions of Postwar Peace Operations*, edited by Roland Paris and Timothy Sisk, 1–20. New York: Routledge, 2009.

Pavkovic, Aleksandar and Peter Radan. 'In Pursuit of Sovereignty and Self-Determination: Peoples, States and Secession in the International Order'. *Macquarie Law Journal* 3 (2003): 1–12.

Peou, Sorpong. *International Democracy Assistance for Peacebuilding: Cambodia and Beyond.* Basingstoke: Palgrave Macmillan, 2007.

Peou, Sorpong. 'The Limits and Potential of Liberal Democratisation in Southeast Asia'. *Journal of Current Southeast Asian Affairs* 33, no. 2 (2014): 19–47.

Pevehouse, Jon. 'Democracy from the Outside-In? International Organizations and Democratization'. *International Organization* 56, no. 3 (2002): 515–549.

Philpott, Daniel. 'In Defense of Self-Determination'. *Ethics* 105, no. 2 (1995): 352–385.

Philpott, Daniel. *Revolutions in Sovereignty: How Ideas Shaped the Modern World.* Princeton: Princeton University Press, 2001.

Philpott, Simon. 'East Timor's Double Life: Smells Like Westphalian Spirit'. *Third World Quarterly* 27, no. 1 (2006): 135–159.

Philpott, Simon. 'Post-Colonial Troubles: The Politics of Transitional Justice'. In *Timor-Leste: Challenges for Justice and Human Rights in the Shadow of the Past*, edited by William Binchy, 237–260. Dublin: Clarus Press, 2009.

Pierson, Christopher. *The Modern State.* London: Routledge, 1996.

Pietsch, Sam. 'Australian Imperialism and East Timor'. *Marxist Interventions* 2 (2010): 7–38.

Pinto, Constâncio. 'The Student Movement and the Independence Struggle in East Timor: An Interview'. In *Bitter Flowers, Sweet Flowers: East Timor, Indonesia and the World Community*, edited by Richard Tanter, Mark Selden and Stephen Shalom, 31–41. Sydney: Pluto Press Australia, 2001.

Pinto, Constâncio and Matthew Jardine. *East Timor's Unfinished Struggle: Inside the Timorese Resistance.* Boston: South End Press, 1997.

Bibliography   221

Pridham, Geoffrey, Eric Herring and George Sanford. 'Introduction'. In *Building Democracy? The International Dimension of Democratisation in Eastern Europe*, edited by Geoffrey Pridham, Eric Herring and George Sanford, 1–6. London: Leicester University Press, 1997.

Purdue, Derrick. 'Introduction: Dimensions of Civil Society'. In *Civil Societies and Social Movements: Potentials and Problems*, edited by Derrick Purdue, 1–16. Oxon: Routledge, 2007.

Purdey, Jemma. 'Legal Responses to Violence in Post-Soeharto Indonesia'. In *Indonesia: Law and Society*, 2nd edn, edited by Timothy Lindsay, 515–531. Annandale: The Federation Press, 2008.

Putnam, Robert. *Making Democracy Work*. Princeton: Princeton University Press, 1993.

Pye, Lucian. *Politics, Personality and Nation-Building: Burma's Search for Identity*. New Haven: Yale University Press, 1962.

Ramos-Horta, José. *Funu: The Unfinished Saga of East Timor*. New Jersey: The Red Sea Press, 1987.

Ramos-Horta, José. *Towards a Peaceful Solution in East Timor*, 2nd edn. Sydney: ETRA, 1997.

Ramos-Horta, José. 'Human Rights, Democracy and Rule of Law in the Asia-Pacific Region'. *Iowa Review* 28, no. 3 (Winter 1999): 1–9.

Rawls, John. *A Theory of Justice*. Oxford: Oxford University Press, 1971.

Regan, Anthony. 'Constitution Making in East Timor: Missed Opportunities?' In *Elections and Constitution Making in East Timor*, edited by Dionisio Babo Soares, Michael Maley, James J. Fox and Anthony Regan, 35–42. Canberra: Pandanus Books 2003.

Reilly, Benjamin. 'Political Engineering in the Asia-Pacific'. *Journal of Democracy* 18, no. 1 (January 2007): 58–72.

Reisman, Michael. 'Sovereignty and Human Rights in Contemporary International Law'. *American Journal of International Law* 84, no. 4 (1990): 866–876.

Renshaw, Catherine, Andrew Byrnes, and Andrea Durbach. 'Human Rights Protection in the Pacific: The Emerging Role of National Human Rights Institutions in the Region'. *New Zealand Journal of Politics and International Law* 8 (2012): 117–144.

Retbøll, Torben. 'The Women of East Timor'. In *East Timor: Nation-Building in the 21st Century*, edited by Gabriel Jonsson, 11–32. Stockholm: Centre for Pacific Asia Studies, Stockholm University, 2002.

Reynolds, Andrew and John Carey. 'The Impact of Election Systems'. *Journal of Democracy* 22, no. 4 (October 2011): 36–47.

Richmond, Oliver. 'De-Romantising the Local, De-Mystifying the International: Hybridity in Timor-Leste and the Solomon Islands'. *The Pacific Review* 24, no. 1 (2011): 115–136.

Richmond, Oliver and Jason Franks. 'Liberal Hubris? Virtual Peace in Cambodia'. *Security Dialogue* 38, no. 1 (March 2007): 27–48.

Roberts, David. *Political Transition in Cambodia 1991–99*. New York: St Martins Press, 2000.

Roberts, David. 'Democratization, Elite Transition and Violence in Cambodia, 1991–1999'. *Critical Asian Studies* 34, no. 4 (2002): 520–538.

Roberts, David. 'Political Transition and Elite Discourse in Cambodia, 1991–1999'. *Communist Studies and Transition Studies* 34, no. 4 (2002): 101–118.

Roberts, David. 'Hybrid Polities and Indigenous Pluralities: Advanced Lessons in Statebuilding from Cambodia'. *Journal of Intervention and Statebuilding* 2, no. 1 (2008): 63–86.

222 *Bibliography*

Roosa, John. 'How Does a Truth Commission Find out What the Truth Is? The Case of East Timor's CAVR'. *Pacific Affairs* 18, no. 4 (2007/2008): 569–580.

Rosenberg, Shawn. 'An Introduction: Theoretical Perspectives and Empirical Research on Deliberative Democracy'. In *Deliberation, Participation and Democracy: Can the People Govern?*, edited by Shawn Rosenberg, 1–24. Houndsmill: Palgrave Macmillan, 2007.

Rosenfeld, Michel. 'The Rule of Law and the Legitimacy of Constitutional Democracy'. *Southern California Law Review* 74 (2000–2001): 1307–1351.

Rotberg, Robert. 'Failed States, Collapsed States, Weak States: Causes and Indicators'. In *State Failure and State Weakness in a Time of Terror*, edited by Robert Rotberg, 1–25. Washington D.C: Brookings Institution Press, 2003.

Rotberg, Robert. 'The Failure and Collapse of Nation-States: Breakdown, Prevention and Repair'. In *When States Fail: Causes and Consequences*, edited by Roland Rotberg, 1–50. Princeton, New Jersey: Princeton University Press, 2003.

Rustow, Dankwart. 'Transitions to Democracy: Toward a Dynamic Model'. *Comparative Politics* 2, no. 3 (April 1970): 337–363.

Sahin, Selver. 'Building the State in Timor-Leste'. *Asian Survey* 47, no. 2 (2007): 250–267.

Sahin, Selver. 'Timor-Leste in 2009: Marking Ten Years of Independence or Dependence on International 'Assistance'?' *Southeast Asian Affairs* (2010): 345–364.

Sahin, Selver. 'Building the Nation in Timor-Leste and its Implications for the Countries Democratic Development'. *Australian Journal of International Affairs* 65, no. 2 (2011): 220–242.

Saldanha, Jose. 'Anatomy of Political Parties in Timor-Leste'. In *Political Parties in the Pacific Islands*, edited by Roland Rich, Luke Hambly and Michael Morgan, 69–81. Canberra: ANU Press, 2008.

Samuels, Kirsti. 'Post-War Constitution Building: Opportunities and Challenges'. In *The Dilemmas of Statebuilding: Confronting the Contradictions of Postwar Peace Operations*, edited by Roland Paris and Timothy Sisk, 173–195. New York: Routledge, 2009.

Sanches, Macario Floriano. *Mengenal Pemerintahan Timor-Leste: Teori dan Serjarah.* Dili: Grafic Patricia, 2010.

Sastrosatomo, Soebadio. *Indonesia di tengah pergolakan perang dingin.* Jakarta: Pusat Dokumentasi Politik 'Guntur 45', 1995.

Saul, Matthew. 'Local Ownership of Post-Conflict Reconstruction in International Law: The Initiation of International Involvement'. *Journal of Conflict and Security Law* 16, no. 1 (2011): 165–206.

Schrader, Peter. 'Elites as Facilitators or Impediments to Political Development? Some Lessons from the "Third Wave" of Democratization in Africa'. *The Journal of Developing Areas* 29, (1994): 69–90.

Schumpeter, Joseph. *Capitalism, Socialism and Democracy.* London: Allen & Unwin, 1976.

Scheeringa, Sandra. 'Enhancing the Local Legitimacy of Transnational Justice Institutions: Local Embeddedness and Customary Law in CAVR'. *East Timor: Beyond Independence*, edited by Damien Kingsbury and Michael Leach, 129–140. Clayton, Melbourne: Monash University Press, 2007.

Shoesmith, Dennis. 'Timor-Leste: Divided Leadership in a Semi-Presidential System'. *Asian Survey* 43, no. 2 (March/April 2003): 231–252.

Shoesmith, Dennis. 'Timor-Leste: Interpreting Violence in a Post-Conflict State'. *The Crisis in Timor-Leste: Understanding the Past, Imagining the Future*, edited by Dennis Shoesmith, 2–30. Darwin: Charles Darwin University Press, 2007.

Bibliography   223

Shoesmith, Dennis. 'Legislative-Executive Relations in Timor-Leste: the Case for Building a Stronger Parliament'. In *Democratic Governance in Timor-Leste: Reconciling the Local and the National*, edited by David Mearns and Steven Farram, 71-84. Darwin: Charles Darwin University Press, 2008.

Shoesmith, Dennis. 'Timor-Leste: On the Road to Peace and Prosperity'. *Southeast Asian Affairs* (2011): 323–338.

Shoesmith, Dennis. 'Is Small Beautiful? Multiparty Politics and Democratic Consolidation in Timor-Leste'. *Asian Politics and Policy* 4, no. 1 (January 2012): 33–51.

Siapno, Jacqueline. 'Timor-Leste: On a Path of Authoritarianism?' *Southeast Asian Affairs* (2006): 325–340.

Simonsen, Sven. 'The Authoritarian Temptation in East Timor: Nationbuilding and the Need for Inclusive Governance'. *Asian Survey* 46, no. 4 (July/August 2006): 575–596.

Simpson, Brad. 'Solidarity in the Age of Globalization: The Transnational Movement for East Timor and U.S. Foreign Policy'. *Peace and Change* 29, no. 3 and 4 (July 2004), 453–482.

Simpson, Brad. ' "Illegally and Beautifully": The United States, the Indonesian Invasion of East Timor and the International Community, 1974–1976'. *Cold War History* 5, no. 3 (August 2005): 281–315.

Singh, Bilveer. 'Habibie Melempar Bola Panas Ke Tangan PBB'. In *Timor Timur Bukan Bagian Dari Nasionalisme Indonesia*, 25–46. Jakarta: Front Indonesia Bersatu, 1999.

Slater, Dan. 'Democracy and Dictatorship do not Float Freely: Structural Forces of Political Regimes in Southeast Asia'. In *Southeast Asia in Political Science: Theory, Region, and Qualitative Analysis*, edited by Erik Martinez Kuhonta, Dan Slater and Tuong Vu, 55–79. Stanford: Stanford University Press, 2008.

Smith, Anthony L. 'The Popular Consultation in the Ermera District: Free, Fair and Secret?' *Guns and Ballot Boxes: East Timor's Vote for Independence*, edited by Damien Kingsbury, 29–41. Clayton, Melbourne: Monash Asia Institute, 2000.

Smith, Anthony L. 'East Timor: Elections in the World's Newest Nation'. *Journal of Democracy* 15, no. 4 (April 2004): 145–159.

Smith, Anthony L. 'Timor Leste: Strong Government, Weak State'. *Southeast Asian Affairs* (2004): 279–294.

Soares, Dionisio. 'Political Developments Leading to the Referendum'. In *Out of the Ashes: Deconstruction and Reconstruction of East Timor*, edited by James J. Fox and Dionisio B. Soares, 57–78. South Australia: Crawford House Publishing, 2000.

Soares, Dionisio. 'Election in East Timor: Some Unresolved Issues'. In *Elections and Constitution Making in East Timor*, edited by Dionisio B. Soares, Michael Maley, James J. Fox and Anthony Regan, 7–14. Canberra: Pandanus Books, 2003.

Soares, Dionisio. 'The Challenges of Drafting a Constitution', *Elections and Constitution Making in East Timor*, edited by Dionisio B. Soares, Michael Maley, James J. Fox and Anthony J. Regan, 25–33. Canberra, Pandanus Books, 2003.

Soares, Dionisio. '*Nahe Biti*: The Philosophy and Process of Grassroots Reconciliation (and Justice) in East Timor'. *The Asia Pacific Journal of Anthropology* 5, no. 1 (April 2004): 15–33.

Soares, Dionisio. 'East Timor: Reconciliation and Reconstruction'. *East Timor Law Journal* 3 (2007).

Soesastro, Hadi and Landry Haryo Subianto (eds), *Peace Building and State Building in East Timor*. Jakarta: Centre for Strategic and International Studies, 2002.

Stahn, Carsten. 'Accommodating Individual Criminal Responsibility and National Reconciliation: The UN Truth Commission for East Timor'. *The American Journal of International Law* 95, no. 4 (2001): 952–966.

224   *Bibliography*

Stahn, Carsten. 'The United Nations Transitional Administrations in Kosovo and East Timor: The First Analysis'. *Max Planck Yearbook of United Nations Law* 5 (2001): 105–183.

Steele, Jonathon. 'Nation Building in East Timor', *World Policy Journal* 19, no. 2 (Summer 2002): 76–87.

Stensrud, Ellen Emilie. 'New Dilemmas in Transitional Justice: Lessons from the Mixed Courts in Sierra Leone and Cambodia'. *Journal of Peace Research* 46, no. 1 (2009): 5–15.

Strating, Rebecca. 'East Timor's Emerging National Security Agenda: Establishing 'Real' Independence'. *Asian Security* 9, no. 3 (2013): 185–210.

Strating, Rebecca. 'Contested Self-determination: East Timor and Indonesia's Battle over Borders, International Law and Ethnic Identity'. *Journal of Pacific History* 49, no. 4 (2014): 469–494.

Strating, Rebecca. 'The Indonesia-Timor Leste Commission of Truth and Friendship: Enhancing Bilateral Relations at the Expense of Justice'. *Contemporary Southeast Asia* 36, no. 2 (2014): 232-261.

Strohmeyer, Hansjoerg. 'Building a New Judiciary for East Timor: Challenges of a Fledgling Nation'. *Criminal Law Forum* 11 (2000): 259–285.

Strohmeyer, Hansjoerg. 'Collapse and Reconstruction of a Judicial System: The United Nations Missions in Kosovo and East Timor'. *American Journal of International Law* 91, no. 1 (2001): 46–63.

Sugden, Craig. 'Timor-Leste's Pursuit of Inclusive Opportunity'. *Asia and the Pacific Policy Studies* 1, no. 3 (2014): 522-540.

Suhrke, Astri. 'Peacekeepers as Nation-Builders: Dilemma of the UN in East Timor'. *International Peacekeeping* 8, no. 4 (2001): 1–20.

Sunstein, Cass. *Designing Democracy: What Constitutions Do.* Oxford: Oxford University Press, 2001.

Sutter, Patrick. 'State-Building or the Dilemma of Intervention: An Introduction'. In *Facets and Practices of Statebuilding*, edited by Julia Raue and Patrick Sutter, 1–14. Leiden: Martinus Nijhoff Publishers, 2009.

Tanter, Richard, Mark Seldon and Stephen Shalom. 'East Timor Faces the Future'. In *Bitter Flowers, Sweet Flowers: East Timor, Indonesia and the World Community*, edited by Richard Tanter, Mark Selden and Stephen Shalom, 243–272. Sydney: Pluto Press Australia, 2001.

Tanter, Richard, Mark Seldon and Stephen Shalom. 'Introduction: East Timor, Indonesia, and the World Community'. In *Bitter Flowers, Sweet Flowers: East Timor, Indonesia and the World Community*, edited by Richard Tanter, Mark Selden and Stephen Shalom, xv–xviii. Sydney: Pluto Press Australia, 2001.

Taylor, John. *East Timor: The Price of Freedom.* Annandale, New South Wales: Zed Books, 1999.

Tilman, Mateus. 'Customary Social Order and Authority in the Contemporary East Timorese Village: Persistence and Transformation'. *Local-Global* 11 (2012): 192–205.

Trindade, José. 'Reconciling Conflicting Paradigms: An East Timorese Vision of the Ideal State'. In *Democratic Governance in East Timor: Reconciling the Local and the National*, edited by David Mearns and Steven Farram, 160–188. Darwin: Charles Darwin University Press, 2008.

Turner, Bryan. 'The Erosion of Citizenship'. *British Journal of Sociology* 52, no. 2 (2001): 189–209.

Um, Khatharya. 'Cambodia in 2013: The Winds of Change'. *Southeast Asian Affairs* (2014): 99–116.

Bibliography 225

Un, Kheang. 'Patronage Politics and Hybrid Democracy: Political Change in Cambodia 1993–2003'. *Asian Perspective* 29, (2005): 203–230.
van Klinken, Helene. 'Taking the Risk, Paying the Price'. *Guns and Ballot Boxes: East Timor's Vote for Independence*, edited by Damien Kingsbury, 43–68. Clayton, Melbourne: Monash Asia Institute, 2000.
Vidmar, Jure. 'The Right of Self-Determination and Multiparty Democracy: Two Sides of the Same Coin?', *Human Rights Law Review* 10, no. 2 (2010): 239–268.
Vincent, Andrew. *Modern Political Ideologies*, 3rd edn. Chicester and Malden: Wiley-Blackwell, 2010.
Weber, Max. *From Max Weber: Essays in Sociology. Edited, with an Introduction by H.H. Gerth and C.W. Mills*. Oxon: Routledge, 1991.
Wesley, Michael. 'The State of the Art on the Art of State Building'. *Global Governance* 14 (2008): 369–385.
Wibisono, Makarim. 'Dunia Meilai Indoneisa Konsisten Dengan Demokrasi'. In *Timor Timur Bukan Bagian Dari Nasionalisme Indonesia*, 47–54. Jakarta: Front Indonesia Bersatu, 1999.
Wilde, Ralph. 'From Danzig to East Timor and Beyond: The Role of International Territorial Administration'. *American Journal of International Law* 95, no. 3 (2001): 583–606.
Wise, Amanda. *Exile and Return among the East Timorese*. Pennsylvania: University of Pennsylvania Press, 2006.
Young, Iris Marion. *Inclusion and Democracy*. Oxford: Oxford University Press, 2002.
Yulianto, Arif. *Hubungan sipil militer di Indonesia pasca Orba: ti tengah pusaran demokrasi*. Jakarta: RajaGrafindo Persada, 2002.
Zaum, Dominik. 'The Authority of International Administrations in International Society'. *Review of International Studies* 32 (2006): 455–473.
Zaum, Dominik. *The Sovereign Paradox: The Norms and Politics of International State-building*. Oxford: Oxford University Press, 2007.
Zifcak, Spencer. 'Restorative Justice in Timor-Leste: The Truth and Reconciliation Commission'. *Development Bulletin* 68 (2005): 51–68.

Government documents

CAVR. *Chega! Final Report of the Commission for Reception, Truth and Reconciliation Timor-Leste*. Dili: Commission for Reception, Truth and Reconciliation, 2005.
CAVR. *Timor-Leste Internal Political Conflict 1974–1975: National Public Hearings, December 15–18 2003*. Dili: Commission for Reception, Truth and Reconciliation Production Team and Translation Unit, 2009.
CAVR. *Timor-Leste Self-Determination and the International Community: National Public Hearing 15–17 March 2004*. Dili: Commission for Reception, Truth and Reconciliation Production Team and Translation Unit, 2009.
Commission for Human Rights Violations in East Timor (KPP-HAM). *Executive Summary on the Investigation of Human Rights Violations in East Timor*. Jakarta, 31 January 2000. Available at www.etan.org/news/2000a/3exec.htm, accessed 24 March 2014.
Commission of Truth and Friendship. *From Memory to Hope: Final Report of the Commission of Truth and Friendship (CTF) Indonesia-Timor-Leste*. Denpasar, 31 March 2008.
Comissão Nacional de Eleições. *Elisaun Prezidente 2007 República Democrática de Timor-Leste: Acta Final Apuramentu Nacional*. Dili, 18 April 2007.
Comissão Nacional de Eleições. *Elisaun Prezidente 2007 República Democrática de*

226　*Bibliography*

Timor-Leste Total Votus Kandidatus Eleisaun Prezidente 2007 Nivel Nacional. Dili, 14 May 2007.

Commisão Nacional de Eleições. *National Provision Results from the 30 June 2007 Parliamentary Elections.* CNE Announcement No. 679/RE-CNE/VII/2007. Dili, 9 June 2007.

Constituent Assembly. *Constitution of the Democratic Republic of Timor-Leste.* Dili, 2002.

Constituent Assembly Secretariat. *Press Release.* Dili, 15 February 2002. Available at http://members.pcug.org.au/~wildwood/02febca.htm, accessed 24 March 2015.

de Araújo, Rui Maria. *Speech by His Excellency the Prime Minister Dr Rui Maria de Araújo on the Occasion of the Swearing-In of the Sixth Constitutional Government.* Dili: Democratic Republic of Timor-Leste Prime Minister, 16 February 2015.

Democratic Republic of Timor-Leste. *The Dili Consensus.* Dili, 28 February 2012.

Democratic Republic of Timor-Leste. *'Goodbye Conflict, Welcome Development': A Citizen's Guide to the 2012 State Budget of the Democratic Republic of Timor-Leste.* Dili, 2012.

Democratic Republic of Timor-Leste National Parliament. *Approving the Statute of the Office of the Ombudsman for Human Rights and Justice.* Decree Law No. 7/2004. Dili, 26 May 2004.

Democratic Republic of Timor-Leste National Parliament. *2nd Amendment to Law No. 6/2006.* Law No. 7/2011. Dili, 2011.

Democratic Republic of Timor-Leste National Parliament. *Law on the Election of the National Parliament.* Law No. 6/2006. Dili, 28 December 2006.

Democratic Republic of Timor-Leste National Parliament. *Law on the Election of the President of the Republic.* Law No. 7/2006. Dili, 28 December 2006.

Democratic Republic of Timor-Leste National Parliament. *1st Amendment to Law No. 6/2006.* Law No. 6/2007. Dili, 2007.

Democratic Republic of Timor-Leste National Parliament. *Law on the Anti-Corruption Commission.* Law No. 8/2009. Dili, 2009.

Democratic Republic of Timor-Leste National Parliament. *Framework of the National Reparations Programme.* Draft-Law No. 2. Dili, 15 June 2010.

Democratic Republic of Timor-Leste National Parliament. *General State Budget for 2013.* Law No. 02/2013. Dili, 1 March 2013.

Department of Foreign Affairs, Australia. *East Timor in Transition 1998–2000: An Australian Policy Challenge.* Canberra: Department of Foreign Affairs, 2001.

Department of Foreign Affairs, Australia. *Australia and the Indonesian Incorporation of Portuguese Timor, 1974–1976.* Edited by Wendy Way, Damien Browne and Vivienne Johnson. Carlton, Australia: Melbourne University Press, 2000.

Department of Foreign Affairs, Republic of Indonesia. *Process of Decolonization in East Timor.* Jakarta: 1976.

Department of Foreign Affairs, Republic of Indonesia. *East Timor: Building for the Future: Issues and Perspectives.* Jakarta, 1996.

East Timor Planning Commission. *East Timor 2020 – Our Vision, Our Future.* Dili: Planning Commission, 2002.

East Timor Planning Commission. *National Development Plan.* Dili: Planning Commission, May 2002.

Government of Democratic Republic of Timor-Leste. *IV Constitutional Government Program 2007–2012.* Dili: Democratic Republic of Timor-Leste Presidency of the Ministers Office, 2007.

Bibliography 227

Government of Democratic Republic of Timor-Leste. *Policy Orientation Guidelines for Decentralization and Local Government in Timor-Leste*. Dili: Ministry of State Administration and Territorial Management, March 2008.

Government of Democratic Republic of Timor-Leste. *Strategic Development Plan*. Dili: Government of Timor-Leste, 2011.

Government of Democratic Republic of Timor-Leste. *Which Social Security for Timor-Leste?* 9 November 2010. Available at http://timor-leste.gov.tl/?p=4254andlang=enandn=1, accessed 20 November 2013.

Government of Democratic Republic of Timor-Leste. *Conference: '10 Years Later: the Contribution of Social Programs in the Building of State Welfare in Timor-Leste'*. 27 February 2012. Available at http://timor-leste.gov.tl/?p=6583andlang=enandn=1, accessed 22 May 2012.

Government of Democratic Republic of Timor-Leste. *'Goodbye Conflict, Welcome Development': AMP Government Snapshot (2007–2012)*. Dili: IV Constitutional Government of Democratic Republic of Timor-Leste, 2012.

Indonesia Departemen Luar Negeri Badan Penelitian dan Pengembangan and Yayasan Pusat Studi Kawasan Samudera Hindia. *Pelaksanaan Politik Luar Negeri Indonesia Pasca Pemisahan Timor Timur*. Jakarta: Badan Penelitian dan Pengembangan, Departemen Luar Negeri, Republik Indonesia, 2000.

Indonesia National Human Rights Commission. *Commission for Human Rights Violations in East Timor (KPP-HAM)*. Resolution No. 797/TUA/X/99. Jakarta, 22 October 1999.

Ministry of Finance. *State Budget 2011: Budget Overview Book One*. Dili: Democratic Republic of Timor-Leste Ministry of Finance, 2011.

Ministry of Foreign Affairs and Cooperation. *Ramos-Horta Addresses the United Nations Security Council*. Ministry of Foreign Affairs and Cooperation Press Release. Available at http://members.pcug.org.au/~wildwood/02janhorta.htm, accessed 24 March 2015.

Minister of State and of the Presidency of the Council of Ministers and Official Spokesperson for the Government of Timor-Leste. *President of the Republic announces the new Prime Minister of Timor-Leste is to be Dr. Rui Maria de Araújo*. Dili: Government of Democratic Republic of Timor-Leste, 11 February 2015.

National Council of Timorese Resistance. *Magna Carta concerning Freedoms, Rights, Duties and Guarantees for the People of East Timor*. 1998. Available at http://easttimorlegal.blogspot.com.au/2009/01/east-timors-magna-carta.html, accessed 16 April 2012.

National Council of Timorese Resistance National Congress. *Draft Resolution on Human Rights*. Available at http://members.pcug.org.au/~wildwood/CNRTCNHR.htm, accessed 24 March 2015.

Prime Minister and Cabinet of the Government of Timor-Leste. *Prime Minister Hails Compact as a Platform for Unity*. Dili: Prime Minister and Cabinet of the Government of Timor-Leste Media Release, 22 March 2007.

Republic of Indonesia. *Government Statements on the East Timor Question*. Jakarta, 1975.

Republic of Indonesia and Democratic Republic of Timor-Leste. *Terms of Reference for The Commission of Truth and Friendship*. Jakarta, 9 March 2005. Available at www.etan.org/et2005/march/06/10tor.htm, accessed 24 March 2015.

Suharto. *Address before the Extraordinary Sessions of the Regional House of the People's Representatives of East Timor*. Dili, July 17 1978. Published Jakarta, 1978.

228   *Bibliography*

United Nations documents

United Nations. *Charter of the United Nations*. San Francisco: United Nations Conference on International Organization, 26 June 1945.

United Nations. *Agreements on a Comprehensive Political Settlement of the Cambodia Conflict*. Paris, 23 October 1991.

United Nations. *Press Conference by Secretary-General Kofi Annan, his Personal Representative for East Timor, and Foreign Ministers of Indonesia and Portugal*. United Nations Press Release S/SM/6922, 12 March 1999.

United Nations. *East Timor National Council Sets Up Truth Commission to Probe Rights Violations*. United Nations Department of Public Information, 20 June 2001.

United Nations Commission of Experts. *Report to the Secretary-General of the Commission of Experts to Review the Prosecution of Serious Violations of Human Rights in Timor-Leste (then East Timor) in 1999*. S/2005/458, 26 May 2005.

United Nations Country Team. *Building Blocks for a Nation*. Common Country Assessment. Dili, November 2000.

United Nations and Democratic Republic of Timor-Leste. *The Millennium Development Goals, Timor-Leste*. 2009.

United Nations Development Assistance Framework. *UNDAF 2009–2013: Democratic Republic of Timor-Leste*. United Nations Development Assistance Framework, 2009.

United Nations Development Programme. *Ukan Rasik A'an: The Way Ahead*. Dili: East Timor Human Development Report, 2002.

United Nations Development Programme. *Human Development Report 2011: Sustainability and Equity: A Better Future for All*. New York: United Nations Development Programme, 2011.

United Nations Development Programme. *Timor-Leste Human Development Report 2011: Managing Natural Resources for Human Development, Developing the Non-Oil Economy to Achieve the MDGs*. United Nations Development Programme, 2011.

United Nations Development Programme. *Timor-Leste: Country Profile: Human Development Indicators*, available at http://hdrstats.undp.org/en/countries/profiles/TLS.html, accessed 20 November 2013.

United Nations Development Programme. *Human Development Report 2013: The Rise of the South: Human Progress in a Diverse World*. New York: United Nations Development Programme, 2013.

United Nations Development Programme. *Sustaining Human Progress: Reducing Vulnerabilities and Building Resilience*. United Nations Development Programme, 2014.

United Nations Development Programme. *United Nations Development Programme: About Timor-Leste*. Available at www.undp.org/content/timor_leste/en/home/countryinfo/, accessed 24 March 2015.

United Nations General Assembly. *Universal Declaration of Human Rights*. United Nations, 1948.

United Nations General Assembly. *Declaration on the Granting of Independence to Colonial Countries and Peoples*. United Nations General Assembly Resolution 1514 (XV), Fifteenth Session, 1960.

United Nations General Assembly. *Territories under Portuguese Administration*. United Nations General Assembly Resolution 1807, Seventeenth Session, 14 December 1962.

United Nations General Assembly. *International Covenant on Civil and Political Rights*. United Nations General Assembly Resolution 2200A (XXI), 16 December 1966.

United Nations General Assembly. *International Covenant on Economic, Social and Cultural Rights*. United Nations General Assembly Resolution 2200A (XXI), 16 December 1966.

Bibliography 229

United Nations General Assembly. *Declaration of Principles of International Law Concerning Friendly Relations and Co-operation Among States in Accordance with the Charter of the United Nations.* United Nations General Assembly Resolution 2625 (XXV), Twenty-Fifth Session, 24 October 1970.

United Nations General Assembly. *Programme for Action for the Full Implementation of the Declaration on the Granting of Independence to Colonial Countries and Peoples.* United Nations General Assembly Resolution 2621 (XXVI), Twenty-Fifth Session, 12 October 1970.

United Nations General Assembly. *Question of Territories under Portuguese Domination.* United Nations General Assembly Resolution 3294, Twenty-Ninth Session, 13 December 1974.

United Nations General Assembly. *Question of Timor.* General Assembly Resolution 3485, Thirtieth Session, 12 December 1975.

United Nations General Assembly. *Question of Timor.* United Nations General Assembly Resolution 31/53, Thirty-First Session, 1 December 1976.

United Nations General Assembly. *Question of East Timor.* General Assembly Resolution 32/34, Thirty-Second Session, 28 November 1977.

United Nations General Assembly. *Question of East Timor.* United Nations Resolution 33/39, Thirty-Third Session, 13 December 1978.

United Nations General Assembly. *Question of East Timor.* General Assembly Resolution 34/40, Thirty-Fourth Session, 21 November 1979.

United Nations General Assembly. *Question of East Timor.* United Nations Resolution 35/27, Thirty-Fifth Session, 11 November 1980.

United Nations General Assembly. *Question of East Timor.* United Nations General Assembly Resolution 36/50, Thirty-Sixth Session, 24 November 1981.

United Nations General Assembly. *Question of East Timor.* United Nations General Assembly Resolution 37/30, Thirty-Seventh Session, 23 November 1982.

United Nations General Assembly. *Question of East Timor: Progress Report of the Secretary-General.* General Assembly Fifty-Fourth Session, A/54/654, 13 December 1999.

United Nations General Assembly. *United Nations Millennium Declaration.* United Nations General Assembly Resolution 55/2, 18 September 2000.

United Nations General Assembly. *Unanimous Assembly Decision Makes Timor-Leste 191st United Nations Member State.* Press Release GA/10069, 27 September 2002.

United Nations General Assembly and United Nations Security Council. *Question of East Timor: Report of the Secretary-General.* A/53/951, S/1999/513, 5 May 1999.

United Nations Independent Special Commission of Inquiry for Timor-Leste. *Report of the United Nations Independent Special Commission of Inquiry for Timor-Leste.* Geneva, 2 October 2006.

United Nations Integrated Mission in Timor-Leste. *International Compact.* Available at http://archive-org.com/page/837976/2012-12-04/http://unmit.unmissions.org/Default. aspx?tabid=12098&language=en-US, accessed 15 June 2015.

United Nations Integrated Mission in Timor-Leste. *Serious Crimes Investigation Team.* Available at http://archive-org.com/page/837976/2012-12-04/http://unmit.unmissions. org/Default.aspx?tabid=12067&language=en-US, accessed 15 June 2015.

United Nations Integrated Mission in Timor-Leste. *Serious Crimes Investigation Team Newsletter.* 7 February 2011.

United Nations News Centre. *UN to Stay Engaged in Timor-Leste after Peacekeeping Mission Ends, Says Senior Official.* United Nations News Service, 12 November 2012.

230 *Bibliography*

United Nations Office of the Commissioner of Human Rights. *Report of the Commission of Inquiry on East Timor to Secretary-General.* United Nations General Assembly, A/54/726, S/2000/59, January 2000.

United Nations Secretary-General. *Peoples of East Timor Reject Proposed Special Autonomy, Express Wish to Begin Transition to Independence, Secretary General Informs Security Council.* United Nations Press Release, SG/SM/7119 SC/6722, 3 September 1999.

United Nations Secretary-General. *Guidance Note of the Secretary General on Democracy.* United Nations, 15 September 2009.

United Nations Security Council. *Resolution 384.* S/RES/384, 22 December 1975.

United Nations Security Council. *Resolution 389.* S/RES/389, 22 April 1976.

United Nations Security Council. *Report of the Secretary-General on the United Nations Integrated Mission in Timor-Leste (for the period from 9 July 2008 to 20 January 2009).* S/2009/72, 4 February 2009.

United Nations Security Council, *Resolution 745.* S/RES/745, 28 February 1992.

United Nations Security Council. *Question of East Timor: Report of the Secretary-General.* S/1999/595, 22 May 1999.

United Nations Security Council, *Resolution 1244.* S/RES/1244, 10 June 1999.

United Nations Security Council. *Resolution 1246.* S/RES/1246, 11 June 1999.

United Nations Security Council. *Question of East Timor: Report of the Secretary General.* S/1999/705, 22 June 1999.

United Nations Security Council. *Resolution 1257.* S/RES/1257, 3 August 1999.

United Nations Security Council. *Question of East Timor: Report of the Secretary-General.* S/1999/862, 9 August 1999.

United Nations Security Council. *Resolution 1262.* S/RES/1262, 27 August 1999.

United Nations Security Council. *Secretary-General Informs Security Council People of East Timor Rejected Special Autonomy Proposed by Indonesia.* United Nations Security Council Press Release, SC/6721, 3 September 1999.

United Nations Security Council. *Resolution 1264.* S/RES/1264, 15 September 1999.

United Nations Security Council. *Report of the Secretary-General on the Situation in East Timor.* RES/1999/1024, 4 October 1999.

United Nations Security Council. *Resolution 1272.* S/RES/1272, 25 October 1999.

United Nations Security Council. *Report of the Secretary-General on the United Nations Transitional Administration in East Timor.* S/2000/53, 26 January 2000.

United Nations Security Council. *Report of the Secretary-General on the United Nations Transitional Administration in East Timor (for the period 27 January to 26 July 2000).* S/2000/738, 26 July 2000.

United Nations Security Council. *Report of the Secretary-General on the United Nations Transitional Administration in East Timor (for the period 27 July 2000 to 16 January 2001).* S/2001/42, 16 January 2001.

United Nations Security Council. *Resolution 1338.* S/RES/1338, 31 January 2001.

United Nations Security Council. *Interim Report of the Secretary-General on the United Nations Transitional Administration in East Timor.* S/2001/436, 2 May 2001.

United Nations Security Council. *Progress Report of the Secretary-General on the United Nations Transitional Administration in East Timor.* S/RES/719, 24 July 2001.

United Nations Security Council. *Report of the Secretary-General on the United Nations Transitional Administration in East Timor.* S/2001/983, 18 October 2001.

United Nations Security Council. *Report of the Secretary-General on the United Nations Transitional Administration in East Timor.* S/2002/80, 17 January 2002.

Bibliography 231

United Nations Security Council. *Report of the Secretary-General on the United Nations Transitional Administration in East Timor.* S/2002/432, 17 April 2002.

United Nations Security Council. *Report of the Secretary-General on the United Nations Transitional Administration in East Timor.* S/2002/432/Add.1, 24 April 2002.

United Nations Security Council. *Resolution 1410 (2002).* S/RES/1410 (2002), 17 May 2002.

United Nations Security Council. *Security Council Establishes One-Year Political Mission in Timor-Leste Unanimously Adopting Resolution 1599 (2005).* SC/8371, 28 April 2005.

United Nations Security Council. *Resolution 1704.* S/RES/1704 (2006), 25 August 2006.

United Nations Security Council. *Report of the Secretary-General on the United Nations Integrated Mission in Timor-Leste (for the period 9 August 2006 to 26 January 2007).* S/2007/50, 1 February 2007.

United Nations Security Council. *Report of the Secretary-General on the United Nations Integrated Mission in Timor-Leste (for the period 27 January 2007 to 20 August 2007).* S/2007/513, 28 August 2007.

United Nations Security Council. *Report of the Secretary-General on the United Nations Integrated Mission in Timor-Leste (for the period 9 July 2008 to 20 January 2009).* S/2009/72, 4 February 2009.

United Nations Security Council, *Report of the Secretary-General on the United Nations Integrated Mission in Timor-Leste (for the period from 21 January 2009 to 23 September 2009),* S/2009/504, 2 October 2009.

United Nations Security Council. *Report of the Secretary-General on the United Nations Integrated Mission in Timor-Leste (for the period from 20 September 2011 to 6 January 2012).* S/2010/43, 12 February 2010.

United Nations Security Council. *Report of the Secretary-General on the United Nations Integrated Mission in Timor-Leste (for the period from 24 September 2009 to 20 January 2010).* S/2010/85, 12 February 2010.

United Nations Security Council. *Report of the Secretary-General on the United Nations Integrated Mission in Timor-Leste (for the period from 21 January to 20 September 2010).* S/2010/522, 13 October 2010.

United Nations Security Council. *Report of the Secretary-General on the United Nations Integrated Mission in Timor-Leste (for the period from 21 September 2010 to 7 January 2011).* S/2011/32, 25 January 2011.

United Nations Security Council. *Report of the Secretary-General on the United Nations Integrated Mission in Timor-Leste (for the period from 8 January 2011 to 20 September 2011).* S/2011/641, 14 October 2011.

United Nations Security Council. *Report of the Secretary-General on the United Nations Integrated Mission in Timor-Leste (for the period from 20 September 2011 to 6 January 2012).* S/2012/43, 18 January 2012.

United Nations Security Council. *Report of the Secretary-General on the United Nations Integrated Mission in Timor-Leste (for the period from 7 January to 20 September 2012).* S/2012/765, 15 October 2012.

United Nations Security Council Mission to Jakarta and Dili. *Report of the Security Council Mission to Jakarta and Dili.* S/1999/976, 14 September 1999.

United Nations Transitional Administration in East Timor. *On the Authority of the Transitional Administration in East Timor.* UNTAET/REG/1999/1, 27 November 1999.

United Nations Transitional Administration in East Timor. *On the Establishment of Panels with Exclusive Jurisdiction over Serious Criminal Offences.* UNTAET/REG/2000/15, 6 June 2000.

232   Bibliography

United Nations Transitional Administration in East Timor. *On the Organization of Courts in East Timor*, UNTAET/REG/1999/1, 27 November 1999.

United Nations Transitional Administration in East Timor. *On the Establishment of a National Consultative Council.* UNTAET/REG/1999/02, 2 December 1999.

United Nations Transitional Administration in East Timor. *On the Organization of Courts in East Timor.* UNTAET/REG/2000/11, 6 March 2000.

United Nations Transitional Administration in East Timor. *Tais Timor* 1, no. 10, 26 June–9 July 2000.

United Nations Transitional Administration in East Timor. *On the Establishment of a National Council.* UNTAET/REG/2000/24, 14 July 2000.

United Nations Transitional Administration in East Timor. *On the Establishment of the Cabinet of the Transitional Government in East Timor.* UNTAET/REG/2000/23, 14 July 2000.

United Nations Transitional Administration in East Timor. *Tais Timor* 1, no. 12, 24 July–6 August 2000.

United Nations Transitional Administration in East Timor. *Selection of National Council.* UNTAET Daily Briefing. Dili, 8 August 2000.

United Nations Transitional Administration in East Timor. *To Amend Regulation No. 2000/24 on the Establishment of a National Council.* UNTAET/REG/2000/33, 26 October 2000.

United Nations Transitional Administration in East Timor. *First Democratic Elections in East Timor to be Held on 30 August 2001.* UNTAET Daily Briefing. Dili, 16 March 2001.

United Nations Transitional Administration in East Timor. *On the Elections of a Constituent Assembly to Prepare a Constitution for an Independent and Democratic East Timor.* UNTAET/REG/2001/2. 16 March 2001.

United Nations Transitional Administration in East Timor. *National Council Defeats Constitution Committees.* UNTAET Daily Briefing. Dili, 27 March 2001.

United Nations Transitional Administration in East Timor. *Timorese Cabinet Considers Consultation on Constitution.* UNTAET Daily Briefing, 28 March 2001.

United Nations Transitional Administration in East Timor. *Training for Trainers on Civic Education.* UNTAET Daily Briefing, 10 April, 2001.

United Nations Transitional Administration in East Timor. *Constitutional Commissioners Deployed in Sub-Districts.* UNTAET Daily Briefing. Dili, 4 June 2001.

United Nations Transitional Administration in East Timor. *Constitutional Commissions Begin Hearings.* UNTAET Daily Briefing. Dili, 19 June 2001.

United Nations Transitional Administration in East Timor. *On the Establishment of a Commission for Reception, Truth and Reconciliation in East Timor.* UNTAET/REG/2001/10, 13 July 2001.

United Nations Transitional Administration in East Timor. *Swearing-In of Constituent Assembly Members.* UNTAET Press Briefing, Dili, 14 September 2001.

United Nations Transitional Administration in East Timor. *East Timorese Government Sworn-In.* UNTAET Press Briefing. Dili, 20 September 2001.

United Nations Transitional Administration in East Timor. *Alkatiri/deMello Press Conference.* UNTAET Daily Briefing. Dili, 16 November 2001.

United Nations Transitional Administration in East Timor. *Assembly Votes to Transform Itself into Legislature.* UNTAET Daily Briefing. Dili, 31 January 2002.

United Nations Transitional Administration in East Timor. *East Timor Assembly Signs into Force First Constitution.* UNTAET Press Briefings. Dili, 22 March 2002.

Bibliography 233

Reports

Australian Council for International Development. *Timor-Leste Civil Society Analysis: Report of an In-Country Consultation and Desk Review for Strengthening Civil Society.* Australian Council for International Development, January–February 2008.

Brandt, Michele. *Constitutional Assistance in Post-Conflict Countries: The UN Experience: Cambodia, East Timor and Afghanistan.* United Nations Development Programme, June 2005.

Brahimi, Lakhdar. *State-Building in Crisis and Post-Conflict Countries.* Vienna: Seventh Global Forum on Reinventing Government, Building Trust in Government, 26–29 June 2007.

Carmona, Magdelina Sepúlveda. *Report of the Special Rapporteur on Extreme Poverty and Human Rights Mission to Timor-Leste.* New York: United Nations Office of the High Commissioner for Human Rights, 24 May 2012.

Chesterman, Simon. *Justice Under International Administration: Kosovo, East Timor and Afghanistan.* New York: International Peace Academy, 2002.

Democratic Governance Support Unit of United Nations Integrated Mission in Timor-Leste. *Compendium of the 2012 Elections in Timor-Leste.* United Nations Integrated Mission in Timor-Leste and United Nations Development Programme, 2012.

European Union Election Observation Mission. *Timor-Leste: Final Report Parliamentary Election 2012.* Timor-Leste: European Union Election Observation Mission, 2012.

Garrison, Randall. *The Role of Constitution-Building Processes in Democratization Case Study: East Timor.* Stockholm: International Institute for Democracy and Electoral Assistance, 2005.

Ghani, Ashraf, Clare Lockhart and Michael Carnahan. *Closing the Sovereignty Gap: An Approach to State-Building.* Working Paper 253. London: Overseas Development Institute, September 2005.

Hart, Vivien. *Democratic Constitution Making.* Special Report 107. Washington: United States Institute of Peace, July 2003.

Hirst, Megan. *Too Much Friendship Too Little Truth.* New York: International Center for Transitional Justice, January 2008.

Hohe, Tanja and Rod Nixon. *Reconciling Justice: 'Traditional Law' and State Judiciary in East Timor.* United States Institute of Peace, January 2003.

International Commission on Intervention and State Sovereignty. *The Responsibility to Protect: Report of the International Commission on Intervention and State Sovereignty.* Ottawa: International Development Research Centre, 2001.

International Poverty Centre. 'Social Protection: The Role of Cash Transfers'. In *Poverty in Focus.* United Nations Development Programme, June 2006.

Inter-Parliamentary Union. *Declaration on Criteria for Free and Fair Elections.* Paris: 154th Session of the Inter-Parliamentary Union, 26 March 1994.

Inter-Parliamentary Union. *Universal Declaration on Democracy.* Cairo: 161st Session of Inter-Parliamentary Council, 16 September 1997.

Meden, Natacha. 'From Resistance to Nation Building: The Challenging Role of Civil Society in East Timor'. In *Development Outreach.* Washington D.C: World Bank Institute, 2002.

Nakamura, Toshi. *Reflections on the State-Institution-Building Support in Timor-Leste: Capacity Development, Integrating Missions, and Financial Challenges.* Oslo: United Nations Development Programme, November 2004.

Organisation for Economic Co-operation and Development. *Monitoring the Principles for Good International Engagement in Fragile States and Situations: Country Report 6: Democratic Republic of Timor-Leste.* OECD Publishing, 2010.

234   *Bibliography*

Oxford Poverty and Human Development Initiative, *OPHI Country Briefing January 2015: Timor-Leste*. Oxford: Oxford Department of International Development, January 2015.

Piguo, Piers. *Crying Without Tears: In Pursuit of Justice and Reconciliation in Timor Leste: Community Perspectives and Expectation*. International Center for Transitional Justice, August 2003.

Reiger, Caitlin and Marieke Wierda. *The Serious Crimes Process in Timor-Leste: In Retrospect*. International Center for Transitional Justice, March 2006.

Robinson, Geoffrey. *East Timor 1999 Crimes against Humanity*. United Nations Office of the High Commissioner for Human Rights, July 2003.

Feijó, Rui Graça. 'Timor-Leste: Challenges to the Consolidation of Democracy'. In *The State, Society and Governance in Melanesia Program In Brief*. Canberra: Australian National University, 2014/2015.

Samuels, Kristi and Sebastian von Einsiedel. *The Future of UN State-Building: Strategic and Operational Challenges and the Legacy of Iraq Policy Report*. New York: International Peace Academy, November 14–16 2003.

Shires, David. *Situation Analysis of Civil Society Organisations in East Timor*. Dili: Report for the United Nations Development Programme, 2002.

Unrepresented Nations and Peoples Organization. *The Question of Self-Determination: The Cases of East Timor, Tibet and Western Sahara Conference Report*. Palais des Nations, United Nations, Geneva, 25–26 March 1996.

Vieira, Luiz. *The CAVR and the 2006 Displacement Crisis in Timor-Leste: Reflecting on Truth-Telling, Dialogue, and Durable Solutions*. International Center for Transitional Justice/Brookings LSE Project on Internal Displacement, July 2012.

Westergaard, Kirsten. *People's Participation, Local Government and Rural Development: the case of West Bengal, India*. Copenhagen: Centre for Development Research, 1986.

World Bank. *East Timor Community Empowerment and Local Governance Project*. Report No. PID8576, December 27 1999.

World Bank. *Health Expenditure, total (% of GDP)*. World Bank Data, 2013. Available at http://data.worldbank.org/indicator/SH.XPD.TOTL.ZS, accessed 24 March 2015.

World Bank. *Strengthening the Institutions of Governance in Timor-Leste*. World Bank, April 2006.

World Bank. *Timor-Leste Overview*. Available at www.worldbank.org/en/country/timor-leste/overview, accessed 24/03/2015.

World Bank. *World Development Indicators 2013*. Washington DC: World Bank, 2013.

World Health Organization. *Timor-Leste*. Available at www.who.int/countries/tls/en/, accessed 24 March 2015.

Civil society documents

Amnesty International. *Amnesty International Calls on the UN to Act Resolutely to Secure Justice for Timor*. Amnesty International Public Statement, 15 July 2005.

Amnesty International. *East Timor: Building a New Country Based on Human Rights*. ASA 57/05/00, August 2000.

Amnesty International. *Justice For Timor-Leste: Victims Await Further Action from the Security Council to Ensure Perpetrators are Held to Account*. Amnesty International Public Statement, 29 April 2005.

Amnesty International. *Timor-Leste: Justice in the Shadow*. ASA 01/206/2010, 29 June 2010.

Amnesty International. *'We Cry for Justice': Impunity Persists 10 years on in Timor-Leste*. ASA 57/001/2009, 27 August 2009.

Bibliography 235

Amnesty International USA. *Annual Report: Timor-Leste 2013.* Available at www. amnestyusa.org/research/reports/annual-report-timor-leste-2013, accessed 24 March 2015.

Asia Pacific Support Collective Timor Lorosa'e. *A Popular Challenge to UNTAET's Achievements.* Available at http://members.pcug.org.au/~wildwood/01seppopular.htm, accessed 24 March 2015.

Association HAK, Australian Coalition for Transitional Justice in East Timor, East Timor and Indonesia Action Network, Human Rights First, International Centre for Transitional Justice, The Commission for the Disappeared and the Victims of Violence, Maria Afonso de Jesus, TAPOL and Timor-Leste University Students' Front. *Joint NGO Statement on the Handover of the Report of the Commission of Truth and Friendship.* Joint Statement, 15 July 2008.

Carter Centre. *East Timor Political and Election Observation Project.* Atlanta: The Carter Centre Democracy Program, April 2004.

Centre for Justice and Accountability. *Background on East Timor.* Available at www.cja. org/article.php?list=typeandtype=198, accessed 24 March 2015.

Della-Giacoma, Jim. *Timor Loro Sa'e is Our Nation: A Report on Focus Group Discussions in East Timor.* Dili: National Democratic Institute for International Affairs and East Timor NGO Forum's Working Group on Electoral Education, March 2001.

East Timor and Indonesia Action Network. *Dare II Agreements.* July 1999. Available at http://etan.org/et99/july/1-7/02dare.htm, accessed 24 April 2012.

East Timor and Indonesia Action Network. *Truth Known, East Timorese Need Justice.* East Timor and Indonesia Action Network Press Release. 9 March 2005.

East Timor and Indonesia Action Network. *On Anniversary of East Timor Church Massacre UN Must Take Responsibility for Justice.* East Timor and Indonesia Action Network Press Release. 6 April 2005.

East Timor and Indonesia Action Network. *East Timor Truth Commission Report Must be Released.* East Timor and Indonesia Action Network Press Release. 1 December 2005.

East Timor and Indonesia Action Network. *Indonesia Must Confront its Past, Accept Responsibility and Deliver Justice for Timor Atrocities.* East Timor and Indonesia Action Network Press Release. 16 February 2006.

East Timor and Indonesia Action Network. *Commission of Inquiry Report can help Timor-Leste Overcome Divisions.* East Timor and Indonesia Action Network Statement. 17 October 2006.

East Timor and Indonesia Action Network. *International Coalition Urges UN to Take Active Role for Promoting Justice for East Timorese.* East Timor and Indonesia Action Network Press Release. New York, 1 June 2008.

East Timor and Indonesia Action Network. *ETAN Renews Call for Meaningful Justice for Victims of Indonesian Occupation.* East Timor and Indonesia Action Network Press Release. 14 July 2008.

East Timor and Indonesia Action Network. *Letter to East Timor President José Ramos-Horta on Justice and Accountability.* 23 March 2010.

East Timor and Indonesia Action Network, La'o Hamutuk, and Australian Coalition for Transitional Justice in East Timor, TAPOL. *Rights Groups Call for End to Farcical Joint Timor-Indonesia Commission.* Press Release. 24 May 2007.

East Timor National NGO Forum. *Letter to Members of the United Nations Security Council.* Dili, 17 March 2001. Available at http://members.pcug.org.au/~wildwood/01marrushed.htm, accessed 24 March 2015.

236   Bibliography

East Timor National NGO Forum. *The Constitutional Process in East Timor*. Briefing Paper to International Donors Conference. Canberra, June 2001. Available at http://members.pcug.org.au/~wildwood/01junconstitution.htm, accessed 24 March 2015.

East Timor NGO Forum. *Expression of Concern at Xanana's Statement Regarding an International Tribunal*. NGO Forum Press Release. 23 April 2001. Available at http://members.pcug.org.au/~wildwood/01aprconcern.htm, accessed 24 March 2015.

East Timor NGO Forum. *Statement to the National Council and the Transitional Government UNTAET/ETTA*. 31 January 2001. Available at http://members.tip.net.au/~wildwood/janngo.htm, accessed 24 March 2015.

Economist Intelligence Unit. *Country Report: Timor Leste*. London: Economist Intelligence United Limited, January 2011.

Economist Intelligence Unit. *Democracy Index 2013: Democracy in Limbo*. The Economic Intelligence Unit Limited, 2014.

Economist Intelligence Unit. *Democracy Index Report: Democracy in Retreat*. http://graphics.eiu.com/PDF/Democracy_Index_2010_web.pdf, accessed 24/03/2015.

FONGTIL, OPVG, Asosiasi HAK, La'o Hamutuk, Victim, Luta Hamutuk, HAFOTS, ETCRN, MDI, Rede Feto, Justice Monitoring System Program, Ba Futuru, GFFTL, CDI, International Center for Transitional Justice – Timor-Leste, FTM, Peace Center, Apheda – Timor-Leste, KBH, Fokupers, Front Mahasiswa, Ratelaek and ANTI. *Dissolve the CTF, Try the Perpetrators of Crimes and Provide Reparations to Victims*. Joint Petition by East Timorese NGOs. 18 March 2008.

FORUM-ASIA. *Open Letter to José Ramos-Horta on Impunity and Rights Violations*. FORUM-ASIA Press Statement. 21 June 2007.

Freedom House. *Freedom in the World 2011*. Available at https://freedomhouse.org/report/freedom-world/freedom-world-2011#.VRChvrccS70, accessed 24 March 2015.

Freedom House. *Freedom in the World 2012: The Arab Uprisings and their Global Repercussions*. Available at www.freedomhouse.org/sites/default/files/inline_images/Table%20of%20Independent%20Countries%2C%20FIW%202012%20draft.pdf, accessed 24 March 2015.

Human Rights First. *Timor-Leste Should Release Truth Commission Report Without Delay*. Human Rights First Press Release. 12 December 2005.

Human Rights Watch. *Justice Denied in East Timor*. 20 December 2002. Available at www.hrw.org/legacy/backgrounder/asia/timor/etimor1202bg.htm, accessed 24 March 2015.

Human Rights Watch. *East Timor: UN Security Council Must Ensure Justice*. Human Rights Watch Press Release. 29 June 2005.

Human Rights Watch. *UN Security Council Must Ensure Justice*. Human Rights Watch Press Release, 29 June 2005.

Indonesia Human Rights Committee. *Call for Action on Truth and Reconciliation Report*. Indonesian Human Rights Committee Media Release. 13 July 2008.

Indonesian Working Group on Truth Recovery, International Center for Transitional Justice, Human Rights Working Group, Kontras, KKPK, People Empowerment Consortium, Ikohi, Network of Cultural Works, Indonesian Human Rights Monitor, Indonesian Legal and Human Rights Association, and East Timor and Indonesia Action Network. *Call for Justice on East Timor Past Mass Atrocities*. Joint Statement. Jakarta, 12 September 2009.

International Center for Transitional Justice. *Truth Commission Report Reveals Shocking Brutality, Calls for End to Impunity*. International Center for Transitional Justice Press Release. 20 January 2006.

Bibliography 237

International Center for Transitional Justice. *Impunity in Timor-Leste: Can the Serious Crimes Investigation Team Make a Difference?* June 2010.

International Center for Transitional Justice. *Unfulfilled Expectations: Victims Perception of Justice and Reparations in Timor-Leste.* 2 December 2010.

International Crisis Group. *Timor-Leste's Elections: Leaving a Violent Past Behind?* Update Briefing No. 134. Dili, Jakarta and Brussels, 21 February 2012.

International Federation for East Timor. *NGO Letter to UN Secretary General on Justice and Accountability.* 18 February 2009.

International Foundation for Electoral Systems. *Election Guide Democratic Republic of Timor-Leste Election for President.* 17 March 2012. Available at www.electionguide. org/elections/id/2227/, accessed 24 March 2015.

Judicial System Monitoring Program. *'Commission of Truth and Friendship' Seeks to End the Search for Justice whilst 'Commission of Experts' Keeps it Alive.* Judicial System Monitoring Programme Press Release. 14 March 2005.

Judicial System Monitoring Program. *Competency of the President to Grant Pardons: Prerogative Right Versus Credibility of the Justice System.* Justice System Monitoring Program Press Release. August 2010.

Judicial System Monitoring Program. *Justice Not Served by Truth and Friendship Commission.* Judicial System Monitoring System Program Justice Update. 25 July 2008.

Judicial System Monitoring Program. *'Truth and Friendship Commission': More Friendship, Less Truth, Impunity from the Law.* JSMP Press Release. 14 January, 2005.

Justica e Paz, Justice System Monitoring Programme, LBH Tane Tumor, Liberta, Clinica da Paz, LBH URA and Asosiasaun HAK. *Justice Must be Given to the Victims of Serious Crimes.* Joint Declaration from East Timorese Civil Society on Justice. 8 July 2005.

La'o Hamutuk. *East Timor: National Council Rejects Bill on Constitutional Commission.* 27 March 2000. Available at http://members.pcug.org.au/~wildwood/01marupdate. htm, accessed 24 March 2015.

La'o Hamutuk. *The La'o Hamutuk Bulletin* 1, no. 1 (21 June 2000).

La'o Hamutuk. *The La'o Hamutuk Bulletin* 1, no. 4 (December 2000).

La'o Hamutuk. *The La'o Hamutuk Bulletin* 2, no. 3 (June 2001).

La'o Hamutuk. *The La'o Hamutuk Bulletin* 2, no. 4 (July 2001).

La'o Hamutuk. *The La'o Hamutuk Bulletin* 2, no. 5 (August 2001).

La'o Hamutuk. *The La'o Hamutuk Bulletin* 2, no. 6 and 7 (October 2001).

La'o Hamutuk. *The La'o Hamutuk Bulletin* 4, no. 5 (November 2003).

La'o Hamutuk. *The La'o Hamutuk Bulletin* 6, no. 13 (August 2005).

La'o Hamutuk. *The La'o Hamutuk Bulletin* 9, no. 3 (November 2008).

La'o Hamutuk. *The La'o Hamutuk Bulletin* 10, no. 1 (June 2009).

La'o Hamutuk. *Justice for Timor-Leste Remains an Unfulfilled International Obligation.* Briefing Paper. August 2009.

La'o Hamutuk. *Letter to UN Security Council on Justice and Impunity in East Timor.* Dili, 20 October 2009.

La'o Hamutuk. *The La'o Hamutuk Bulletin* 11, no. 1–2 (February 2010).

La'o Hamutuk. *Seats Resulting from Parliamentary Elections.* 8 July 2012. Available at http://laohamutuk.blogspot.com.au/2012/07/seats-resulting-from-parliamentary.html, accessed 24 March 2015.

La'o Hamutuk. *RDTL General State Budget for 2012.* 18 September 2012. Available at www.laohamutuk.org/econ/OGE12/10OJE2012En.htm, accessed 24 March 2015.

La'o Hamutuk. *RDTL General State Budget for 2013.* 19 October 2013. Available at www.laohamutuk.org/econ/OGE13/12OGE13.htm, accessed 2 March 2015.

238   *Bibliography*

Scheiner, Charles. *First Round Presidential, by District, CNE Final Results.* Available at www.etan.org/etanpdf/2007/SOMET%20VoteResultsByDistOfficial.pdf, accessed 19 November 2013.

Scheiner, Charles. *Statement to the Alternative Public Hearing against the Truth and Friendship Commission.* Dili: International Federation for East Timor, 29 September 2007.

TAPOL. *International Tribunal Proposal for East Timor Welcomed.* TAPOL Press Release, June 29 2005.

TAPOL. *Though Limited by its Mandate, the CTF Revealed a Great Deal.* TAPOL Press Release, 21 July 2008.

TAPOL, Amnesty International, Human Rights Watch and Progressio. *Timor-Leste: Letter to Parliament Honoring Report of the Commission for Reception, Truth and Reconciliation.* 14 March 2007.

The Commission for the Disappeared and Victims of Violence (Kontras). *Tarnishing the Spirit of 'Friendship' of Both Nations.* Joint Statement on Commission of Truth and Friendship. Jakarta, Bali and Dili, 23 Feburary 2007.

Timor-Leste National Alliance for an International Tribunal, Australian Coalition for Transitional Justice in East Timor and International Federation for East Timor. *Joint Letter to Kofi Annan on Commission for Reception, Truth and Reconciliation Report.* 24 March 2006.

Walsh, Pat. 'East Timor's Political Parties and Groupings: Briefing Notes', *ACFAO Development Issues 9.* Australian Council for Overseas Aid, March 2001.

Walsh, Pat. *From Opposition to Proposition: The National Council of Timorese Resistance in Transition.* 1999. Available at http://members.pcug.org.au/~wildwood/CNRTPat.htm, accessed 24 March 2015.

Walsh, Pat. *The Human Rights and Future of East Timor Workshop.* East Timor and Indonesia Action Network, 2000. Available at www.etan.org/issues/9-00reprt.htm, accessed 24 March 2015.

Yayasan HAK. *A People's Constitution for East Timor.* Press Release, 29 May 2001. Available at http://members.pcug.org.au/~wildwood/01mayconstitution.htm, accessed 24 March 2015.

Yayasan HAK. *East Timor: Elections in the Context of Nation-Building Press Release.* Dili, 3 September 2001, http://members.pcug.org.au/~wildwood/01sepyhak.htm, accessed 24 March 2015.

Yayasan HAK. *The HAK Association.* Available at www.yayasanhak.minihub.org/eng/aboutus.html, accessed 24 March 2015.

Yayasan HAK. *MajGen (ret) H R Garnadi.* Available at www.yayasanhak.minihub.org/mot/Garnadi.htm, accessed 24 March 2015.

Conference papers, media and other

Agence France Presse. *Tetum and Portuguese Named Timor's Official Languages.* 11 December 2001. Available at www.etan.org/et2001c/december/09-15/11tetum.htm, accessed 3 May 2012.

Allard, Tom. 'Timor PM Protecting "Corrupt" Cabinet Members'. *The Sydney Morning Herald*, 26 November 2014.

Author Unknown. 'No Clean Sweep'.*The Economist*. Dili, 30 June 2012.

BBC News. *East Timor Joins the UN.* 27 September 2002. Available at http://news.bbc.co.uk/2/hi/asia-pacific/2284596.stm, accessed 28 February 2012.

Bibliography 239

da Silva, Antero. 'Popular Social Democracy of the RDTL I 1975–1978'. In *New Research on Timor-Leste*, edited by Michael Leach, Nuno C. Mendes, Antero B. da Silva, Bob Boughton and Alarico da Costa Ximenes, 171–180. Hawthorn: Swinburne Press, 2012.

Dodd, Mark. 'Gusmão Gives UN Team a Serve: "We Don't Want a Legacy of Cars."' *Sydney Morning Herald*. 10 October 2000.

Everingham, Sara. 'East Timor, 10 Years On'. *ABC Radio 744 AM*. 19 May 2012. Available at www.abc.net.au/news/2012-05-19/east-timor-10-year-on/4021254, accessed 21 May 2012.

Ginsberg, Thomas, Zachary Elkins and James Melton. 'The Lifespan of Written Constitutions'. *American Law and Economics Association Annual Meetings* 33 (2007).

Global Finance. *Timor-Leste Country Report*. Available www.gfmag.com/gdp-data-country-reports/162-timor-leste-gdp-country-report.html#axzz2bo2PenKJ, accessed 13 August 2013.

Guedes, Armando. 'Power-Sharing in the Tropics and the Ubiquitous "Presidential Drift": The Mechanics and Dynamics of Unstable Equilibrium in the 'Semi-Presidentialism' of East Timor'. In *Understanding Timor-Leste*, edited by Michael Leach, Nuno C. Mendes, Antero B. da Silva, Bob Boughton and Alarico da Costa Ximenes, 131–138. Dili: Timor-Leste Studies Association Conference, July 2009.

Hoadley, Stephen, *The Future of Portuguese Timor*. Occasional Paper no. 27. Singapore: Institute of Southeast Asian Studies, March 1975.

Jolliffe, Jill. 'East Timor Approves Draft Constitution'. *Sydney Morning Herald*, 11 February 2002.

Knoema. *World Data Atlas: Timor-Leste – Sanitation – Total Population – Proportion of Total population served with Improved Sanitation (%)*. Available at http://knoema.com/atlas/Timor-Leste/topics/Water/Sanitation--Total-Population/Improved-Sanitation-percent, accessed 23 November 2013.

Land, Jon. 'East Timorese Convention a Success'. *Green Left Weekly* 317 (Wednesday 13 May). Available at www.greenleft.org.au/node/17770, accessed 23 April 2012.

Lipscomb, Leigh-Ashley. 'Beyond the Truth: Can Reparations Move Peace and Justice Forward in Timor-Leste?' *Asia Pacific Issues* 93, East-West Centre (March 2010).

Lutz, Nancy. *Constitutionalism as Public Culture in East Timor*. Pittsburgh: Law and Society Association Meeting, 7 June 2003.

Matsuno, Akihisa. 'The UN Transitional Administration and Democracy Building in Timor-Leste'. In *Democratic Governance in Timor-Leste: Reconciling the Local and the National*, edited by David Mearns & Steven Farram, 52-70. Darwin: Charles Darwin University Press, 2008.

Matsuno, Akihisa. 'Analysing Timor-Leste Electoral Politics from a Socio-Economic Perspective'. In *Understanding Timor-Leste Conference*, edited by Michael Leach, Nuno C. Mendes, Antero B. da Silva, Bob Boughton and Alarico da Costa Ximenes, 330–334. Dili: Timor-Leste Studies Association Conference, 2–3 July 2009.

Michelmore, Karen. 'Ramos-Horta Cuts Jail Terms for Militia'. *Sydney Morning Herald*, 23 May 2008.

Morison, Michael. 'Democratisation and Timor-Leste after UNTAET: Towards Participatory Intervention'. In *Understanding Timor-Leste Conference*, edited by Michael Leach, Nuno C. Mendes, Antero B. da Silva, Bob Boughton and Alarico da Costa Ximenes, 179–184. Dili: Timor-Leste Studies Association Conference, 2–3 July 2009.

Murdoch, Lindsay. 'Truth Out of Indonesia's Scorched Earth'. *Sydney Morning Herald*. 11 July 2008.

240 *Bibliography*

Pension Watch. *Country Fact Sheet: Timor-Leste*. Available at www.pension-watch.net/country-fact-file/timorleste/, accessed 20 November 2013.

Pereira, Agio. 'Timor-Leste Transforming Belligerent Democracy into Consensus Democracy'. *Tempo Semanal*. 24 January 2014.

Pereira, Agio. *Working Together with Timor-Leste: the Next Ten Years Keynote Presentation*. Preston, 24–26 July 2014.

Petroleum Economist. *Going for Broke*. March 2013. Available at www.laohamutuk.org/Oil/TasiMane/2013/PetroEconLeaderMarch2013.pdf, accessed 20 November 2013.

Reilly, Benjamin. *Government Structure and Electoral Systems*. Canberra: Australian National University, February 2003.

Ressa, Maria. *Indonesia's Habibie Faces Daunting Task*. CNN, 2 June 1998. Available at http://edition.cnn.com/WORLD/asiapcf/9806/02/habibie.interview/, accessed 11 February 2015.

Saad-Filho, Alfredo. *Growth, Poverty and Inequality: From Washington Consensus to Inclusive Growth*. DESA Working Paper No. 100, AT/ESA/2010/DWP/100, November 2010.

Shoesmith, Dennis. 'Remaking the State in Timor-Leste: The Case for Constitutional Reform', *17th Biennial Conference of the Asian Studies Association of Australia*. Melbourne, 1–3 July 2008.

Stephenson, Carolyn. *Nation-Building*. January 2005. Available at www.beyondintractability.org/bi-essay/nation-building, accessed 12 February 2015.

Tempo Semanal. *Alkatiri seeks Transitional Council for Old Generation and FRETILIN seeking Coalition with CNRT*. Dili, 10 July 2015.

Tempo Semanal. *Xanana Prefers CNRT to be the Opposition, or to Govern with a Strong Opposition*. Dili, 15 July 2012.

Tempo Semanal. *Taur Concern with the Violance [sic] and Say Sorry to the Country*. Dili, 17 July 2012.

Tempo Semanal. *East Timorese Fifth Government: An Oligarchy*. Dili, 6 August 2012.

Tempo Semanal. *PM Xanana Present to TL Parliament the Programs of Government*. Dili, 12 September 2012.

Tjandraningsih, Christine. *East Timor Announces Cabinet Lineup*. Dili, 20 September 2001. Available at http://members.tip.net.au/~wildwood/01sepannounces.htm, accessed 19 February 2015.

Vanaja, Tanya. 'East Timor: Tensions Rise as Elections Nears'. *Green Left Weekly* 445 (25 April 2001).

Index

Page numbers in *italics* denote tables, those in **bold** denote figures.

Aceh 57
activism *see* civil society
Afghanistan 1, 77
Alatas, A. 54, 57, 59, 60–1, 70n169, 72n239
Alkatiri, M. 10, 21, 23, 26, 30, 49–50, 87, 106, 109, 124, 129–33, 140, 144, 146, 164
Alliance for Parliamentary Majority (AMP) 138, 140–2, 144, 146–7, 163–72, 176n60, 194
Alves, M.O. 158
Amnesty International 49, 51, 54, 185, 187, 189
Angola 21
Annan, K. 61–3, 65, 72n241, 183
Anti-Colonial Information and Documents Centre 52
Anti-Corruption Commission 141–2
Anwar, D.F. 58, 69n149
Araújo, A. 50, 53
Araújo, G. 50
Asia Watch 49, 52
Asia-Pacific Coalition for East Timor 55
Asia-Pacific Conference on East Timor 54
Asian Development Bank 89
Asian Financial Crisis 56, 59
Association of Southeast Asian Nations (ASEAN) 38
Australia 2, 5, 23, 26, 48–9, 51–3, 55, 59, 61, 64, 65, 68n106, 69n149, 133, 186
Australian Catholic Relief 53
Australian Coalition for Transitional Justice in East Timor 195
Australian Council for Overseas Aid 53, 81
Australian East Timor Association 51
authoritarianism: in Cambodia *see*

Cambodia; 'competitive' 9, 78, 124, 131; general 3, 7, 38, 78, 83, 113, 123, 124, 128, 130–2, 138, 149, 205, 207; New Order *see* Indonesia; resilience 2
authority: charismatic 16n62, 124, 128, 129, 140, 148; rational-legal 7, 132, 148, 167, 179, 186; traditional 132, 16n62, 148, 179

Badan Koordinasi Intelijen Negara see Indonesia
Balibo Declaration 29, 62
Belo, C. 39, 49, 51, 54, 62, 64, 115
Belo, J.A. 141
Bosnia and Herzegovina 1, 180
Borges, F. 188
Brazil 3
Britain *see* United Kingdom
British Coalition for East Timor 54
Bush, George W.H. 54

Cambodia: constitution-building 103, 106; *coup* 125; elections 3, 49, 77–8, 103, 109, 124, 131, 135; elites 78, 109, 125, 135; human development 166; Paris Peace Accords 78, 135; political culture 78–9, 124–5, 135, 137; transitional justice 180, 183; United Nations Transitional Administration in Cambodia (UNTAC) 1, 77–8
Campaign for an Independent East Timor 52
Caritas Dili 80
Carmona, M.S. 165
Carrascalão, J. 22–3, 27, 43n96, 87, 137
Carrascalão, M. 21–3, 27, 29, 42n67, 56, 109, 141

242　*Index*

Carter Centre 108, 111, 129
Carvarinho, A. 30
Catholic Church 21, 62, 80, 81, 85, 87, 90, 105, 108, 113, 115, 189–90
Charlesworth, H. 162
Charter for Women's Rights 161
Chesterman, S. 115
China 27, 29, 31, 78
Chopra, J. 8, 85–6, 89–90
Christian Democratic Party (PDC) *139, 145,* 109
citizenship: definition 156, 159; rights 8, 11, 19, 39, 74, 77, 82, 156–9, 161–2, 173–4, 179, 186, 207; social democratic 91, 157, 159, 161–2, 164–5, 173–4
civic education 17n84, 82–3, 90, 100, 107–8, 112, 114, 117, 194
civil conflict 1, 4, 19, 21, 26–9, 37, 39, 64, 73, 78–9, 181, 193; post-conflict societies 81, 83, 107, 117, 128, 147, 172, 187–91, 204
civil society **206**: activism 11, 56, 63, 83, 112; defined 12–13; roles and activities 3, 8, 10, 11–13, 34, 48–60, 65, 73–4, 77–8, 80–4, 86–8, 90–1, 96, 99–102, 104–8, 110–17, 123, 131, 133–4, 144, 147–8, 157, 158, 164, 170–1, 180, 182, 184–9, 191, 193, 195–7, 205–6; solidarity movements 13, 49, 51–3, 55–6, 58, 26
Civil Society Consultative Commission on Development 162
Clinton, B. 55, 62, 64
Cold War 5, 29, 30, 31, 48; end of 1, 20, 36, 49, 53, 60, 78
Commission for Reception, Truth and Reconciliation (CAVR) 14, 28, 52, 180, 182, 187–94, 196–7; *Chega!* Report 20, 27, 29, 37, 50, 52, 180, 189, 192–4, 196; Community Reconciliation Procedures 192, 194, 197; National Reparations 194
Commission for the Rights of the *Maubere* People 49, 52
communism 5, 31, 36, 40; Maoism 30–1; Marxism 20, 24, 30–4; Marxist-Leninism 27, 30–2, 51
Conselho Nacional Juventude Timor-Leste 81
Constituent Assembly 13, 38, 96, 99–101, 103–4, **104,** 105–15, 117, 123, 129, 138, 162
Constitution of East Timor 8, 9, 13, 38, 40, 91, 98, 123–5, *127,* 128–30, 133–4, 138, 140–1, 148–9, 156–9, *160,* 161–2, 165,

173, 180, 186, 191, 207; Bill of Rights 159, 173; drafting 82, 84, 98–11, 130, 157, 161
constitutionalism 99, 101–2, 114, 116, 179
corruption 2, 25, 138, 141–2, 144, 147, 183
Coup d'etat 27, 45n170; Cambodia *see* Cambodia; Carnation Revolution *see* Portugal
crisis (2006) 2, 129, 131–3
Crouch, H. 57
Cuba 30
customary governance 7, 8, 14, 21, 74, 84, 101, 161, 162, 179, 181–2, 190–3, 197; *badame* 190; *nahe biti* 190, 192, 195

da Costa, G. 24
da Costa, Z. 141
da Costa Mouzinho, C.A. 22
da Cruz, F.L. 22
Damayanti, Y.R. 58
Dare I and II 39
de Araújo, F. 109, 137, 140, 143, 146
de Araújo, R.M. 10, 148
de Mello, S.V. 7, 76, 84–5, 87, 90, 106–7, 110, 190
de Oliveira, D. 22–3, 29
decolonisation 3–5, 19–22, 27, 40, 52
democracy *passim*: social *see* social democracy
Democratic Party (PD) *109,* 137–8, *139,* 140, 143–4, *145,* 146
Democratic Republic of Timor-Leste (RDTL) 4–5, 23, 50–1
democratisation 1–3, 8–11, 13, 19, 23, 56–7, 73, 77–9, 96, 131, 134, 146, 164, 180, 205
Dewantono, H. 57
Diamond, L. 90, 205
Diaspora, East Timorese 34, 51–3, 55, 59, 65, 133, **206**
Dili Consensus 148
displaced people *see* refugees
do Amaral, F.X. 21, 23–7, 30, 109, 129, 137, 140–1, 143
do Nascimento, B. 39
dos Reis Araújo, A. 24, 29
Downer, A. 59
Dunn, J. 21, 23, 25–9, 52–3

East Timor Action Network (ETAN) 49, 54–5, 185
East Timor Agriculture and Development Project Foundation 80

Index 243

East Timor Jurist Association 157, 159, 174n12
East Timor Political System: Council of Ministers **104**, 110, 125, *127;* government structure and organs 123–5, *126–7*, 128–9; Semi-Presidentialism 124–5, 128–30, 133
East Timor Public Administration (ETPA) **104**, 110
East Timor Relief Association 49, 55
East Timor Security Institutions 6, 9–10, 131–2, 132–3, 135, 144, 148, 170, 181
East Timor Students Solidarity Council 80
East Timor Transitional Administration (ETTA) 87, **104**, 110, 184, 189
East Timorese Catholic Youth Organisation 20
East Timorese Social Democratic Association 138
elections 3, 4, 9, 12, 32, 37–9, 49, 77–8, 83, 87, 89, 96, 114–15, 123–5, 134, 179
elections, Cambodia *see* Cambodia
elections, East Timor 75, 123, 132, 134, 147–9, 204; 2002 presidential elections 124, 129; 2007 parliamentary 130, 138, *139*, 140–1; 2007 presidential 130, 137–8; 2012 parliamentary 2, 142, 144, *145*, 146–8, 171, 204; 2012 presidential 2, 142–4, *145*, 147, 204; Constituent Assembly 13, 87, 96, 103–5, 108, 112, 114–15, 120n98, 129; independence referendum *see* referendum; pre-1999 27, 62; proportional representation system 13, 108, 110, 123, 134–5, *136*, 141, 147
Elites 8, 10, 11, 19, 25, 57, 78–9, 86, 89, 102, 106, 109, 115, 123–4, 131–2, 161
ETWAVE 80
European Union 37, 144

fascism 27
Feijo, R. 128, 130
Fernandes, A. 30
Fernandes, C. 55, 60
Fokupers 80
Fonesca, J. 105
FORKOT 57
FORTILOS 49, 56
Freire, P. 24
FRENTI-Mudança 143–4, *145*, 146
FRETILIN 4, 19–20, 23, **26**, 25–31, **32**, 32–3, **33**, 34, **35**, 35–6, 42n52, 43n96, 45n170, 49–53, 62, 85–7, 98–100, 105–6, *109*, 109–11, 112–15, 117,

120n114, 124, 129–33, 135, 137–8, *139*, 140–4, *145*, 146, 148, 171, 205, 206
Fry, K. 51

Gama, J. 61
Garnadi, H.R. 64
gender equality 39, 158, 161–2, 169, 172; quotas 138
Gill, G. 10, 134
Gini index 167
'Goodbye Conflict, Welcome Development' 167–8
Gomes, S. 53
Gonçalves, G. 24
Government Coalition Bloc (BGK) 146, 166, 171–3, 194
Guinea-Bissau 21
Gusmão, X. 10, 20–1, 23, 28, 30–8, 40, 49, 54, 58, 64, 85–8, 100, 106–7, 116, 124, 129–31, 133, 137–8, 140–4, 146–8, 157, 162, 171, 173, 174n8, 188, 193, 195, 204
Guterres, Abel 53, 55
Guterres, F. 137, 140, 143
Guterres, J.L. 143
Guterres Lopes, Anecito 106, 190

Habermas, J. 12, 98, 105
Habibie, B.J. 49, 57–65, 205
health 26, 28, 39, 80, 93n85, 159–60, 162–74, 194, 196, 204
Hill, H. 30
Howard, J. 59, 61, 69n149
Human Rights Monitoring Network 83
Human Rights Watch 51, 183, 195
Hun Sen 3, 78, 124–5
Huntington, S. 10, 181

Indonesia; ad hoc Human Rights Court in Jakarta 180, 184–6; Commission for Human Rights Violations in East Timor 184; foreign relations/diplomacy 30, 48, 54–6, 59–62, 64, 69n149, 75–6, 183, 185–6, 193, 195–6; military (TNI) 28, 29, 31, 34, 53, 55–8, 59, 61, 63–4, 183–6, 193, 196; National Human Rights Commission 184; New Order regime 56–7; occupation of East Timor 2, 4, 5, 13, 19, 22–33, 35–7, 39, 44n134, 48–51, 53–4, 58–9, 65, 67n45, 80–1, 130, 158, 179, 187, 191, 205; on decision to grant East Timor a referendum *see* referendum; pro-democracy movement *see Reformasi*; response to referendum result *see*

244 *Index*

Indonesia *continued*
  Operation Clean Sweep; transition to democracy 3, 10, 34, 49, 56–8, 65, 205; withdrawal from East Timor 75–7
Indonesia-Timor-Leste Commission of Truth and Friendship 195
inequality 166–7
infrastructure 23, 64, 103, 144, 148, 163, 165, 167, 169–72, 174, 177n121, 178n135, 180, 182
International Centre for Transitional Justice 190
International Covenant on Civil and Political Rights 38, 101, *160*
International Covenant on Economic, Social and Cultural Rights 38, 194
International Criminal Court 184
International Crisis Group 148, 171
International Force for East Timor (INTERFET) 65, 75, 180
International Monetary Fund 58, 156
International Stabilisation Force (ISF) 2, 133, 141, 146, 172
international intervention 1, 2, 8, 77, 84, 88, 207; peace-building 2, 50, 73, 133, 196; state-building 1, 2–3, 6–8, 11, 13, 40, 73–4, 77–87, 90, 100–2, 123, 163–4, 169, 184, 206
Iraq 1, 77

Jacob, F. 87
justice, forms: customary *see* customary governance; distributive 11, 174, 193–4, 196; transitional 14, 179–97; reconciliation *see* reconciliation; restorative 180–2, 187–92, 193, 197; restitutive 180–2, 192–7; retributive 180–9, 193, 195, 197; social *see* social justice
justice system, re-building 76, *126*, 179–80
Justice System Monitoring Programme 185
Jolliffe, J. 21

Katjasungkana, N. 56
Kiernan, B. 30, 43n96
Kingsbury, D. 44n121, 74, 113
Kosovo 1, 49, 77, 180; United Nations Mission in Kosovo 77, 92n42
KOTA 29, 41n3, 85, *139*, *145*
Kouwenberg, S. 53

La'o Hamutuk 82–3, 86, 89, 94n116, 100, 102, 105, 111, 115, 117, 161, 170, 185, 189–90, 192

Laos 29, 166
Leach, M. 138, 140–1
Levitsky, S. 9, 78, 131
Linz, J. 99–100, 148, 204
Lipset, S. 9
literacy 24, 30, 163, 165, 169
Lobato, L. 114, 141–2
Lobato, N. 21, 23–4, 27, 43n100
Lobato, R. 50, 133
Lutz, N. 112–13

Magna Carta concerning Freedoms, Rights, Duties and Guarantees for the People of East Timor 38–40, 113, 140, 157–9, 173
Malaysia 56, 170
Maoism *see* communism
Marcal, A. 111, 158
Marshall, T.H. 159
Martin, I. 63
Martinkus, J. 63
Marker, J. 5, 60
Marxism *see* communism
Marxist-Leninism *see* communism
Mauberism 24, 26, 33, 35, 37
May 5 Agreements 61–2, 75, 186
Migdal, J. 74
militia 61, 63–4, 78, 184, 186
Millennium Development Goals 166, 168, 172–3
Mozambique 21, 50, 130; Constitution 113; Mozambique Liberation Front (FREMILO) 25
Murtopo, A. 27

nation, civic 7, 12, 18n95, 73–4, 79–80, 86, 88, 192
nation-building: definition 7, 73; processes 8, 13, 73–4, 79–80, 82, 86, 88–90, 162, 192
national: identity 40, 79, 102, 112; unity 28, 31, 32, 37, 39, 45n170, 57, 79–80, 106, 109, 116, 128–9, 135, *136*, 140, 156, 181, 188
National Armed Forces for the Liberation of East Timor (FALINTIL) 10, **26**, 28, 31–2, **32**, **33**, **35**, 64, 131, 143
National Congress for the Reconstruction of Timor-Leste (CNRT) 138, *139*, *145*, 138, 140, 143–8, 171, 173, 188
National Consultative Council (NCC) 74, 85–7, 95n137, 95n150, **104**, 183–4
National Council (NC) 74, 86–9, 91, 103, **104**, 104, 106–8, 110, 189–90
National Council of *Maubere* Resistance

Index 245

(CNRM) 10, 20, 31, **33**, 33, 34, **35**, 35–7, 40
National Council of Timorese Resistance (CNRT) 20, 31, 34–6, 38–40, 62–4, 81, 85, 87, 90, 95n156, 103, 106, 113, 118n47, 157, 158, 189; Magna Carta *see* Magna Carta concerning Freedoms, Rights, Duties and Guarantees for the People of East Timor; National Congress 103, 158, 189; National Convention 38
National Democratic Institute 88, 102, 105, 108, 115
National Development Plan 162–4, 174
National Popular Association 21–2
National Resistance of East Timor Students (RENETIL) 20, 56, 95n150, 140
nationalism 33
nationhood 63, 80, 102, 188
NATO 28
neo-colonialism 6, 96, 133
Netherlands, the 51, 59
New Zealand 133, 186
NGO Forum (FONGTIL) 81, 82, 84, 87–8, 100, 104–6, 107–8, 110–11, 117, 157
Nhen, L.K. 53
Niner, S. 36, 44n126
Nobel Peace Prize 49, 51, 54
non-governmental organisations (NGOs) 12, 28, 48, 49, 52–5, 58, 65, 80–4, 87–8, 90, 93n79, 93n85, 94n116, 94n120, 100, 106, 114, 117, 157, 165, 172, 183, 185, 189–91, 195, 203n205

oil and gas reserves 5, 142, 144, 165–7, 171
Operasi Komodo 28
Operation Clean Sweep 64, 75, 182
Our Nation, Our Vision 162–3
Oxfam 81

Pact for Peaceful Elections 144
Pact of National Unity 39, 108, 109, 129
Papua New Guinea 166
Parliamentarians for East Timor (PET) 51
peace-building *see* international intervention
Pereira, A. 148
Pereira, C. 106
Pereira, L.T. 52
Pessoa, A. 87
petitioners group 131, 138, 141
Philippines 10, 55

Philpott, S. 32, 189
Piguo, P. 186
Pires, E. 142
Pires, M. 87
pluralism 3, 32, 34–6, 38–40, 82–3, 99–100, 102–3, 105, 108, 110, 116–17, 124, 130, 135, 207
Poland 3
political equality *160*, 179, 181
Popular Assembly of East Timor 29
popular consultation *see* referendum
Popular Democratic Association (APODETI) 19, 24–5, **26**, 28–9, **32**, **33**, **35**, 42n67, 85
Portugal: administration of Timor 4, 21, 27–9, 37, 179; Carnation Revolution 4, 19, 21, 25–6, **26**, **32**, **33**, **35**, 40, 173, 205; constitution 113; civil society 48–9, 51–3, 55, 59; decolonisation process 4, 19, 22–4, 27, 37, 40, 41n3, 50, 60–1, 75, 133; language 40, 62, 111; military 21, 28, 67n42
poverty 30, 157–9, 162–72, 193, 196
Pro-Democracy Movement *see Reformasi*
Pronto Ata Serbi 80, 93n85
Proportional Representation *see* East Timor Elections
Putnam, R. 102

quasi-states *see* state, forms

Rainsy, S. 124
Ramos-Horta, J. 10, 21–4, 27, 29, 35–7, 49–51, 54–5, 59, 87, 129, 133, 137, 140–3, 157, 159, 195–6
Ranariddh, N. 124–5
Rawls, J. 175n28
reconciliation 14, 35–6, 39–40, 107, 116, 133, 142, 180–3, 185–96, 207
referendum 2, 5, 13, 20, 37, 39, 48–50, 57–65, 75–7, 80–1, 103, 123, 179, 182, 187–8, 196, 205–6, **206**
Reformasi movement 49, 56–8, 60, 65, 68n103, 205, **206**
refugees 29, 51, 53, 61–2, 75, 132, 142, 166–7
Reinado, A. 141
Revolution: Carnation *see* Portugal, Cultural 30; Vietnamese 30
Revolutionary Council of National Resistance (CRRN) 31, **32**, **33**, **35**, 35, 40
revolutionary ideology 19–21, 25, 30, 33–5, 40

246 *Index*

Revolutionary Movement for the Liberation of Timor (MORELT) 21

rights: children 39, 80, 112, 158, 162–3, 167–9, 172, 193–4; citizenship 8, 11, 19, 77, 82, 156–9, *160*, **161**, 161–5, 173–4, 179, 186, 205; civil, political and legal 4–5, 9–11, 13–14, 19, 24, 37–40, 58, 60, 79, 90, 101–2, 106, 108, 112, 115, 130–2, 134, 149, 156–9, *160*, **161**, 161, 163, 173, 179, 181–2, 186; constitutional rights 38, 124–6, *127*, 128–9, 134, 147, 149, 161; cultural 38–40, 156, 158–9, *160*, **161**, 162, 170, 173; gender 39–40, 80, 89, 93n85, 112, 158, 161–2, 167; human 3–6, 8, 13–14, 19–20, 23–5, 27, 32, 36–40, 48–9, 51–7, 59–60, 64–5, 75, 80–3, 93n85, 95n137, 103, 104, 106, 113, 116, 123, 133, 140, 156–9, **161**, 161, 163–4, 170, 174n8, 174n12, 179–83, 185–91, 193–6, 204–6; institutions 6, *126*, 183–4, 187–9; negative 11, 159, 165; positive 11, 159, 165–6, 194, 196; self-determination *see* self-determination; socio-economic 11, 13–14, 25, 38–40, 74, 132, 156–9, *160*, **161**, 161–5, 167–71, 173–4, 179–82, 193–5; violations 27–9, 37, 49, 52–5, 61, 75, 83, 158, 179–92, 194–7

Roberts, D. 78, 124, 137

Robinson, G. 64

Robinson, M. 184

Rodriques, R. 50, 53

Rome Statute *see* International Criminal Court

Roth, S. 55

Ruak, T.M. 10, 129, 132, 143, 146, 171

rule of law 2, 7, 38, 75, 79, 82, 99, 114, 123, 132, 141, 158–9, 179–81, 183, 186–7, 189–90, 193, 195–7

Rustow, D. 13

Rwanda 183

Sabam, S. 60

Samuel, T. 58

Sani, A. 29

sanitation 80, 93n85, 163–4, 168

Santa Cruz massacre 49, 53–5

Schumpeter, J. 12, 134

Security Sector Reform 172

self-determination 1–6, 9, 10, 13, 15–16n39, 19–24, 28–30, 34, 37–8, 40, 48–60, 62–5, 76–8, 80, 84, 101–3, 111, 116, 123, 134, 156–7, 195, 206

self-government *see* sovereignty

Serious Crimes process 180, 185–7

Simpson, B. 52, 55

Soares, Abilio 184–5

Soares, Aderito 105, 115

Soares, D.B. 57, 108, 113, 147, 162

social democracy 3, 14, 20, 24–5, 36, 40, 74, 115, 117, 123, 144, 156, 159, 162, 166, 181–2, 194, 107; defined 11–12

Social Democratic Party (PSD) *109*, 109, 138, *139*, 141, *145*

social justice 3, 8, 11–12, 14, 24–6, 38, 40, 123, 163–5, 167, 172–3, 181–2, 190, 193–5, 197, 207

socio-economic development 9, 83, 165, 172

Solidarity for Peace in East Timor (SOLIDAMOR) 56, 58

solidarity movements *see* civil society

Solomon Islands 166

Somalia 75, 207

South Sudan 50

Southeast Asia 2, 3, 9, 29, 142, 166, 169–70, 187

sovereignty: 'as responsibility' 1; external 1, 13; internal 1, 7, 11, 13, 74, 86, 98, 101, 103, 116, 164, 167, 173, 181; popular 6, 9, 79–80, 94n120; positive 73, 75, 207; recognition of 1–6, 20–3, 28, 31, 36, 48, 50, 59–60, 63, 75–7, 106, **206**; rights 6; shared 76, 84; supported 207; violation of 77

Soviet Union 29, 31, 36

Stahl, M. 53

state, forms: fragile/failed 1, 2, 6, 73, 131–2, 142, 207; post-colonial 1, 3, 4, 24, 124, 142, 172; quasi- 4; Weberian 6–8, 73, 98; welfare *see* welfare

state-building *see* international intervention

Strategic Development Plan (SDP) 163–4, 172, 174

Stepan, A. 99–100, 148, 204

Suharto 34, 48–9, 56–8, 60, 65, 205

Suratman, T. 63

Taylor, J. 21, 24–6, 42n67

Tempo Semanal 146, 148

Thailand 170

Timor Gap *see* oil and gas reserves

Timor-Leste National Alliance for an International Tribunal 195

Timorese Democratic Union (UDT) 19, 22–3, 25–6, **26**, 27–9, **32**, **33**, 34–5, **35**, 37, 43n96, 53, 85, 87, 109, 137, *139*, *145*, 205, 106

Index 247

Timorese Social Democratic Association:
political party *109*, 109, 129, 137–8,
139, 140–1, *145*; resistance body 19,
23–6, **26**, **32–3**, **35**, **37**, 206
Trabalhista 29, 41n3
Transitional Administration: in Cambodia
see Cambodia; in East Timor *see* United
Nations Transitional Administration in
East Timor; in Kosovo *see* Kosovo
Truth and Reconciliation Commissions
187–9; between East Timor and
Indonesia *see* Indonesia-Timor-Leste
Commission of Truth and Friendship; in
East Timor *see* Commission for
Reception, Truth and Reconciliation
(CAVR)

UNDERTIM 138, *139*, *145*
United Nations 2, 3, 48–52, 54, 57–9, 62,
64–5, 75, 77, 84, 131, 133, 183, 186,
188; charter 4, 38, 76, 157; reports
142–4, 147, 165, 168–70, 185, 188
United Nations Development Programme
81, 164–5, 167, 170
United Nations General Assembly 4, 54,
61
United Nations Integrated Mission in
Timor-Leste (UNMIT) 133, 142, 164,
187, 204
United Nations Mission in East Timor
(UNAMET) 5, 16n48, 50, 62–4, 70n184
United Nations Mission of Support in East
Timor (UNMISET) 131
United Nations Office in Timor-Leste
(UNOTIL) 131
United Nations Security Council 2, 4–6,
16n39, 29, 50–1, 62, 75–7, 84, 107, 111,
131, 133, 180, 182, 185, 187–8
United Nations Transitional
Administration in East Timor

(UNTAET) 8, 82–90, 100–4, **104**,
105–8, 110–11, 114, 117, 129, 131, 157,
159, 179–80, 182–90, **206**, 206, 207;
criticisms 6–8, 74, 79, 86–8, 90–1, 100;
mandate 2, 6, 73–5
United States of America 5, 30, 48, 50,
54–5, 59, 62, 64–5, 78, 186
Universal Declaration of Human Rights
38, 159, *160*

Vanuatu 166
Vietnam 15n24, 29–30, 78

Wahid, A. 183
Walsh, P. 35
Wanandi, J. 29
Washington Consensus 156
Way, L. 9, 78, 131
wealth distribution 3, 11, 23–4, 39, 108,
112, 114, 144, 159, 162, 166–7, 169,
171, 173–4, 194
welfare 11, 144, 157, 159, 161, 163–7,
169, 171–4, 175n28, 207
West Papua 57
West Timor 24, 64, 75, 85, 191
western values 3, 6, 8, 77, 101, 157
Wiranto 57, 72n239, 185–6
World Bank 83, 130, 156, 166–7, 171–2,
176n80, 204; Community Development
and Local Governance Project 74,
89–90

Yayasan Bia Hula 80, 85n93
Yayasan HAK 64, 80, 82–3, 85n93,
94n120, 100, 105–6, 112, 115, 117, 157,
190
Yugoslavia 92n42, 183

Zaum, D. 73, 75, 101
Zedong, Mao 30

eBooks
from Taylor & Francis

Helping you to choose the right eBooks for your Library

Add to your library's digital collection today with Taylor & Francis eBooks. We have over 50,000 eBooks in the Humanities, Social Sciences, Behavioural Sciences, Built Environment and Law, from leading imprints, including Routledge, Focal Press and Psychology Press.

Choose from a range of subject packages or create your own!

Benefits for you
- Free MARC records
- COUNTER-compliant usage statistics
- Flexible purchase and pricing options
- All titles DRM-free.

Benefits for your user
- Off-site, anytime access via Athens or referring URL
- Print or copy pages or chapters
- Full content search
- Bookmark, highlight and annotate text
- Access to thousands of pages of quality research at the click of a button.

Free Trials Available
We offer free trials to qualifying academic, corporate and government customers.

eCollections

Choose from over 30 subject eCollections, including:

Archaeology	Language Learning
Architecture	Law
Asian Studies	Literature
Business & Management	Media & Communication
Classical Studies	Middle East Studies
Construction	Music
Creative & Media Arts	Philosophy
Criminology & Criminal Justice	Planning
Economics	Politics
Education	Psychology & Mental Health
Energy	Religion
Engineering	Security
English Language & Linguistics	Social Work
Environment & Sustainability	Sociology
Geography	Sport
Health Studies	Theatre & Performance
History	Tourism, Hospitality & Events

For more information, pricing enquiries or to order a free trial, please contact your local sales team: www.tandfebooks.com/page/sales

www.tandfebooks.com